Praise for Arcade Perfect

I loved reading David Craddock's *Arcade Perfect*. I had forgotten how hard it was for developers/programmers to convert an arcade game to the SNES or Sega Genesis home consoles, and David captures those stories in great detail. **–Tom Kalinske, former CEO of Sega of America**

A crucial yet overlooked part of our industry's past is the art of the arcade port to console. David's book sheds light on the stories of some of the biggest games that made that transition and is a must-read for anyone looking to understand the process. -**John Tobias, "ko-kreator" of Mortal Kombat**

I don't know of another book like this one that focuses on arcade ports—it's unique and I had a blast reading it. **–John Romero, co-founder of id Software (Commander Keen, Wolfenstein 3D, Doom, Quake)**

In *Arcade Perfect*, David lets us inside the unique, insanely difficult world of video game porting. I learned a lot, and I've been making games professionally for 32 years. You like video games? READ THIS NOW. **–Tom Hall, co-founder of id Software (Commander Keen, Wolfenstein 3D, Doom)**

Rather than copy press releases designed to turn business executives into heroes, David steps into the trenches to share the stories of the people who brought our favorite games into being. **–Jennell Jaquays, director of game design at Coleco Industries (1982-'85), designer on Quake II and Quake III: Arena, Hall of Fame member: Academy of Adventure Gaming Arts & Design**

When I smell pepperoni pizza, I can hear "GET OVER HERE!" and "BOOM-SHAKKA-LAKKA!" vividly. It was wonderful to read about the work that went into those games, and it's something I never considered until *Arcade Perfect*. **–Adam Bromell, co-founder of System Era Softworks and co-creator of Astroneer**

Home versions of arcade hits drove the growth of the video game industry. *Arcade Perfect* brings to light how this was done. **–David Bamberger, former senior brand manager of marketing at Sony Computer Entertainment America (Final Fantasy VII)**

Arcade Perfect is a great look into the work our industry pioneers had to put into bringing games home before technology should have allowed it to be possible. – **Patrick Scott Patterson, historian and Guinness World Record-holding pro gamer**

The history of the creation of great arcade games has been exhaustively covered, but adding in how they were converted to home consoles and computers? That's a fascinating, under-explored angle. **–Simon Carless, executive vice president of GDC (Game Developers Conference)**

Arcade Perfect is a deep exploration of one of the most overlooked aspects of game development, and a celebration of the creativity found in the limitations developers face when porting games from powerful arcade cabinets to the inferior hardware of consoles. **–Gabe Durham, founding editor of Boss Fight Books**

A must-read for any gamer old enough to have hoisted a controller in the 1980s and '90s—and should be required reading for today's budding designers. **–Doug Walsh, author of *The Walkthrough: Insider Tales From a Life in Strategy Guides***

David Craddock builds a time machine out of thoughtful storytelling and attention to detail that puts you right in the room with game developers charged with the impossible: to bring the greatest video games in the world into millions of homes. **–Jesse Schell, author of *The Art of Game Design*, Professor of Entertainment Technology at Carnegie Mellon University**

Craddock's DiMaggio-like streak for providing readers with compelling video game history is still going strong. **–Wes Locher, author of *Braving Britannia: Tales of Life, Love, and Adventure in Ultima Online***

I loved learning about some of the most important ports that helped bring the arcades to our homes. **–Adrian Wallett, co-host of the Arcade Attack podcast**

From the arcade classics of yesteryear to the Arcade1Up movement of today, Craddock tells the behind-the-scenes stories of some of your favorite games. – **Patrick Hickey, Jr., author of *The Minds Behind the Games* series**

Copyright

Arcade Perfect: How Pac-Man, Mortal Kombat, and Other Coin-Op Classics Invaded the Living Room

ISBN-13: 9781079275544

Published in the United States of America.
Press Start Press
www.arcadeperfectbook.com

ARCADE PERFECT

How Pac-Man, Mortal Kombat, and Other Coin-Op Classics Invaded the Living Room

By David L. Craddock

Table of Contents

About the Author

David L. Craddock lives with his wife, Amie Kline–Craddock, in Canton, Ohio. He is the author of several books including the bestselling *Stay Awhile and Listen* trilogy, and the critically acclaimed Gairden Chronicles series of epic fantasy novels for young adults. Follow David online at davidlcraddock.com, facebook.com/davidlcraddock, and @davidlcraddock on Twitter.

Stay up-to-date on David's latest releases by signing up for his newsletter.

If you enjoy *Arcade Perfect*, please consider leaving a review on Amazon and/or Goodreads: **https://www.goodreads.com/book/show/46841504-arcade-perfect.**

To Amie
Always

Author's Note

Arcade Perfect is a narrative account based on research and information received from dozens of interviews. All the games discussed in this book are at least ten years old. Given their age, some inconsistency in information was bound to occur. When necessary, I recreated scenes based on details from my interviews, research drawn from previously published interviews, reviews, preview features, and biographies, and my best judgment of what happened, when, why, and how.

None of the dialogue in this book has been manufactured. All of it came straight from the mouths of the developers who shared their stories with me.

Introduction: I Got Next

I HAVE WANTED to write this book my entire life. Well, since I was nine, at least. Around that age, Mom would let me hang out in the mall's video arcade while she shopped for clothes and school supplies and other dreadfully boring things. Upon setting foot in the arcade, Jolly Time, I'd take a minute to bask. The flashing screens and whirring lights; the beeps and grunts and explosions whine of laser beams.

Then I hit the change machine. Inserted the dollar bill Mom had given me. Listened for the clatter of quarters slaloming down the chute. Scoop them out of the cup, and scoped out my targets. My favorite games tended to be along the righthand wall, for whatever reason. This was just before the dawn of *Street Fighter II* and *Mortal Kombat*, so most of the games I played were beat-em-ups: *Golden Axe* by Sega, *Final Fight* by Capcom. I'd drop a quarter into the first favorite machine I laid eyes on. Then I'd make a counter-clockwise circuit around the arcade to scout new games.

One afternoon, as I came around the last bend, I saw it. *Teenage Mutant Ninja Turtles*. The cabinet was huge, with a spacious deck for four players. I stood there for several seconds, totally gobsmacked while the attract mode played. Turtles in groups of two, three, or four, hunted Foot Soldiers through city streets and sewers. There was a *clang* as one of Leonardo's katana swords slashed free a parking meter and sent it flying into a cluster of purple-clad Foot Clan. Moments later, a rumbling *KA-BOOM* as the robotic ninja soldiers exploded.

Frantically I patted the pockets of my shorts. Empty. Of course. I'd splurged on games I'd already played to death on earlier visits. When Mom came to pick me up, I pleaded and cajoled for more. I would take out the trash, unload and load the dishwasher, dust all the lamps and the piano keys, vacuum—any chore if I could borrow just one more quarter. Well, maybe two. Nope. Mom set limits: The money she gave me was the extent of my funding for each arcade visit. I could play the game next time. And I did. As Leo, as Mikey, as Donny, as Raph. Over and over, by myself or amid swarms of other players looking to kick shell as a team.

Much later, during our weekly sojourn to the local video store where my kid sister and I were allowed to rent two of any combination of games and movies for the coming weekend, I was perusing the store's generous selection of NES cartridges, and there it was. *Teenage Mutant Ninja Turtles II: The Arcade Game*. I picked up the box, mesmerized by the screenshots on the back: There was

April's apartment building, on fire; the city streets I'd walked with three strangers in Jolly Time; and—

A snow level? A ninja dojo? What?! Those levels weren't in the arcade!

As soon as we returned home, I jammed the cartridge into my NES and jabbed the power button. Right away, something seemed off. The characters were smaller, and used fewer colors. Levels such as April's burning apartment and the sewers underneath New York City felt longer. Foot Soldiers could no longer be destroyed by certain environmental obstacles such as speeding cars on the freeway or the inexplicable gigantic bowling balls crashing down stairways in April's apartment. (Seriously, who was up there rolling bowling balls on the off-chance they'd scatter turtles like pins? Well, it worked. More times than I care to admit.)

I pondered these differences. The NES only had two controller ports, so obviously a four-Turtle brawl wasn't an option. But why wasn't the gray NES cartridge otherwise identical in function, if not form, to the cabinet into which I'd sunk dozens of my (Mom's) quarters?

For a long time, ports—a term I wouldn't understand until later—of arcade games were markedly different from their source material. I had to play *T2: The Arcade Game* on my Game Gear without the benefit of a plastic sub-machine gun. In the arcade, *Mortal Kombat II* displayed character names within each player's life bar; on Super Nintendo, the names were written below life bars. Yeah, I noticed that stuff, okay? I'd spend hours poring over issues of *Nintendo Power*, *GamePro*, *Electronic Gaming Monthly*, and other magazines as the home release of one of my favorite coin-op games drew nearer, scrutinizing screenshots and re-reading articles a dozen times.

I wanted to know everything, because I loved those differences. Primordial releases of arcade-to-home games were graphically inferior almost to a fault. Over time, though, those inferiorities evolved into something greater: Personality.

A friend of mine had *Mortal Kombat* for Genesis; I had it for Super NES. My version had crisper graphics, but no blood, and sluggish controls. His version was grainier, but snappier—oh, and there was blood. So much blood. You could argue that the Genesis version was superior because it more closely matched the arcade's controversial violence, but I didn't care about that, really. I just found alterations fascinating, and saw merit in both versions.

As hardware got better, the gap between arcade games and ports shrank. Audiovisual elements lagged, but in terms of gameplay, ports took liberties with their source material. The resultant experiences were undoubtedly unique, but in many cases, they were also superior. Sure, the Turtles and the Foot Clan were larger in the *TMNT* arcade game, but the new bosses and levels of the NES port made it its own beast.

Arcade perfect. That's what we called those rare home versions that looked, played, and sounded like the monolithic cabinets in arcades. They were few and far between during the epoch of Genesis and Super Nintendo. By the mid-nineties, the gap had narrowed a hairline crack. By the mid-2000s, the gap had closed.

And that's for the best. Agnosticism in gaming hardware means aside from the occasional hiccup in frame rate, your version plays like my version plays like every version. Still, I have to admit I miss all those disparities. They made ports unique. Better or worse than others, yes. But unique. All worth playing, comparing, and exploring.

Arcade Perfect: How Pac-Man, Mortal Kombat, and Other Coin-Op Classics Invaded the Living Room exists as a method of not only charting those disparities for over a dozen titles, but explaining why and how they'd come about in the first place: Differences in graphics and sound, mostly, but also differences in gameplay that elevated the home adaptations over their forebearers.

I spent several months interviewing developers from Probe, Sculptured Software, Binary Design, Digital Eclipse, and other studios—many of which no longer exist—about the particulars of porting arcade games to a wide array of platforms. Each chapter focuses on one or more ports of a single game. Chapters have been ordered in rough chronological order of when the arcade versions of those games were released. This way, you'll get to enjoy a tour of the primordial ooze of the coin-op industry, to the golden age when yellow pizzas and blue-and-yellow-clad ninjas feasted on quarters, to the twilight of coin-op development, when consoles matched and then exceeded arcade hardware.

We hear a lot about a game's original creators: Ed Boon and John Tobias made *Mortal Kombat*, Shigeru Miyamoto came up with *Donkey Kong*, Toru Iwatani ordered a pizza at lunch and created *Pac-Man*, thereby changing video games and popular culture forever. And those people are awesome. You'll even read some of those stories in this book. But you know who you don't hear about nearly as often? The unsung heroes who were given the nigh-impossible task of taking arcade games and shrinking them down to cartridges. Imagine someone coming up to you and saying, "See that mountain over there? I want you to make it fit in my house, but be just as tall and scenic and awesome. Oh, and you're the only person assigned to this project. Have fun!"

This book exists as much to tell the stories of just a few of those unsung heroes as it does to point out why ports of games on Super Nintendo tend to look fatter than the same port on Genesis. It exists to introduce you to people, and so they can share their experiences, warts and all.

I chose games to write about based on several factors: critical and commercial success; favorites from my gaming history; and who was available to talk. I've written a lot of these narrative-style history books about games, and my objective with this one, as with all that came before and all that will come after, was to talk to people rather than regurgitate Wikipedia. I like telling stories no one has either heard, or heard in detail. What that means, in short, is if a developer could not be reached for interviews, or declined to talk, you won't read anything—or as much—about their game in this book.

As an extension of that point, I've also done my best to avoid retreading ground. Some repetition is unavoidable; retro gaming is nearly as trendy as contemporary gaming. However, since no one from the development team that made *Tetris* for Game Boy—inarguably the most popular version ever—was available, and since that version has been discussed too many times to count, don't expect me to dig too deeply into it. Again, my intent is not to slight your favorite ports, only to focus on others that better lend themselves to examination.

While each of these stories is written in a narrative style, I do get into some nitty-gritty technical details: processor speeds, assembly language, color palettes, background modes. This is necessary to comprehend the tough decisions that had to be made for even the most rudimentary of ports to exist. I have taken steps to dig into that material deep enough that more technically inclined readers will appreciate it, while also making sure it's palatable for those readers who just want to know why *Mortal Kombat* on Super NES had sweat instead of blood.

Several chapters cover the same hardware, such as the chapters on *Pac-Man* and *Donkey Kong* for the Atari 2600. In these cases, I try to switch things up by talking about different aspects of the hardware so you're not reading the same information over and over, and/or to approach the same platform from a different angle. (For instance, the Atari 2600's playfield is mentioned in chapters two and three, but I don't really roll up my sleeves and dig into how it affected home ports until chapters four and five.) This was bound to lead to some repetition, but I tried to avoid that as much as I could.

Finally, there's no way one book or one author could write about every arcade port, or every platform to host arcade ports, or even the best platforms for arcade ports. If you finish *Arcade Perfect* and your first thought is, "Hey, that guy didn't mention Port X on Platform Y!", have mercy on me. I am but one author whose ambition greatly outweighs the constraints of reality under which we all operate.

(Also, if you've read other books of mine such as *Stay Awhile and Listen: Book I*, you know I dig sequels. Just saying.)

-David L. Craddock

2 June 2019

I also noticed a big difference in the number of colors in Donkey Kong. The arcade version used four colors, but the Famicom/NES only used three. For the arcade version, we combined two three-color panels, but that wasn't technologically possible with the Famicom/NES. But it was incredible enough that an arcade game became a home game.

-Shigeru Miyamoto

Chapter 1: Pong

Part I: "If This Doesn't Work, We're Dead"

NOLAN BUSHNELL FELT like he was sitting down to a high-stakes poker game instead of lunch in the Sears Roebuck cafeteria.

Bushnell, the co-founder of Atari, had entered the cafeteria with Joe Keenan, president of Kee Games, a subsidiary games company. Their guide was Tom Quinn, a buyer at Sears and Atari's champion who was pushing Sears to sell the company's home version of *Pong*.

Quinn steered his guests over to a table where a group of Sears executives waited. "You're the guy from Atari?" one of the men asked Alcorn as he pulled up a chair.

Bushnell sized him up. "Yep. What do you do?"

The man smiled thinly. "I'm the traffic manager at Sears. We are holding the release of our Christmas catalog for this one product from Atari."

Bushnell and Keenan from Atari paused in mid-chew.

"I want you to know that the last time we did that was for the Marvin Glass slot car set," the manager continued. "We built 50,000 of them, and the car wouldn't get past the first turn. We had to take all those 50,000 units back. Okay?"

They nodded, and finished their food. Back at Atari, Keenan pulled Al Alcorn, the company's lead engineer, aside.

"Is this going to work, Al? Because if this doesn't work, we're dead."

Alcorn prided himself on his poker face. "Oh, yeah. Sure. What could go wrong?"

Inwardly, he fretted. Atari was in unfamiliar territory. Arcade games, they knew. Building games for the living room was different. Riskier. "When you're in the consumer electronics business, you had to guess in the first three months of the year how many units you would sell, and the last three months of the year. If you guessed too few, you missed sales. If you guessed too many, you had stock in the warehouse. It was a crapshoot."

Pong. The game was Alcorn's blessing. The game was Alcorn's curse.

Nolan Bushnell had broken into the amusement games business by creating a coin-operated version of *Computer Space*, a game where players captained ships and fired missiles at one another. It was based on *Space War*, a computer game developed by students at MIT. Bushnell's coin-op versions had performed moderately well, but *Computer Space* was complicated. Factors such as the pull of a nearby gravity well and the trajectory and velocity of each player's missiles had to be taken into account.

Bushnell knew coin-op video games had potential. He just needed more, and ideally titles that consumers could grasp within seconds. Recruiting for Atari, the company he'd co-founded with fellow entrepreneur Ted Dabney, Bushnell hired Allan "Al" Alcorn, an electrical engineer who had experience with computers. On the subject of video games, however, Alcorn knew next to nothing. To get his feet wet, Bushnell told Alcorn he'd landed a contract with General Electric to develop and manufacture a coin-operated version of table tennis. It should be simple, he explained. Two paddles, a ball, a net, and score counters to keep track of points.

Alcorn built the game from circuits that functioned using gate logic: on, or off. The concept of his ping-pong game, which was named *Pong*, was indeed simple. Wiring circuits together was considerably less so. Still, he finished the job with time to spare, so he added more features to spice up the rudimentary gameplay. Each paddle, a vertical rectangle on the screen, consisted of eight segments. Depending on where a ball connected, it would ricochet at a different angle and velocity. Alcorn also wired up logic to increase the ball's speed the longer it remained in play. As soon as one player scored, the ball's speed reset.

Ted Dabney was impressed by the prototype, but he wanted a virtual crowd to boo when players lost a round. Alcorn knew he was bumping up against the limits of his resources. Every feature required more electronics, increasing the price of manufacturing, the difficulty of troubleshooting breakdowns—which circuit had malfunctioned, and why?—and, quite simply, he had no idea how to generate sound effects. He experimented with a sync generator and discovered that it could create simple beeps at different tones. A far cry from Dabney's booing and hissing crowd, but it was something.

Alcorn's prototype consisted of a $75 black-and-white TV set made by Hitachi, a four-foot wooden cabinet, and wires soldered into boards. When Dabney and Bushnell got their hands on it, they were floored. What had started as a warm-up test had developed into a potential product that was easier to pick up and infinitely more addictive than *Computer Space*.

In August 1972, Alcorn and Bushnell wheeled the prototype of *Pong* into a local watering hole, Andy Capp's Tavern. The proprietor, Bill Gaddis, allowed them to test their machine on his grounds because Atari supplied him with pinball games. They placed the prototype on a table near a jukebox, plugged it in, and then sat down at a nearby table to drink and observe. Eventually, a patron wandered over to inspect the machine. He ran his hands over the controls: spinner dial on the left, another dial on the right. Then he inserted a quarter. Someone else ventured over, dropped in another quarter, and the two patrons hunched over the machine, laughing and exclaiming as they volleyed the square ball back and forth.

Over the next week and a half, Gaddis kept Atari informed of *Pong*'s growing popularity. More customers gravitated to it each day. In fact, Gaddis exclaimed, people were starting to visit the bar just to play the game, which was pulling in thirty-five to forty bucks a day, an unprecedented amount in the coin-operated amusement business. Bushnell knew they had a hit on their hands and packed up another prototype to demonstrate to executives at Bally/Midway, a manufacturer of amusement games based in Chicago. Atari had a contract with Bally/Midway, and Bushnell believed building and distributing *Pong* would fulfill it better than a driving game he'd promised.

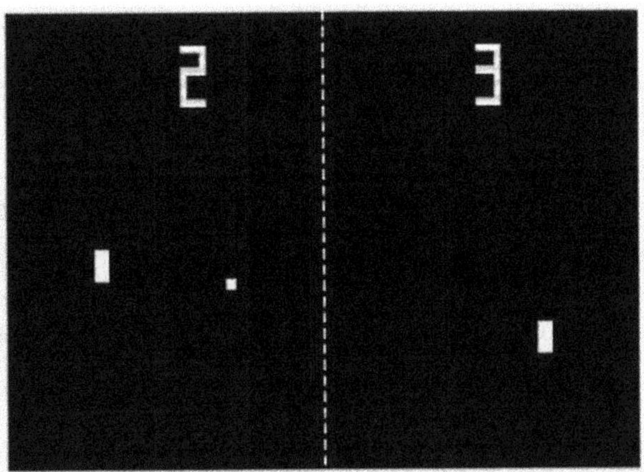

A few days after Bushnell left, Alcorn received a call from Gaddis. *Pong* was acting up. Alcorn drove to the bar, popped open the money hatch, and inspected the milk carton he'd set up inside to collect quarters. To his amazement, quarters had filled the carton and overflowed, jamming the machine.

Pong went into production soon after, and became a hit. The more machines Atari manufactured and sold, the higher demand rose. Soon, they were able to charge operators three times as much as the game cost to produce, generating enormous profit.

As *Pong* spread through arcades, Atari's growing staff discovered that not every version had come from their Sunnyvale, California-based offices. "We were plagued by copycats," Alcorn said. "Atari became the advanced development group for all of our competition. In fact, we even had one of our vendors for printed circuit boards that turned out to be quite a crook. He was shipping our boards, occasionally minus our name on them, to the competition. These guys didn't have any engineering talent at all. They'd just put the parts in the board, plug it into a cabinet, and sell it."

Bushnell ranted about the copycats, referring to them as jackals. There was no point, he espoused to Alcorn, Dabney, and anyone who would listen, in slapping imitators with patent infringements. These operators were sleazy: They'd just drop off the radar for a while and resurface under a different name. Bushnell's rage was more than a little ironic. *Pong*'s success had attracted the attention of engineer Ralph Baer, who'd invented a game console called the Magnavox Odyssey that played variations of a table tennis game. Baer had been working on the Odyssey since 1966, and had demonstrated the system and its built-in tennis game on several occasions. Bushnell had attended one of those demonstrations, and had even signed his name in the guestbook. Baer's employer, Sanders Associates, pushed Magnavox to pursue legal action against Atari and other "jackals" who had ripped off Baer's design. In April

1974, Magnavox filed a lawsuit against Atari, Bally/Midway, and other manufacturers of ping-pong copycats. At first, Bushnell claimed he didn't remember viewing a demonstration of the Odyssey, only to later recant and say that he had attended one of the events, but that he didn't find the game that clever. After Bushnell's lawyer explained that Atari would likely win, but at expenses of at least $1.5 million, Bushnell settled with Magnavox out of court. Magnavox made Atari a licensee for only $700,000, a figure that paled in comparison to the money Atari would go on to make from *Pong* variants.

Regarding the "jackals," Alcorn agreed with Bushnell's reasoning. Atari would simply have to stay two steps ahead. "As soon as they'd get going with a knockoff of our game, we'd have another game out to render theirs obsolete."

The strategy worked for a while. Then Alcorn grew annoyed. Atari was churning out *Pong* variants—two-on-two, soccer, hockey, all essentially the same game with slight wrinkles—and the jackals kept ripping them off. Coin-op games were successful for Atari, but only just. They needed a more profitable strategy.

Bushnell was just as irritated. In April 1973, he circulated an internal memo that outlined a six-point plan to finish off the jackals once and for all: have at least four production-ready machines in development at all times; engineer a new style of coin box; bulk up the staff so one engineer could be on call for "emergency projects" at a moment's notice while the rest of the team develops games; and, listed at item number six, develop a consumer version of *Pong*.

The memo ended tersely: *Statements concerning our manufacturing capacity [are] inapplicable to the above design schedule.* Meaning, in short, keep any objections to yourself and just make it happen. Alcorn, by that time appointed vice president of engineering and thus expected to deliver on these expectations, flagrantly ignored the last directive and wrote back: *Is the fact that we have no money germane to this discussion?*

Bushnell's response: *No*.

"That was basically the creation of the consumer video game business: Item six," Alcorn recalled, laughing.

***

HAROLD LEE WAS cut from the same cloth as Al Alcorn. He was an electrical engineer with a master's degree in EE, and a designer as adept at developing circuits as he was these newfangled microchips that were creeping into computing technology.

He was, to Alcorn's thinking, the perfect engineer for this job.

"I want to think about designing a chip that we can use in all our games," he told Lee one afternoon. "A custom chip. It would make our board harder to copy if you don't have the chip."

Following a few months of R&D, Lee came to Alcorn with a verdict. "You know, we could do that. But your technology is evolving so fast that by the time the chip came out, it'd probably be useless. But I think technology has progressed to the point where we could do the dumbest, simplest game ever made on a chip."

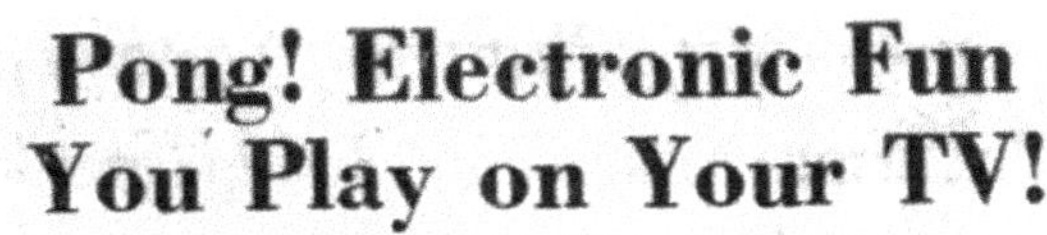

Pong! Electronic Fun
You Play on Your TV!

13
14
99.95
Newest word in family fun—Pong! It plays a lot like table tennis, but with an electronic difference: the computerized console attaches to your TV set! Scores are posted on the screen, with synchronized "pong" sound effects! Buy now for holiday, and year-round fun!
TELE-GAMES
ELECTRONIC GAMES

Alcorn knew exactly what Lee meant. *Pong*. What's more, he knew he wanted to be more involved with developing a consumer *Pong* game than simply assigning Lee to the task and waiting for a prototype to show up on his desk. He was twenty-five years old and tired of managing engineers. He was an ex-football player who was used to working with his hands, an engineer at heart, not a corporate suit who could spend ten-plus hours a day managing people to do things he wanted to do himself.

"Let's try to do this," Alcorn told Lee.

Lee recommended he hire Bob Brown, another engineer. Alcorn also brought in his wife, Kate, an accomplished engineer, to pitch in. To Steve Bristow, Alcorn passed his baton of VP of engineering. Let Bristow deal with people and their emotions; he was going back to the trenches of development.

The team divided their talents. Lee would design the logic for the chip based on modifications to *Pong*, which Alcorn had to make so the game functioned efficiently on a chip rather than a series of binary circuits. "To be fast enough to do *Pong*, the chip had to run at three or four megahertz," Alcorn explained. "In those days, any consumer chips were used in calculators or watches, and they were slow." He attained the necessary processing speed by using MOSFET's N-channel enhancement mode, a type of operation that enhances the conduction of electricity.

Lee mocked up designs for the chip, and Alcorn handed over the schematics to Kate, who would wire-wrap them, the process of mounting electronic components on an insulating board and connecting them with insulated wire. Alcorn debugged the wire-wrapped board and, once it was ready, gave it to Lee. Harold Lee drafted it on a computer aided design (CAD) terminal he'd rented, mapping out the chip's construction.

After weeks of back-and-forth, iterative work, the group received the first prototype of the chip. "And goddamn it, the chip worked, and that was quite a surprise to me. I was shocked," Alcorn admitted. "I remember vividly the day we got the chip back from AMI—American Micro Systems Incorporated was the semiconductor company that ran the prototype for us—and we put it in the test rig, and my god, it worked. I felt like a dog chasing a car: What do you do if you catch it?"

The answer, per item number six on Nolan Bushnell's memo, was to sell it. No one knew precisely how to do that. Atari had no business plan written in greater detail than Bushnell's memo. Without any idea where to start, they rattled off consumer companies. Someone suggested Sears Roebuck, and Alcorn perked up. Sears Roebuck was a big company that sold products to consumers. Specifically, it sold Ralph Baer's Magnavox Odyssey.

Gene Lipkin, president of Atari's coin-op games divisio, phoned Sears, got an operator, and asked to be connected to the department that sold the Odyssey. The operator paged through her catalog and arrived at Department 606, Sporting Goods. She connected Atari to Tom Quinn, the department's buyer, who immediately expressed interest in Atari's home *Pong* game. That came as something of a surprise to Alcorn and the others, who assumed—dreaded—that Magnavox had the home market locked down. As it turned out, the company's advertising suggested that the Odyssey system would only run on Magnavox TVs. In effect, Magnavox viewed Ralph Baer's little box as a way to sell more televisions. Quinn, who saw potential in home games, was frustrated by Magnavox's strategy, which seemed to make him more receptive to take a look at Atari's device.

Quinn told Alcorn he'd stop by Atari the next time he passed through California. Two days later, he showed up at Atari's factory in Los Gatos at eight a.m. looking sharp in a suit. Quinn strode to the front desk and let the secretary know who he was and why he was there. Nonplussed, she phoned Lipkin. Equally flummoxed, Lipkin showed Quinn to the manufacturing floor. A few engineers, all in t-shirts and jeans or shorts, milled around the area. Nolan Bushnell hopped in a box and rode it down a conveyor belt like a kid sledding down a snowy hill.

Alcorn got in around nine and steered Quinn away from the shenanigans at Atari—which included hot tub parties and passing around marijuana, although it was, fortunately, too early in the day for that level of debauchery—and toward the prototype of what was being called *Home Pong*. Quinn liked what he saw and arranged for Atari reps to demo the game at Sears Roebuck's headquarters in Chicago.

The day before the meeting, Allan Alcorn flew out to Chicago with Bushnell, Joe Keenan, and Lipkin. Worried that their prototype might be stolen, they arranged to store it at a friend's apartment for the night. The next morning, they retrieved the prototype and drove to Sears Tower, where they rode the elevator to the thirty-seventh floor. The view of Chicago's skyline was spectacular, all glittering skyscrapers and warrens of streets teeming with Micromachines-sized cars.

Setting up in a conference room, Alcorn tried to appreciate the scenery while his stomach did flips. They needed this contract. All the executives gathered around the table, coughing and fidgeting while they waited, knew they'd look like fools if they signed on the dotted line with this company full of twenty-somethings and turned out a product that didn't work. Atari had everything to lose. Worse, Alcorn fretted, what if the prototype—a barely contained rat's nest of wires—had been a fluke? There were a few bugs, too. What if they'd come all this way to secure a contract for a product they wouldn't be able to build?

The meeting began. Everyone watched as Alcorn unwrapped the prototype box. "We hadn't got the chip done yet, so it had the wire-wrapped board in it that my wife had built. It was in a wooden box about two feet wide, a foot and a half deep, six to seven inches high. It had a wooden model of what the final package would look like, because we didn't have the tooling done either. We had no chip and no tool."

Alcorn connected the prototype to a television, switched the TV to channel three, and powered on the box.

Seconds passed. The screen remained blank.

Gritting his teeth, Alcorn popped a panel off the prototype and examined its innards while Gene Lipkin went through a song and dance: *Home Pong* will be a smash sensation! Families across the country—nay, the world—will be ecstatic to play rousing games of table tennis from the comfort of their own home!

Alcorn tuned out his partner. Ignoring the stares of executives boring into his back was not so simple. Everything depended on this meeting. If he and Lipkin embarrassed Atari, they'd blow their shot at forming a relationship with the country's retail giant, and Atari would likely tank.

At last, Alcorn found the culprit. The building was more than just Sears Roebuck's corporate headquarters. As one of the tallest buildings in Chicago, it was also used to broadcast radio and TV transmissions. An antenna on the roof was also beaming out on the same channel as his prototype.

Taking a breath, Alcorn switched his modulator to output to channel four, changed the channel, and powered on the box again. This time *Pong*'s familiar interface painted the screen. Two paddles, a ball, a line down the middle representing a net, two scores.

Lipkin operated the other paddle and played a round against Alcorn. The Sears executives smiled, laughed, and exclaimed. *They're into it*, Alcorn thought, his heart beating faster.

When they finished, Alcorn and Lipkin opened the floor to questions. Carl Lind, a department head, cleared his throat. "Mr. Alcorn, you're telling me that you're going to take that big rat's nest of wires and put in on a piece of silicon the size of your little fingernail?"

"Yes, sir," Alcorn replied.

Lind's eyes widened. "Mr. Alcorn, how are you going to solder the wires to it?"

Alcorn wanted to jump through a window. *This is a total mismatch*, he thought. These guys didn't get technology. They were getting hung up over wires that won't even be an issue once the microchip was finished.

If it was finished.

Not that he could air his fears in front of these men. Alcorn rallied. "I don't know what we told them, but they came out and visited Silicon Valley a month or two later. We made a point of giving them a tour of a semiconductor fabrication line so they could see how it was done. They still didn't get it, but somehow they went along with the gag and it all worked out. It was a weird, weird feeling."

Part II: The Luckiest Engineer in the World

THE MEETING ADJOURNED, and the Atari crew joined Quinn in the cafeteria for lunch. They got an earful from the traffic manager of Sears, who made it clear he didn't like the idea of Sears putting so many eggs in Atari's basket.

Nolan Bushnell felt the same way. The last thing he wanted was for Atari to depend on Sears. What if Sears's terms weren't agreeable? What if Sears went belly up?

In January 1975, Alcorn and a few others took the *Home Pong* prototype to the Toy Fair in New York City. They assumed the annual event was like any other marketplace. Anyone with a product to sell would set up shop at a table, and potential buyers would flock to them. Plus, they were Atari. They had *Pong*.

Reality hit like a punch to the gut. Arriving at the expo, they discovered that most business took place behind closed doors a week before the show opened. Most products had already been assessed and rejected. Buyers milled around the floor, looking for scraps. Alcorn and the others sat on their hands until late in the afternoon when Tom Quinn stopped by and asked how things were going. Great, they replied through too-wide smiles.

Things were not great. Every night, they had dined by themselves instead of with buyers. Adding insult to injury, the jackals were out in force. "Next to us in a booth was National Semiconductor, and they were selling a rip-off of our game," Alcorn recalled. "We go, 'What the hell?'" Atari got revenge a few years later when it hired away most of National's engineering team to help build its Video Computer System (VCS), a cartridge-based game console.

Refusing to let Quinn know he'd been the only one to express interest in *Home Pong* so far, Bushnell and the others signed a contract with Sears. The terms made Alcorn and the rest of the engineers nervous. Atari floated the idea of having 75,000 *Home Pong* units ready for Christmas, but Quinn shook his head. Sears wanted 150,000. Atari didn't even have a case.

"The big fly in the ointment was designing the case. I had completely underestimated that," Alcorn admitted.

***

BACK AT THE office, Alcorn poured his energy into *Home Pong*. If the team could build a chip for $10 or less, they'd be in business. Quickly, he realized the plastic case posed a much higher engineering hurdle. Alcorn, who knew nothing about designing cases, got a crash course in high-volume, injection-molded plastic shells. First, a designer had to make plans. They shopped the plans to a tool-and-dye maker, who would need around three months to cut out a mold base, a 300-pound block of steel from which they would make tools to insert in an injection-molding machine. If any part of that three-month process went sideways, they had to start over.

George Faraco, a designer at Atari who'd built the cabinet for the company's *Gotcha* arcade game—including a prototype that featured breast-shaped controllers, another example of the company's male-dominated culture—told Alcorn he had a buddy down in Los Angeles with a company that could do the tooling. "Sounds great," Alcorn replied. "Take care of it."

The company was a tool-and-dye shop that specialized in injection-molding, transfer-press tools. "Their primary business was doing the transfer mold," Alcorn explained. "You've seen integrated circuits? The black, plastic caterpillars with fourteen pins on them that you see all the time? The way those are made: There's a metal reel of all the pins, flat; you glue the chip down to it, attach the wires to it, and put it in this special, injection-molding press tool that holds all of the parts and connects around a metal lead so tight that when you squirt plastic into it, the plastic doesn't squeeze out. This is a very difficult tool to make."

Faraco's buddy would have been up for the job if not for a slump that had hit the semiconductor business. "You know," said a buyer visiting with Alcorn, "you're being screwed by this guy in L.A."

"What?" Alcorn said. "How can that be?"

"It's not going to happen," the buyer said. "Let's go down and do a visit to your tool-and-dye maker and see how it's going. If you're happy, fine. But I'm a little concerned."

Alcorn arrived on the floor to find 2,000 square feet occupied by two engineers, a single Bridgeport lathe, and near-total silence. "We're screwed," he said. Two months had gone by, and Atari was no closer to a case for *Home Pong*.

Alcorn gave Bushnell a status update. Bushnell took action by assigning in-house engineers in the coin-op group to throw together a wooden case. "We could use it as a backup to ship this thing, because we had nothing else to put it in," Alcorn said. "I wouldn't work on it because I figured I'd put all my effort into [helping make the chip], and I couldn't juggle two or I'd screw them both up."

In the meantime, Alcorn received a tip about another tool-and-dye company called Krass West. When he showed up for a visit, he felt like he'd stepped into a different world. The shop was huge, and the floor crawled with engineers working at machines. "They were pros, and they were able to put half their shop on this job. And by the way, you had to build several of these bases if you were going to order hundreds of thousands. You needed lots of tooling in case one failed."

The chip that would power *Home Pong* came with its own set of problems. Alcorn knew the general process. "You didn't own the tooling. You just bought the chip," said Alcorn. Atari's situation was unique. "We owned our own tooling, and we could say, 'Hey, could you build this for us?' and they'd go, 'Well, we can look at it.'"

Before production could kick into high gear, AMI, the company that had built the *Home Pong* prototype, and the supplier Atari wanted to mass-produce its chip, got cold feet. Atari's finances were still shaky, and AMI's executives worried that Bushnell wouldn't be able to pay. Alcorn and Joe Keenan compromised by urging AMI to produce a certain number of chips just to get them started. Another semiconductor company called Synertek agreed to manufacture the rest.

The only part of building *Home Pong* that went smoothly was the design of the paddles attached to the machine. "It was a dedicated game," reasoned Alcorn. "Even if you wanted wired controllers, there'd still be no point in unplugging them. But this was almost meant to be made at the lowest cost."

Alcorn leaned into low-cost solutions to design *Home Pong*'s audio/visual components. One detail communicated in Bushnell's infamous memo was that the consumer game be displayed in color. Alcorn's coin-op version had displayed output on black-and-white screens. Audio was also a concern, one Alcorn solved by pumping sound effects from a speaker built into the case rather than from the player's television. "There's a reason for that, a big reason," he said.

Audio and video could either work hand-in-hand, or battle for dominance. "The trick is, you've got a base video signal that has color information and sound information on it. The way I did it was so cheap with one diode, just three parts, that if you tried to modulate

Home Pong became Sears' most successful product to date and earned Atari a Sears Quality Excellence Award.

Their victory was short-lived. The jackals were back, and in greater numbers. Magnavox released updated versions of the Odyssey; Coleco, a leather-company-turned-toy-maker, rolled out a console that played *Pong* clones; even Nintendo, a Japanese company that had made playing cards before its president, Hiroshi Yamauchi, pivoted to coin-operated video games after *Space Invaders* took Japan by storm, ripped off *Pong*.

Home Pong was just the beginning. To combat the jackals, Atari needed to take consumer games to the next level: A game system that played games on interchangeable media, similarly to how VCRs played different movies by inserting different tapes.

But that was the next battle. For a moment, Alcorn relished the whirlwind of events that had led him on a journey from paddles, to ping-pong balls, to a mega-hit product that paved the way for arcades as well as home games.

"Things went wrong, and we solved them as fast as we could. The whole thing was a big surprise. I was twenty-five years old. This was not in my plans at all. It was a wonderful exercise working with great guys. We had a great rapport. We were all friends without any politics. Looking back on it, I just think I'm the luckiest engineer who ever walked the face of the earth to have been in this spot. There were guys who were a lot smarter than me, no doubt about it.

But I happened to be in the right place at the right time, with the right skills and experience to get it done. I managed, by luck, to hire the right people who could do this. You know what I mean?"

Chapter 2: Space Invaders

Part I: The Rosetta Stone

ON A COOL Christmas Eve in Japan, schoolchildren flooded the streets and pointed up at the sky. Excited chatter filled the air. Any minute, now. Any minute.

Toshihiro Nishikado stood among the children, and was the first to spot it. There, an object so distant he couldn't make out a shape. He smiled. It must be Santa's sleigh. But where were the reindeer?

Another object appeared. This one he could make out. It hung lower in the sky, and grew larger, bulkier, as it descended.

His smile slipped. The object had legs that dangled like tentacles.

Another creature appeared. Another. Another. Hundreds descended, blotting out the stars with their misshapen forms and their tendril-like legs and antennae that twitched as if they were receiving signals. Nishikado opened his mouth to cry out a warning, but could not speak. More invaders appeared, row after row after row, marching from left to right as they drifted closer and closer to Japan. People were screaming, and the children were running.

Not all of them, he saw. Some of the children, the clever ones, rallied together and assembled a laser blaster out of spare parts: spark plugs, a hubcap, and a car battery. They tracked the aliens' movements from left to right, right to left, and blasted them as they rained down, lighting up the sky like a fireworks display. The aliens fired back. Missiles shattered buildings and blew craters in the roads. But the children stayed their course, firing back. Within minutes, it was over. Japan, and the earth, were saved.

Nishikado opened his eyes. It was a dream. It was a video game.

On the morning after his dream in 1977, Toshihiro Nishikado raced to his job as an engineer at Taito, a manufacturer of mechanical and electronic amusement games, and he took stock of the company's technology. Japan had been using microcomputers for a short time, but they were behind the curve of other countries such as the United States, where personal computers like the Commodore PET and Apple II were making their way into homes and offices. Nishikado saw the advantages of building games using a microprocessor. One of his earlier titles, *Western Gun*, had been built using discrete logic circuitry, chips that represent binary decisions such as AND and OR. Later, in 1975, the American developer Midway created *Gun Fight*, an adaptation of Nishikado's game powered by a microprocessor, allowing for better graphics and smoother animations.

So, like the industrious children in his dream, Nishikado improvised. Over the next year, he designed and rounded up tools and hardware to make his literal dream game, which he'd taken to calling *Space Invaders*. The arcade board ran an Intel 8080 central processing unit (CPU), and drew characters and special effects using simple lines, a technique known as raster graphics. Perhaps the most inventive component was the backdrop itself. Nishikado knew the technology at the time would have accommodated only a plain black background. Instead, he constructed an intricate setup: a screen positioned in the bottom of the unit, facing upward, and reflected back at players through an overlay glass adorned with painted images.

The on-screen layout of *Space Invaders* was inspired by *Breakout*, the 1976 coin-op game from Atari. Players would control a blaster that could move left and right along the bottom, like *Breakout*. Above the blaster were three mountain-like barriers that could absorb missiles from the rows of aliens marching downward from the sky. Once the barriers were destroyed, players would have to rely on their reflexes to dodge missiles as they fired on the alien army.

Space Invaders also drew from *Space Monsters*, a mechanical game Taito had released in 1972. The title had premiered at the dawn of an era when arcade manufacturers were more concerned about factors such as the cost of hardware and sales opportunities, and less about game design. A microprocessor afforded Nishikado the luxury of focusing on improving and streamlining the design. Hardware continued to frustrate Nishikado. He overcame some limitations by turning them to his advantage. For instance, he noticed the screen refreshed faster when there were fewer aliens to draw. Rather than alter his code, he kept the invaders' faster movement and touted it as part of the game's difficulty.

In the early summer of 1978, Taito released *Space Invaders* as a cocktail table with black-and-white graphics. (An upright-cabinet version followed later, featuring strips of orange and green cellophane over the screen so the monochromatic graphics appeared to display in color.)

The game's first three months on the market did not bode well. Few arcade operators purchased it; machines out in the wild sat desolate. The word-of-mouth campaign paid off. Within a few weeks, players were forming lines that stretched for city blocks. *Space Invaders* became so popular that many operators cleared out their arcades and stocked the game exclusively. Taito struggled to meet demand, rushing to assemble tens of thousands of cabinets and blanketing Japan like the alien invaders from Nishikado's dream.

Space Invaders was a game of many firsts. It was the first game to save a high score, tacitly challenging future players to beat it; the first game in which AI-controlled objects attacked players; the first game that gave players numerous "lives," and that required them to fight back against waves of enemies; the first game where players could take cover; and the first game to use a continuous soundtrack, consisting of four simple notes that sounded like a heartbeat and that sped up as the aliens' speed increased.

In short, *Space Invaders* was the arcade game that birthed arcades. Before it, games like *Pong* were found almost exclusively in bars, laundromats, bowling alleys, and eateries. The growing popularity of *Space Invaders* prompted operators to create spaces dedicated solely to it and, later, coin-operated games like it.

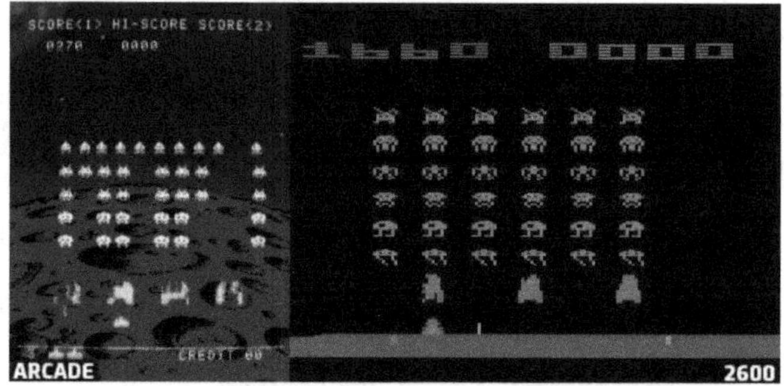

By late 1978, Taito had sold over 100,000 machines and earned the equivalent of $600 million US dollars. Supposedly, players were dropping so many 100-yen coins into *Space Invaders* cabinets that Japan suffered from a shortage. (Historians and academics have since debunked this myth, pointing out that the supposed shortage was due to Japan producing fewer 100-yen coins than usual over 1978 and '79. In addition, arcade operators would have been emptying coin boxes and depositing them in banks during the craze, where they would have been withdrawn and pumped back into the economy.)

Over in the United States, Atari engineer Richard Mauer thought he must be going crazy. He had played *Space Invaders* and enjoyed it, but no one else at the office seemed all that intrigued. Finding merit in its design, he had started building a version of the game for the Atari 2600. His first milestone was developing the game loop: draw space invaders, get them marching in rows that gradually descend, and devise input so players can move the ship and fire at the aliens.

After a few months, he showed the game to colleagues, and was surprised when no one seemed interested. Some programmers went so far as to say that original game ideas were more valuable than clones of arcade hardware. Mauer shrugged and tabled his port of *Space Invaders*.

One day, Atari president Ray Kassar, who had replaced Nolan Bushnell as president, caught on to the craze. Midway had signed a license with Taito to bring the arcade game to the U.S. and was raking in quarters. Kassar pounced and landed exclusive rights to develop a cartridge-based adaptation of the game for Atari's VCS/2600 in 1980, making that port the first arcade game licensed to a console.

Suddenly, Atari's programmers cared very much about *Space Invaders*, and who was going to bring it to the 2600. Mauer, who had been working on a game called *Maze Craze*, pointed out that he had already made excellent progress. Management urged him to finish.

Mauer was close, except for one nagging issue. For reasons he could not comprehend, objects on the screen were flickering like mad. After several weeks, he solved the problem, and incorporated new aliens drawn by an artist who had sketched them out on graph paper.

At last, Mauer was finished, except for one problem. Each Atari cartridge contained a ROM (read-only memory) chip capable of storing up to four kilobytes (KB) of data. Mauer's code weighed in at seven kilobytes. Over the next month, Mauer pruned his game, wincing as he cut features and routines he was proud of: a byte here, a few bits there.

When *Space Invaders* invaded retailers later in 1980, demand was unprecedented. Atari sold through two million cartridges in the game's first year, making it the first game to hit the vaunted one-million-units-sold milestone. Sales of the Atari 2600 quadrupled, marking another first: Buying hardware specifically to play a single program, anointing *Space Invaders* as the first "system seller" or killer app for a game machine.

Just as significantly, *Space Invaders* was the first port to push the envelope of its source material, and break through it. While there were fewer aliens on the screen, Mauer created new types and gave them unique point values, encouraging players to prioritize targets. Players could also load variations that altered the gameplay. Moving Shields added barriers that drifted back and forth, making the aliens harder to hit; Fast Laser Bombs caused Invaders to attack faster; and gameplay modes such as one that rewarded one player with points when their partner took a hint, adding another layer to competitive play.

Space Invaders on Atari's little console represented a rallying cry to game designers. Even though Mauer's port differed in many ways—the graphics weren't as crisp, the sound effects were jarring—it existed on a home machine, which meant other coin-op games could, too.

"The convenience factor of not leaving the house to play a hit game was the real motivator, I think—even though clearly a quarter was less money than $30 USD or whatever, there was a sense that you were investing in something you could own and not just 'wasting quarters,'" said Dan Amrich, formerly known as Dan "Elektro," editor for *GamePro* magazine. "Certainly I got that line a lot: 'If you save those quarters then you can buy the game and own it.' Ownership plus convenience equaled a market."

***

DECADES LATER, PROGRAMMERS like Eric Mooney continue to answer that rallying cry.

Mooney began playing games at age three, starting on a TI-99 computer that came with a version of the BASIC programming language. He taught himself to code by typing out listings published in magazines. When he was old enough to cross the road to the library by himself, Mooney walked back and forth, checking out more magazines and studying program listings as he punched them in.

His family bought an Atari 2600, and it was fun to play games on, but couldn't be programmed. When they upgraded their computer to a Tandy PC with GW-BASIC, another dialect of the language, Mooney learned how to draw graphics and produced clones of games he'd played on the 2600 and TI-99. Eventually he outgrew BASIC and taught himself assembly language.

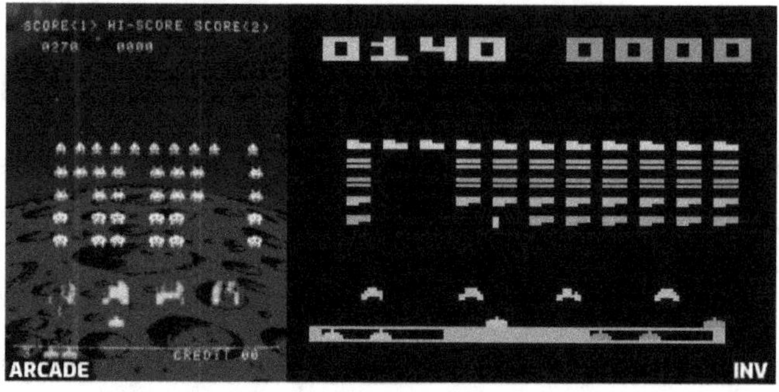

Mooney remained fascinated by the 2600 through high school. So did hundreds of other players. Every time he logged on to the rec.games.video.classic newsgroup, which he discovered in 1997, more amateur developers had posted new messages asking questions about coding the machine. Others shared works-in-progress of games they were writing for the hardware.

The availability of information enabled Mooney and countless others to try their hand at writing software for legacy hardware. "I already knew how to write PC x86 assembly, and saw what they were doing with the simpler 6502 pretty quickly. It seemed amazing in 1997 that programming a game console with cartridges would be within reach of a home hobbyist, so I joined in and read along."

Mooney had written clones of Atari 2600 games, but had never attempted coding software in 6502 assembly, the dialect used by the 2600's processor. He continued reading newsgroups as well as the Stellalist, a sort of newsletter sent out to subscribers. The issue that blew his mind was a guide written by fellow programmer Nick Benssema titled "How to Draw a Playfield," the screen space where 2600 objects and backgrounds appeared: the maze of walls and castles in *Adventure*; the blocky battlefield of *Combat*. "This was the Rosetta Stone of 2600 programming, the seminal document from which all else followed," Mooney explained. "From this, I understood the principles of the 2600's graphical display, the scanline-based nature, that the CPU has to rewrite the graphics registers as the electron beam draws each scanline. I could immediately see how my favorite games from childhood were constructed, what was going on down at the assembly language level."

His early experiments in graphics were simple, nothing close to a finished, playable game, but they demonstrated his growing comprehension of how the machine displayed objects and backdrops. As he finished demoes, he uploaded them to his website, dos486.com, for anyone to try. "I like the one called *River Rampage*, a tech demo showing a scene like *River Raid* with lots more sprite and missile firepower," he said.

Of particular interest to Mooney was the 2600's graphics registers, like mailboxes in memory where data was stored, sent from, and retrieved as the playfield was updated. One day he painted a mental image of how *Space Invaders*' iconic five-by-eleven array of aliens would be stored in registers. Excited, he set about writing his own version that would run on the Stella emulator based on Atari 2600.

Maybe, he thought, his version could be better. One of Mauer's sacrifices during the final month of production had been downsizing his layout of invaders to a six-by-six arrangement.

"I always thought the six-wide invader setup on the 2600 *Space Invaders* port was lame, so I wanted to show and prove the console could do an arcade-accurate recreation of *Space Invaders*' gameplay," Mooney said. "I never even thought about a title and just named the file *INV* as a placeholder."

Mooney restricted himself to the same parameters Atari's programmer had worked within: the 2600 hardware, plus a 4K ROM. "In 1997, we didn't yet have the homebrew capability for bank-switching cartridges or anything else," he said, referring to a technique that allowed Atari programmers to take advantage of greater ROM sizes such as 8K, "so I never targeted anything other than completely-standard 4K. It wasn't exactly a goal, more like it was the only feasible option at the dawn of the homebrew scene."

Drawing an arcade-perfect recreation of the invaders became the central purpose of *INV*. Before Mooney could realize this purpose, he had to take a breather. "Back in 1997, I lost interest before I ever finished *INV* as a playable game. Part of that was that we on the Stella mailing list discovered a hardware trick to get extra repeating copies of sprites by disassembling 2600 *Galaxian*, which does it."

Another homebrew programmer utilized the trick to develop his own port, dubbed *Space Instigators*. Mooney updated his work-in-progress as well, dubbing it *INV3*. Once he knew how to duplicate sprites—a 2D image typically assembled as a composite of smaller images—there was no need for a version that looked as blocky as a 2600 game. He could have started over, but he didn't want to rewrite systems he'd already finished, so he abandoned the game.

Seven years later, he was stunned to find cartridges containing *INV*'s source code being sold on AtariAge, a popular web community for Atari aficionados. Programmer Albert Yarusso of AtariAge had copied his code onto ROM chips and produced cartridges that users could buy and run on authentic 2600 consoles. The discovery bothered Mooney, not because he wasn't making money off sales, but because he disliked the idea of anyone paying money for a game he'd left unfinished. He began tidying up code he'd written back in 1997 and rebranded the game. "By then, the game had become well known for years as *INV*, and someone suggested *INV+* as the best way to make the succession clear and mark the new version as distinct," he said.

A finished version of *INV+* was made available for download in 2004, skirting the edge of Richard Mauer's 4K limit. "I could have gone higher with the later *INV+* version in 2004, but didn't see any need. In fact the 4K limit was even a convenient excuse to stop there rather than continuing to scope-creep on features."

Mooney went for years without thinking about *INV+*. He had moved on to adulthood and regular jobs. Reflecting on the game stirred up mixed emotions. "I'm proud to have been part of the birth and development of the homebrew scene. But honestly I started to wish that I'd put that effort into a real original game, rather than what frankly is a fairly dull *Space Invaders* clone," he admitted. "I do a lot of writing about games, particularly the *Civilization* series; all that is at dos486.com as well. I don't really do much programming outside of my day job nowadays. Actually I've been doing something else entirely recently: I learned to sew and have been doing costume stuff for conventions. By the way, there is an Easter egg in *INV+*, in true classic style. Try waiting and hitting the saucer with your very first shot of the game!"

Part II: Evolving Nicely

DAVID LEITCH HAD given entrepreneurship a good try. The time had come to pack it in.

Leitch and fellow programmer and friend Paul Carruthers had made a go of running a company together. Both had years of experience porting arcade games to consoles but never managed to get their company off the ground. For his next move, Leitch called on Cameron Sheppard, another friend and programmer. In 1998, Sheppard had co-founded Crawfish Interactive, a company with a reputation for developing quality titles on Nintendo's family of Game Boy handhelds.

"I hadn't done any Game Boy stuff before, but it was a similar level of tech to Master System and Game Gear stuff. It was a nice fit, and a good project to do, because in principal it should be a simple game. Generally you approach these projects from a pragmatic standpoint and do the best you can with it. Some things evolve nicely, some things don't."

Leitch's first assignment was to remake Taito's legendary *Space Invaders* for Game Boy Color. He wasn't too fussed about it. The core game loop was so addictive, so simple, it would be hard to mess it up. Plus, he didn't have to figure out ways to differentiate his remake from the then-twenty-nine-year-old original. The way Sheppard and the rest of Crawfish's co-founders worked was, higher-ups would pitch projects to publishers based on design documents they had drafted, and once a publisher accepted a project, the design document was given to programmers charged with carrying it out.

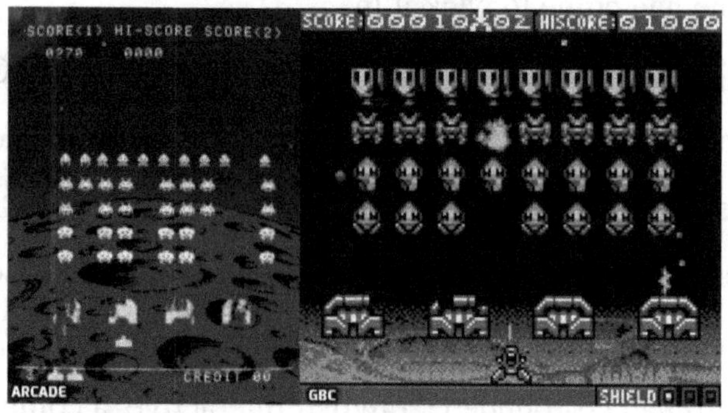

"That way there will be an expectation on the part of the programmer for what the game will be like; when I come on board *Space Invaders* as the programmer, I have a set of parameters I have to stick to. Mitchell Slater did the design for that. He's a nice lad, and it was a nice, simple take: Some tweaks, a few more alien ideas, and then the rest evolved as we were doing it."

Leitch broke *Space Invaders* into manageable chunks. To his thinking, the background was simple: a black screen, some twinkling stars made of sprites scattered across the rows where objects were drawn. The tricky part would be drawing and animating the aliens. Game Boy Color could place a maximum of ten sprites on a line, same as the original Game Boy, but aliens weren't the only sprites Leitch would have to work with. He'd need to conserve space for the player's laser cannon, the mountains that blocked shots, and special effects such as missiles, laser blasts, and explosions.

"How that scene is constructed—I have to brag a little—is kind of clever," Leitch said.

Nintendo's Game Boy and Game Boy Color represented backgrounds as a grid known as a character map. A scroll mechanism could be used to draw and redraw elements of the character map on a horizontal interrupt, a signal informing the processor that another action should interrupt the current process. For instance, the top row of space invaders gave the illusion of movement by setting the position of the character map and then changing it as the screen was redrawn using a horizontal interrupt to "show" the aliens shuffling to the right, then shuffling another step, and another, until they hit the edge, at which time they'd drop down one line and shimmy to the left. However, part of the screen—the part drawn according to an interrupt—never changed.

"It sounds complicated, but it's a fairly commonplace thing," Leitch said. "Many Game Boy and Game Boy Color games have scrolling backgrounds, but there will be a chunk of the screen memory for the display: The score information, [health, ammo, armor, and other information] that will be locked in place. This fixed chunk will probably be the full width of the screen."

Leitch rendered the aliens as background elements, as part of the character map, instead of sprites. That enabled him to move them fluidly. When the bottom-most row reached the horizontal line on the screen just above the barriers that absorbed shots, they were converted into sprites. “They have to turn into sprites because the barriers are part of the character map as well,” Leitch explained.

The alternative, drawing the aliens as sprites in the foreground, would have made for an inferior product. “You'd have to have very small space invaders, with no more than eight in a row or they'd flicker all the time,” said Leitch. Sprite flickering occurred when programmers exceeded the maximum number of sprites that could be drawn on a single line.

Leitch spent most of development perfecting his objects-as-background-elements technique. The rest of the project consisted of generating simple content such as sprites for items and effects, the main menu, and bosses, special aliens that weren’t present in Toshihiro Nishikado’s *Space Invaders*. He designed whizbang effects like explosions to look impressive without distracting from more important on-screen elements, namely the aliens in the background’s character map. One effect was a wave that rolled across the screen, sweeping away space invaders in its path. “The wave is a little curve. It doesn't have a lot of sprites in and of itself,” Leitch said. “The only complication with that was that as each space invader was picked up and blown away, it had to be turned into a sprite. But you could time it so you didn't end up with a bunch of transformations from character map to sprite all at once. You just wanted to time it well so they weren't all lifting up at the same time to avoid the sprites-on-a-line issue.”

In *Space Invaders* for arcades and early consoles like the 2600, the screen simply cleared at the end of the level, and another formation of aliens popped into existence. Compared to old hardware, the Game Boy Color's resources were a spoil of riches. Leitch designed a cool transition effect that drops in the next wave of aliens, as if they were the next force sent by the invaders to take the place of the fallen, at the start of the next level. "It helps you keep up momentum between levels, rather than: finish, fade out, fade in, and play again," he said.

As an Easter egg, he stashed away a version of the game that looked like the original: black-and-white graphics, minimal special effects. "I took a quick look at some version of the original somewhere. The mode you unlock is based on the same engine as the rest of the game. It's just tweaked to make the gameplay more rigid, more like the original."

If his *Space Invaders* remake for Game Boy Color had a fatal flaw, it was one shared by every other version of the game. "After a while, the charm wears off. It's also got kind of a crappy save system, where you have to enter about a dozen characters [as a password]," he continued. "That's because the publisher was too cheap to splurge on an EPROM. They'll try and cut corners anywhere. They're ruthless businessmen."

The significance of leaving his mark on arguably video gaming's most iconic franchise was not lost on Leitch. "It's a cute game, the way it turned out. The effects, the power-ups—it's just got a nice pace to it. You've got a strong, original game mechanic, but just tweaked a bit."

What Leitch appreciated most about his remake was that he avoided adding too many extra bells, whistles, and frills. "Activision was doing more complex remakes on consoles, but I think the Game Boy Color one is the best out of that pack, because the rest are too slick. The coin-ops from that era were all sort of tiny. It was the bare minimum of interaction, and if you want to keep the spirit of that, that's what you need to aim for. Better effects and graphics makes the experience less authentic to me. It was just one of those projects that you know works. Not all projects are like that, but that was one of them for me."

Chapter 3: Missile Command

Part I: Death From Above

ROB FULOP COULDN'T believe his ears, or his luck.

He'd been studying at University of California, Berkeley, in 1980 when he'd landed an internship at Atari. What started as a summer gig blossomed into a full-time career, and since there had been no space in the coin-op division when he came on board, he was working on consumer games for the 2600.

Fulop, along with programmers Tod Frye and Howard Scott Warshaw, were the crest of Atari's second wave of soon-to-be-legendary programmers, and were eager to leave their mark. "There wasn't much else to do other than military work at that time. There was no PC industry, so software jobs were Lockheed and Atari. It was just very early."

Now that he was full-time, he assumed he'd be assigned to projects. On his first day, his manager came up to him and said five magic words: "Just go make a game."

Fulop was stunned. Go make a game? Any game? "Atari was probably the most independence I've ever had over thirty years in this industry," he recalled. "They had absolutely no management. You didn't even have to tell them what you were making."

Some programmers took initiative and wrote original games. Fulop was just starting out, and preferred to stand on the shoulders of giants by doing conversions of coin-op titles. “It was a lot easier to work with the 2600 if you knew in advance what you want to make. If you were trying to explore on the 2600, it's not a very forgiving machine. It's easier for someone to say, ‘Go make *Night Driver.*’ I know what to do. Make a pylon, make a sound—that I could do.”

Image courtesy of Rob Fulop.

Influenced by earlier driving games such as Midway’s *280 ZZAP* and Micronetics’ *Night Racer*, *Night Driver* originated as a coin-op title in which players piloted their car along a winding road. The game was set at night, natch, which kept the display simple: A black screen with a track of lights that marked the curvature of the road. Released in 1976, *Night Driver* was one of Atari’s more immersive games. Arcade operators could purchase cabinets in a standard upright configuration, or in a cockpit-style mold that let players drive using a steering wheel and pedals. The game also presented a pseudo-first-person view by positioning the camera inside and slightly above the car's dashboard, making *Night Driver* the first first-person driving game.

Fulop never saw source code for *Night Driver*, nor did he need it for a conversion. Sixteen dots, eight on the left and eight a little ways to the right, forming a lane. That was the game. The Atari 2600's TIA (Television Interface Adapter) allowed programmers a limited number of on-screen objects, referred to as hardware sprites, that could be recycled to create duplicates of graphics such as the dots that marked out lanes.

Reusing objects wasn't as simple as copying-and-pasting them all over the screen. They could only be reused at a critical moment, when the electron beam in the television moved from the bottom-right corner of the screen back up to the top-left to redraw imagery. "You'd have to reuse these hardware sprites, and the program had to keep track of exactly where the television beam was," Fulop explained. "That's how we synced our program. Only later did they come up with a system where you could write something to memory and it would then pop up on the screen. That's what made the 2600 so difficult: Managing that display."

Fulop likened the experience of working with the 2600 to how early directors of silent movies must have felt: Telling as complete a story as possible with a paltry supply of resources. "We had to figure out the primitive, raw materials that could make a game. I think the best games from back then had very simple play patterns, and were games that already existed [in arcades] so you could just make them work on the TV."

Night Driver's display was relatively easy to manage. Fulop simulated the experience of acceleration by moving the game's two columns of dots down the screen. The tricky part was repositioning the dots so the "road" wound and curved, keeping players engaged. At first, Fulop struggled to render a graphic of a car, so he cut out a picture of a vehicle from a magazine and taped it to the bottom-center of the TV screen at his desk. The way he displayed the vehicle and dots was by taking advantage of the television's internal display capabilities. Televisions manufactured in the USA ran at sixty frames per second, so every few frames he'd draw one image, then draw the next one during other frames. The trick was to not let too many frames pass without displaying one image or another, or they would flicker in and out of existence, causing a flashing effect. "We had to be careful: If you had fifteen frames a second and [only updated] every fourth, that could trigger epileptic fits in people that had epilepsy."

Not all televisions were created equal. TV sets in Europe ran at fifty frames per second, which meant programmers had to tweak the code for international products to redraw frames at different intervals. Only one TV set in Atari's office had been jerry-rigged to run at fifty frames per second so programmers could test their code. "The timing was all different," Fulop said. "You're always keeping track of how many seconds it's been since something happened. You have to know the time at every moment, down to the frame. You'd have to re-test it. There was a lot to think of because it was very precise. We' have to mess around with it, and that could take another week. No one wanted to do that when they'd just finished a game."

Despite the literal and figurative headaches caused by frame rates and electron beams, the limitations of designing games for the 2600 encouraged creativity. *Night Driver* weighed in at 2,048 bytes—or two kilobytes—on its cartridge, roughly half the capacity on a standard cartridge. "You also only had 128 bytes of RAM [random access memory] to work with, so the computer could remember 128 things. That was it," he said. "We learned how to write this really efficient, bizarre kind of code. I don't believe it really matters anymore, because you don't care about memory as much now. But at that time, we cared very much. And you had to make a game good. It was too much. Any original game, to me, was a masterpiece. Anything new was a miracle. It took a real piece of talent to make that work."

Fulop's second project was a conversion of *Space Invaders* for Atari's 400 and 800 personal computers. Like *Night Driver, Space Invaders* was a vertically aligned game, with objects at the top of the screen slowly moving to the bottom. Feeling confident in his burgeoning skills, he took some liberties with the original design, such as adding a large, foreboding mothership that sent forth aliens at the beginning of a level rather than having the next wave of enemies appear out of thin air. After the product shipped, members of Atari's marketing group complained.

Fulop was taken aback. No one had told him he should stick to a game's original blueprint. For his third job, he chose to convert *Missile Command* to the 2600. This time, he'd do whatever was necessary to turn out as accurate a port as possible. It was another vertical game, and therefore, he thought, would be simple to reproduce.

***

DEATH RAINED FROM the heavens. Dave Theurer squeezed his eyes shut tighter, refusing to see the cause of the bright flashes against his eyelids.

He could still hear. Booms. Cracks and thuds as buildings shattered and clogged streets with dust and debris. The screams were the worst.

Theurer's eyes snapped open. He took a moment to process his surroundings. He was at home, in his bed, sweat-soaked sheets twisted around him. The nightmare. Always the same: Bombs dropping from a black sky, each trailing a colorful tail behind it like contrails from airplanes, each reducing earth's cities to rubble and their populations to zero.

A few weeks ago, the idea, which wasn't even his, had thrilled Theurer. Gene Lipkin, Atari's president of coin-op and vice president of sales, had read a magazine article about a satellite built with state-of-the-art radar screens. Lipkin had clipped the article and sent it to Steve Calfee, Theurer's manager, with instructions to have a programmer make a game that used a radar to track missiles falling from the sky. Calfee had called Theurer into his office and given him the mission: Create *Armageddon*, the title of the game where ICBMs (intercontinental ballistic missiles) rain down on cities stationed along the bottom of the screen, and players shoot them down before impact.

Theurer shuddered as he remembered walking out of Calfee's office, his spine tingling with excitement. The concept was simple, but would be a blast to create. He stayed grounded in the idea of ICBMs destroying cities. He wanted *Armageddon* to be a defensive game: No attacking other countries, no killing their people. Players would only be able to defend cities by scrambling to blast ICBMs before impact. That, he believed, would open their eyes to the game's bigger story. As time lapsed, the missiles would descend faster and in greater numbers, forcing players to focus on cities that could be saved, and growing resigned to the fates of those that couldn't.

Nestled between the cities were three bases stocked with a finite supply of missiles. Players aimed at ICBMs by rolling a trackball to move a cursor on the screen. The trick was to aim just below an ICBM so their missile would have enough time to launch from a base, soar through the sky, and hit its target. If players aimed too high or too low, they'd waste a missile.

Early in development, Theurer realized that neither he nor anyone else at Atari grasped the full meaning of the word Armageddon. Not only that, Theurer pointed out that no one could spell it. It was too confusing. Management agreed, and the name was changed to *Missile Command.*

Other facets of the game changed. Theurer planned to incorporate railroads that players had to protect so trains could transport missiles to restock bases. A radar would sweep across the screen, revealing missiles at certain portions as it passed. Railroads and radars ended up being too complicated and were cut. The focus remained on protecting six cities based in Atari's home state of California: San Francisco, Santa Barbara, Los Angeles, San Diego, Eureka, and San Luis Obispo. Theurer eventually dropped the names, trusting players to substitute names of cities that meant something to them, which would tighten their connection to the game and its outcome.

The simplicity of the display—a black sky, three bases and six cities along the bottom, and colored trails with blinking weapons of mass destruction at the end—dogged Theurer the longer he worked on the game. It was, he came to realize, born of the Cold War nightmare that still plagued the world: The belief that the skies could open and nukes could reduce the world to charred rubble.

Soon, Theurer had nightmares of his own. He happened to live close to Moffett Field, where the Air Force would launch spy planes that roared during takeoff. Sometimes, after the nightmare, he would wake up, hear the roar, and forget—just for a split second—that what he heard was the roar of a plane engine and not the detonation of a nuclear bomb. Sometimes, he dreamed he was hiking through the mountains over the Bay Area, and that when he looked up to take in the view, he'd see colorful trails of smoke moments before the world went white.

Theurer channeled his fear into *Missile Command.* The game could not be won. Eventually, attacks would fall too fast and in too great a number. *The End* would appear on the screen. That, Theurer said, would drive home the idea that *Missile Command* was telling a story.

No matter how hard players fought, they, like everyone else, were doomed.

Arcade (left), Atari 2600

PLAYERS FLOCKED TO *Missile Command* cabinets when Atari rolled them out in 1980. Rob Fulop decided to port it because he, too, enjoyed the game. Unlike Theurer, he wasn't bothered by it being a parable for nuclear war. Someone at Atari was rewriting the story that would be detailed in the 2600 version's manual, renaming all the cities with weird titles to give the impression that players were defending an alien civilization.

Plus, Dave Theurer was his buddy. When Fulop wanted to talk about particulars of the game so he could nail them in his conversion, he joined Theurer for lunch and picked his brain. When he had trouble digesting the algorithms Theurer had written for routines like detecting the trajectory of falling ICBMs, Fulop could walk over to his friend's desk and study them.

Theurer's close proximity ended up being vital as Fulop waded deeper into the project. When, for instance, do the ICBMs appear? What routine did Theurer write to make them fall? Why do players sometimes hit them, but sometimes miss when it seems like they should have made contact? What are the minute differences between the generic ICBMs and other enemy attacks such as smart bombs? Those conversations opened his eyes to the subtle and compelling methods Theurer had used to make the game's difficulty rise on a curve.

"You could make a smart bomb infinitely smart so the player can never hit it," Fulop explained. "It can be as smart as I want, because I'm programming it, and I know exactly where the explosion is. I could make it impossible to hit, or really easy to hit. But how do I make it so it's easy to hit at first, but not that easy, and it gets harder to hit later, but not so hard that you can't do it? That kind of [granularity] is the real art of making a game."

Some obstacles were technical. Tilting the 2600's joystick to move an on-screen cursor was slower and less accurate than spinning a trackball. A related problem was that in the arcade version, players fired missiles from any of their three bases by pressing the button corresponding a specific base. Each of the three bases held ten missiles. The 2600's limited controls—a stick with a single button—offered no elegant way to select bases. Fulop solved the problem by consolidating all thirty missiles in a single base. Players still had to defend six cities, but they only had to fire from one location.

There arose another problem. The arcade's hardware had been powerful enough to draw several smart bombs and player-guided missiles on the screen at once. On the 2600, Fulop was only able to render a maximum of two missiles fired by players. Between fewer missiles and the inferior joystick, players would only be able to handle so much challenge before the game became overwhelming. Dialing in missile accuracy would make or break Fulop's conversion.

Fulop learned that Theurer had massaged accuracy by making bombs harder or easier to hit using a table of numbers he'd arrived at through calculations. Fulop was able to convert the table to the Atari 2600. "It depended on the level and how close [the cursor] was to the smart bomb itself. The further away you were, the slower a bomb would move. If you were really close, it would try to jump away. The table had maybe 100 numbers, and it was the secret sauce for the smart bomb system."

Determining whether players scored a hit introduced another snag. Players didn't have to make direct contact with a bomb. Their missile exploded as soon as it arrived to where they'd deployed it, creating a blast radius that destroyed any smart bombs falling through it. That meant Furor had to know the difference between a bomb's current position and a player-guided missile's blast area. Complicating matters was the fact he always needed that information: ICBMs were always falling, which meant players would be firing missiles at different spots to hit them.

The formula entailed finding square roots and adding them together. Unfortunately, calculating square roots was not the Atari 2600's strong suit. Fortunately, Fulop figured out a shortcut. He could round off by using integers instead of real numbers, meaning numbers without a decimal point: 2 instead of 2.235113, for instance. "Once I figured that out, I can figure out distance really fast, because I can find three-eighths of something pretty quickly."

Fulop wasn't in the clear yet. The Atari needed several machine cycles to perform his truncated calculation. The best time to do that was during the brief period when the electron beam jumped from the bottom-right corner of the screen back up to the top-left before redrawing the screen. "That's when I can figure out what happens in the next frame. If you spent too much time thinking, the computer wasn't going to be able to draw the next frame. It was a real nightmare to work on. It was like nothing else, a bizarre thing to learn how to do that really didn't have much long-term value."

Between reference tables and intense calculations, *Missile Command* blasted its way through Fulop's four-kilobyte cartridge space and 128 bytes of memory. Every byte could be used to keep track of one thing: bomb locations, how many missiles players had at their disposal, even the score. "I knew from the beginning that it was going to be a bitch to go back at the end and cut it down. Every time I'd get it down by one extra byte, I was so proud. That was by far the hardest part. I would say half the time I spent making the game, and the other half was spent squeezing it into memory."

By the time Fulop was done, he'd chopped out roughly twenty percent of the code he'd started with. "I couldn't save all the features. I lost a few I really liked, but that's how it works: You've gotta kill your babies."

Some of his babies survived. One was artificial, an illusion, but an effective one. As players increased their score, the Atari's speaker chirped as points were totaled. After a certain high score, the chirp would last several seconds, as if the number of points players had earned was so high the counter could barely keep up. "We can count exactly, but it made it seem like, 'Oh my god, you broke the game by getting so many points!' It's complete bullshit, but people love that kind of stuff."

Fulop wasn't given credit for *Missile Command*'s conversion. So he slipped in an Easter egg that functioned like a flashy autograph. "We were given complete autonomy, but also, we were kids," Fulop admitted. "We did things because we could. We figured we could slip Easter eggs in there, and no one in the company is ever going to find it."

Fulop's Easter egg was appropriately obtuse. On level 13, players must deplete their missiles without scoring a single point. Their game will end, but the initials *RF,* for Rob Fulop, will be transposed over the farthest city on the right. The secret was discovered by Joseph Nickischer, a player who shared his find in a letter to the editor published in the July/August 1982 edition of the *Atari Age* newsletter. It became the second Easter egg to be publicly acknowledged by Atari, but was removed in later versions of the cartridge after Fulop left the company to work for Imagic, one of the competitors founded by former Atari engineers.

Fulop reaped rewards from his conversion a lot sooner. Propelled by glowing reviews from critics and players, *Missile Command* for the 2600 sold over 2.5 million cartridges, making it one of the top ten bestselling games on the system. Fulop was satisfied; he'd made good on his promise to deliver as close to an arcade perfect conversion as possible, and he earned a fair bit of money due to his royalty deal with Atari.

"I really wanted it to feel like playing the arcade game. The more successful early games were conversions. Death from above—that was the theme of the games."

Part II: Something to Do

KEITH BURKHILL SAT back in his chair and weighed his options.

He'd just come back from playing *Missile Command* at his local arcade. The game was beautiful. The stark yet elegant simplicity of bombs spiraling down toward cities, their colorful trails cutting across the night sky like serrated knives; the basic yet addictive nature of rolling a trackball to target and shoot down bombs that erupted like pixelated flashbulbs.

Burkhill let his gaze trail across the room until it landed on the brand-new ZX Spectrum, an 8-bit personal computer popular in European countries. His family had bought it just recently, but there were no games to play. Suppose… suppose he wrote his own? "I was just looking for something to do," Burkhill said of his motivation to clone *Missile Command.*

After six months of work, Burkhill approached companies with his conversion. One, a publisher called Anirog Software, expressed interest and paid him a small advance. Burkhill and the team named the game *Missile Defence* to avoid confusion with Atari's original game.

Burkhill talked over certain aspects of the game with Anirog's developers, who helped him iron out some gameplay decisions. "You could fire from any silo if you used the keyboard," he explained. "I gave it to the company, and they said it needed to support one of these newfangled joysticks."

Burkhill had realized, as Rob Fulop had, that playing with a joystick was innately slower—and could therefore be more frustrating—than using a trackball. "We discussed it for a few minutes, and I said, 'Players could select which silo to fire from.' We agreed to just use the middle silo, and transferred the missiles from the other two to the middle," he remembered.

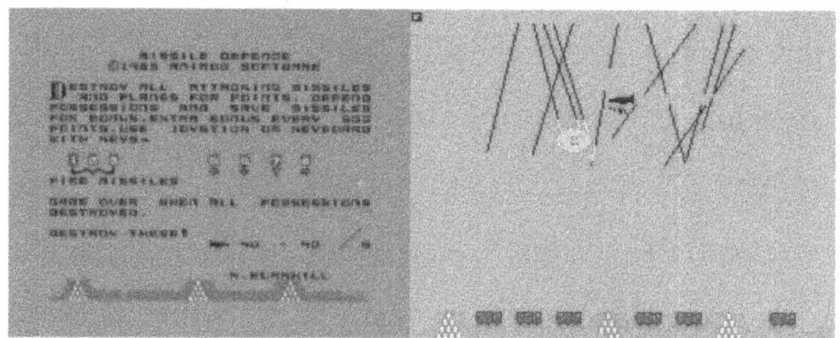

Missile Defence

The resources of the ZX Spectrum necessitated that Burkhill take some creative liberties. He changed the background from black to blue, and colored the blast radius white. He also took a different approach to determining the locations and impacts of bombs and missiles. The ZX Spectrum stored images in a memory map, a grid of pixels stored in memory at a specific address. There were twenty-two lines, or rows, and thirty-two columns, comprising a memory map of 704 positions for characters. Each character consisted of an eight-by-eight square of pixels. Every pixel could be individually accessed, read, and manipulated by programmers, an innovation from previous models of ZX computers.

In effect, all he had to do was tell the game to look at the screen in memory. "You can look at the actual byte where the bomb is positioned on the screen. If it's a white pixel, that's an explosion, a hit."

Anirog and Burkhill made a tidy profit from sales of *Missile Defence*. The fact that he had cloned someone else's game, and that Anirog had sold it without obtaining licensing rights, never bothered him, because it never crossed his mind. "No one cared back then," he said. Not until the mid to late eighties would publishers start to crack down on blatant clones such as *Apple Invaders*, a clone of *Space Invaders* published by *The Print Shop* and *Where in the World is Carmen Sandiego?* publisher Broderbund. Burkhill wasn't out to rip anyone off. He was just a kid who deduced that the best way to learn how to make games was to copy one that already existed, which would open doors for him in the future.

"I was just a kid living at my parents' house," he said. "From day one, I wanted to sell it. I wanted to get into the industry."

Chapter 4: Pac-Man

Part I: Essence

TOD FRYE STEPPED into his boss's office and found another programmer, Bob Polero, already waiting. Frye sat down beside Polero and listened as his boss made a pitch.

"We have two coin-op conversions that need to get started," he said.

Frye raised an eyebrow. Only two? It was April of 1981, and everyone at Atari was hustling. Two years earlier, several key employees had quit and founded Activision. The idea of any studio other than Atari producing games for the Atari 2600 console was still hard to fathom, but Activision's growing team had already put out several hits such as *Pitfall!* by David Crane, a former colleague of Frye's. Refusing to cede hot properties to the competition, Atari had been signing licenses to convert coin-op games to cartridges for the 2600.

Atari's first big coin-op-to-console release had been *Space Invaders*. There were many more to come. Shoot-em-ups like *Defender*, *Missile Command, Asteroids*, and *Galaxian*; racing games like *Rally-X* and *Pole Position*; maze crawls like *Pac-Man*, *Berzerk*, and *Wizard of Wor*; platformers—run-and-jumpers—like *Donkey Kong*.

The two up for discussion during today's meeting were *Defender* and *Pac-Man*.

"You're available to do one, and so is another programmer," the manager said to Frye. "You guys figure it out."

Frye and Polero talked it over. "I don't care," Frye said, shrugging. But he did. He'd played *Pac-Man* and *Defender*, and vastly preferred the shooter. *Defender* had players defending humanoids on an alien planet from enemy ships. Describing the game as difficult was like describing the Pacific as a small body of water. *Defender*'s controls consisted of five buttons and a joystick. Enemy aircraft flew in patterns and bombarded players and the planet with unique attacks. Most players lasted mere seconds their first time out. Yet the game's high degree of challenge drew them in rather than scared them off. Players learned strategies and timing as they played, and beating the game became an honor worthy of bragging rights.

Pac-Man, to Frye, was nothing more than a yellow pizza with a missing slice running around a maze, munching dots and avoiding four ghosts. Porting either game would be a headache. *Defender*'s graphics and multi-button controls would need to be severely truncated or compacted to work on the 2600; *Pac-Man*'s graphics were simpler, but more flamboyant, and the patterns of the ghosts would be important to incorporate so arcade players would feel at home. But if Frye had his choice, he'd choose—

"I'll take *Defender*," Polero said.

Frye pasted on a smile. "Fine. No problem. I'll do *Pac-Man*."

***

TEN YEARS AGO, Tod Frye had been kicking around Berkeley High School and kicking around life. When he wasn't cutting class by ducking into closets to smoke weed, he kept busy by finding ways to avoid being busy. Athletics, acting—nothing appealed to him.

Frye drifted until he discovered the school's Wang 3300, a computer that connected to typewriter-like terminals called teletypes. Users typed instructions, and the teletype sent the instructions off to the computer over its connection and printed output on a giant roll of paper. Suddenly, Frye than interested in something. Now when he cut class, he could often be found in the computer lab, feeling his way through the BASIC and FORTRAN programming languages.

"One of our students had a father who worked in a computer center that let high school students use it—all three of us who were interested in it back then—and had some interns from UC Berkeley working there."

Two of the interns working at University of California, Berkeley were Larry Kaplan and Ian Shepard. After graduation, Shepard and Kaplan found jobs at Atari. Frye's path to making games was rockier. He dropped out of high school during his junior year and, homeless, panhandled on the streets. Eventually he reconnected with Kaplan and Shepard, who went on to work at Atari.

Atari seemed the right place for Frye, based on other companies where he'd interviewed. At Apple, he figured he would have been writing boring applications like word processors and spreadsheets. Another company had been looking for software engineers to create industrial controls. At Atari, he'd get to program computers—all he wanted to do—and making games sounded a lot more interesting than making digital checkbooks.

His first project lived up to his expectations. His objective was to convert *Breakout*, the brick-paddle game Steve Wozniak and Steve Jobs had written before going on to co-found Apple, to a handheld game. The game would be rendered at 32x32 resolution on an LCD screen, the very definition of cutting-edge tech in 1980—a little too cutting-edge.

"It turned out that that particular piece of hardware could not be manufactured profitably for a mass market project," Frye said.

His prototype consisted of a processor on a microchip, the S2000, with sixty-four nibbles of RAM and 2,000 kilobytes of program storage. Every spot on the 32x32 on-screen grid was represented by a bit in memory. As players batted balls at bricks along the top of the playfield, Frye's code shifted bits—performed mathematical calculations—that caused individual screen locations to light up or go dark.

"While I count it as one of my games, it didn't actually get published. It was a piece of custom hardware that never got manufactured," he said. "It was crazy stuff, man. Crazy stuff. Once you got used to it, it was fine. It was very, very simple games with very, very simple hardware. There was an interesting paradox where you almost didn't have enough power to accomplish anything, but you also didn't have enough rope to hang yourself."

His second project, a conversion of *Asteroids* for Atari's 400- and 800-model personal computers, made it to production. After applying finishing touches, Frye was given the choice to port *Pac-Man* or *Defender* to the 2600 consoles.

"It was very much a work of solo authorship. Things have changed," he said.

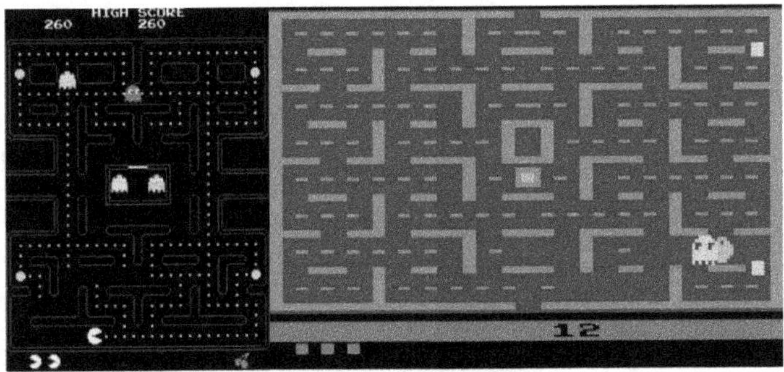

Arcade (left), Atari 2600.

Pac-Man had been made by Namco, a company that, much like Atari, had operated according to the one-programmer-job rule. Businessman Masaya Nakamura founded Nakamura Manufacturing to create coin-operated children's rides for retail stores in

Yokohama, Japan. When video games caught on, the company was renamed Nakamura Amusement Machine Manufacturing Company, or NAMMCo (later renamed Namco). One of its first hits was *Namco F-1*, a racing game released in 1976. When Atari's Japan-based operation struggled, Nakamura swooped in and bought the company for $500,000, outbidding Sega's offer of $80,000.

Under the agreement's terms, NAMMCo exclusively licensed and distributed Atari coin-op games in Japan. Nakamura's company, later renamed Namco, produced plenty of its own titles. *Galaxian* became the first arcade game to use multicolor sprites when it launched in 1979. That spring, inspiration struck engineer Toru Iwatani when he removed a single slice of pizza and observed that the remainder looked like a head with an open mouth. He refined the concept by rounding out the Kanji character for *mouth* (くち).

On the surface, *Pac-Man* was simple. Players guided the titular hero, shaped like a yellow hockey puck—or a pizza with a slice missing, or a rounded-off kanji character—around a maze full of dots. Four ghosts, each a distinct color, started in a square pen in the center; a few seconds after the game began, they freed themselves and gave chase. Players had to munch the breadcrumb trail of dot-shaped pellets along each corridor of the maze. Once they gobbled up the last pellet, the maze was repopulated, and a new session began. Players could either avoid ghosts as they roamed the corridors, or gobble up one of four power pills in the maze to devour the ghosts, which banished them back to their pen for a few precious seconds and increased players' score.

Japanese players paid little attention to *Pac-Man* when it appeared in arcades in 1980, preferring to drop yen on action games like *Space Invaders*. America was a different story: In its first year, players spent over $1 billion in quarters on *Pac-Man*. Coin-op manufacturer Bally/Midway purchased the rights to distribute *Pac-Man* arcade cabinets in North America in 1980, but Atari—then owned by Warner Communications, Inc.—capitalized on its relationship with Nakamura in Japan and secured exclusive licensing rights to distribute cartridge versions of the game.

Atari's marketing department pulled out all the stops to advertise the forthcoming VCS/2600 adaptation of *Pac-Man*, taking out ads in magazines, on televisions, even billboards. Tod Frye viewed the job as just that.

"Now admittedly, now we know that those were important days. But back then it was just another day on the job. I do not remember *Pac-Man* having any sort of pressure. I started on it, and I worked on it, and it did need to get done."

Pac-Man's arcade board sported a Zilog Z80 processor clocked at 3.072 megahertz, two kilobytes of video memory, another two kilobytes for standard system memory, the ability to render sprites with video hardware, and a wavetable sound generator to play audio. Its data consumed sixteen kilobytes of storage. Up to eight sprites could be displayed on the screen at once—more than adequate for *Pac-Man*'s hero, four ghosts, a few pieces of fruit that gave players bonus points, and power pellets—in up to sixteen simultaneous colors.

Atari's console plodded along at 1.19 megahertz, made do with 128 bytes of system memory—less than thirty-one times the amount on the arcade game's board—and programmers had to squeeze data onto four-kilobyte ROM chips.

"The amount of computing power in a Namco coin-op board for *Pac-Man* was orders of magnitude more than the computing power of the Atari 2600," Frye said.

There were other quirks unique to *Pac-Man*. For instance, the game's mazes were taller than they were wide, a feat Iwatani accomplished by installing a vertically mounted, nineteen-inch monitor. Television sets were more horizontal than vertical. There was no way Frye could recreate *Pac-Man*'s mazes one-to-one. So, he didn't.

"That's all context for: I abstracted *Pac-Man*," Frye explained. "I abstracted the heck out of it. I did not even try to make the game like the coin-op. I looked at *Pac-Man* and said, 'What do I think the essence of this is, and how can I make something that evokes its spiritual essence, the essential character of *Pac-Man*? How can I make something on the Atari 2600 that, even if it doesn't look the same, captures the essential character of this game as I understand it?' And in truth, I feel very good about how I did that."

***

EVERY GAME, TOD Frye knew, consisted of two components: appearance, and functionality. To abstract *Pac-Man* from a coin-operated game into a cartridge, he evaluated both at the same time.

"You're thinking about that as you go: drawing horizontal and vertical walls, some gaps, rows of dots, dots that can disappear, and drawing four ghosts and a Pac-Man. For me, all these years later, that's still the essence of it. It was an interesting juggling act."

In the arcade version, the walls of *Pac-Man*'s maze were constructed from blue lines set against a black background. According to Frye, Atari had a company-wide policy that only space games could use black backgrounds. The reason was that televisions in both black-and-white and color flavors were made with phosphor on the screens, and that phosphor would cause a burn-in effect when colorful images were set against a black backdrop for too long. Space games were an exception, per Atari management, because no other color could accurately represent the deep darkness of space besides black.

"That's why a lot of 2600 games have what's called an attract mode, where when you're not playing, it draws some pictures but swaps colors around a lot," Frye explained.

(Other ex-Atari personnel recalled this policy differently, or not at all. Al Alcorn remembered no such mandate before his departure in 1981. Rob Fulop, who converted *Missile Command* for the 2600, shared one reason why black screens would have been used for space shooters, as well as preferable to any other color all around. "There was a hardware register called HMOVE that was hit whenever an object was being reused, and a consequence of hitting HMOVE was an annoying black line appearing on the left side of the display extending about one inch long. A black background covered this annoying HMOVE artifact, thus black backgrounds were preferred. I don't recall any rule about dictating the color of the background, but I left after finishing *Missile Command*.")

Frye changed up the color scheme to orange lines set against a blue backdrop. To him, that just made sense. A blue-and-black color scheme never struck him as integral to the game's character. As long as there was a maze full of dots and ghosts, why make a fuss?

"I am here to tell you, almost forty years later, that it would have cost me nothing to make that change, and I pretty much wish I had," Frye admitted with a laugh. "If I could go back, I'd say, 'You know what? It doesn't look like *Pac-Man* unless I have a black background and a blue maze. Can I get a variant on that guideline?' If I knew then what I knew now, I'd say, 'It's hard enough to make this look like *Pac-Man*. I need you to cut me some slack by letting me use blue on black.'"

Dots posed another problem. Atari 2600 pushed graphics to TV screens using a proprietary TIA, or Television Interface Adapter. All audio/video capabilities stemmed from the TIA. That didn't leave Frye with much wiggle room to create on-screen graphics as deceptively simple as circular dots.

"You have no idea how crazy this shit is," he said.

The TIA had the capacity to draw a playfield, defined as the area on the screen where graphics appeared. Twenty bits of playfield data could be stored on one side; another twenty bits could be repeated or reversed (mirrored) on the other side. That meant Frye could draw half of a *Pac-Man* maze and have the TIA mirror it to create the opposite side, but there wouldn't be enough capacity to render all the individual dots. However, there was a loophole. The TIA had just enough graphical data for him to draw little dashes instead of dots. Those dashes would be treated by the TIA as part of the playfield, but Frye could make them disappear—flipping a dash's bit in memory from on to off—when Pac-Man traveled over them.

"That's what I decided to use for the dots," he said. "It was really insanely hard, and was not sensible at the time, to try and make the round dots. The dashes was a practical accommodation to the hardware limitations of the 2600."

Each maze was supposed to have smooth, rounded corners. That was a cinch for manufacturers like Namco, who were developing boards that cost hundreds of dollars. When arcade game makers discovered new technology, they could add to an existing board or make a new one from scratch. Consoles like the 2600 were set in stone. One option for improving games was to add chips to cartridges that expanded their functionality, but at a hefty cost to Atari. Frye was stuck with the original hardware.

By the time the world came down with a case of "*Pac-Man* fever" in 1980, the 2600 was already three years old. Smoothing out the corners of *Pac-Man*'s mazes would take computing power the 2600 did not have, so Frye made them sharp instead.

"All of that stuff, such as finer details on the maze, round dots, nicer-looking fruit—all a question of computing power," he said. "The Atari 2600 simply did not have the ability to draw the same things that Namco's *Pac-Man* hardware did. Wasn't even conceivable."

Every maze had a tunnel. One entrance was on the left side, the other on the right. Going into one passage led players and ghosts out of the other. Frye found it impossible to simply recreate *Pac-Man*'s horizontal tunnel on the 2600.

"In theory, I could have made a really narrow maze and left most of your television screen blank." He paused. "I'm not even going to think about that right now."

Frye's *Pac-Man* conversion included a module that drew rows in pairs. Within that code, it was easier to draw the tunnels on the top and bottom of the maze, with extra code to generate the pen in the center where ghosts begin each game.

"My sense, rightly or wrongly, was that the essential character of *Pac-Man* was that you had a tunnel. I did not have the sense that *Pac-Man* require a horizontal tunnel instead of a vertical tunnel. And you have to remember, the cartridge was almost impossible to write. It was a little easier to make the tunnels at the top and bottom, so I did that."

To Frye's thinking, the ghosts' movement patterns were as integral to *Pac-Man*'s functionality as the maze, dots, and ghosts were to its aesthetic. He knew that players who performed the same movements each time they played the game could trick the ghosts into steering clear of the Pac-Man character. That gave players free reign to snack on dots (dashes) at their leisure. Without the arcade game's source code, Frye had to write his own movement routines. He relished the challenge, and designed a pseudo-random number generator that produced a fixed sequence of numbers. Every frame—sixty every second—he would advance the pattern.

"What that does is keep the number appearing to be random relative to the timeline of the player. Since the game is moving along at sixty frames per second, the player's moves are very rarely always at the exact sixtieth of a second," Frye explained.

Normally, a random number generator produced a seed that altered routines every time the game ran. To ensure that the ghosts could be manipulated, they had to follow the same routine every time. Frye wrote his generator so it always spat out the same seed, resulting in the sequence players expected, but only at the start of the game.

"I used a fixed generator that would only check what players were doing infrequently, and had ghosts choose patterns based on that," he said. "It used players' moves to affect the pattern: Depending on what the player did, you would get one of several patterns. It felt like the ghosts were doing something different every time, but they would actually do the same thing. That made it feel like the ghost were smart. I captured the essence of that idea in a much simpler way. That is an essential characteristic of *Pac-Man*, and I did that. I'm very proud."

There was one other characteristic of the arcade game Frye considered integral to its functionality. In arcades, two players could switch on and off each time one player lost a life.

"I had no idea—and I had no marketing information to back this up; no one knew anything—how many times the coin-op game was played by one player or two players. It may be that no one played two-player. The odds seem to be against that, but I felt it was important that you have a product in your living room where you can play back and forth with each other the way you could in the arcade."

Frye had only four kilobytes of space on the game's ROM chip to work with. A two-player mode seemed so important that skipping it in and implementing other features—or refining rough edges such as turning dashes to dots or smoothing out maze corners—never crossed his mind. The final product would be a little less fancy due to the space a two-player option would take up, but kids with a case of *Pac-Man* fever would be spared fights breaking out over who got the controller next.

"I didn't feel like I was in trouble. If I'd felt that way, I'd have considered putting two-player on the chopping block. I didn't. I was feeling good."

Part II: Creative Solutions to Impossible Situations

TOD FRYE BEGAN working on *Pac-Man* for the Atari 2600 in the summer of 1981. That left approximately six months to write and finalize his code and artwork, and four to six weeks to manufacture cartridges, box them up, and ship them to retailers in time for the holidays. But Frye recalled no pressure to finish the game before the holiday season.

"There have been some myths about me being pressured to have it done for Christmas. That's not true," he said.

Frye finished *Pac-Man* in five months, a number he remembered as being just below the average time frame for writing a cartridge game in the early eighties. A year later, his friend and colleague at Atari, Howard Scott Warshaw, would be tasked with developing a game based on Steven Spielberg's E.T. in under two months. That, Frye knew from talking to Warshaw, was pressure. "He did it in five weeks, and that is ridiculous. In the history of the Atari 2600, *Pac-Man* and *E.T.* really stand out. Not from all the other games, but as notable events within the history of the VCS. *E.T.* had the highly compressed schedule pressure. It has seemed to me, in listening to people who were not there, that they get confused sometimes, and think that what happened with *E.T.* happened with *Pac-Man*. That is not the case. I do not honestly recall any particular pressure to finish it early."

In the five months Frye worked on *Pac-Man*, the industry changed. *Electronic Games*, the first magazine devoted to consumer video games, premiered in the U.K. in November of 1981. (Magazines such as *RePlay*, founded in 1974, came first, but were trade publications aimed at arcade operators. Journalists had been writing about games in newspapers and magazines since the late seventies, but those publications weren't dedicated to coverage of the gaming industry.) In early 1982, just before *Pac-Man* released, Tod Frye approached his manager, George Kiss, and told him that he and Warshaw had been offered jobs at Twentieth Century Fox, where executives wanted the two programmers to helm a new video game studio. Ray Kassar, the chief of Atari, feared a repeat of the disgruntlement that had led employees to leave and form Activision and Imagic in years past. Moreover, Frye and Warshaw were the only two senior programmers he had. He needed them more than they needed him, and they knew it. Kassar appeased both engineers by drawing up new contracts that promised them a share of royalties per cartridge sold.

Atari threw its weight behind a marketing campaign for *Pac-Man*, canvassing newspapers and magazines with advertisements that billed April 3, 1982, as National Pac-Man Day. However, the game's on-sale date was elastic depending on when retailers received shipments and stocked shelves. Three Capps stores in Madison,

Wisconsin, received ninety-six copies each in mid-March, and put the game on sale on March 16.

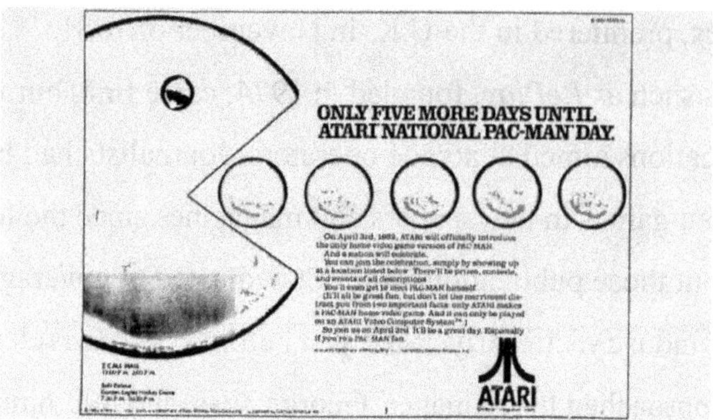

No matter when and where *Pac-Man* went on sale, retailers sold through stock and placed orders for more copies. Atari was ready. The company had ramped up to meet demand, cranking out millions of cartridges in anticipation of at least $500 million in sales. Seven million of those cartridges found their way into consumers' homes. Tod Frye, who received ten cents per cartridge sold, earned hundreds of thousands in a few months.

Almost overnight, critics and consumers went from excited to appalled. *Pac-Man*'s visuals on the Atari were nowhere close to the arcade version. The ghosts flickered constantly, a byproduct of how Frye used and reused the Atari 2600's limited game objects, a catch-all term for graphics such as the player-character and the ghosts. He had approached management with a solution to the problem: Give him eight kilobytes of ROM per cartridge instead of the usual four. Doubling the cartridge's capacity would, when paired with a memory management technique known as bank-switching, eliminate the problem. Frye had even come up with a proprietary solution to the flicker effect, but tabled it after management expressed concern. Atari had one shot to get *Pac-Man* right. This wasn't the time to try something untested.

Besides, management added, *Pac-Man* was a guaranteed bestseller regardless of whether the game shipped on four-kilobyte cartridges or eight kilobytes. The cost to double ROM sizes was miniscule for an individual cart, but that cost would be multiplied by the millions of cartridges it planned to build.

That was another thing. Marketing data in Atari's possession showed that out of the twenty million 2600 consoles they had sold to date, approximately ten million were still in use. The company was going to pump out more cartridges than there would be consumers still playing their 2600s. Perhaps, Frye thought, management assumed that the availability of *Pac-Man* would spur consumers who had offloaded their console to buy another, or dig their first one out of the attic.

Frye was vexed by complaints over his game's flickering. "If you look at *Defender*, the other Atari cartridge made at the time, it has vastly more flicker than *Pac-Man* does. And I am not dissing on the engineer who put together *Defender*. I'm saying we were reaching the point where flicker was getting hard to avoid on the 2600. That has to do with stretching the fixed form factor of the

Atari 2600, and the way coin-op machines kept getting more and more computing power."

Atari enjoyed a boost during the game's first few weeks at retail, but in time, pundits cited it as one of the key failures—along with factors such as Warshaw's poorly received *E.T.* game, a glut of consoles by Atari and other companies that wanted in on the consumer-game gold rush, Atari's hesitation to release a successor to the 2600, and, indirectly, the founding of Activision by ex-Atari developers, opening the door to other third-party developers who rushed poorly made titles to retail—that led to the crash of North America's video game market in 1983.

"I finished *Pac-Man* and moved on to the next thing, and I wasn't paying attention to or thinking about reviews," Frye admitted. "When they came out, I resented the bad reviews. Also, there was nothing I could do about it."

Reflecting on *Pac-Man* is bittersweet for Frye. "Looking back, so many things were being done for the first time. When I converted *Pac-Man*, what it was to determine what parts of a video game were essential to its character weren't particularly well-understood. Certainly not by me. I really love programming computers, and I really loved solving these difficult programming problems. Getting *Pac-Man* to run was not easy. I don't want to minimize how difficult the work was: I enjoyed it, but in a sense, it was made easier by the fact that you couldn't do much. It was almost impossible to do anything, but the system was so limited that you couldn't give yourself enough rope to cause problems. I really enjoyed that, and the fact of the matter is that a $60k-a-year salary for twenty-five-year-old Tod in 1981 would have been all the compensation I cared about. I worked really hard, and I'm really proud."

As proud as he is of the impossible task posed to him, he does think about what he'd do differently. "How could that have gotten out of our department with how wrong it was?" he said of his orange-and-blue maze. "No one knew it was wrong. Plenty of people will look back and say, 'That's obvious,' but I didn't know I'd need an exemption from Atari's policy. I would change that, but otherwise I'm really proud of what I was able to accomplish. My one regret is not trying harder to reduce the flicker."

Chapter 5: Donkey Kong

Part I: Barrel Full of Monkeys

SICKLY GREEN LIGHT washed over the stubble and pale complexion of the man hunched in front of his computer monitor. Beside it sat a television, black except for five horizontal, crimson-colored bands running from top to bottom like lines on notebook paper.

Garry Kitchen closed his eyes, but the straight red lines were burned into the backs of his eyelids. Behind him came a steady pounding: *pound—pound-pound-pound.* He didn't rise to the bait. He knew what he'd see. On the arcade cabinet's screen, a giant ape the size of King Kong had just scaled a construction site made of straight red girders. With every stomp, the platforms had twisted and bent until they were slanted like ramps. Standing tall at the top, the ape intoned his grating, mechanical laugh.

Kitchen gritted his teeth. His replica of the construction site was almost perfect. Steel girders, a flaming barrel, a little man in red-and-blue overalls, an ape at the top.

There was just one glaring, maddening difference. His platforms refused to bend. That was going to be a problem.

The advent of technology in one industry causes ripple effects that touch others. In 1968, Viatron Computer Systems coined the term *microprocessor* to describe the integrated circuit found in its System 21 computer. One year later, Intel engineer Ted Hoff invented the first commercial microprocessor, a technology that triggered change throughout hardware and software development. Engineers could store enormous processing power in a single chip and produce them en masse, greatly reducing manufacturing costs. Those savings could be transferred to consumers in the form of more affordable technology ranging from calculators, printers, and microcomputers, or PCs, affordable and compact enough to take their place in homes and offices.

In 1972, Mark Lesser was living with his in-laws in Laguna Niguel, California, when he answered a job ad for a circuit designer at Rockwell. Lesser was brought up to speed after joining the microelectronics division. Toy company Mattel had approached Rockwell to convert calculators into a handheld game, and George Klose and Richard Cheng, two of the division's engineers, pitched an auto racing title. The idea of animated graphics was pure science fiction in the early to mid-seventies. Instead, they described a blocky handheld unit with tiny controls and an LED screen. The player would be represented as a vertical red blip at the bottom, and would use a small control stick to swerve around other blips—rival vehicles—in their mad dash to the top of the screen.

Klose and Cheng envisioned the game, but had no idea how to build it. Mark Lesser did. He consulted with Rockwell engineers and determined that a single chip from an LED calculator would do the trick. Each chip had 511 bytes of ROM for a program, and every bit and byte would need to be used elegantly to display information such as the blips representing racecars, generating beeps when vehicles collided and the steady growl of the engine as the player shifted gears, and processing input from the player. Lesser wrote a multiplexing (combining multiple signals into one) routine to display the playfield as well as information such as the score using digit drivers in memory; a single line of code that toggled the speaker and produced tones based on the timing of certain variables; and maintenance for the game logic, scoring, and time-keeping—all in 511 bytes of code, several times smaller than the tiniest Microsoft Word document.

The humbly titled *Auto Race* launched in 1976. Lesser's next project was another handheld game, titled *Football.* It used a different chip than *Auto Race*, but still permitted no more than nine yard positions on the display at once. Mattel signed a deal with Sears to carry *Auto Race* and *Football*, only for Sears to back out. The company's executives believed the games were too crude to catch on, and told Rockwell to cease production after 100,000 units had already been made. Six months later, by mid-February of 1978, they had sold through their supply and then some. Over 500,000 units were being sold per week.

Garry Kitchen watched the success of Mattel's electronic games with interest. Just a few years ago he'd been a college kid chasing an art degree and working part-time at Wickstead Design

Associates, a firm that built consumer products like calculators and other digital electronics. “I ended up getting involved in microprocessor engineering because I kind of had to,” Kitchen recalled. “During this time period, I'd switched from art in school to electrical engineering. I was learning engineering on the job, so why not finish my degree in engineering? We were a small company, I got dragged into doing work of a much higher caliber out of necessity. There was one guy who could, but he wasn't available.”

By the time he’d finished learning the basics, he was able to design, build, and solder boards himself. Kitchen stayed on at WDA as one of four employees, and discovered that *Football* used the same microprocessor found in their electronics. “Let’s try to do something fun with this,” Kitchen said to his bosses. “That’ll be much more interesting than clocks and calculators.”

His managers agreed and, in the late seventies, signed a deal with Parker Bros. to make electronic toys. Kitchen’s first was *Wildfire*, a handheld pinball game equipped with LEDs and a four-bit microprocessor. *Wildfire* had been someone else’s design; Kitchen had simply followed orders and built it. For his next project, he designed and engineered *Bankshot*, a billiards-style handheld, and patented his work.

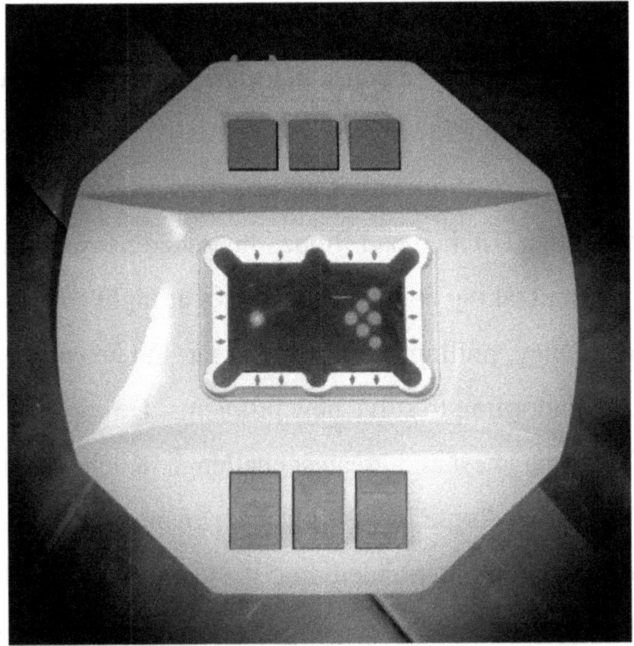

Bankshot. (Image courtesy of Garry Kitchen.)

By 1978, consumer electronics were evolving from handheld electronics to Atari's 2600 machine. While Atari had started out as the sole manufacturer of games for its console, Activision opened that December and developed games for personal computers and the 2600—a tacit admission to developers everywhere that anyone could write games for Atari hardware. Kitchen went to his bosses. "Look, electronic toys are being hurt in the marketplace by video games," he said. They stared blankly. Video games? Kitchen pressed on: "Everybody's jumping on this Atari thing. We should look into it."

Kitchen asked around and received little feedback. Atari couldn't stop Activision and other studios from making games for its device, but it didn't have to help. There was no software development kit, no prototype console designed to write and test code. Activision's founders only knew how to make games for the 2600 because they'd worked with it while at the company.

By that time, Kitchen had flipped his schedule, working at WDA full-time and taking engineering classes at night. He wasn't making much money, pulling in $11,000 a year, but he enjoyed waking up every morning to solve new problems. Developing games for the 2600 was his latest and greatest challenge. Kitchen scraped together $1200 for an Apple II—the most expensive of 1977's "holy trinity" of personal computers, including the Commodore PET and Radio Shack TRS-80—and dissected his new machine to learn its ins and outs. It ran on a 6502 8-bit processor, which he picked up on quickly having worked with microprocessors on electronic toys.

Once he wrote code, he knew he'd have to find a way to put it on an Atari 2600 cartridge. His solution was a custom-made board with a chip he'd soldered on to play Atari ROMs. Testing code required him to run a ribbon cable from the chip on his board to the teeth in the 2600's cartridge slot.

Six months later, he'd completely reverse-engineered the 2600 using his jerry-rigged setup and written a game, *Space Jockey*. The program weighed in at two kilobytes, four times the size of Mark Lesser's 511-byte handheld games, and was much more complex. A shooter, *Space Jockey* scrolled the screen to the right as the player shot down enemy ships. Kitchen took his creation to his bosses at WDA. He had daydreamed about Atari and Activision getting into a bidding war over *Space Jockey*, one of the first Atari games written outside either studio's walled garden. Instead, Donald Yu, one of his bosses, published it through US Games, a separate entity they'd founded to publish electronic toys. Yu licensed *Space Jockey* to his company and prepared to put it on the market.

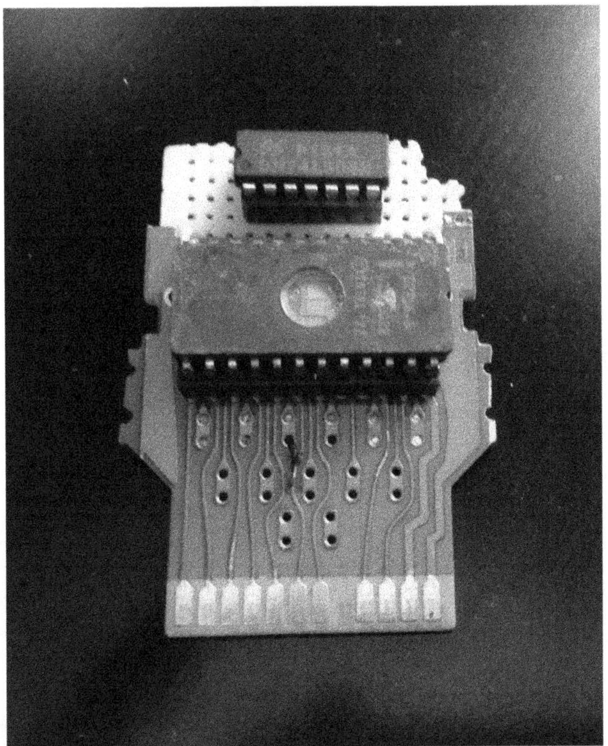

The ROM chip containing Space Jockey. (Image courtesy of Garry Kitchen.)

Before, when Atari had employed the only engineers capable of writing software for its console, games had appeared at a steady drip. The advent of Activision and engineers such as Kitchen increased the drip to a steady flow. Consumers, thirsty for new titles, lapped them up, but Garry Kitchen wouldn't see a penny from any sales of *Space Jockey* when it released. His bosses, as the game's publisher, would reap any rewards.

"You know," he said to Yu and the others, "I should be making more money than $11,000." *Bankshot* and *Space Jockey* had become two of WDA's biggest products.

"We don't think you're worth that much," they replied.

Kitchen quit in early 1982.

***

GARRY KITCHEN DIDN'T leave Wickstead Design Associates alone. His brother, Dan, went with him. They threw in with a couple of other engineers and set up shop in Garry's basement. Within a few hours of their first meeting, it resembled a mad scientist's lab.

The owner of the house Kitchen was renting had left the basement unfinished. Exposed pipes and wiring hung from the open ceiling. Several workbenches had been shoved against the walls, and the four engineers spread out, cluttering every surface with computers and other equipment. Everyone did their own thing. Some guys experimented with the Apple II. Others tinkered with Atari's 2600. As yet, no one had a contract to develop anything. They were just tooling around until something came up. Coleco was the first to offer up a something.

Founded in 1932 as the Connecticut Leather Company, Coleco pivoted to toys in the 1980s with Cabbage Patch Kids dolls. Now the owners were eyeing video games. Kitchen was confused when he received a call from a contract company offering him a deal with Coleco. "We have an in there," the recruiter said, and explained that word had gotten around about Kitchen's aptitude for programming 2600 software. "They're looking for somebody to do a port of *Donkey Kong* on the Atari. Are you interested?"

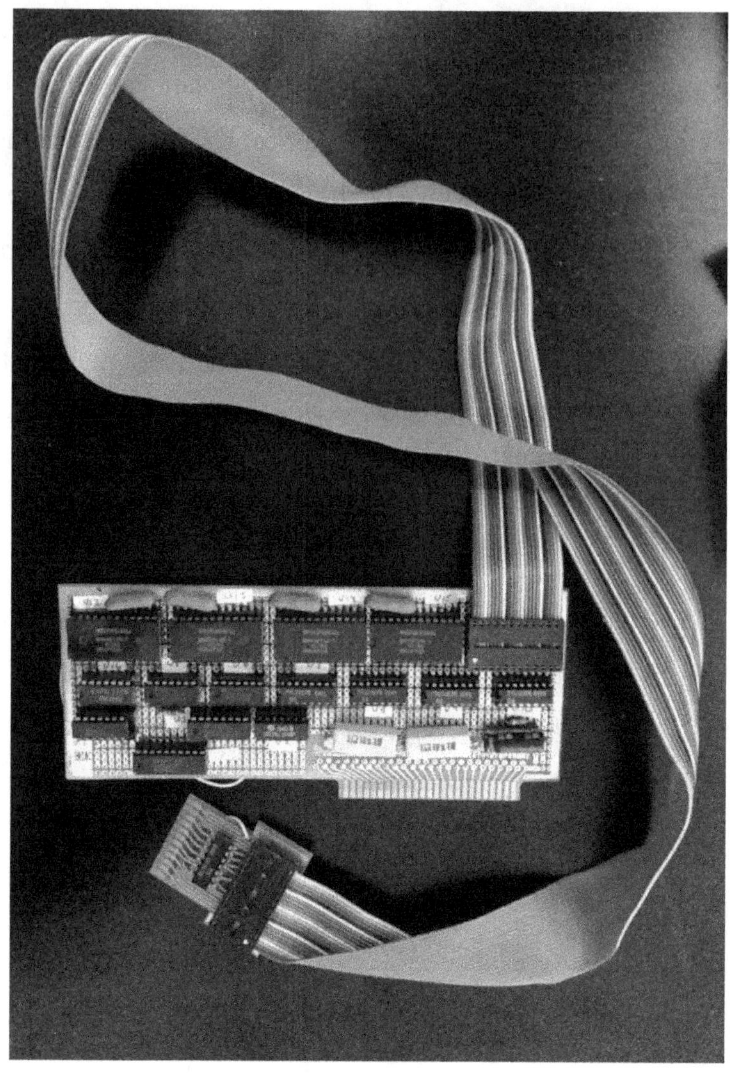

Garry Kitchen's homemade dev kit for the Atari 2600. (Image courtesy of Garry Kitchen.)

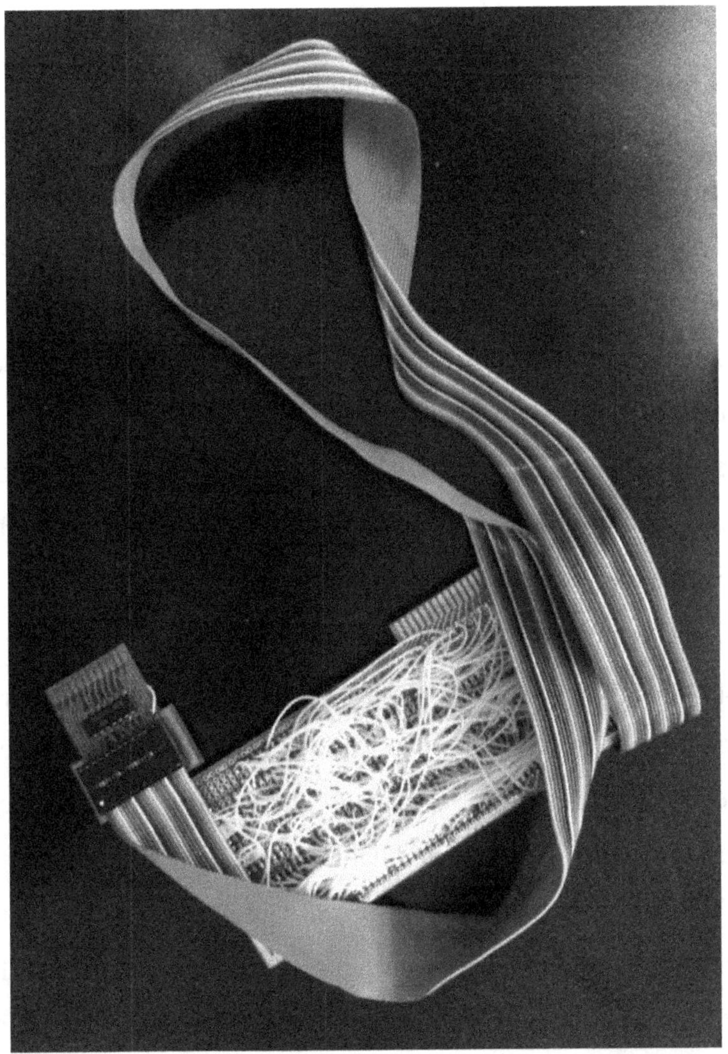

Garry Kitchen's homemade dev kit for the Atari 2600. (Image courtesy of Garry Kitchen.)

Kitchen brightened. "Sure."

The terms of Kitchen's partnership with the contract company dictated that they would split their share of the profits down the middle. Coleco wanted to ship *Donkey Kong* for the Atari in September. That meant production had to be finished by May to leave time for production and shipping.

Landing the deal made Kitchen's day twice over. It meant steady work and steady pay, and it meant an opportunity to work on something red-hot. "It was the best one out at that point, head-and-shoulders above anything else in the marketplace," he said of *Donkey Kong*. "It had a backstory, it had beautiful animation, and it wasn't blobs of unrecognizable graphics on the screen, unlike a bunch of other arcade games. There was a guy who ran around and jumped, and it looked very nice. I was aware it was a very high-profile adaptation."

The guy who ran around and jumped was aptly named Jumpman, and a few years later would be rebranded as Mario. In *Donkey Kong*, Mario/Jumpman was a carpenter—later plumber-turned-rescuer-of-princesses—whose girlfriend Pauline had been abducted by the titular ape and hauled up to the top of one of Mario's construction sites. The player's goal was to guide Mario across four levels, or boards, each a single screen consisting of platforms and obstacles like rolling barrels, fireballs, gaps in floors, ladders, and lifts. Falling too far would kill Mario in cartoonish fashion, so precise jumps and careful timing were key.

Donkey Kong had been released in 1981 by a Japanese coin-op manufacturer called Nintendo. The game had single-handedly made the career both of its creator, a young industrial designer named Shigeru Miyamoto, and Nintendo, which had been struggling to get a foot in the door of the coin-op business with colorful but derivative rip-offs of shooters like *Space Invaders* and *Galaxian*. Kitchen had gravitated to the game's colorful graphics and unique gameplay, setting it apart from the droves of shooters popular in arcades in the early eighties, as well as storytelling segments such as the cutscene that showed Donkey Kong climbing to the top of the construction site, Pauline clutched under one arm, and stomping the platforms to shatter and tilt them. Nintendo of America, the marketing arm of Osaka, Japan-based Nintendo Company Limited, sold through its initial run of *Donkey Kong* machines shortly after the game's premiere in July. By October, NOA was shipping out 4,000 cabinets a week and still barely keeping up with demand.

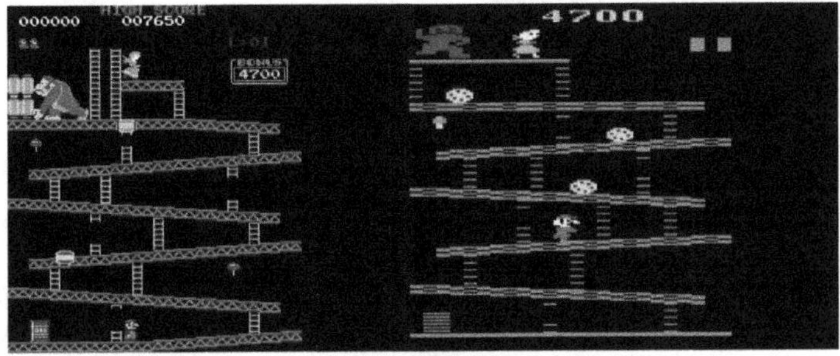

Arcade (left), Atari 2600.

Kitchen received a *Donkey Kong* coin-op to reference the game's graphics and gameplay as he worked. "Since I was primarily concerned with the iconic first level with the slanted ramps and rolling barrels, that's the one I focused on first. It's also the level that was hardest to do, and took up the majority of my time."

He scrutinized every pixel of *DK*, studying how characters and objects such as barrels and fireballs moved to recreate them on the 2600. He even took photographs of the screen and placed them by the Apple II keyboard. As he'd done for *Space Jockey*, Kitchen wrote code for *Donkey Kong* on his Apple. He'd left his custom-made board and ribbon cable at Wickstead Design Associates, but he whipped up another in a month, one-sixth of the time he'd needed to build the first one.

Kitchen had more wiggle room on *Donkey Kong* than he'd had on *Space Jockey*, but only just. Instead of having to constrain his design to fit a two-kilobyte cartridge, he had double that amount. The rest of his toolset was just as spacious: Merlin, an assembler on Apple II that turned out a program in a few seconds, and a homemade chunk of 6502 assembly for the Apple II that took the binary file Merlin spit out and copied it into the memory on his 2600-compatible board. "I would assemble, wait thirty seconds, flip on the Atari, and there was the code, running on the Atari," he said.

Merlin was barebones. There was no way for Kitchen to check the contents of a variable—a container to hold data such as scores, hit points, and character names—as he used them. "The one thing you could do was, in the code where you displayed the score on the screen, I could change that code—which I did often—to display variables in the game. So if you were having a problem with a function and you wanted to know why it wasn't working, you could look at the variable's [data] in the score space on the screen."

When Kitchen had reverse-engineered the Atari 2600 back at WDA, he'd started by writing a *hello world* program. *Hello world* is typically the first program a programmer writes when learning a new language, because it encompasses the basic building blocks of programming: Send a message to the screen. Once he'd gotten a handle on the basics, Kitchen delved into particulars. The 2600's screen, which the system's engineers had designated the playfield, functioned like a container. It could display scenery against a colored background, and hold five moveable objects named by Atari's engineers: two players, two missiles, and a ball. Player objects served as avatars of sorts. They could be tanks as in Atari's *Combat*, paddles like in *Pong*, spaceships as seen in *Space Invaders*—anything an artist could draw and a programmer could fit in memory. The missile, player, and ball objects could be moved around the screen as the programmer manipulated data held in the system's memory registers.

Each of the five moveable objects had predefined capabilities. For example, it only took a single instruction in code to move a player object, but the playfield had to be completely redrawn to reflect movement. Redrawing an object meant clearing every scan line, defined as one row of pixels. This, Kitchen knew, was where drawing *Donkey Kong*'s first level got tricky.

Working with the Atari 2600 was difficult because of the timing and handling engineers had to exert over its resources, as well as those of the television to which it output graphics and sound. Upon booting a game, programming routines synchronized the 2600 with the television set. The processor allocated memory for the five moveable objects, and each object consumed one bit of memory. The playfield took up forty bits, twenty for each half of the screen. Each slate of twenty bits could be told to duplicate or mirror the opposite side, and every individual pixel on the screen stored color information so the screen knew what color to put there. (The two missile objects assumed the color of their respective player objects.)

A raster television's electron beam could be thought of as a paintbrush, and the pixels in each memory register as colors of paint on the artist's palette. The brush started in the upper-left corner of the screen and, dabbing its bristles into the paint colors stored at each pixel's position in memory, colored them in from left to right. When it finished with the first row, the brush moved down to the leftmost position of the next line and painted pixels again one by one, zooming across to the right.

Over and over, down and down it went until it reached the bottom-right corner. At that location, the electron beam—the brush—shut off and moved back up to the top-left corner. During that brief interim, routines written by programmers could reload memory registers with the next set of graphics data. Then the whole process started again. Any objects that had moved—say, the positions of the square ball and rectangular paddles in *Pong*—were redrawn. The entire process was blink-and-you'll-miss-it fast, so that players never detected so much as a flicker.

Where Kitchen and other programmers ran into trouble, and what separated the good Atari 2600 developers from the bad, was in figuring out how to multiply those five moveable objects. Most games involved more than five on-screen elements, and *DK* was no exception. The first level called for Mario, a fireball or two, barrels rolling down the spaced stack of slanted horizontal platforms, and Pauline and Donkey Kong standing at the top, each waiting for Mario to ascend. "*Combat* and *Pong*," Kitchen said. "Those were the only two games that chip was meant to do. *Pong* was two paddles—player one and player two—and a ball, which was a one-bit object that bounced between them. That was all of it. Now, based on all of that, how do you do more? You come up with tricks."

Kitchen knew, for example, that every time a player object rotated or moved, the code pointed to a different block of graphics data so the object would be drawn at the correct orientation: facing right, or lower-right, or left, and so on. Each object consisted of pixels drawn over multiple scan lines. The Atari allowed programmers to designate which set of graphics an object could use on which lines, repeated two or three times. To duplicate any object, all he had to do was write code that told the game to reuse one object over and over.

Games like *Pong* and *Freeway*, a game where players must guide a chicken across horizontal lanes of traffic, made use of a common trick among 2600 developers. "You'll notice many, many Atari games were done with horizontal bands," Kitchen said, describing the game. "You just isolated an area of the screen and said, 'For the first forty lines, player one is going to be used for the cars in lane one. For the next forty lines, player one is going to be used for the cars in lane two,'" he continued, referring to how *Freeway* recycled objects. "You'd divide the screens into bands, and you'd reuse player one and player two as necessary to make it look like there were a lot of objects on the screen."

For *Donkey Kong*, Kitchen designated Jumpman as the player one object. Every girder was a horizontal band. The barrels were player two objects repeated as needed, and represented one of Kitchen's coding tricks. Unlike the cars in *Freeway*, which flowed from left to right but never moved up or down to switch lanes, the barrels in *DK* rolled from higher horizontal bands to lower rows. The code he wrote was dynamic, so the band that held a barrel could move down while never overlapping with another barrel.

"There were times you could have three barrels rolling down the screen, and they were relatively close to each other because one of them may have taken a shortcut and rolled down a ladder, while another one was near the edge of a ramp, and the third was near that same edge of the ramp but below it," he explained. "Those barrels were really close to each other, but they never overlapped horizontally. They rolled down the screen in dynamic bands that moved and changed in height, but I always made sure the game logic kept them apart vertically so they never overlapped. They couldn't overlap, because those barrels were all the same object."

Kitchen was proud of his first trick, but it was a mere hack compared to his second.

Part II: Doing Backflips

DONKEY KONG'S MECHANICAL laughter grated on Garry Kitchen's last nerve. He'd had it with the ape's taunts and the arcade version's crooked platforms. He knew how to split the Atari's playfield down the middle, and how to duplicate or mirror one side of the screen based on the other. He had done so to make the ramps in *Donkey Kong*'s first level. The problem was the two sides were not supposed to be symmetrical. Every ramp was slanted, some sloping down to the right, others drooping to the left so that barrels rolled down them like marbles rolling through chutes in a Rube Goldberg-like device.

He'd been hammering at the problem for weeks and had finally reached a breaking point.

"The ramps can't be slanted," he told his brother and fellow engineers. "I'm going to do them flat, just like level two."

From the beginning of the development, he'd suspected it might be impossible to replicate the arcade game's slanted girders. The second level of the Atari conversion, which was the fourth level in the arcade, was another construction site, but composed of flat, blue girders. Players cleared the stage by walking over the rivets in each platform to remove them. After all girders had been removed, the site would collapse, Donkey Kong would plummet to the floor, players would reunite with Pauline, and the game would begin again.

Soon enough, Kitchen had level one finished. Its red girders were flat, but at least he had barrels and fireballs. By early April, he estimated he was seventy percent through the project with five or six weeks to spare. It was time to think about what came next. *Donkey Kong*'s high-profile conversion would open doors anywhere he wanted to go. His first thought was Activision. One afternoon he called the company and got their main switchboard.

"Can you give me the guy in charge of product development?" he asked. The receptionist admitted she had no idea who that would be, and put Kitchen on hold. Half an hour ticked by. Kitchen was ready to try back later when another woman picked up. She was secretary to the vice president of product development, Tom Lopez.

"Can I talk to him?" Kitchen asked. She checked to see if he was busy. He wasn't, so she put the call through.

"I write Atari games," Kitchen said when Lopez picked up. "Are you interested in having me write games for you?"

"Nobody writes Atari games," Lopez responded immediately, automatically. "Only Activision and Atari can do that."

"There's a game coming out from US Games," Kitchen replied. "*Space Jockey*. I did it. I reverse-engineered the machine, and right now, I'm working on *Donkey Kong* for Coleco."

Lopez's breath caught. This was too good to be true. A game programmer, self-taught, who knew the inner secrets of Atari's black box, and was about to drop possibly the biggest arcade-to-living-room conversion to date.

"Where are you?" Lopez asked.

"New Jersey."

"I'll be there tomorrow."

Kitchen estimated that maybe fifteen people in the world outside of programmers at Activision or Atari knew how to program the 2600. He was one of them, and was determined to prove it to Tom Lopez.

Lopez caught a flight to New Jersey and showed up at Kitchen's the next afternoon. They exchanged pleasantries, and then Kitchen took him down to his mad scientist's lab and showed him *Donkey Kong*. The first level played nearly identically to the arcade. Lopez picked up the Atari's one-button joystick and guided Jumpman/Mario up ladders and over barrels.

He set the joystick down and admitted he was impressed. The game checked almost all the boxes. Almost? Kitchen's brow furrowed. Lopez smiled, gathered his things, and made his way up the stairs and to the front door. Kitchen followed and asked about plans for the future. Lopez said he'd think about it, and shook Kitchen's hand.

"One more thing," Lopez said, pausing in the front doorway. "If you were working for Activision, you'd figure out how to make those ramps slanted." Then he left.

***

KITCHEN DRAGGED HIMSELF back downstairs to his Apple II. Lopez had left the obvious truth unspoken. *Donkey Kong* would be played by millions of players, and Kitchen knew all of them would take one look at the first level and ask, "Why aren't the ramps slanted?" He knew it because he'd been the one who'd prioritized the first level as the game's selling point.

He pulled up his code and searched for a way it could be done. He found one by reading between the lines. "In between scan lines, you can make changes to the position of an object so you can reuse it on later scan lines. By synchronizing your TV, you could do that. Well, what if I could sync to an even finer degree?"

Crafting the solution wasn't a matter of writing a few extra lines of code. He'd have to start over. Motivated, he recreated most of what he'd had, then deployed his greatest trick. He would fill in twenty bytes of memory for one side of the playfield as the electron beam swept across the screen coloring in pixels. Before it reached the right side, he'd change those bytes by loading in and drawing a completely different image. "I rewrote the entire kernel to, in the middle of the screen, store another twenty bits of information to the right side. I'm actually changing the graphics on the fly as the raster goes across the screen, and I had to time it down to the pixel so you wouldn't notice anything."

The 2600 had not been engineered to draw a separate image on either side of the screen. He was effectively pushing the system when it had been made to pull. By the time he was finished, Kitchen had bent the girders to his will, but at the cost of an enormous amount of the 4K he had available to store the game. Consequently, most of *Donkey Kong*'s ROM went to level one. Levels two and three from the arcade, a pie factory and a series of elevators, were cut.

Kitchen worked on his rewrite for three weeks. In May of '82, he entered the final sprint on *Donkey Kong.* Coleco, eager to have the game in hand, flew him out to the office so he could be on-hand to zap any bugs the testing department found. Kitchen was miserable. For the entire month, he sat in a cubicle with Leonard and Arnold Greenberg, Coleco executives and sons of founder Maurice Greenberg, breathing over his shoulder. "Is it done yet?" they would ask nearly every hour.

Kitchen worked for eight hours a day over the first three weeks. For the final three days, he coded and tested nonstop. "Under that stress, I couldn't add a third level because I had no [extra ROM] and I had no time. It would've been an extra four million dollars out of their pockets."

At last Kitchen wrapped up *Donkey Kong* and returned to hunting for his next contract. By now, Atari and Activision were aware of his technical savvy and had rolled out the red carpet. When

Kitchen called Tom Lopez and arranged an on-site meeting at Activision: flying him out first class, putting him up in an opulent hotel, and treating him to lavish dinners. He received a tour of the campus and met the company's growing roster of engineering superstars including David Crane, Bob Whitehead, and Al Miller, who had quit Atari in 1979 to found Activision.

Back in his hotel room, Kitchen mulled over his decision. On paper, Atari was the better option. Manny Gerard, an executive from Warner Communications who had guided the sale of Atari to Warner, had essentially offered him a blank check. But if he was being honest, he was more impressed by Activision. "I liked the Activision guys, and I thought the quality of Atari's games wasn't as good," he said.

Kitchen was young and full of pomp. He'd wrangled the biggest arcade game of 1981 onto an Atari 2600 cartridge. Any company would be lucky to have him, but Activision placed a greater emphasis on designing quality software. He could get paid anywhere. He wanted to be associated with the best.

After returning home, Kitchen called Steve Mayer, one of Atari's founders and the engineer behind the Atari 2600 and the 400- and 800-model personal computers, and told him he'd be going to Activision. "Are you available?" Mayer replied. "I want to come see you tomorrow."

Mayer pulled up in a limousine the next day. They rode to the Warner Communications building in New York City, took an elevator to the top floor, and swept into the office of Manny Gerard. Gerard shook Kitchen's hand and offered him a seat. "I understand from Steve that we need to get a deal done," Gerard said. "What do you want?"

Kitchen hemmed and hawed, enjoying this courtship dance. Gerard remained pleasant, but pressed him. "What do you want? Name your price."

Kitchen shrugged. "I'll be honest with you," he said. Then he took a breath.

Pac-Man had just released for the Atari 2600. Kitchen had played it, and was aghast. The game flickered like crazy and only remotely resembled the arcade title. Even so, Kitchen had come a long way and had given Atari's offer considerable thought, so it was only fair that he tell Manny Gerard and Steve Mayer why he would be taking his talents elsewhere.

"You can offer me anything you want. But I couldn't work for a company that put out a piece of shit like *Pac-Man*."

The meeting ended quickly.

"I don't know things like how long Tod [Frye] had, and I didn't know that he had many of the same pressure I had, so maybe I'm wrong," Kitchen admitted. "Maybe I couldn't have done a better job, just like so many people said they could have done a better job with *Donkey Kong*. But I believed I could have done better. And I have nothing against Tod. I just think that would have been able to do it, but I don't really know, because I don't know the specifics."

***

GARRY KITCHEN, ADMITTEDLY a young pup full of himself when he spouted off to Manny Gerard, shared more in common with Ted Frye than he'd known. Both Kitchen and Frye had been hamstrung by the same hardware and management limitations, and both programmers caught hell from consumers and critics upon the release of their respective conversions.

Due to the amount of space consumed by the two levels he'd been able to reproduce, *Donkey Kong* for the 2600 lacked the game's fun and inventive middle levels. The game's graphics suffered as well. Donkey Kong himself resembled a gingerbread man more than Shigeru Miyamoto's fearsome ape, and barrels looked like chocolate chip cookies. Jumpman, too, was cut down to scant frames of animation, and his trademark red-suit-and-blue-overalls was changed so he looked like he was wearing red pajamas. Sound effects amounted to screeches and beeps. All extraneous animations, such as Donkey Kong grabbing Pauline and climbing up to the next level after Mario climbed to their height, were scrapped.

Kitchen would have been able to squeeze all of the missing content in if he'd been given permission to upgrade *Donkey Kong*'s cartridge. Unbeknownst to him, Coleco's management put up the same roadblocks that Frye had encountered at Atari. "The 2600 had just gotten the ability to run 8K ROMs using a technique called bank switching, but Coleco didn't want to spend the money. Two kilobytes was cheaper than 4K, was cheaper than 8K," he said.

Bank switching increased a system's memory beyond the amount able to be accessed by the processor. The technique originated around 1971, though Atari engineers Larry Wagner and Bob Whitehead were the first to get it working on the 2600. Atari's conversion of *Asteroids* was the first home video game to be released that utilized the technique. However, Coleco saw no reason to upgrade *Donkey Kong* to 8K of ROM. Why spend more money when consumers would buy the game no matter how it looked or played?

Under its licensing agreement with Nintendo, Coleco published home versions of *Donkey Kong* on the Atari 2600 and bundled another version with its ColecoVision console due to arrive in stores that August. The ColecoVision port looked and played nearly identically to the arcade. (In the decades that followed, rumors that Coleco sabotaged its ports of licensed games such as *Donkey Kong* for other platforms so ports running on its ColecoVision would look that much better by comparison.)

Atari's 2600 version benefitted by being more widely adopted, and was no slouch at retail: Coleco sold over six million copies of *Donkey Kong* across home platforms, earning over $153 million but turning over five million in royalties to Nintendo per their agreement. Kitchen, too, pocketed a share of royalties. "To get anything was great, but if you got a dime off four million cartridges, you would've gotten $400,000. I didn't get $400,000. I got far less. Even Coleco had to pay an enormous amount of money to Nintendo. They got so squeezed by Nintendo, because Nintendo owned the game, that they had very little to share with the programmers. It's even amazing we got any royalties."

Kitchen was displeased and a little surprised at the negative reaction to *Donkey Kong* on the 2600. Even today, many consider it one of the worst arcade-to-home ports of all time, along with Tod Frye's conversion of *Pac-Man*. Dan "Elektro" Amrich, a former editor at *GamePro* magazine, believes Frye deserves more empathy. "Tod was judged too harshly. When you learn about the limitations of the hardware and the circumstances of that development cycle, the pressure he was under… it's nuts. People forget that developers literally create something from nothing—they start with a blank screen. It's an achievement to get anything that looks good or makes sense. Now add the emotional investment from players who want the arcade version at home but have no idea how the sausage is made—anything other than what they saw in the arcade is going to be criticized."

Amrich admitted that he'd been crushed by the *Pac-Man* that he played on his Atari 2600 as a kid, like millions of other kids in

1982. “But once I got older and learned more, I came to understand what a creative solution it was to an impossible situation. I’m never going to expect that people will put themselves in the developer’s position, but I encourage that kind of empathy. Education tempers expectations.”

The same sentiment can and should be extended to Kitchen, who harbors regrets of his own about his conversion of *DK*. “I had to do it,” he said, referring to giving *Donkey Kong*’s first and most iconic stage the most attention, and acknowledging that other parts of the game suffered as a result.

“So when people say to me, ‘Ugh, *Donkey Kong* on the 2600 was shit, nothing like the arcade game,’ I take umbrage because of the back flips I did to get it so close.”

Chapter 6: Ms. Pac-Man

Part I: "There Was No Contract"

FRANZ LANZINGER DIDN'T want to come off as boastful, but he was, in fact, a world-renowned cyberathlete.

On December 6, 1981, he walked into an arcade and dropped a quarter into *Centipede*. When he finished playing hours later, he had set a world record of 2,999,999 points. His score was recorded by a referee from Twin Galaxies, an organization founded that year to verify and preserve record-making and record-breaking feats in video games.

Despite his prestige, Lanzinger remained humble. "That's kind of overstating my abilities," he said of his world record. "A lot of it came down to luck. I wasn't the best player, but I figured out how to marathon the game. I did it for six hours, and no one else cared to play it that long."

In November 1982, a Twin Galaxies referee verified Lanzinger's score of 1,081,900 points in *Burger Time*. On many occasions he played games with a friend, Brian McGee, who clinched world records of his own. One day, McGee walked into an arcade with a pocketful of quarters and walked out with a job. Representatives from Atari were scouting talent at arcades in Sunnyvale, California, and noticed McGee's skill. They brought him in for an interview, and hired him to develop games. A short while later, McGee reached out to Lanzinger, then employed as a researcher for the U.S. Department of Defense. In a whirlwind series of events, Lanzinger went to Atari for an interview and left his job as a defense contractor to make video games for a living. "It was a dream job for me," he said. "I liked my old job. It's not like I was looking to work elsewhere. But I was such a big fan of games that to get a job at Atari all the sudden was a dream."

IMAGE COURTESY OF FRANZ LANZINGER.

Lanzinger joined Atari's coin-op department. His first project was programming a game called *Crystal Castles*, a platformer that challenged players to navigate environments crawling with monsters while collecting crystals. Lanzinger wrote every line of code except a boilerplate section that processed coins and translated them to in-game credits. "That was pre-written from other games. All the animated art, the sprites, were drawn by somebody else. But the backgrounds were my doing, mostly. They were generated by code."

Lanzinger was proud of *Crystal Castles*, but a legend at Atari tempered his excitement. "Atari had a rule that your first arcade game was always a big bomb, and it would not succeed," he explained. The rule was known as Dave's Law, named after *Missile Command* creator Dave Theurer. The law came by its name ironically: It held true before Theurer created *Missile Command*, his first game and a smash hit that paved the way for him to create *Tempest*, an even greater critical and commercial success.

Crystal Castles turned out to be another exception to the rule. Not only was it fun, it was one of the first arcade games to feature an ending. The most popular games of the time such as *Donkey Kong*, *Pac-Man*, and *Missile Command* continued until players ran out of lives or quarters.

Lanzinger humbly chalked up the game's success to age and the programming know-how he brought to Atari. "We were all young, under thirty, but I was twenty-six and already had four years of coding experience."

After *Crystal Castles*, Lanzinger returned to defense contracting. In 1989, he returned to game development when he was hired by Tengen, a label of Atari focused on developing games for home platforms. "They were looking for somebody who knew how to program 6502, and there weren't many people who knew it back then. That was the processor used in arcade games in the early eighties, and also on the NES," he said.

An 8-bit microprocessor crafted by a small team at MOS Technology led by electrical engineer Chuck Peddle, the 6502 held several distinct advantages over competitors such as Intel's 8080 and

Motorola's 6800. It was faster, and much more affordable at $25 compared to $200 for Intel's and Motorola's tech. Apple co-founder Steve "Woz" Wozniak had chosen the 6502 to power his Apple-1 and Apple II personal computers. Before long, CEOs and entrepreneurs followed in Woz's footsteps: Commodore chose the 6502 to be the brains of its PET and 64 PCs, as did Atari for the 2600, and Nintendo for its 8-bit Famicom console that launched in Japan in 1983.

Setting its sights on North America's consumers, Nintendo rebranded the Famicom as the NES, and redesigned its case. It was gray and white instead of red and cream-colored, and boxier compared to the Famicom's toy-like shell. Nintendo and the NES faced an uphill battle. North American retailers had sworn off video games after the market's crash in 1983, so the Japanese company positioned the NES as an *Entertainment System* rather than a video game console.

The system's specs were modest but affordable: a 6502 variant clocked at 1.79 megahertz, two kilobytes of system memory, another two kilobytes for video RAM, a generous resolution of 256x240, a color palette of fifty-two with up to twenty-four able to be displayed at once, and cartridges—branded as Game Paks—able to hold 192 kilobytes of data compared to the Atari 2600's four.

Lanzinger was pleased to find that although the NES was significantly less powerful than arcade hardware, its specifications afforded developers more resources to turn out conversions that were closer than any console had been able to achieve to date. His first project at Tengen was a conversion of *Toobin'*, a river-racing game where two players ride innertubes down a river, avoiding obstacles as they zip along. The arcade title was vibrant, but Lanzinger's NES port held its own with a good sense of speed and river layouts that differed from the arcade's maps.

"It didn't have the resolution or the processing power," he said of the NES. "There was no multiply operation, no divide. You could add and subtract. If you wanted to multiply, you would shift bits [in memory] and hope your multiplication was by a power of two. That's the kind of thing you had to deal with when writing code for these things. It took very specialized knowledge to write games."

Following *Toobin'* and another conversion, Lanzinger was put on his highest-profile job to date. "*Ms. Pac-Man* is an interesting story because the original game was not made by Atari," he said of the arcade cabinet. "That was Namco. If I remember, the deal was a single letter. There was no contract. The letter was from Namco to Atari, and it said, basically, 'Yes, you can do this game.'"

***

PAC-MAN WAS GOOD, a few programmers at General Computer Corporation decided. But it could be better.

GCC was the brainchild of Doug Macrae and Kevin Curran, two MIT students who met when Macrae, who ran a pinball room out of his dorm, partnered with Curran to purchase more machines. Soon, they were running twenty coin-operated games across four dorms. One, *Missile Command*, was their highest earner until players grew bored with it. Macrae and Curran decided to custom-engineer enhancement kits that adjusted the game's difficulty and added new features. Players who had tired of *Missile Command* suddenly had reason to return to it and master its new tricks.

Macrae and Curran were having more fun operating arcade games than they were going to class. They had dropped out of MIT and were renting a house in Brookline, Massachusetts, with a handful of other programmers. The friends co-founded GCC and advertised their kit, *Super Missile Attack*, to arcade operators looking to breathe new life into games that were no longer earning. Operators bought the kit in droves, and GCC's developers turned their talents to enhancing other classics such as *Asteroids* and *Pac-Man*. Namco's game was beloved by millions of players. They had a different take: It sucked. The maze was always the same, and the four ghosts followed the same patterns. It was too simple, but data showed that the game raked in quarters, so they followed the money by designing an enhancement kit.

GCC aimed to release their upgrade, named *Crazy Otto*, to arcades in late 1981, when they estimated that temperatures spiked by *Pac-Man* fever would lower. Their goal was to keep players on their toes by introducing new maze configurations and randomized chase patterns for the ghosts. Effectively, the game's charm would never wear off because, unlike default *Pac-Man*, *Crazy Otto* would present fresh experiences.

Production halted when Atari sued General Computer Corporation over *Super Missile Attack*. Atari claimed the kit's creators were profiting on its intellectual property, even though the right for third parties to modify games via kits—or for a game's creator to attempt to penalize them—was uncharted legal territory. However, the fact that Atari threatened legal action may have been enough of an impetus for GCC to approach the gaming giant with a compromise: It would continue selling conversion kits, but with Atari's consent. Atari agreed. That gave GCC's team another idea.

Arranging a meeting with executives at Midway, the licensee of *Pac-Man* arcade games, the team pitched *Crazy Otto* as a sanctioned upgrade. They were in the right place at the right time. Midway was frustrated with *Pac-Man*'s creators, who were taking too long to release a sequel, *Super Pac-Man*. Far from being angry at *Crazy Otto*'s existence, Midway bought the rights to the conversion, made a few changes, and spun it off into a separate game, *Pac-Woman*. The protagonist would be a female Pac character taken from *Crazy Otto*'s cutscene-like interludes where *Pac-Man* met and fell for another yellow, disc-shaped pellet-gobbler distinguished by lipstick, a pink bow, and eyelashes. Within two weeks of the initial meeting, the game's name was finalized to *Ms. Pac-Man*.

Ms. Pac-Man performed well in arcades, drawing in huge numbers of female players, who had also enjoyed *Pac-Man*. Namco was less than thrilled. Its executives had never given permission to Midway or GCC to release a new *Pac* title. Namco regained the rights to the property, and its distribution deal with Midway fell apart. Consumers still benefitted, however. The coin-op led to numerous home versions, including an Atari 2600 cartridge that went a long way toward soothing any ill will remaining after 1981's *Pac-Man* conversion. While the graphics were inferior to the coin-op, they were much closer to the source material than Frye's port, as were the cart's sound effects and smoother gameplay.

Eight years after *Ms. Pac-Man* devoured quarters, Lanzinger was charged with developing an NES port for Tengen. He had no source code to work from. Fortunately, he had the next best thing, a *Ms. Pac-Man* cabinet squeezed into his cubicle. Lanzinger dusted off his arcade skills and sunk dozens of hours into the game, eventually scoring over 100,000. This time, he wasn't out to set any world records.

"In order to understand how the later maze stages worked, I needed to improve my abilities. That's how I justified playing the game a lot. That's one of the nice things about being a game developer: You play games and get paid for it."

Lanzinger didn't play the game the same way arcade-goers had back in '82. Another engineer wired up a separate button to his cabinet, and pressing the button paused the game, letting him get a good look at the artwork. Every time he paused, he studied the screen and then swiveled around to his computer to recreate them pixel by pixel.

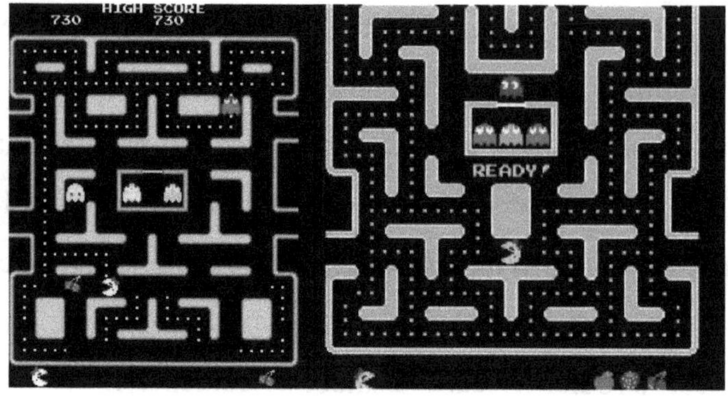

Arcade (left), NES.

His biggest challenge was creating a facsimile of the patterns followed by the ghosts. "True fans of *Ms. Pac-Man* might object to this, but we did not get the same AI logic in the game as in the original. It was close, but not quite the same."

Playing *Ms. Pac-Man* gave Lanzinger a general idea of how its logic worked. He knew the red ghost made a beeline for players as soon as possible, that the orange ghost roamed the maze without much of an idea of where players were, and that the pink and blue ghosts would go near the player but wouldn't close in right away. His facsimile of the arcade version's logic channeled rather than reproduced that spirit.

"Expert *Ms. Pac-Man* players had developed elaborate ways to bunch the ghosts into groups, and those wouldn't work with my port. Maybe they could bunch my ghosts using some different technique, but the strategies they'd learned in arcades wouldn't work. But that only affected experts. Most people who bought these ports were fairly casual players: They were happy to get through a few rounds of mazes, and that was it."

The most substantial change to Tengen's adaptation affected gameplay and visuals. Namco had released an NES port of *Ms. Pac-Man* some years earlier, and Lanzinger was unimpressed. Namco's version scrunched the playfield and interface so everything would be displayed on the same screen. Downsizing the assets—industry jargon for file such as artwork—made the maze's tight corridors and tiny objects such as pellets truer to the arcade, at the cost of making objects harder to see. Scrunching the graphics also reduced the original game's crisp visuals and animations. The upside was that the entire maze could be displayed without having to scroll the screen as players moved.

Lanzinger took a different tack. "I had to scroll because there weren't enough pixels on the screen to display the original art without loss of resolution," he explained. "I didn't have to scroll side to side, only up and down. I thought that was a reasonable compromise. I thought it would be better to keep the art without loss of resolution."

Scrolling permitted Lanzinger to recreate *Ms. Pac-Man*'s pleasing visuals almost perfectly, but at a slight cost to gameplay. Players wouldn't know if any ghosts above or below the viewable area, or if they were missing any dots they needed to eat to finish the level, until the screen shifted up or down.

Lanzinger had other surprises in store. "I went wild and added a lot of new stuff. There was two-player cooperative play, and two-player competitive play, and a whole bunch of new mazes."

Creating new mazes was simple. He and some of Tengen's artists would sketch a layout on paper. Next, Lanzinger wrote a tool that let him construct mazes by typing characters into a text file. "The way it worked was, I would only type in the left half of the maze, and each letter was a code: a wall, a tunnel. All I had to do was type in whether there was a wall there or not, and my code would put in the right piece, whether it was a curved piece or a straight piece."

Every maze in *Ms. Pac-Man* was symmetrical, so he simply typed in symbols for the left side, and his code mirrored it on the right. The game shipped with a wide array of mazes: the originals, which scrolled up and down; smaller and larger types with variable degrees of scrolling, and a few extra-challenging labyrinths for experts.

Other new features were derived from conversion kits like the one that had inspired *Ms. Pac-Man*. One of the more popular tweaks in many kits was a speed boost that made every character in a coin-op game move faster. Lanzinger incorporated the ability so players could accelerate by pressing and holding a button. Her ethereal pursuers moved at the same pace, so the speed boost could be used to escape scary situations such as when all four ghosts closed in at once.

"If I had to do it over again, I wouldn't do any new content," Lanzinger admitted of his port. "If you [deviate from the original design], you're mixing a recreation of a classic game and an entirely new game. You're sort of stepping on the creative vision of the original creators. I just feel a little bit queasy about it, looking back thirty years later. I think I did a good job. The new mazes are fun, but a better approach is to simply update the technology, but don't mess with the original game as much. I guess marketing, at the time, thought that was good, and that it would sell more units. And putting those features in probably did help sell more units."

***

FROM ACCEPTING THE project to handing it over for mass production, Lanzinger wrote Tengen's *Ms. Pac-Man* in approximately five months. "Nowadays, with modern tools, you could do it in a month. But for those days, it was pretty quick, especially for doing it all in assembly language."

He was grateful for help from Tengen's quality assurance (QA) department. Testers played every new iteration—or build—of the game and got back to him with feedback. The process was slow out of necessity. "It was a different time than today, because these games ended up on a ROM, and you could not change that ROM. You would submit that ROM, wait six weeks for it to be made, and then it would get shipped, and that was the game. There was no chance of putting out an update. We had to test the games a lot just to make sure there were no serious bugs."

To avoid shipping buggy games, Tengen and Atari mandated that testers play a game for at least 150 hours without encountering a single problem. "If they found a bug—and they often did—then we would start from square one: fix the bug, start the clock again, another 150 hours," Lanzinger remembered.

Some phases went more smoothly than others. While working on *Toobin'*, a tester reported that the game was crashing repeatedly. He didn't know why, only that every time he came to a certain spot in a certain maze configuration, the game halted. Lanzinger's eyes went dry as he watched a VHS tape of the tester's play session over and over, determined to pinpoint the problem but unable to find anything amiss. "It took me a week to figure out why it was crashing, and five minutes to fix it. That was a horrible week. I remember there were five conditions that had to be met [to recreate the bug]. But I didn't know what those five things were, or that there even were five conditions."

Fortunately, *Ms. Pac-Man* speed-boosted her way through testing. “I don't think we had any bug issues. I think we went straight through the 150 hours,” Lanzinger said.

After *Ms. Pac-Man* released, Lanzinger left to form his own company. A short time later, he discovered that Tengen had taken his NES code, reproduced it for the Sega Genesis, and spruced up the graphics. The Genesis version was published to sales of over one million units, a prestigious accomplishment in 1991. Because the updated graphics didn’t consume much space, and because the code came from Lanzinger’s NES version, the Genesis cartridge was cheap to manufacture and retailed for less than other software, offsetting its age.

Atari and Midway reaped enormous profits due to the game’s small footprint, but Lanzinger never saw a dime even though the Genesis adaptation ran on his code. “This is one reason I left the company. They had what they called a bonus plan, and the plan was a percentage of sales—it was fairly low, two percent or something—would go to the team that made the game, and the team would split the money, and it would be handed out as bonuses. If you ever left the company, you would get nothing. Once I left, I never saw anything.”

He wondered, however, if he’d have earned much even if he’d still been employed by Atari when the Genesis port was released in July 1991. “Their policy was that only the people who worked on a version got bonus money for it. People who contributed to predecessors got nothing. It's ancient history. I'm not bitter about it now, but I was for quite a while."

Lanzinger's bitterness is in the past, but his gratitude at being able to work on such an iconic property remains constant. "I couldn't even believe they got that license. It was not an Atari property. That was awesome. I felt very fortunate to work on this. I got lucky, I guess. I'm glad I did it."

Part II: "The Apogee of the Rocket Ride"

WHILE JEROME STRACH'S friends put their allowance toward baseball cards and trinkets, he got serious, entering the workforce at age thirteen and saving up for an Atari 400 PC. The 400, along with its 800 successor, were the first personal computers to use sprites for graphics. For aspiring game creators like Strach, that meant more colorful software.

Strach taught himself to program while keeping an eye on the 2600's progress. One day, he would write games for an Atari platform. First, he had to get through college. He enrolled at a local university in 1985 and found its computer science program lacking, but easy. He breezed through, able to rely on what he'd taught himself years earlier. When Atari offered him a job, he jumped at it. "I left school and started doing quality assurance work, or video game testing. From there, I quickly jumped into the fray because Atari had just bought from Epyx the Atari Lynx system."

The Lynx handheld started life at development studio Epyx, designed by the engineers who had created the Commodore Amiga. Epyx had a reputation for addictive action games that sold well on the Commodore 64, a PC popular among educators and teenage boys until the latter crowd abandoned their computers to pick up NES gamepads and journey through games like *Super Mario Bros.* and *The Legend of Zelda*. Epyx refused to kowtow to Nintendo. In 1989, engineers Dave Morse, Dave Needle, and RJ Mical, all of whom had worked at Commodore, built a prototype for a handheld system called the Potato. When the time came for a public unveiling, they christened it the Epyx Handy. Morse, Needle, and Mical showed it off to buyers at the '89 Winter Consumer Electronic Show, making each individual sign non-disclosure agreements to stay hush about what they saw and played. Executives from Nintendo swung by, but passed on making deals. Their engineers were deep in the process of developing the Game Boy. All but one prospective buyer passed on the tech.

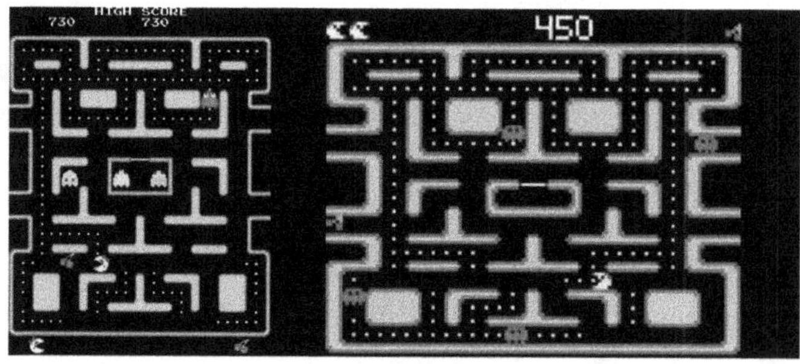

Arcade (left), Atari Lynx.

Epyx and Atari had had run-ins before, but this Atari was different. Cutthroat businessman Jack Tramiel, who had founded Commodore, had edged out Texas Instruments, Mattel, and Timex Corporation to acquire Atari for a steal. Per terms of the agreement, Tramiel gave Warner no money for the company. Instead he granted Warner executives a thirty-two percent interest in his new venture, with Warner holding on to Atari's coin-op division.

Tramiel had bought Atari knowing Warner had been in a position of weaknesses, still recovering from the crash of North

America's game market in 1983. Now, thanks to rocky finances at Epyx, he had designs on scooping up the Handy at a fire sale price. With no other suitors, the handheld's creators sold the hardware. Atari away stripped all traces of the Epyx name. Epyx was reduced to the status of a "software partner," no different than Midway, Activision, or any other third-party publisher.

Atari rebranded the Handy as the Lynx. Regardless of its name, the handy little system seemed capable of taking on Nintendo's Game Boy, a black-and-green brick still in development. The Lynx boasted color graphics, a 16-bit processor, a color palette of 4,096, and sixty-four kilobytes of memory.

Jerome Strach was thrilled by the Lynx, but was not in an official position to develop software for it. He was a QA tester. Still, Atari had no rule forbidding testers from writing software in their spare time. "*Ms. Pac-Man* seemed like a good game to do since I knew it really well, and since it seemed easy to make. That was the first game I worked on."

Strach approached his friend and fellow tester, Eric Ginner, to collaborate. "What was different about his background was he competed in game-playing professionally," Strach said of Ginner. "When we wanted to come up with a game to make on the Lynx, he suggested *Ms. Pac-Man* because he was so familiar with the game. It was just two young guys who were hungry to make games and created an opportunity."

"I wasn't really one of the best," Ginner added modestly, "but I played pretty much everything. I was going for world records. *Robotron* was the game I played the most, probably. Any time a new game came out, I'd get really good at it."

Ginner had been recruited by headhunters who'd prowled arcades looking for pros to come test games. He was intrigued by porting *Ms. Pac-Man*, but foresaw one problem. He was a player, not a creator. What he brought to the table was a deep knowledge of what made the conversion-kit-turned-arcade-sensation tick. "I knew the game really well," explained Ginner. "I knew how the ghosts moved around and all that, because I'd played it a lot. There wasn't much more to be learned from playing more at Atari."

Ginner did play occasionally. Atari kept a *Ms. Pac-Man* cabinet in one corner of QA's domain. "That's how we answered detailed questions we had," Strach said. "We'd play and listen, then go back to our desks and nail it. It was there as a research tool, but we didn't need to use it that much."

Strach offered to teach Ginner how to program as they made progress. He was learning, too. The Lynx, like most platforms, required developers to learn its idiosyncrasies. Luckily, the Lynx environment was a blast to use and easy to pick up. "If you wanted to play a sound, you'd give it a command to play a sound," Ginner said. "You didn't need to know how it worked or why it worked. If you wanted to draw something at a certain position, you'd just tell it to do that. You didn't have to know all the technical details. I do iOS development now, and it's very similar to working with the Lynx. You can spend more time on design than on the more technical parts."

"When we were shown what the hardware could do by the guys at Epyx, they really designed a state-of-the-art piece of hardware that really surprised people because of their sprite-display capabilities," Strach added. "It wasn't like the Atari 2600 where you had 2K to figure out how to make things work. "They provided so many excellent sub-routines. Drawing sprites was easy to do. *Ms. Pac-Man* was perfect for what we had to pull off: learn how to program 65C02 assembly; learning the debug environment; and learn hardware from scratch."

Strach and Ginner had to wait until the end of the workday to moonlight as Lynx developers. When other testers packed up and went home, they brought out development kits and continued programming. "Because we were so familiar with quality assurance, we were able to debug our software on the fly as well," said Strach, who became more of a producer as the project went on, making himself available to help test Ginner's incorporations of *Ms. Pac-Man*'s routines and logic. "Once he got into it and was feeling comfortable, it didn't take long for him to take off and do his thing, and I was doing my thing," Strach continued.

At first, collaboration was tricky because they had no source control, a means of checking out a piece of code so other programmers can see who's working on what. "We had to combine our work manually, and figure out how to split things up," Ginner remembered. "We'd have to compare our two versions of a file, then combine all the changes into one file and hope nothing got left out."

Their primary joint effort was a series of drawing routines to display mazes. From there, they wrote generic code to get the ghosts up and stalking. The next step was all Ginner. "Anything related to the gameplay—that was one thing I knew better than he did," he said. "It can't be perfect, but it's close, I hope."

Movement routines for the ghosts comprised the heart of *Ms. Pac-Man*. The fact that each ghost had a distinct personality—some chasing players, some floating around until players wandered by—combined with the more random nature of their movement was what made the game challenging, and was what Ginner concentrated on translating to a Lynx cartridge. "One way you can move around *Ms. Pac-Man* is you can group the ghosts together depending on what you do," he explained. "You can force them to go certain directions by the way you're facing. We didn't get all of that into the game, but we tried."

"If you were good at the arcade game, you'd be able to play our port and not be surprised or disappointed. Eric was obsessed with that. He worked on polishing the algorithms," Strach recalled.

Their chief technical challenge was the Lynx's 160x102 screen resolution. The maze, pellets, power pills, fruit, Ms. Pac-Man, her ethereal stalkers—lots of minute objects had to fit the handheld's tiny display. Scrolling the screen was an option, but Ginner found it unappealing. "I didn't like scrolling because I think it's important to see the entire maze, so you can see what you have remaining to do. Getting everything on the screen was more important than making objects bigger."

Similarly to Lanzinger's NES port made at Tengen, Strach and Ginner developed custom mazes to entertain players after they had mastered the game's default set. "After we finished the port, we created more levels that built off the theme of what the original *Ms. Pac-Man* was all about," said Strach. "We had a little flexibility, but it was all very much in the flavor of the original game."

***

JEROME STRACH AND Eric Ginner sat in adjacent cubicles. They never worked on their port outside of Atari, sticking to late nights and the occasional weekend at the office. "We were young, hungry, and just excited. Mostly we were running on adrenaline. Our artist sat right behind us," Strach said.

Atari's artists were like loose cargo on the deck of a ship, sliding here and there as development storms raged. Susan McBride was the captain of one of those ships. As director of animation, she'd built the team from two up to a group of ten. "The only ones in Lynx development who worked full-time on a game were engineers," McBride explained. "There wasn't really a need for a full-time artist [on a single project] because once you supply the art, you're done. The coding took much longer."

McBride clicked instantly with Ginner and Strach when she was brought on to their *Ms. Pac-Man* project to render the game's cutscenes, simple interludes that showed Pac-Man and the game's protagonist meeting and falling in love. "A lot of our early development was done on the Amiga," she said. "We used Deluxe Paint, and would generate a lot of graphics. Then we'd give them to the programmers, and they'd convert them to go into the code."

Most of the characters and objects had been drawn by Ginner and Strach. When something was slightly off, such as a color palette, McBride would pull up her artwork, make the change, and resubmit files. "If ever we needed something that involved more animation—and *Ms. Pac-Man*'s not that sort of product—we'd go to Susan, and she'd provide extra assets along those lines," recalled Strach. "Susan did provide a lot of advice for various aesthetics: how font looked against backgrounds, any dithering that needed to be done. She was more an adviser, and was much more important to future games."

The game's audio library was generated by Paul Bonsey, another friend of Strach's. "I knew him prior to starting my job at Atari," Strach said. "He was the guy who got me all fired up about pursuing computers again. We were working at an electronics firm.

We'd been working together six months. Because he was also an Atari 400/800 kid, we would always talk about those computers. When the Atari opportunity came up, I think he was as excited that we were going to Sunnyvale to do it as I was. The stars were all aligned."

Bonsey cranked out sounds quickly, due in no small part to *Ms. Pac-Man*'s modest library of sounds. "I think he did the sounds in two, two-and-a-half weeks. He did it all from scratch, and I think it sounds pretty good," Strach said.

Over nearly seven weeks of full-time day jobs and long nights and weekends, what started out as a hobby project grew into a title that Atari intended to publish. "We'd finished the game by the time we knew it was going to be an actual product," Ginner said. We were just out to make a game, and if it never turned into a product, that was fine. It's a lot easier to copy a game than make an original game. That's helpful for learning, trying to duplicate something."

"The hardware was so new that Atari needed games quickly," Strach said. "I think we were one of the first several games that came out on Lynx, if I remember."

Ms. Pac-Man went on sale in 1991, roughly two years after the Lynx arrived in stores. The conversion featured new mazes, a speed boost gained through a power-up, and a new intermission cutscene animated by McBride. The game was nearly arcade perfect, with the only difference of note being the portable's smaller screen.

Ms. Pac-Man sold well, but the Lynx was less fortunate. Nintendo's Game Boy came to market one month before Lynx went on sale, and while it was technically inferior, its lengthy battery life and pack-in copy of *Tetris* acted like a magnet to customers eager for gaming on the go. Although Lynx's color graphics and sophisticated software made a splash when it launched, the product's threadbare release schedule, virtually nonexistent marketing budget, higher price point for games and hardware, and tendency to chew through batteries doomed it to an early grave.

Today, Strach and his friends don't remember sales numbers. They remember the bonds they formed while working on a passion project that just happened to draw money for Atari and a tidy profit for themselves. "We thought we did a wonderful job considering we were never provided any code or algorithms," Strach recalled. "It just turned out really well, we thought, and we did it in no time flat. Atari Corp. paid us each $5,000 and got a steal on the software we'd cranked out in no time."

"I have to say, it's great that we are lifelong friends now from working at Atari," said McBride. "We all had a lot of respect for each other. I don't know Paul Bonsey as well—he was more a friend of Jerome's—but I do know him. Jerome, Eric, and I still get together. It was a great experience, because it was their first time learning the Lynx. It's wonderful when you have a passion for something, and their first programming project was such a huge brand."

Strach and Ginner still work together, partners developing apps for Apple's iOS-powered products like the iPhone and iPad. "I switched from a tester to a programmer, and I wouldn't have been able to do that without that game," Ginner said.

"It was a really good time for both of us to jump in and change our career trajectory," Strach continued. "I have yet to find a work environment and level of passion and execution that matches *Ms. Pac-Man*. We all got along so well, and those people are still my friends. That was an exceptional time. That game was really, really special to us. My takeaway was: Always make sure you're working on something you're passionate about, because it will show in the end product. I've worked at Pixar, Sony, some high-level places. That time working on *Ms. Pac-Man* was the apogee of the rocket ride. We were young and passionate."

Chapter 7: Double Dragon

Part I: The Whiz Kid

BASIC WAS TOO basic, David Leitch decided. As a matter of fact, everything about his setup seemed a bit too rudimentary.

Taking a break from his college studies, he was seated in front of his ZX-81, a microcomputer that British PC manufacturer Sinclair rolled out in March 1981 with a price tag of $149.95 U.S. dollars. It was a successor to the ZX-80, and although it ran at the same speed as last year's model, it boasted an updated version of Sinclair's dialect of the BASIC language. The ZX-81 made waves across Europe thanks to its affordable price tag and a lean design that consisted of the ZX-80A processor clocked at 3.25 megahertz, one kilobyte of RAM with room to expand up to a decadent 64K, and a custom Ferranti logic chip designed to handle input and output operations. It did not include a monitor; few personal computers did. Instead there was a port in the back for users to connect the computer to a television. Graphics were displayed in black-and-white, and that was fine, at first. A simple machine with easy access to a programming language was all Leitch needed.

The problem he was up against on this night was that although BASIC was easy to grasp—predicated on English commands such as PRINT to display text and INPUT to take data from the keyboard—it was limited in what it could do for Leitch's purpose: Writing computer games. He'd gone as far as he could, publishing a few code listings in magazines. Ready to move on, he taught himself how to program in assembly language. Assembly was much more complicated. It gave programmers a tremendous amount of power by letting them manipulate computers down at the machine level, such as moving data in and out of memory registers. The tradeoff to its complexity was more efficient code and infinitely more possibilities.

IMAGE COURTESY OF DAVID LEITCH.

As his self-teaching progressed, Leitch moved beyond publishing code in magazines. "The first thing I got published in shops was a *Pengo* clone, *Freez'Bees*. That was for a company called Silversoft in London."

Published on the ZX Spectrum in 1983, *Freez'Bees* represented a cumulative exam of everything Leitch had learned in his quest to program games. Based on Sega's *Pengo* arcade game, *Freez'Bees* was a puzzler in which players guided a penguin through mazes of blue blocks while steering clear of red, jelly-like monsters. "These were the days when you could just decide you wanted to write a *Space Invaders* knock-off. Coin-op publishers didn't demonstrably seem to care," Leitch said.

Freez'Bees earned just enough for him to decide he was done with higher education. Truth be told, he'd had one foot out the door for a while. He had switched majors from history to computer science but was still unhappy: classrooms, syllabi, and exams had lost their limited appeal. "I thought, *Fuck it. I'll leave, get a job, be a computer whiz kid, and make games professionally.*"

Leitch was making a bold move. The game industry existed only nominally in many parts of the world. Fortunately, he was in Manchester, a major metropolitan area and a hotbed of development. It hosted the Interactive Museum of Science & Industry, culture centers, and, in the mid-eighties, several budding studios. One of the biggest was Ocean Software, whose teams produced dozens of games for platforms widespread in the UK such as the ZX Spectrum and Commodore 64 PCs. Leitch was more intrigued by another company, Binary Design, Ltd., a development house that made budget-priced titles published by bigger names such as Quicksilva and Mastertronic. Many of the titles in Binary's catalogs were arcade conversions, projects right in Leitch's wheelhouse.

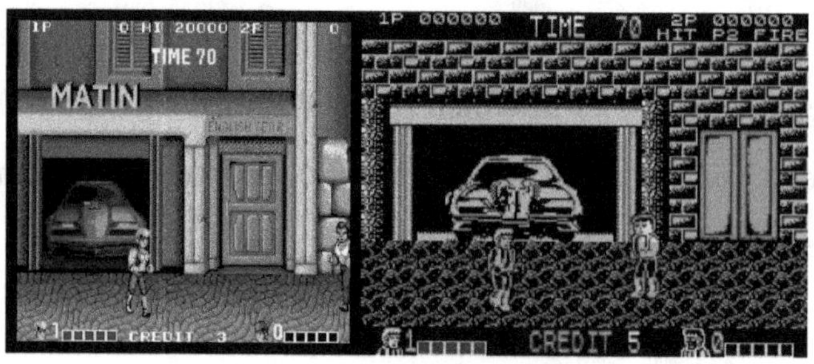

Arcade (left), ZX Spectrum.

On his first day on the job, he was tasked with converting *Double Dragon* to the ZX Spectrum. "That's how Binary worked: 'Here's an available body that knows how to program the Spectrum. What project is next on the conveyor belt?'" Leitch recalled. "This elephant just fell into my lap."

Developed by Technōs Japan, *Double Dragon* was a beat-em-up that was at once iterative and innovative. The first game to center on fisticuffs was Sega's *Heavyweight Champ*, a boxing title released in 1976 and displayed from a side view. Eight years later, Data East's *Karate Champ* employed the same view but featured a wider array of attacks, and popularized martial arts-themed games in arcades. Successors broadened repertoires and game mechanics: 1984's *Bruce Lee* incorporated two-player combat, multiple characters, and collecting items; *Renegade* allowed players to move up and down the screen, a new idea in the genre, as well as the standard left-to-right progression.

Technōs Japan's *Double Dragon* ushered in a golden age of beat-em-ups when it released in 1987. The game's panoply of hand-to-hand and weapon-based attacks made it deeper than competing titles. For instance, players could punch and kick, but certain attacks such as jumping kicks only hit enemies behind the avatar, requiring players to consider their placement. Overlapping the player-character with an enemy caused the player to grab them; from there, players could get fancier than simple punches and kicks by kneeing enemies in the head or heaving them over their shoulders. Environments ranged from wide street lanes where players could roam in any direction, fences and ladders to climb, and conveyor belts that often ended at pits, which players could knock enemies into, unless they got surrounded and knocked in first.

Two-player cooperative play featuring protagonists Billy and Jimmy Lee cemented the game as more than just another mindless button-masher. The icing on the cake was a surprise twist. After defeating the final boss, both players must fight to the death to decide who will ride off into the sunset with Marion, the damsel in distress who'd been kidnapped by the gang during the game's introduction.

Leitch was vaguely aware of *Double Dragon*'s popularity, but was too excited to digest the pressure such a momentous assignment carried right away. He was in his early twenties, and confident he was the right man for such an auspicious job. "You get into it, and then you realize maybe it's not as great as all Christmases coming at once," he said.

***

MAYBE TECHNŌS JAPAN would have provided code from *Double Dragon*'s arcade source, or maybe not. Nobody thought to ask. Binary Design had a coin-op machine in the office, and David Leitch played it for hours while a senior engineer tried to extract graphics from its chips. "You want to know how something works? You play the coin-op, then go back and try to interpret that as best you can," he remembered. "It was a look-and-feel interpretation," Leitch continued of his port of *Double Dragon* for the Spectrum. "Try to get as much of this game in as possible."

Four to six months was typical for an arcade conversion at Binary Design, and Sinclair's ZX Spectrum was a substantial upgrade over the ZX-81, with a base of 16K of RAM expandable up to 128KB, a Z80 3.5 megahertz processor, and a dynamic keyboard with keys able to perform multiple functions. The Spectrum's most impressive ability was generating a palette of sixteen colors, a feat made possible by graphics engineer Richard Altwasser, and a range so impressive for the time that Sinclair dubbed the computer Spectrum.

The ZX Spectrum caught fire in the United Kingdom after being touted on BBC's The Computer Programme special. It was not, however, so great for games. Other PCs stored graphics data in a character map, a sort of grid where sprites and background tiles could be referenced and drawn to the screen one or more at a time using assembly code. The Spectrum was a different beast. In order to meet an affordable price point, Sinclair Research and manufacturer Timex Corporation cut corners that introduced limitations for artists and programmers. It lacked a dedicated graphics chip—Sinclair and Timex likely saw no reason to equip it with one, since the Spectrum had been designed as a business machine—so it had to set aside 6,912 bytes of RAM to hold a display file of 256x192, or 49,152 individual dots. All that pixel data was stored in a bitmap made up of 32x24 blocks, and each block held two bytes' worth of values: one byte for foreground and background colors, and a second for a "blink" value so the block could be switched on or off.

All those big blocks meant every time the screen scrolled, programmers couldn't simply check to see which parts of the grid in memory needed to be updated; the entire viewing area had to be redrawn. "It just looked clunky. Technology-wise, it wasn't that complex, but the game would inherently be slow," Leitch said.

Slowdown was only one problem inherent in the ZX Spectrum. Color clash was another. Binary's artists did a commendable job pulling level graphics from the *Double Dragon* arcade board and reproducing them on the Spectrum. Streets, ladders, pits, and moving platforms made the jump, but color clash painted backgrounds in headache-inducing swatches of bright, single colors: blue over one expanse of terrain, yellow over another, then green, then maybe pink, and so on, turning the player's screen into a garishly colored quilt. On one screen of *Double Dragon*, players walked along a blue road, and the building in the background was painted in yellow bricks. An open garage door revealed a yellow automobile—a block of characters that shared the color coding of its immediate surroundings—but the garage's side borders were done up in blue while the top border, where the shutter rolled up, was white. To the right was a set of double doors colored green.

Despite the simple color scheme, background elements were quite detailed. Bricks in walls and cobblestones along roads stood out, as did automobiles, holes punched through walls, and doors. Sprites for characters such as the player's avatar and enemies were another matter. The Spectrum displayed them as transparent outlines, like drawings in an untouched coloring book, and they assumed the background color of blocks of graphics data as they moved: blue as they marched along a street, yellow as they moved up to a brick wall—all a manifestation of color clash. "That was a fairly common thing in Spectrum games," Leitch said. "For each of those 32x24 positions, you can only have one foreground color and one background color."

Game programmers working on the Spectrum tended to approach graphics in one of two ways. They could band colors according to level design, or have foreground objects such as items and characters take on the background's color, a much simpler solution. "The basic methodology, if we dare call it that, for *Double*

Dragon was choosing to have the sprites take on the backgrounds," Leitch said.

Double Dragon came together in bits and pieces. Enemies possessed unique fighting styles to give players a challenge, and weapons such as oil drums and whips could be thrown and swung to deal extra damage. While the character sprites lacked the arcade's smooth animations, most attacks such as punches, kicks, and grabs were at players' disposal. Two players could work together to clean up the game's mean streets, but one would be saddled with the Spectrum's one-button joystick while the other played on the keyboard. "That added another layer of complexity. This was complicated for the Spectrum," said Leitch, who was new to juggling multiple input methods.

Leitch's biggest obstacle was storage. The ZX Spectrum ran programs from cassette tapes. For players, that meant long load times between levels. For programmers, it meant the possibility of losing hours of code when—not if—something went wrong. BASIC is an interpreter language, meaning computers process one line of code at a time. If the interpreter finds an issue in the code, it spits back an error message, and programmers fix it and run the program again.

Assembly language was less forgiving. "With machine code, if you've got a problem, it's more than likely going to crash the system," Leitch explained. Some errors were severe enough that he'd have to unplug his computer and plug it back in. "This means that anytime you write something substantial, you've got to save your code. Say you spent a couple hours writing a couple hundred lines of code. There's an element of jeopardy if you say, 'I'm just going to run it because I'm confident it's going to work.' But if it crashes, you've lost your work. You want to have saved it someplace."

Saving was a tough choice. Writing to a cassette took minutes, not milliseconds. Saving too often meant losing time that could be spent coding. Not saving enough meant losing progress when an error occurred. Due to the tight turnaround times of conversions, programmers didn't have the luxury of writing code for hours and then testing once or twice. They needed to test a routine or new idea every few minutes. Fortunately, Binary Design had two pieces of equipment that formed a safety net. One was the Microdrive, a small device that ran two quarter-inch, cartridge-like disks able to hold 100KB each with a transfer rate of 16KB a second. Sinclair announced the Microdrive in April 1982 and promised it would revolutionize home computer storage. Like all Sinclair hardware, the Microdrive was cheap, significantly less expensive than the emerging 5.25-inch and 3.5-inch floppy drives. Also like all Sinclair hardware, its price tag came with limitations, namely less data per diskette and slower read/write speeds. Microdrive's media did hold one advantage over cassettes, however. "They were about as reliable as a cassette tape, i.e., not very. But they were a lot faster," said Leitch.

Binary's second piece of equipment at Leitch's disposal was a Tatung Einstein, a PC much more capable than competing machines with its four-megahertz processor and banks of dedicated system and video memory.

"The main thing in the Einstein's favor was it had a proper disk, disks with hard cases. Swappable media. I was basically programming *Double Dragon* on a little machine, and then sending code across to the Spectrum," Leitch said, explaining that a cable connecting the machines was used to transfer files. "That way I could test whatever I'd done."

***

TO PARAPHRASE FORMER U.S. Air Force pilot Chuck Yeager: Any landing a pilot can walk away from is a good landing. David Leitch viewed his port of *Double Dragon* to the ZX Spectrum as a rough landing, with a wing cracking off and more than a few components sputtering out. It was not as faithful to the arcade as he would have liked, but it was a complete game, and he had finished it on time and on budget.

"If you were a big *Double Dragon* fan and you loaded this into your Spectrum on Christmas Day, you'd think, *Jesus, man. This sucks*. You might say, 'Oh, thanks, Dave Leitch,'" he said, laughing. "But for the publisher, it was a success, because they knew people were going to buy it anyway. Whenever this comes up, nobody likes it. I don't particularly like it, either. It wasn't the first game I'd published, but it was the first professional project. After I'd done it, I was pleased with it. But the pleasure stemmed from getting it done."

The timeline had been grueling. The sacrifices he'd had to make just to get the game running were frustrating. The hours had been interminable. But even in the moment, Leitch had had the time of his life. "In hindsight, it was fairly stressful, and would have been for anybody so young. Overall, I have no regrets. It sort of worked out."

Binary Design rewarded him for his timeliness by giving him a significant bump up in pay. They also assigned him two more projects. The first was *Shinobi*, another arcade beat-em-up where players controlled a ninja, that he was able to write from his flat. His boss even gave him an Einstein computer to take home. *Shinobi* was written under the same restraints as *Double Dragon*, but it had more going for it. For one, Leitch was a fan of *Shinobi*, whereas *Double Dragon* had been just another brawler to him. For another, his experience on *Double Dragon* had taught him more about the Spectrum, and how he could turn shortcomings like color clash to his advantage. He and the artist were more selective with the machine's color palette so that levels more closely matched the personality and flow of their arcade source.

Leitch also believed the color scheme worked because unlike *Double Dragon*, which let players roam pseudo-3D environments, *Shinobi* unfolded across a straight line. Players could jump, crouch, and move left or right. There was no depth to the playfield, which made the programming as well as the coloring easier to juggle.

"*Shinobi* was one of the good Spectrum games, I think," he said. "I enjoyed the coin-op. Not knowing much about *Double Dragon* influenced the quality of that project, so *Shinobi* was a better project for me. I liked the pace to it."

Part II: "This Nebulous, Ethereal Thing"

PETE ANDREW HAD fallen down a rabbit hole. Like Alice, he had landed in a place that seemed too small for him. Once upon a time, it had fit just right. Back then, the walls had stretched up to ceilings lost in shadows. Corridors as wide as twelve-lane superhighways carried tidal waves of students lugging books and backpacks.

Every time Andrew returned to his old high school, the ceilings seemed lower, like a deathtrap that would eventually catch him. Once spacious corridors had narrowed to claustrophobic chokepoints. He tried to think more about that, about the wonder of it, and less about the reason he was here.

The halls were quiet as he took a deep breath and peeked his head into his old computer lab.

It was empty. The computers, off-white towers likely running Pentium processors, hummed quietly. Ghostly images from screensavers painted the walls. Andrew's gaze slid to the desk where his former teacher had sat. It figured that Andrew had come all this way to make his grand announcement, to tell the man he had been wrong, only to find him gone.

For a long time he just stood there, soaking in the room's details, and remembering.

Pete Andrew was a bright student. Maybe that's why his high school's singular computer science course called to him. He was ahead of the curve in math, and he picked up on every lesson in BASIC, the language he was studying in a classroom full of BBC Micro PCs, the dominant platform in the United Kingdom, within minutes. The class was split between two rooms: one dedicated to the practical application of code, and another where the teacher lectured. After handing in assignments, he would wander into the other classroom. He was such a quick learner that the teacher sometimes called on him to lead a discussion in one room while the teacher worked with students in the other.

The first bit of trouble came when his teacher gave him a C on a mid-term. It was preposterous: Andrew's solution worked. The teacher had marked off due to a difference in opinion of coding styles. But, whatever. Andrew could make up the point difference. Then the second bit of trouble occurred.

One afternoon in the theoretical classroom, his teacher paced back and forth as he lectured. "Computers are a big, new thing," he said, waving one hand to take in the machines. "What are you hoping to get out of this? Where do you think these skills will take you?" He paused and waited for someone to answer.

Andrew spoke up. "I want to make video games."

Silence greeted his answer. Andrew cleared his throat and readied himself to continue. To explain that in fact, he had already taken the first steps on his chosen path. He and a buddy planned to form a two-man team: He, Andrew, would be the artist, and his friend would write code.

Then his teacher laughed. "That's not a real industry. That's not a way anybody could make a real living."

Andrew sat frozen. All around him, other students chuckled or barked laughter.

"Now, it wasn't a bullying situation, because these were good kids, and I had a love-hate relationship with that teacher," he said in reflection. "But still, it was like, dude: That's not cool."

Andrew knew his teacher was wrong. The United Kingdom's retail scene had exploded with computer and home video games overnight. There was Mastertronic's budget line of titles starting at £1.99 when £5.99 was the going price. Developers like Ocean Software charged as much as ten pounds, but the games were worth it. Of more immediate concern was the fact that the availability of these games proved conclusively to Pete Andrew that someone out there was making them, and getting paid for their efforts.

He almost missed his chance to join their ranks. His mom worked at a factory, and his dad made sheet metal. They had money for house payments, food, and clothes, but not for frivolities like computers. Or at least that's what Andrew thought. "To buy me my first computer was a big stretch for them financially. I never would have entered this industry without that lift from them. I had convinced them, 'Get me a computer and I'll do all these things for you!' I had no idea, but they saw I was passionate about it."

To his frustration, Andrew didn't pursue a career in games after graduating his high school. He didn't know where to start. And, secretly, he feared his teacher had been right.

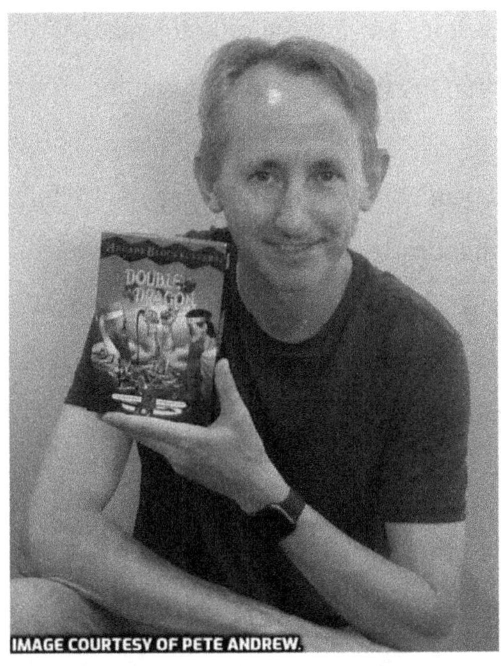
IMAGE COURTESY OF PETE ANDREW.

Andrew went to the Royal Air Force to join up, hoping it would give him some direction. Recruiters took one look at his resume and told him to go get more education first. He enrolled in university, but was unmotivated. Three months later, he quit. After another three months looking for work, Andrew was running out of ideas. Entering a job center, he approached the front desk.

"What are you looking for?" the receptionist asked.

"Anything, really," he admitted. "Something that has prospects. I know I've got no background in anything just yet."

She considered. "What are your interests?"

"Well," he said slowly, buying himself time to think. "I rode in on my bike. I like doing that." He continued in a rush, "I also like video games, but I know there's no jobs there."

At first, the receptionist said nothing. Andrew's heart sank. His teacher had been right after all. Then she brightened. "Wait a minute," she said, digging through papers. "There might be."

She handed him a sheet for a program called Youth Training Scheme. As Andrew read it over, his mood brightened.

The United Kingdom's Young Training Scheme originated in 1980, when industrialist Norman Tebbit laid out plans to train the unemployed during their first year after graduating high school. Over time, the program gained a reputation for plucking young people away from potential careers and into unpaid positions where they stocked shelves. This was false. The goal of YTS was to train and educate people across a range of fields and industries. Enrollees would have to meet certain standards set by employers who agreed to take them on, effectively combining education with hands-on experience in a real job within a real industry.

"There's a company not far out of town that makes video games," the receptionist said. "They're in the Youth Training Scheme program. Are you interested?"

This, Pete Andrew thought, *is too good to be true.*

Days later, he was in a small room with Doug Anderson, a programmer at M.C. Lothlorien, also known as Icon Design. The studio was known for war games, and had been founded by three school chums who decided to start a company together after one man's wife bought him a ZX-81 computer as a Christmas gift. Now Andrew was here, at a game studio, being interviewed by a guy who made video games for a living.

The dream job was real, and it was his to lose.

So far, Anderson had asked Andrew three questions. Actually, they were more like chit-chat about computers and games. Nevertheless, Andrew believed—desperately hoped—he had impressed the other man so far. Then came a real question: What if you had four numbers, and you used mathematical operations to add them together?

Andrew's breath caught. Could this really be as simple as mental arithmetic? He gave his answer, and Anderson broke into a smile. "Okay. You're in." Anderson shook his hand and got up to leave.

"Wait," Andrew said. "I thought you were going to ask me more questions."

"I just did."

"Right," Andrew said, "but I thought that was just talking. I thought we'd be getting to the really tricky questions."

Anderson shrugged. “Nope. You’re in.”

Everything happened so fast. Andrew went from unemployed to earning £27.50 a week, the equivalent of $34.89 US dollars in 2019. The pay was low, like most jobs acquired through the Youth Training Scheme, but Andrew didn’t care. He was making games. Sort of.

He started out making coffee runs for programmers, but seized every opportunity to pick the brain of the engineer who sat next to him. Eventually they gave him a computer and told him to learn assembly language. “At this point, I'd never done assembly. I was a Commodore 64 programmer, but I'd only ever done BBC BASIC. In the real world, you couldn't make a game in anything other than assembly. So I was learning 6502 assembly on the spot.”

When he made a breakthrough, Andrew would politely ask the engineer to look at what he’d written and critique it. The man’s eyes would scan left to right like the platen in a typewriter. Then he’d take a swig of coffee and say, “Well, that’s one way of doing it,” before walking Andrew line by line through ways he could tighten things up.

“Obviously I was just making it up and working it out, but that's how you had to do it: Lots of experimentation and exploration,” Andrew recalled. “You have to fail many times before you understand what the lessons of those failures are on the coding side.”

Andrew had heard of programming caves, windowless rooms where programmers wrote code long into the night. Icon Design took the term literally. He was seated in the basement, and other students from the Youth Training Scheme joined him over the following weeks and months. They used the term "student" sarcastically: They were there for expert training, but other than the engineer who critiqued Andrew's code, they mostly interacted with each other, a group of kids struggling to teach themselves.

One day, Andrew, the most experienced in assembly, fell into the role of teacher. The YTS group rallied under his instruction and made progress on the project Icon's managers had assigned them. "They gave us a game to make, an Atari 8-bit [computer] game. There was a *Pong* mode, and three or four other games inside it. From there, things progressed. I got a reputation for knowing what I was doing."

Just when the group's confidence was at its peak, Icon Design's finances were dwindling. Projects fell through, and paydays came and went. The co-founders had to let people go until only three full-time employees remained: Doug Anderson, another engineer called John Buckley, and Andrew. Buckley had been the engineer mentoring Andrew in his spare time. The three friends resolved to stick out Icon Design, until the situation grew untenable. "They were hoping to have this one game we were working on get funding, but it fell through. That's when I had to move on," said Andrew.

Andrew didn't need long to get back on his feet. The experience he'd gained at Icon Design helped him land a job at Software Creations, where his first task was a port of *Solar Jetman* from the 8-bit NES console to Atari's ST computer. It gave Andrew the opportunity to learn how to write assembly code for the 68000 processor, which he found difficult to wrangle. "It was a game where you flew around caves, and you could rotate your ship, and drop a rope to pick something up. The rope behaved with physics, and I could not get the math right. I was writing everything in 68000 assembly. We had something acceptable working, but it had bothered me."

While he worked on the Atari ST port, John Buckley sat nearby converting the game to Commodore 64. The ST version was cancelled prior to release, and Andrew tried his best to salvage something from the situation. While he had been unhappy with his port, he had developed an efficient horizontal-scrolling engine, quite a feat on the Atari ST. He'd done it by pre-rotating graphics in every position for quicker loading and reducing the number of colors as well as the play area.

There was also the trifling inconvenience of his appendix bursting during production.

All in all, he thought glumly, his first gig at Software Creations had been a bust, and had done little for his self-confidence.

"Then *Double Dragon* came along," he said.

***

ONLY ONE OTHER engineer at Software Creations had more experience writing 68000 assembly than Pete Andrew. That made them the only candidates to write games for Sega's Genesis console, known in the UK as the Mega Drive. Andrew's job was to port *Double Dragon* to the Genesis.

At first blush, the job seemed relatively simple. *Double Dragon* was an arcade game from 1987. It was 1992, and the Genesis was a sophisticated piece of hardware. Andrew dissected it, seeking to answer the usual questions he asked himself when learning a new platform: How many sprites on-screen at once? How does scrolling work? How many background layers?

"At first it felt overwhelming, but when I look back at how constrained the information set was, it was a lot easier to wrap your head around it. Plus, that's where your head lived. When you had new hardware come along, like the Super Nintendo versus the NES, the things people cared about were, 'Look at the number of colors it can do,' and 'It's got these different graphics modes, and here's how they work,' and 'How do the character blocks work?'"

Every experiment revealed answers. There were two planes, a foreground running on Plane A and backgrounds on Plane B.

Planes could be used in myriad ways, from giving all the space to the foreground to parallax scrolling, accomplished by moving certain rows of tiles at different rates, a technique for which the Genesis was becoming well-known. Backgrounds were stored in a character map constructed as a grid of tiles, where each tile was an eight-by-eight block of pixels.

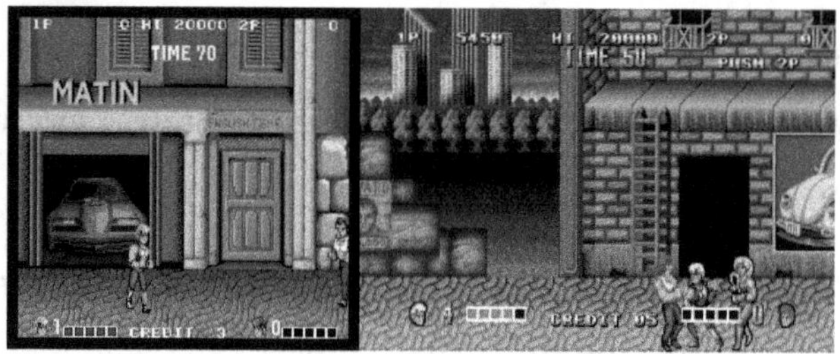

Arcade (left), Genesis.

Next, Andrew tested his growing knowledge by writing simple programs that grew in complexity as he learned. Those programs amounted to demos, but they gave him a framework in which to store housekeeping tasks such as performing an anti-piracy check when a cartridge booted. He could recycle that framework for each Genesis game he wrote, saving time at the beginning of every project.

And he needed every spare minute. *Double Dragon* had to be finished in three months, four at the most. “That was the typical timeline back then: one programmer, one artist, and maybe an audio person. Just, go-go-go-go. I was a kid and loving every minute of it.”

Andrew was self-aware enough to know he was still green. Everything he knew about the Genesis was relative to the Atari ST, the most advanced platform he'd developed on prior to being given the beat-em-up. As his familiarity with the hardware increased, so did his confidence. "Just having hardware that allowed me to do certain things like scroll with sprites, and what we could do with the way the screen was displayed, which was called character mapping—those were huge. It felt like, 'Okay, here's a whole bunch of stuff I don't have to worry about to do the task I've been given.'"

There was no source code, but Software Creations did order in an arcade unit. Andrew played and played and played, absorbing what he saw on the screen and thinking how to best replicate it in 68000 assembly. "On the Sega Genesis, there was a lot more storage capacity. At this point, I'm working out, how do I get the materials I need to make the game from the arcade system, and what is going to be the structure of the game with regard to how I put this content [onto the Genesis]? The two pieces of content were, what is the gameplay? That's the programming, how things work, how the fights work. Then, how will I get the art into the game? I needed background art; the sprites needed to be animated."

IMAGE COURTESY OF SIMON STREET

Simon Street was the artist paired with Andrew. Like his new partner, he'd been interested in games as a kid. Unlike Andrew, he'd had an easier time catching a break thanks to his older brother, who had entered the industry first. He diagnosed himself as a hopeless programmer but was significantly more adept at creating art. To get a job, he'd painted renditions of the covers of boxes for games made by Ocean Software and given them to his brother, asking him to show them to his boss. "Thankfully, he took a chance, as the pictures were okay, but nothing special," Street remembered. "I had to learn a paint program on the Commodore 64 and draw them in record time, but that was my foot in the door."

Street had begun by cleaning up artwork for 8-bit computers before he and Andrew joined forces on *Double Dragon*. The beat-em-up was his favorite project so far. "I was already a massive

Double Dragon fan," Street recalled. "I had played it for years in the arcades; it was always my go-to machine if I wanted to waste a few hours. I was very good at it. I knew all its secrets, and I could actually play through the entire game on its hardest setting using only the headbutt, and complete it with no loss of health."

Street's in-depth knowledge of the game came in handy for extracting artwork. First, Andrew took the arcade cabinet apart, pulled out the board, and removed the EPROMs—erasable programmable read-only memory chips—that contained the game's sprites and backgrounds. "I wrote a tool on the Atari ST that could take data and, based on different keys I pressed, represent the data," said Andrew. Every press of the key revealed graphics data and, instrumental to his part of the project, its format. "That allowed me to fill the screen with the data I had, and interpret it through these different formats. Eventually, when you've pressed enough keys and gone through enough examples, you're like, 'I recognize something.' Then you can hone in on, 'Oh, here's the actual format they're using.'"

"The colors were all over the place," Street recalled of his first look at the data. "Nothing was genuinely tiled in the backgrounds, and the sprites were massive and fragmented."

With the graphical data at his fingertips, Street set about rebuilding the game's first screen, a street near Billy and Jimmy's garage, using Deluxe Paint. Like Andrew, he was looking for answers. No, he determined, the arcade screen was too tall for the Genesis's resolution, and had too many colors. That called for downsizing. "We could cut certain elements out of the arcade graphics and set them to correct sixteen-by-sixteen boundaries, and not have to alter them too much," Street said.

Even so, the cuts were not as dramatic as, say, the ones David Leitch had to make for his port to ZX Spectrum. "We just had to make sure that the levels and sprites all fit to our colour palette and make sure we didn't run out of VRAM," Street continued. "The Genesis definitely made it a lot easier to create something faithful to the arcade original."

That didn't mean Street could slap something together. Recreating a single screen blew his sprite and color budgets, so he partnered with another artist, Martin Holland, to cut the backgrounds into tiles. "It was a mix," Street admitted of porting stages over to the Genesis. "There were some assets that we could take and, with a little manipulation, we got them to fit. But on the whole, [the levels were] a recreation. We had all the arcade graphics, so we could rebuild our art right next to the original, on the same screen, that allowed us to be faithful as possible."

Every screen of *Double Dragon* consisted of a pseudo-3D effect, where players were free to move vertically, horizontally, and diagonally along wide lanes. Pits, ladders, moving platforms, and other objects could be placed anywhere, such as against buildings in the background, and the code needed to know what to do when players stepped onto any location: conveyor belts should move them in a set direction, pits should cause them to fall and lose a life, and so on. Once a few screens were in place, Andrew created a data set that said, in code, what type of terrain a sprite was on, and what should happen to the sprite based on that terrain.

Andrew cheated by creating two data sets. One gave every character a height within the pseudo-3D environment. The other mapped the total height of the game world as well as where players should be located based on their height relative to the height of the space where they stood. Even though the on-screen perspective was skewed, Andrew's code treated it like a 2D map displayed from overhead. The further up the screen an object was located, such as a ladder or conveyor belt, the further he had to move coordinates to determine which tile in the height map players overlapped with.

The operation was complicated by *Double Dragon*'s jumping ability. "When you want to represent 3D, there's always a problem of, when things are in the air, they can be in the air anywhere," Andrew explained. "If I'm close to the edge of the screen, and I jump, I could actually be on the ground two or three tiles back from a visual perspective, the way the game renders in 2D."

Andrew tracked where players were in his height map relative to the terrain that should be beneath them, such as a platform or a pit. He also added data such as ladders to the height map, which characters would grab on to if they stood on its spot within the map coordinates. "That was everything I needed to do to allow the artist to leverage what I was giving him, and to allow the art to work in the game."

Sprites were trickier. Street scaled them down from the arcade game—smaller sprites ate up less space on the cartridge—and cleaned them to fit into the Genesis's color palette. "We would use a sixteen-colour palette for characters, with one transparent, so fifteen colors: four for skin, three for hair, four for primary clothing, and four for secondary," he said.

That palette could be replicated for player two by using the same avatar model, changing the clothes from blue—player one's color—to red, and darkening the other model's skin tone ever so slightly. Every step amounted to memory saved, since the game wouldn't have to load another model with unique graphical data.

Enemies posed challenges of their own. "Some enemies even used the same sprites as the main characters, only with different head sprites," Street said. "However, the enemies used eight-color blocks, not sixteen as the player sprites, so some of them do look a little washed out."

The solution was to create enemy sprites as single entities, then break them up to make them more flexible: hands that could clutch weapons, feet with different footwear, and so on. Alignment was critical, but could be jiggered. "For example, if a punching arm was eight pixels high by sixteen wide, we would fit that arm into two sprites, even if they did not line up," explained Street. "Then it was down to Pete to align them in code. We had to be as efficient as possible so we could fit more in."

Andrew's role in programming sprites was complicated by the fact that he and Street had to build them by look and feel, since he lacked data from the source code specifying that, say, sprite seven on a certain character should be placed next to sprite four in frame thirty-five. Street took charge of those details, but he needed format information for Andrew, whose primary concern was drawing the frames in such a way that used the Genesis console's resources efficiently. "I used a PC to take images Simon had drawn, where he had taken their source art and palette-mapped it to a structure that would make sense on our hardware. Then my PC tool would take it and say, 'Okay, the most efficient way to break this up is to map it to thirteen individual sprites,' looking for the smallest boxes it could put together."

That approach was effective because it avoided scenarios such as allowing white space underneath a character's arm—leftover from cutting the sprite out of its tile—when he or she leaned forward to punch. "If you do that as one big image, that's a waste of memory, and we couldn't afford that. So we had a tool that would take the artist's art and create little metadata sets of, 'These are the different [pieces] you want.'"

Andrew's tool also kept an eye out for duplicate frames that could be trimmed to save on storage and memory. "For example, if the bottom half of the body isn't changing when the top half does something, the burden was on the artist to make sure things didn't change if they didn't need to. Even if the original artwork had more detail and nuance, we would have made changes just to fit things into the cart."

Resource limitations meant not every enemy made the cut. "It was down to how many colors we had to play with. The graphical data was there, but we only had a certain amount of blocks of that we could dedicate to sprites," Street said. "There are a lot of arcade conversions out there that, for no fault of the artists or coders, don't really look like their source material due to limitations of the hardware. We got the look of *Double Dragon* spot on in my opinion, although the deadline was quite a short one, if memory serves."

More than graphics, Andrew struggled with artificial intelligence and collision detection. "It was spotty," he admitted of collision detection. "This was the first [brawler] game I'd ever done, and the first game with any kind of pseudo-3D. There were a couple of problems in trying to match the arcade game that made sense."

Even with his height map, *Double Dragon*'s pseudo-3D, skewed perspective threw off calculations during combat. When an enemy punched, for instance, Andrew had to decide how deep into a height map location the punch was allowed to go. He mishandled some calculations, resulting in occasions where players or enemies swung and missed despite being close enough for the hit to connect. “The characters to need to line up on the exact pixel line you were on. There needed to be some depth, there, and I didn't do anything clever with that depth. It would effectively been a cube around his fist; I should have made it spherical.”

A spherical hit cube, as opposed to hitbox, would have probed more spots on the height map than a square. As it was, Andrew’s hitbox activated when the animation started and switched off afterwards. “It wouldn't have been left on until the end of the animation, because of course if you just leave your fist hanging out, people shouldn't walk into it and get hurt,” he said. “I just wasn't that good at it back then. I wish I could have done better. I know it's not great, but it was what I could do at the time.”

State management, what players or enemies can do when they were grappling versus not touching, was another challenge. Andrew had trouble adapting his code to effectively change what players could do depending on whether their sprites overlapped with an enemy.

As deadlines loomed, he focused on hitting milestones. Synchronized movement, stemming from AI, seemed determined to keep him from completing the project. *Double Dragon* allowed enemies to converge on players from all directions, hence the importance of players being able to strike at enemies in front of and behind them. The arcade game was programmed to coordinate enemy movement such that characters closed in on players at different rates. Unfortunately, Andrew left out character-on-character collision, so enemies piled onto each other, sprites overlapping like a folded paper doll.

"They would freely walk through each other," Andrew remembered. "What I'd say was, if the spot next to you or behind you isn't available, there should be other desirable spots to go to. When there are lots of enemies around you, you'll see them moving in sync, almost like some sort of dance system we'd set up. How they would come at you and fight you was very limited. It was, 'They're going to try and get into that position, and then they'll throw a punch at you.' There was no coordinated AI. I couldn't tell you how much that existed in the arcade game, because the time I had to investigate that was limited."

Double Dragon ended well—or as well as could be expected, depending on each developer's perspective. Simon Street was thrilled with the final product. "For me, there was no downside to working on this game. I loved it. It was one of my favorite arcade games as a kid, and I got to port it over onto one of the most successful consoles of the day."

Andrew's feelings on the Genesis port had been mixed at first. He was aware of its shortcomings and resisted the urge to feel personally attacked when critics carved off their pound of flesh.

Even so, he had been pleased that he'd finished the game at all. It had been his toughest and most ambitious project to date, and the fact that it existed, that characters on the screen moved and fought and lived and died according to code he had written, was a small miracle.

The project had boiled down to moments: the moment he figured out where artwork had been on the EPROMs; the moment a level had taken shape before his eyes; the moment he had touched a controller and made the player-characters move.

"You spend time saying, 'I want this thing to happen,'" Andrew remembered. "You're creating something in this weird, nebulous way where once you've created it, it acts, and it behaves. There's something really thrilling about that. It doesn't matter how simple the thing you're doing is. It still gives you that rush of, 'I made it work.' That moment is just thrilling. I guess that's it. The moment you can take something from your head, this nebulous, ethereal thing that doesn't exist outside of your imagination, and turn it into something tangible and tactile—there's something magical about that. That's true of every creative endeavor: art, music, writing, video games—it's a common motivator."

***

PETE ANDREW BROKE his reverie. He trailed back down the corridor toward the exit.

Although no one would remember his adaptation of *Double Dragon* as arcade perfect, Software Creation's higher-ups had thought it more than good enough. When management announced they needed someone to go to the United States and work on an adaptation of Disney's *Beauty & the Beast* for the Genesis, Andrew made his case for why he was the right programmer. They agreed.

"They never would have sent me if I hadn't had some success and built up some trust. I never would have come to America, and I never would have gone down this path."

Beginning there, every job Andrew accepted represented one rung up a career ladder. He accepted a lead programmer position at Electronic Arts' Seattle office, went from there to Volition and then to THQ where he was technical director for two years, then to EA in Canada as technical director, all the way to D3 Publisher of America, where he was promoted from VP of product development, to VP of publishing, to his current position as senior VP of product development across the entire studio.

Andrew took one final look around, then pulled out of the lot.

"I really wanted to say to him, 'Look what I did,'" he reflected of his teacher. "The whole thing is, what he was really saying was, 'I have no idea how that happens. I have never witnessed anybody doing it. It's not in my realm of experience. Therefore, it doesn't happen.' Well, the world's bigger than your realm of experience, and the things you have touched."

Chapter 8: Tetris

Part I: Atari and Atari

ED LOGG KNEW a thing or two about lines. He'd co-created *Asteroids* at Atari, a game where players piloted a ship and blasted the eponymous space rocks into smaller and smaller bits. Released in 1979, *Asteroids* was in black and white, but the animation was slick and fluid thanks to raster graphics, a technique that rendered graphics from lines.

But the game he was staring at was beyond anything he'd ever seen. On the monitor of an Atari ST, segmented lines in different shapes—a proper "L," a mirrored "L," a plus-shaped block, a straight line that could be flipped horizontally or vertically—rained down from the sky into stacks at the bottom. There was no one at the controls. It was an automated demo, what arcade developers called an attract mode.

As Logg watched, the AI guided the lines to fill in gaps in the stack. The lines could be flipped to face different directions as they fell, like puzzle pieces adjusted to fit their spaces. When blocks formed a horizontal line, it flashed and disappeared, and the score increased. Logg tapped a key and began to play. With every block he dropped and every line he filled out, his addiction grew. It was a puzzle, almost mathematical in its precise execution. Blocks fell, and he had to maneuver them into place to form horizontal lines as quickly as possible before the screen filled up.

Logg went to track down a manager. This game, *Tetris*, could be the next big thing on home consoles, and he would be the one to write it.

ED LOGG (LEFT) ATTENDING A LAUNCH PARTY FOR TENGEN'S TETRIS FOR NES.

Curiosity guided Logg to computers. In high school, he enrolled in programming classes as a means of learning what made the machines tick. Programming fed the part of his brain that was addicted to problem-solving. After studying computer science in college, he was hired by Control Data Corp, where he wrote a little bit of this and that: games, Snoopy calendars, printable artwork. "I did conversions of the original *Adventure* and *Star Trek* between

CDC Fortran and the IBM Fortran," he said. "So although I was paid to support CDC software, I often did games on the side."

Logg discovered *Adventure*, Atari programmer Warren Robinett's game in which players controlled a square and explored simple dungeons and caves, at a Christmas party where someone had brought a prototype of the Atari Video Computer System (2600) game console. The following year, he built his own computer and wrote games for it. Games remained a hobby until a friend at CDC got a job at Atari, which happened to be across the street from the CDC offices. His friend encouraged him to apply, and he was hired in February 1978.

Logg worked in a group led by Dave Stubben, an engineer known among the team for what the rest of Atari called the "Stubben test." A monster of a man at roughly 350 pounds, Stubben would beat, bend, twist, and perform handstands on hardware to test its durability. Logg's first project was to finish *Avalanche*, a reflex-based game where players caught rocks as they tumbled from rows at the top of the screen to the bottom. The game had been started by Dennis Koble before he'd moved over to the consumer division to write games for the 2600. After *Avalanche*, Logg wrapped up another Koble title, *Dirt Bike*, but it failed Atari's field test—putting a cabinet in the wild to see how players responded to it—and did not enter production.

Atari's coin-op engineers had just made an era-defining transition around the time Logg joined. Until recently, arcade games like *Pong* and *Breakout* had been constructed from transistors. In 1975, *Gun Fight*, a western-themed shooter where two players engaged in a shootout from opposite sides of the screen, became the first coin-op title to use a microprocessor. The change represented a quantum leap rather than a baby step forward. When a processor-based game glitched, it was easier to troubleshoot code than it was to rebuild a chain of transistors.

But Logg and other coders still had to jump through several hoops to get games up and running, and restrictions like processor speed and available memory only scratched the surface. "Now, programming in those days was very interesting," he said. "The development system did not have a compiler or any means to save our source code. This was all done on a PDP system and there were two ladies who did all the data entry. We provided a listing or marked up sheets of paper and they made the desired changes to the game code and provided us a listing and a paper tape—as best as I can remember it was paper tape—for us to load into the 'black box' development system. This system would allow us to stop and start the program as well as examine memory."

Logg hit his stride when, in 1978, he answered Atari co-founder Nolan Bushnell's call for an expanded version of *Break Out*. The game, which Logg dubbed *Super Breakout*, bridged Atari's past with its future. Before co-founding Apple Computer with engineering whiz kid Steve "Woz" Wozniak, Steve Jobs worked at Atari as an engineer and, in 1974, was tasked by Bushnell to convert *Pong* from a two-player tennis game into a single-player game where players guided a paddle across the bottom of the screen to knock balls against rows of colored bricks at the top. In those days, most arcade games need anywhere from 150 to 170 transistors. Bushnell promised Jobs a $700 bonus if he could build the game using fewer than fifty transistor-transistor logic (TTL) chips, which would save Atari money when the cabinet went into production.

Jobs promised to do the job in five days. As soon as everyone left, he called in Woz, his friend who worked for Hewlett Packard at the time, and told him Bushnell's requirements. Over four sleepless days, Woz worked with Jobs by his side and got the job done. Unfortunately, his design was so complex that Atari's engineers couldn't duplicate it before *Breakout* entered production. Jobs still earned the bonus, and gave Woz his share of $350. (According to Woz, Jobs mentioned nothing about the royalties he would earn as the engineer credited with *Breakout*, and pocketed thousands of dollars from Woz's work. Woz, more sentimental than jobs, was devastated when he found out years later.)

Super Breakout arrived in arcades in 1976, and became Logg's first commercial hit. He rode his momentum when designer Lyle Rains proposed they team up to write a space game like *Space*

Invaders, but with ships and asteroids that could move in any direction. That game became *Asteroids*.

Things were looking up for Logg, but looking grim for Atari Nolan Bushnell. Atari's co-founder had sold the company to Warner Communication in 1976, a move he admitted was "stupid" in retrospect, and stemmed from his failure to grasp the machinations of Wall Street. To shore up the company's wild culture, Warner brought in Ray Kassar, a professional from the textiles industry, as a consultant. Kassar recalled wearing a suit on his first day only to be greeted by Bushnell wearing a t-shirt with *I love to fuck* printed on the front. During a meeting later the same day, Bushnell interrupted proceedings to offer Kassar a cannabis joint. It was, Kassar went on to discover, only the tip of the iceberg of freewheeling drug use within the company. He left the meeting immediately. Smoking pot didn't bother him. This was California; everybody lit up. He was bothered by the fact that they were lighting up at work.

In late 1978, following an argument with Emanuel "Manny" Gerard, the Warner executive who had pushed his bosses to acquire Atari, Bushnell was fired by Warner. (Bushnell claimed the decision was mutual in his account of the incident, and that he decided to quit around the same time Warner attempted to fire him.)

Kassar wasn't sad to see him go. Atari couldn't operate at tip-top efficiency with two bosses. Now firmly in charge, Kassar made the call to throw all of Atari's weight behind the aging 2600 console, which Bushnell had wanted to put out to pasture. He swept away the clutter and chaos of the company's laidback culture and replaced it with one rooted in order and efficiency. Instead of advertising its games only during Christmas, Kassar worked with marketing to promote the Atari brand year-round. Under his leadership, Atari, Inc.'s sales exploded from $75 million in 1977 to $2.1 billion in 1980. Shareholders were thrilled. Programmers were less enthused. They still weren't receiving public credit for their work and had to resort to burying Easter eggs in their games. "It seemed more of a small company atmosphere except Time Warner did own us at the time," Logg remembered. "There was certainly less management when I started than there was later."

Moreover, not everyone felt the company's financial compensation was fair. "Coin-op employees always had a bonus program," said Logg. "The Consumer Division did not. We were a little miffed that they were taking credit for making all this money on our titles and we did not get anything. Of course they were miffed that they did not receive any credit for programming the games nor any bonus. Ray Kassar more or less laughed at them."

Kassar went further than laughing. He called the programmers "high-strung prima donnas" in a comment that Kassar later said was supposed to be off the record, but was overheard. Still, he believed he was right. What's more, he couldn't blame them. Atari's programmers were creative, but mercurial, just like all artistic types. Once, he suffered through five hours listening to a programmer read poetry he'd written because he recognized the man's importance to Atari's bottom line.

In 1979, after programmer David Crane and others had complained about the unfairness of compensation, the marketing department drafted a memo breaking down the most successful cartridge games. The purpose of the memo was to alert programmers to the types of software most popular with consumers so they could pivot to writing more games in that vein. Crane and several others interpreted the memo differently: Right there, in black and white, were sales stats for each game they'd made. To them, it was proof that they, the high-strung prima donnas, were valuable. In fact, Crane found that games he had programmed on his own had generated over twenty million in revenue. So why was he working overtime every week on a salary of $20,000?

Another programmer, Alan Miller, pitched Kassar and other executives on a compensation plan that would give programmers credit and royalties on their software. When management shot them down, Miller, along with Crane, Bob Whitehead, and Larry Kaplan decided to leave. Their cohort had made Atari over $60 million, and went directly to Kassar to inform him as much. According to Crane, Kassar told them they were no more important than the workers on assembly lines who dropped cartridges into boxes.

The "Gang of Four," as they became known, walked away from Atari and founded Activision, the first third-party publisher to release games for hardware another company had manufactured, in 1979. At Activision, Crane went on to develop titles including *Pitfall*, an action-platformer that became the second-bestselling game on the 2600, after Tod Frye's *Pac-Man* conversion.

Atari and Activision soon found themselves on common ground in 1983, when North America's video game market collapsed under its own weight. Atari's heavy involvement in the games business caused Warner to weather a loss of $425 million, leading the communications company to sell the PC and consumer divisions to computer tycoon Jack Tramiel for a song. Tramiel rebranded his acquisition as Atari Corp., while the arcade division continued as Atari Games under the auspices of Warner.

Through the turbulence, Logg continued to pump out games. One of his biggest hits was 1985's *Gauntlet*, a dungeon-crawl where up to four players hacked and slashed their way through labyrinths displayed from a top-down perspective. *Gauntlet* was a success, but on a different scale than earlier games due to the aftereffects of the market crash. Over 7,800 *Gauntlet* cabinets were sold in '85, but that was a far cry from the 70,000 *Asteroids* machines in operation around the world, making it Atari's most lucrative coin-op title and the seventh highest-grossing coin-op video game of all time.

Logg, employed by Atari Games, soon gained a crystal-clear understanding of how far the company's split went. "I had done a version of *Centipede* for the NES around 1986 when we learned that it was not clear if we could release our own titles in the consumer group," he said. Logg had partnered with Atari engineer Dona Bailey to co-design *Centipede*, a shooter in which players open fire on a gigantic centipede as it wriggles its way down the screen, back in 1981. "So we had to [ask] the other company to find out what we could do. The result was we no longer owned any coin-operated titles created before the split in 1985, so I could not release my version of *Centipede*."

Namco sold Atari Games to Atari Corp. in 1985, but there was another obstacle in the path to releasing home ports of Atari's coin-op games. Nintendo had been credited with single-handedly resurrecting the North American games market that Atari had been somewhat responsible for killing. Recognizing that a lack of quality control over software had been one of Atari's faults, Nintendo, riding high on the success of the NES, wielded near-total control over who could make NES games, how many, and how often. "A pain in the ass is a mild way to put it," Logg said. "Think anti-trust."

Atari's designers went from being furious to cautiously optimistic when they exploited a loophole in Nintendo's publisher-developer contract. According to its draconian terms, Nintendo permitted developers of NES software to release no more than five titles per year, a form of quality control to make sure the market wasn't flooded with subpar games. Atari Games wanted to branch out from coin-op. To do so, it would have to form a consumer division of its own, separate from Atari Corp. It chose the name Tengen, Japanese for the central part of the strategy game Go's board. Other publishers exploited the same loophole to produce more NES titles, such as *Contra* and *Castlevania* studio Konami establishing Ultra Games as a shell corporation that launched titles such as *Teenage Mutant Ninja Turtles* and *Metal Gear*.

Nintendo permitted Tengen to publish games on NES. The two entities co-existed until 1988, when *Tetris* tore them apart for good.

Part II: Heartbreak

SOVIET RESEARCHERS ALEXEY Pajitnov and Dmitry Pavlovsky knew that all work and no play made for dull scientists. Employed at the Computer Center of the Russian Academy of Sciences, Pavlovsky noticed sixteen-year-old Gerasimov writing an encryption program for Microsoft's DOS command-line operating system. They began to chat, and Pavlovsky said he liked to write games in his spare time, and introduced Gerasimov to Pajitnov. The trio decided to write a computer game of their own, with Gerasimov taking point as programmer and graphics designer. They warmed up by converting some of Pavlovsky's older projects and daydreamed about selling a collection of their work, which they called a computer funfair.

A few weeks into their working relationship, Pajitnov came to his friends with an idea. A while back, he'd written a game called *Genetic Engineering* in which the player moved four-square pieces, called tetraminos, into groups. Gerasimov thought the game sounded like a bore, until Pajitnov rattled off ways he'd thought of improving it. Tetraminos would fall from the top of the screen into a glass jar-like enclosure, and would pile up unless the player grouped them to form horizontal lines, causing them to disappear. Excited, the three friends expanded the idea so two players could challenge each other to see who could clear lines the fastest. They called their game *Tetris*.

Though excited by their creation, the trio couldn't simply drop floppy disks in a Ziploc bag—common packaging in the days before colorful boxes—and sell it in stores. They lived in a communist country, meaning the state owned *Tetris*, not its creators. Instead, they uploaded it to a network, where it spread across computers. Robert Stein, president of publisher Mirrorsoft, caught wind of it and approached Pajitnov with a worldwide distribution offer for *Tetris*. Stein secured publishing rights and turned them over to Spectrum HoloByte, where engineer John Jones-Steele converted it to the Atari ST.

That was when Ed Logg discovered it. Entranced by *Tetris*'s easy-to-pick-up-too-addictive-to-quit nature, he went to Robert Stein and negotiated distribution rights for Atari Games. Per their agreement, Atari Games would bring the game to arcades, while Logg would develop an NES port under the Tengen label. "I thought it was best for the home market because of the possibility of never-ending game play," Logg explained. "I asked our management to get the license for the home market which they did via a sub-license through a couple of parties. It turned out later the contract was not very ironclad and the parties were not the most trustworthy to deal with."

Tengen's Tetris.

Logg kicked off the project by writing *Tetris* for Nintendo's 8-bit Famicom. "I completed one version for the Consumer Electronics Show before the coin-operated game was started. When someone wanted it for the coin-operated market, another team took over," he said.

Right around the time Logg was ready to get started, Nintendo threw up another roadblock. According to the manufacturer, there were shortages of the ROM chips that held code for NES games on cartridges. In order to satisfy demand, Nintendo would determine which companies would receive cartridges, and how many. Fed up, Tengen's engineers decided to reverse-engineer the lockout chip, a little piece on every NES cartridge intended to prevent pirates from bootlegging software. They called their modification the Rabbit chip.

Logg found out about the project when he walked into Tengen's lab and asked the three engineers huddled around a table full of hardware what they were up to. One of them looked up and said, "Don't ask."

Meanwhile, Logg continued his conversion of *Tetris*. He used no code that Pajitnov and the other Russian engineers had written, designing a look-and-feel replica by playing the game on a PC and retooling it with his own code. The basic logic, making pieces fall, was easy enough to implement. Within weeks, his game looked slicker and played more smoothly than the original. Logg focused on fleshing out what *Tetris*'s creators had built, adding a competitive multiplayer mode as well as a cooperative style of play where two players worked together to clear lines. Another improvement was gradually increasing the speed of falling blocks over time, a more subtle, flowing method than Pajitnov's jumps in pacing. Whereas the original game's tetraminos were each made of a solid block painted a single color, Logg's were black and white at first.

"The first version for the January CES was probably more mono-chromatic," he recalled. In advance of the June Consumer Electronics Show, he added colors and applied textures that gave each piece a segmented, 3D appearance.

"I had the ability to burn EPROMs and test them on the NES," Logg explained. "I used a special PCB [printed circuit board] that would allow me to play on the NES in this manner. I wrote all my code on a VAX using a 6502 cross complier. I do not remember the development system I used at the time for this. I suspect there was a PCB plugged into the NES that would simulate the EPROMs because I would not burn EPROMs for each build."

When Atari's programmers were ready to develop an arcade cabinet for *Tetris*, Logg supplied his code as a foundation. The inverted process marked one of few examples when the console version of a game influenced arcade hardware.

Atari Games assigned two engineers to handle *Tetris*, Greg Rivera and Norm Avellar. Logg helped them get the code up and running on coin-op hardware before returning to his work. "For many years there was just one programmer per project as were the Atari 2600 console titles," he recalled. "There was also an engineer and technician assigned to several titles. The engineer was to design the hardware and early on the audio for the game. The technician was to keep the development hardware running and to get the test units ready for testing. There was no need for more than one programmer. Our development systems were designed based on one-programmer projects. I think around 1984 to 1985, we started looking at getting two programmers on a project. In my case, I believe *Gauntlet* was the first project with more than one programmer. I am not counting Mark Cerny on *Millipede*, who volunteered to create the attract mode to show all the game characters and to add the 'game of life' mode to change the mushroom pattern."

***

AFTER THREE YEARS of work between the NES and arcade adaptations, Tengen sent its NES version of *Tetris* to Nintendo for approval in the spring of 1989. Once again, Nintendo hit the brakes, this time by ordering a pitifully small quantity of cartridges.

Behind the scenes, the company's agents were working on locking down *Tetris*. That March, Bullet-Proof Software executive Henk Rogers flew to Moscow and met with bureaucrats to discuss licensing. The bureaucrats were happy to listen. They were aware of *Tetris*'s burgeoning popularity and were eager to make money off of the work completed by its creators. To their amazement, Rogers offered five million in exchange for the rights to all console and handheld adaptations, a much higher proposal than they had expected. Rogers bowled them over again by delivering a promise from Nintendo that the Japanese gaming giant would make up any differences if their royalties failed to reach the five million marker.

The rights to *Tetris* were summarily divided up like a holiday pie. Nintendo signed paperwork giving it worldwide rights (except in Japan) to *Tetris* on March 22, 1989. Mirrorsoft claimed Europe and, through its Spectrum HoloByte division, North America. Atari Games kept the rights to release its arcade version, and Bullet-Proof allowed Nintendo to bundle a portable version of *Tetris* with its Game Boy, due out later in the year.

Nintendo of America legal counsel Howard Lincoln wrote and submitted a cease-and-desist letter to Tengen on March 31, declaring that his company had secured all console rights. If Atari didn't pull its Tengen-developed version of *Tetris* for NES from shelves, the two companies would settle the matter in court. All-out war followed, but both companies had fired shots earlier.

In December 1988, Atari filed a lawsuit accusing Nintendo of monopolistic practices centered on the company's lockout chip. That same day, Atari Games announced that Tengen would release games without going through the proper channels established by Nintendo. There were three, *Pac-Man*, *R.B.I. Baseball*, and *Gauntlet*, with more on the way. *Tetris* would be the tip of that spear.

Nintendo couldn't allow Atari to get away with selling unlicensed software for NES. Its executives believed its policies were the dam that held back a flood of poor software that would kill the North American game market for good. More to the point, Nintendo wanted control. The company responded by delivering a one-two punch. First, it countersued Atari for patent infringement on February 2, 1989. Concurrently it threatened retailers: Anyone who carried unlicensed game software for Nintendo's hardware would suddenly find that its well of Nintendo products had run dry. Retailers capitulated. They had no choice. Nintendo was red hot, and they would rather lose a few Atari and Tengen games than their relationship with Nintendo.

Other software manufacturers in North America sympathized with Atari. Nintendo's practices were draconian, but the fact was they depended on Nintendo for money. Atari sued again, demanding $250 million in damages from Nintendo.

The war raged until May 17, 1989, when Tengen, true to its word, released *Tetris* for NES. Not that anyone could find it. Few stores were brave enough to stock it, and Nintendo doubled down by filing yet another suit eight days later. Now both companies were accusing the other of infringing upon its rights to develop *Tetris* for consoles.

In June, Nintendo delivered a knockout blow when a Federal judge ruled in its favor, decreeing that Tengen and Atari were prohibited from selling any home version of *Tetris*, and had to recall all unsold cartridges. Executives from Atari and Tengen estimated that around 50,000 copies of the game had been sold. Hundreds of thousands were returned. Although Tengen continued to develop games—understandably throwing its weight behind Sega hardware, which rose up to challenge Nintendo's iron grip on the console market—Ed Logg was devastated. He had fallen in love with his version of *Tetris* over working tirelessly for three years, only for a figurative handful of consumers to get to enjoy it.

"Heartbroken is a good summary. It was so much better than the version Nintendo did," he said.

Critics and players tended to agree. While there was no denying the addictive simplicity of the Game Boy port, the inclusion of which made Nintendo's brick-sized portable a global phenomenon, Logg's NES version boasted richer features and game modes than Nintendo's cart.

"I was glad I had started working in the consumer area. I am greatly disappointed that my early efforts, *Centipede* and *Tetris*, did not make it out to the public," Logg said. His awareness of support for his work buoyed his spirits and justified his labor. "To back this up, many years later when I worked for another company and we wanted to do a *Tetris* version on our platform, our management went to Blue Planet, I believe, who owned the rights to *Tetris* at the time. During the discussion they pointed out the best version they had ever seen was the version behind them. It was the Tengen version of *Tetris*."

Chapter 9: Teenage Mutant Ninja Turtles

Part I: "Everybody Has Their Pac-Man"

SCOTT BACHRACH CONSIDERED the items arranged on his desk. It was the usual assortment of stuff. Action figures, trinkets, apparel—

One item caught his eye, and he slowly leaned forward. It was an arcade cabinet, but miniaturized, no larger than a shoebox stood on one end. The cabinet was painted canary-yellow, and the character on the front was shaped like a pizza with one missing slice.

Bachrach smiled. *Pac-Man* had been his favorite arcade game as a kid. He remembered rushing to arcades and dropping a few quarters into the cabinet once or twice a week, watching his score rocket upward the longer he dodged the ghosts patrolling the maze and gobbled up fruit and pellets.

He switched the cabinet on and played. Within seconds, his smile dipped downward. The cabinet was cute, inarguably a nice collector's item, but the tiny joystick and buttons were hard to manipulate. Also, he was no longer a teenager. It was June 2017. Bachrach was pushing fifty, and he had to squint to follow the action on the miniature cabinet's miniature screen.

A couple of days later, Bachrach sat down in a development meeting and mentioned the frustrating experience to the room at large. "That's because you're not running an arcade ROM," one of his employees said.

"What does that mean?" Bachrach asked.

"Well," the other man said, "arcade games like *Pac-Man* can be played a multitude of ways. You can play it on your mobile device, or a plug-and-play device. But the version in the arcade is the original ROM," he continued, elaborating that a ROM was a chip that contained the art and code that made the game run.

Bachrach and a few of the others strolled through a local arcade. He spotted a *Pac-Man* machine and went up to it, waggled the joystick, tapped the buttons. This was it. The real deal.

"Why can't we make a home version of this?" Bachrach asked.

As a matter of fact, Bachrach and his team were in the perfect position to create just such a product. He was the president of Tastemakers, LLC, a company that specialized in the manufacturing, licensing, and development of toys and collectibles, a domain Bachrach had inhabited for thirty years. Since 1996, he'd been involved in building and selling products stemming from Disney's Hannah Montana, to Toy Story, to High School Musical, to dolls of Gene Simmons and the KISS band.

In mid-2017, Bachrach's experience playing a miniaturized *Pac-Man* cabinet dovetailed with statistics reporting a perpetual rise in nostalgia. Home versions of arcade cabinets seemed a natural fit, but Bachrach had a form and function in mind. *Pac-Man*, *Asteroids*, *Galaga*—those games had been his bread and butter.

Other companies such as MyArcade and New Wave Toys appealed to collectors and players by selling miniaturized cabinets like the one Bachrach had played. They looked good on desks and bookshelves, he told his team, but he wanted to offer actual cabinets. Or, rather, facsimiles of actual cabinets. The logistics of coin-op machines made owning one more of a dream for the average consumer than a possibility. They were huge and bulky, weighing at least 250 pounds, and cost upward of $1500. If the circuit board or ROM chips failed, the machine was as good as dead unless consumers were willing to pay for someone to come to their house, dismantle the machine, diagnose and fix the problem, and put it back together.

Newer titles—relative to *Pac-Man*—like *Mortal Kombat* and *Street Fighter II* had come and gone without his notice; by the time the one-on-one fighter craze of the 1990s hit, Bachrach had left arcades and was focused on his career.

But what did that matter? The important thing was authenticity. “I started to realize very quickly that everybody has their *Pac-Man*,” he said. “The same identification I had with *Pac-Man* was the same identification a younger person had with *Mortal Kombat* or *Ninja Turtles*. Everyone had their favorite.”

Bachrach and his team conceptualized arcade cabinets. They called the initiative Arcade1Up, a brand to be developed and sold by Tastemakers. “Candidly, what happened was Arcade1Up was the item that became the line that became the category that became the brand that has become a business," he said.

Bachrach's team—four including himself—proposed an alternative. "Without knowing an exact size, we knew we wanted to slim our product down, which would do two things," he explained. "From a cost-exercise standpoint, it would bring the price down; and we wanted to bring down the weight so cabinets would be easier to move around. At the same time, we wanted to have as close to an authentic experience as possible."

Most arcade cabinets stand approximately six feet tall. The first samples they ordered stood roughly four feet tall, and measured just under a foot and a half in width and shy of two feet in depth. "We made a size that was within six inches of what we ended up with, and it just looked good," Bachrach remembered.

Naturally, the first sample to roll off assembly lines was a *Pac-Man* cabinet. Standing before it, Bachrach had to bend at the waist to reach the controls. He pulled up a chair and planted himself in front of the machine. "This is amazing," he said, working the joystick and tapping buttons. "I'm fifty years old. I don't want to stand for an hour anymore."

"I want to stand," one of his team members spoke up.

Bachrach knew his colleague had a point. Although he liked being able to take a load off, many consumers would want as authentic an experience as possible. That meant designing cabinets tall enough to be played without having to bend over and develop a kink in his back.

The team hit on an alternative. While poking around a bar/arcade, they noticed risers, blocks of wood that cabinets stood on to raise them off the floor. Arcade1Up could sell themed risers, painted to match a cabinet's décor, for customers who preferred to stand, and for those who wanted an accessory that matched their showpiece.

"They just wanted to be able to interact with the game in about the same position as they'd done years ago," Bachrach explained of the research they'd done into their prospective customer's mindset. "We developed the risers in such a way that they took up no more space in length or width, but what it did was make it so as you were standing, your hand was in almost the same place, from a height standpoint, of where it'd been on the old machines."

Arcade1Up's team discovered that authenticity in certain areas of cabinet design was more important than in others. The artwork that adorned a cabinet needed to be spot-on. The control deck, the spread of buttons and joysticks, needed to look and feel like the genuine article so players familiar with the game could step up to an Arcade1Up cabinet and play without missing a beat. "You can go out and buy fighting sticks for one hundred to one hundred and fifty bucks, but it's just a different experience," Bachrach said.

"We like to say that we're making and selling an experience. We're taking you back to a point in time that you remember, or introducing someone new to a point in time that was long before they remember."

The first *Pac-Man* cabinet to incorporate the artwork and control deck Bachrach remembered bowled him over. He felt like a kid again, investing hours into eating pellets in a maze where four colorful ghosts hunted him down.

Not every cabinet Arcade1Up aspired to recreate came off without a hitch. "What's funny is many of these games were created so long ago that some of the original artwork doesn't even exist," Bachrach said. "The licensors don't have it. So, it becomes a field mission, for lack of a better term, to figure out who owns what rights, gather up those rights, make sure sign-offs are done, and replicate cabinets to the best of our ability so we can make sure we're paying homage in the right way."

One of the toughest contracts to land was *Mortal Kombat*. Midway had created the franchise, but had filed for bankruptcy in 2009 after being unable to climb out from under $240 million in debt. That July, Warner Bros. bought the rights to *Mortal Kombat*, the Midway logo, and another title for $49 million. The *MK* branch, formerly Midway Chicago, was rebranded as NetherRealm Studios. Arcade1Up's team approached co-creator Ed Boon with an offer to design a *Mortal Kombat* cabinet in 2017. "We want you and your team to play it with your technology, and tell us if we're on the right track," Bachrach said.

It was important for Boon to give the thumbs-up. Bachrach recalled a time in 1998 when he'd sat down with Gene Simmons to show the famous musician an early model of the KISS doll bearing his likeness. "No," Simmons had said, turning it this way and that, "my face is more like this," he continued, and struck a pose. Getting direction from Simmons had resulted in a better product, and getting the green light from *MK*'s co-creator would benefit Arcade1Up's machine.

The trouble was that Boon did not have the final say for *MK*-licensed products. "All of a sudden, you go into Warner Bros.'s licensing department, and they're used to licensing Batman," Bachrach explained. "That's a robust brand: they have archives, ledgers of artwork. They didn't have that for *Mortal Kombat*."

Arcade1Up's team worked for nearly a year to nail down the *MK* cabinet's artwork and technical details such as the speed of gameplay for *MK 1*, *II*, and *III*, all of which would be included. Like Simmons, Boon went back and forth with Arcade1Up's team until the trilogy of *MK* games looked, played, and sounded the way he remembered designing them.

"The cool part," Bachrach explained, "the common denominator between both of those experiences, is we're going back to the people who are the gatekeeper of a brand and saying, 'We're delivering right on message,' but they can say, 'No, you're not, and here's why you have to change it.'"

***

JERRY CUMMINS, LEAD designer for Arcade1Up's products, believed in their mission. "We've got something here," he told Scott Bachrach.

Cummins had made products for Hasbro and Mattel, the who's-who of toys and collectibles. When he believed in an idea, Bachrach was inclined to agree. Arcade1Up had potential. They were two of the only people who thought so.

At the early stages of the project, Bachrach told a dozen or so friends and associates about his plan to build, license, and distribute replica arcade machines based on some of the hottest video game brands of yesteryear. Everyone looked at him like he was crazy. Bachrach tried not to let their doubt get under his skin. But what if consumers failed to understand that Arcade1Up cabinets weren't supposed to equal the 250-pound behemoths that cost as much as a month's rent in many American cities?

In July of 2018, thirteen months after Bachrach and his team hit on the concept for Arcade1Up, cabinets began shipping out to retailers. Walmart, Target, and GameStop were three of a select number who agreed to stock the product. There were five cabinets total, all three-quarters to the scale of their originals, each featuring three to four games and carrying a price tag of $250 to $300. Titles ranged from classic maze games such as *Pac-Man*, to shooters like *Centipede* and *Galaga*, to button-mashers such as *Rampage* and *Gauntlet*. To ease their concerns that their products would fail to register a blip on consumers' radars, the team sat around and talked about arcade games and their hopes for the brand. "You know," someone said, "if this ends up being too expensive, it's still so freaking cool. We could make it into a wastepaper basket, and someone would still buy it."

Bachrach laughed with the others. "There's something really cool about having a cabinet that's three-quarters-size of the real thing with the real artwork and real game running on it. It just looks cool."

Consumers agreed. Tens of thousands of cabinets flew off shelves after arriving in stores that fall. After quick and easy assembly, "mini arcades" held places of honor in living rooms, dens, garages, and game rooms. In February 2019, Arcade1Up received the coveted Tech Toy of the Year Award, one of the Toy of the Year (TOTY) Awards looked upon by manufacturers and distributors as the Oscars of their industry, in recognition of the product's high-quality display, sound, and overall composition.

Getting to a point where their brand could win awards had been an uphill battle. One of Arcade1Up's most popular three-quarter-size cabinets was *Street Fighter II*, a machine that packed in *SFII' Champion Edition*, *Super SFII*, and *Super SFII Turbo*. Within weeks of the cabinet's availability, Tastemakers was deluged with complaints. "We got jammed by north of roughly 25,000 phone calls in a very short span of time," Bachrach recalled. "People were saying, 'I just bought this machine. I spent 300 bucks on it, and the deck is fading.'"

The artwork on the control deck, where players' wrists naturally rested while working the joystick and buttons, was wearing off. Arcade1Up's team, still scrappy, wracked their brains to determine why the art was fading. The answer seemed obvious in retrospect: A gland under skin pores produced a natural oil called sebum that kept skin hydrated, giving humans their natural shine, and the combination of that oil and occasional brush-ups against the artwork was rubbing it away.

Arcade1Up's team leaped into action, building and shipping out deck protectors to customers at no charge. "I can tell you that that was a seven-figure expense," Bachrach said. "But we did that because we felt we owed it to our customers who had trust in us. I stand by that today. I'm proud of our group, not just because we came up with the financing to do that, but to actually do it. To get the customer system set up and in place; to figure out a system to get goods in and ship them out to people on time. It cost us dearly financially, but in the long-term view of the brand, it was the right thing to do."

In 2019, the next wave of mini cabinets—*Mortal Kombat*, *Space Invaders*, *Karate Champ*, *Golden Tee*, and *Final Fight*—made their way to stores. With high sales and awards under their belts, Arcade1Up's team considered what to do next.

The answer seemed obvious: Throw a pizza party.

Part II: Cowabunga

ON A QUIET street in New York City, the manhole cover trembled. Moments later it burst into the air, riding a beam of pulsating purple light that shot out of the sewer and up into the night sky like a beacon. Four green forms catapulted out after it, clutching weapons in three-fingered hands and somersaulting through the air.

In some parts of the world, they were ninjas. In others, they were heroes. Everywhere, they were teenage, mutant, and turtles.

Created by comic book writers/artists and friends Kevin Eastman and Peter Laird, the Teenage Mutant Ninja Turtles—later known as the Teenage Mutant Hero Turtles in the United Kingdom after the BBC felt the word "ninja" implied excessive violence for a kids' show—were four anthropomorphic fighters, and the hottest kids' property of the late '80s and early '90s. The four brothers dwelled in the sewers beneath New York City with their sensei, a rat named Splinter, and protected the Big Apple from the Foot Clan, a group of robotic ninja soldiers controlled by Shredder, a warrior dressed head to toe in blades.

Premiering in the late 1980s, TMNT rode a wave of popularity that grew into a tsunami. The Turtles were everywhere: on cartoons after school, in the pages of stylish black-and-white comic books, on silver screens as a blockbuster live-action movie distributed by New Line Cinema. In 1989, Konami, brought the four brothers to the NES in a platforming games where players swapped between Leonardo, Michaelangelo, Donatello, and Raphael on the fly. At the same time, the publisher/developer rolled out an arcade game that became one of the hottest titles of the season.

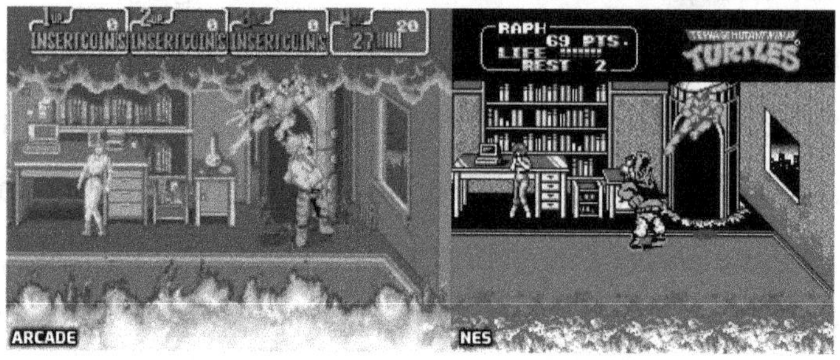

Teenage Mutant Ninja Turtles, the arcade game, was straightforward. As one of the four turtles, players fought through burning apartments, city streets, sewers, and underground fortresses to defeat Shredder and his minions. The game used a two-and-a-half-dimension system, like *Double Dragon*, that let players move through environments in any direction. An eight-way joystick controlled movement, and jump and attack buttons provided means of offense and defense. Pressing both simultaneously triggered a special attack: Leo, Mikey, and Donny jumped and swung their weapons, dealing enough damage to Foot Soldiers to destroy them in one hit; Raphael performed a rolling kick that was weaker than his brothers' attacks, but afforded him more maneuverability, useful for escaping mobs of enemies.

Although the control layout was simple, a variety of attacks could be performed by pressing the two buttons at different rhythms. Jumping into the air, waiting a beat, and then pressing attack performed a giant swing that destroyed Foot in one hit; pausing for half as long launched the Turtles into a diving kick; and tapping jump and then immediately pressing attack executed a faster leaping kick that stunned enemies, giving players an opening to launch into combos—performed by mashing the attack button—as soon as they hit the ground. The environment could be turned against both Foot Soldiers and the Turtles. Some Foot popped out of sewers and launched manhole covers, but players could knock it back like a game of *Pong* to send it careening into the enemy. Mashing attack to hit enemies with combos resulted in the Turtles occasionally performing specialty maneuvers such as an over-the-shoulder throw that, if they were close enough, could send enemies flying into buildings.

At a time when most arcade games consisted of simple sprites and backgrounds, *TMNT*'s graphics looked like the hit cartoon come to life. Sprites were large and fluidly animated, but the real attraction was the cabinet itself. Released in a two-player format that was more prevalent in Japan and Europe, *TMNT* was most commonly found as a four-player machine that sported four sets of colored joysticks and buttons. Players could select their character in the two-player version, but the four-player version assigned each of its four coin slots to a specific character.

Predictably, Konami ported the game to a variety of home computers and consoles. The most popular conversion landed on the

NES in 1990, and was markedly different than its source material. *Teenage Mutant Ninja Turtles II: The Arcade Game*—the Roman numeral and subtitle added to distinguish it from the first game on the console, also titled simply *Teenage Mutant Ninja Turtles*—downsized sprites and details, but expanded each level to twice its original length, adding more enemies and bosses, incorporating two new stages that hadn't been featured in the arcade, and, unfortunately, cutting four players down to two. Attacks were trimmed to basic swings and slices, one type of flying kick, and the jump-and-swing special move.

Individually, those changes amounted to slight deviations. Combined, they produced a home experience unique from the arcade. Adding more Foot Soldiers created scenarios where players had to fight an assortment of enemies and prioritize which ones to take down first based on their attacks. Foot Soldiers that threw packs of dynamite had short range, but dealt more damage than counterparts that threw boomerangs. Additionally, the accuracy of the Turtles' super-attack, pressing both buttons to swing their weapons in a one-hit K.O., was greatly improved from the arcade. Knowing that, and that Foot Soldiers could only attack once they had a Turtle in their line of sight, allowed players to come up with strategies such as approaching a Foot Soldier diagonally and performing a super-attack before the enemy even knew what hit them—exactly what one would expect of a ninja, or a "hero." The strategy was so much more effective than approaching enemies head-on and giving them a chance to attack that players could use it to clear most levels unscathed, saving their health meters for boss fights.

Substituting bosses worked out for the better as well. Originally, players fought Shredder's henchmen Rocksteady and Bebop—a mutated rhino and warthog, respectively—at the end of levels one and two, only to have to face both of them in a parking garage-themed stage later on. On the NES, the tag-team of Rocksteady and Bebop is replaced with the mutated fly incarnation of Baxter Stockman. Developer Ultra Games may have made the change because the NES would have struggled to render two bosses and two player-characters at once. Whatever the reason, players and critics applauded it. Not only was a brand-new boss more exciting than recycling two old encounters, Baxter's fly form was a popular character from the hit cartoon series, which made for a pleasant surprise for players familiar with the coin-op version.

Going further, players had fought Baxter as a human scientist in the sewers, the stage before the parking garage. Encountering him in the next level post-mutation added a narrative thread—characters were changing, just like in the cartoon—that made the beat-em-up seem deeper than it really was.

TMNT II sold well, but as years passed and nostalgia settled over the gaming industry like a cozy blanket, players who had frequented arcades in the late eighties and early nineties reminisced about *Teenage Mutant Ninja Turtles* and its coin-op sequel, *TMNT: Turtles in Time*, ported to Super Nintendo in 1992.

Fifteen years later in 2005, Microsoft's Xbox 360 console launched with a big splash in November. Over the next year, the console grew more popular as exclusive games made their way to the platform. Part of the 360's appeal was the Xbox Live Arcade service, where a smattering of new, smaller titles accompanied re-releases of arcade games priced between five and ten dollars apiece. Steve "Snake" Palmer, a programmer at Digital Eclipse, had worked on XBLA's lineup of classic coin-op games such as *Joust* and *Gauntlet* before the 360 had launched. Palmer followed websites such as IGN and GameSpot closely, keeping an eye out for polls that asked players which arcade games they'd like to see on XBLA. "Most of them had *TMNT* as number one, and *The Simpsons* as number two," Palmer recalled, "so I figured we were going to get asked to do these at some point."

In his spare time during late 2004, over a year before the Xbox 360 launched, Palmer had written an emulator that played arcade ROMs for *Teenage Mutant Ninja Turtles* and *The Simpsons*, another licensed four-player brawler by Konami. As icing on the cake, he added support for *Turtles in Time*. That way, he figured, Digital Eclipse would be ready if Microsoft asked for the games.

For a time, Palmer thought his foresight had been for naught. “We got told that due to licensing issues with the IP and the original developer this was probably not going to happen,” he said.

His emulator gathered dust until a Monday afternoon in 2007, when Microsoft informed Digital Eclipse that management wanted the original *TMNT* on Xbox Live Arcade. “They're also asking for alpha by Wednesday,” Palmer remembered, because “they needed to rush it out in time for a new movie,” referring to the computer-animated film dubbed *TMNT* slated for release in theaters that spring. “Given I was already very busy with something else, it was a good thing I'd already done most of the work!”

Palmer spent a day getting the emulator up to snuff with XBLA’s newest protocols, then handed it off to another programmer, Corey “Ozzy” Asbreuk, to finish. Arcade games displayed in low resolutions that would looked pixelated and blurry on newer TVs, so Asbreuk added new artwork that bordered the game’s playfield like a picture frame, preserving the resolution and showing off the Turtles’ new designs based on the movie. Next, he added a front-end menu for things like options that hadn’t been available in the original arcade ROM. Last, Asbreuk and Palmer teamed up to implement achievements, point-based rewards players earned for completing specific goals.

"I don't remember how many days it was in total before the final version was sent off, but it has to be the fastest turnaround in history," Palmer said.

Published by Ubisoft, *Teenage Mutant Ninja Turtles* hit XBLA on March 14, 2007, at the bargain price of 400 Microsoft Points, or five bucks. Rebranded as *TMNT Arcade '89*, the game featured multiplayer for up to four players. Both it and a remake of *Turtles in Time* enjoyed a four-year run on XBLA before licensing issues caused both games to be pulled from the service in late June of 2011.

Retro gaming only grew over the next six years. Prices of classic games skyrocketed as collectors sifted through trade shows and showed off their collections on YouTube. All the while, arcade games continued to be re-released in anthologies put out by publishers such as Capcom and Sega. The turtles, however, seemed to have gone underground for good.

***

SCOTT BACHRACH TOOK a moment to soak it all in.

On the morning of Tuesday, June 11, 2019, the Los Angeles Convention Center was silent. At noon, the doors would open, and over 10,000 consumers, journalists, and developers would pour in for the first day of E3, the annual trade show where publishers show off their latest games.

Bachrach and his team practically trembled with excitement. For the first time since Arcade1Up's founding two years earlier, they had a booth on the show floor. Their station was in South Hall, one of two cavernous spaces in the Convention Center where Ubisoft, Nintendo, Microsoft, and Capcom constructed booths festooned with statues and decorations. Theirs was less a booth, Bachrach thought, and more an arcade. That was the point. Mini arcade cabinets were everywhere. Most stood on risers. Stools decorated with logos from games such as *Street Fighter II* and *Mortal Kombat* were scattered around the floor. Once the doors opened, anyone could wander by and play Arcade1Up's offerings, including a sixteen-feet-tall cabinet that played *Marvel Super Heroes*, a special attraction to promote the mini-cabinet version of the one-on-one fighting game.

Before the madness began, Bachrach took a moment to address his team. Two years ago, he had been one of four. Now Tastemakers employed thirty-five individuals dedicated to working on the Arcade1Up brand. "I've been in the business thirty years," he told them. "I've done a lot of products. I've been really fortunate to be around some very smart people who let me ride their coattails. But I've never been as proud of this company as I am today."

Bachrach had reason to be excited. Days earlier, Arcade1Up had revealed two of its three new three-quarter-size machines. The first was *Marvel Super Heroes*, which included two other superhero-themed titles. The second featured *Teenage Mutant Ninja Turtles* and *Turtles in Time*. "The best thing is, the fans are the best way to find out if we're on track or not," he said. "A lot of times we're going out and saying, 'What games do you guys want to see?' So many people came back with *Marvel* and *Turtles*. I was blown away."

Securing the licenses for both *TMNT* games had been a year-long endeavor. In some cases, publishers still owned licenses to their arcade games. That made the team's job easier. *Teenage Mutant Ninja Turtles* had been a different matter. Nickelodeon had acquired the rights to the property from co-creator Peter Laird in October 2009, but Konami had held the rights to develop and publish video game adaptations. To develop mini cabinets based on the two coin-op titles, Arcade1Up would have to win over both. "Konami wrote that code, and partnered with us as well as Nickelodeon, the owner of *TMNT*," Bachrach said. "Some of the games you'll see us put out through 2020 will be like that, with three stakeholders involved. There are various reasons for that: game publishing, game rights, artwork. It becomes a legal minefield."

Arcade1Up's team had spent the past twelve months running in different directions to acquire licenses for every piece of the arcade games, from the rights to use the Turtles, to the games themselves, to the iconic cabinet artwork. Initially, both licensors expressed disinterest. "'What makes us difference is we're the at-home, affordable arcade experience,'" Bachrach had explained. "You can play *Turtles* and *Pac-Man* on Xbox or PlayStation, or you can play it on our platform. We've become just another platform. Until we're able to establish that platform, it was a learning process. No one had thought of doing a home arcade at an affordable price."

Just when contracts were ready, Nick and Konami underwent changes in management, and Bachrach and the team found themselves back at square one. Luckily, they had a new card to play: 2019 happened to be the twenty-fifth anniversary of the Teenage Mutant Ninja Turtles comic book, the characters' first appearance. That, Arcade1Up's team explained to the licensors, was a golden opportunity. TMNT's popularity had ebbed and flowed over the years, but launching a new cartoon all but guaranteed renewed interest in the brand. "Being in that format, we were able to find common ground that made sense, and find strategy that made sense," Bachrach continued. "*Turtles* then became a great anchor item for them to create a groundswell."

With all licenses secured, the next step was deciding on branding. Each Arcade1Up cabinet houses multiple games, but each cabinet can only exhibit artwork for one. In some cases, deciding on a marquee title was easy. *Mortal Kombat* and *MK3* had been successful games, but fans and critics pointed to *Mortal Kombat II* as the pinnacle of the franchise in its early days, so *MKII*'s artwork was plastered on Arcade1Up's cabinet.

Choosing *Teenage Mutant Ninja Turtles '89* as the marquee was another obvious choice. *Turtles in Time* was beloved, but the first arcade game had launched when the TMNT fandom had reached critical mass. "So much of our product is about what looks cool. We think part of our mission is to make sure each cabinet speaks to what its brand is. There are cabinets with three or more games on them, but those don't speak as well."

The highlight of the cabinet was speccing out a four-player control deck, a first for Arcade1Up. "We couldn't use our existing deck size," Bachrach explained. "It needed to be larger so we had enough room, but, we didn't want to design a cabinet that was over-sized compared to what we had already? It would have defeated all the other strengths of our product: the cabinet would have been too bulky, too heavy."

Arcade1Up's team settled on a wider deck affixed to its cabinet. While the deck isn't as wide as either *TMNT* arcade title's control panel, it's more than spacious enough for four players to play side by side (by side by side) without anyone in the middle feeling sandwiched, or the players on either end having to crane their necks to see the screen. In fact, the height of the cabinet remained unchanged, as did the space on the deck where players naturally placed their hands while playing.

Authenticity has become Arcade1Up's guiding light, one that illuminated its space at E3. Over the three days of the show, thousands of attendees stopped by to challenge one another in *Mortal Kombat* and *Street Fighter II*, to demolish buildings in *Rampage*, and to shred the Shredder and his Foot Clan in *Teenage Mutant Ninja Turtles*. When the *TMNT* mini arcades arrives in stores in the fall of 2019—around the same time the brand will release its *Marvel Super Heroes* and *Star Wars* machines—it will deliver the most authentic experience possible without paying thousands of dollars and lugging around a 250-pound cabinet.

As far as Scott Bachrach is concerned, Arcade 1Up has nowhere to go but up. "It's dumb luck," he said of the business's recent success. "People say there's a very fine line between a genius and an idiot, and it's called success. If you do something that works, you're a genius; if it doesn't, you're an idiot. I think you have to have enough experience or wherewithal to execute on something, but you also have to be lucky and be at the right place at the right time."

Chapter 10: Street Fighter II

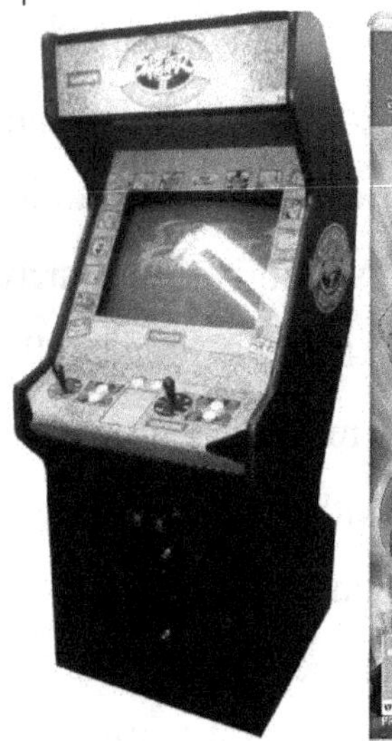
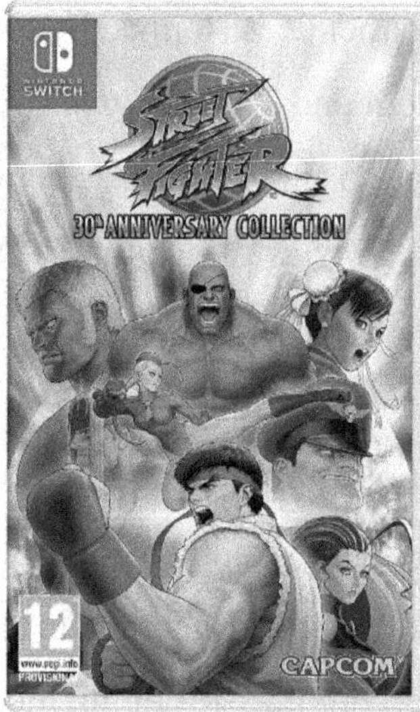

Part I: Resurgence

MIKE MIKA SWITCHED off his monitor before picking up the phone. "Hello?"

"QA came back," the voice on the other end of the line said. "They said safeties don't work."

Mika cupped one hand over the phone and leaned back to talk to Tom Russo, a fellow editor at *Next Generation* magazine. "What the hell is a safety?"

Russo didn't even blink. Editors at gaming rags were always asking each other questions about types of games they didn't normally play. A safety, Russo explained, was a scoring play that awarded a team one or two points. Safeties could occur in a number of ways: a ball carrier tackled in his end zone, or through a conversion, or…

Russo paused. Mika's eyes had glazed over.

"It was going to be so much work," Mika recalled. "Just to support safeties would break everything I'd been doing."

There were people who wrote video games, and then there were people who wrote about them. Mike Mika was one of the rare breed who did both. He got his start writing games for computers such as Commodore's 64 and Amiga machines. As his programming skills evolved, a company called Titus France contracted him to port *Titus the Fox*, a side-scrolling action game that had been published on a variety of computing platforms, over to Nintendo's black-and-green portable.

"I'd gotten really good at coding for Game Boy because it was something I was doing as a hobby, then I started doing it more professionally."

Riding the momentum from *Titus the Fox*, Mika agreed to meet with a contractor who wanted to pitch him on converting another title to Game Boy. The meeting took place on the upper deck of a McDonald's in Burlingame, California, which amused Mika. His contact was Andrew Ayre, co-founder of Digital Eclipse Software, Inc., the studio charged with arcade-to-Game-Boy conversions on behalf of Midway. Ayre had three jobs up for grabs, two of which, *Mortal Kombat 4* and *NFL Blitz* for Game Boy Color, were high-profile. Mika signed up for both.

On his way back to work, he mulled over how he was going to break the news that he'd found other work to his boss. Mika's day job was writing and editing articles for *Next Generation* magazine. He worried that the editorial managers would forbid him from taking side jobs; after all, working with publishers posed an obvious conflict of interest, since Mika and the rest of the staff reviewed games made by those studios. Luckily, his bosses granted him permission to moonlight as a game programmer. He didn't cover the Game Boy Beat, so no conflicts of interest should arise.

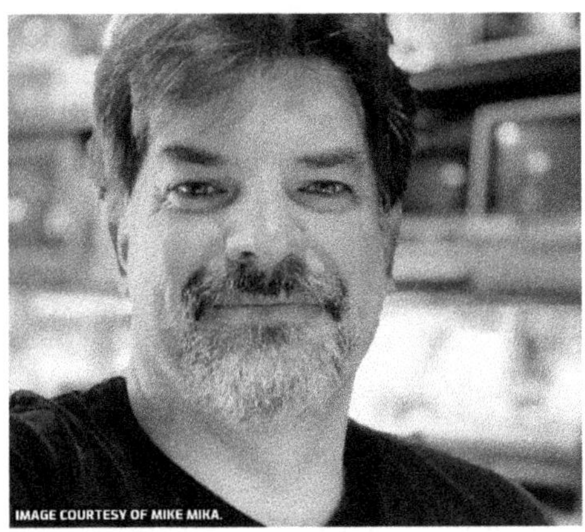
IMAGE COURTESY OF MIKE MIKA.

Seven days a week, Mika went into *Next Generation* early in the morning, worked for nine to twelve hours, went home to wolf down dinner, programmed his conversions until four or five in the morning, crashed for a power nap, then showered and changed before heading back to *Next Gen*. For three months, he was having the time of his life juggling both jobs. He was also sleep deprived, but he made his schedule work. Working on properties like *NFL Blitz* and *Mortal Kombat* was too good to let something like mental and physical exhaustion keep him down. "Every game I'd worked on to that point was just a secondary thing, but now I was working with a bigger company, Midway, and the company in charge of it, Digital Eclipse, was new to Game Boy. I didn't know what I was getting myself into. If you add to that the fact that I knew nothing about football, I was in for quite a treat."

NFL Blitz was a 1997 coin-op game captained by Mark Turmell, the arcade designer at Midway responsible for *NBA Jam*. Like *Jam*, *Blitz* stripped away all the slow, monotonous plays from the sport it was based on and beefed it up with hard-hitting, adrenaline-fueled action. Players didn't just tackle opponents, they spun them around and slammed them to the ground like pro wrestlers. Unlike *NBA Jam*, which had released four years earlier, *NFL Blitz* was a fully 3D game. That made it perfect for newer home systems like the PlayStation and Nintendo 64, but a round-peg-square-hole situation on Game Boy Color.

Even before the daunting trial of coding safeties, Mika had been scratching his head over *NFL Blitz*. Game Boy Color had a two megahertz processor and specialized in sprites, not polygons. As if that weren't challenging enough, Nintendo told Midway it expected *Blitz* to be compatible with the older, black-and-white Game Boy, which ran slower than the Color. Over a week, Mika psyched himself up by seeking to emulate Atari programmers like Tod Frye and Howard Scott Warshaw. He knew they had made *Pac-Man* and *E.T.*, respectively, by endeavoring to capture the spirit of their source material rather than attempting to recreate it perfectly on low-end hardware. "I said, 'On Game Boy, I can't do 3D.' Some people maybe could have, but there was no way I could have pulled it off. The closest I could get was isometric, so I made it *Zaxxon*-style isometric."

A coin-op game developed and published by Sega in 1982, *Zaxxon* was a shooter in which players blasted their way through fortresses. Scenery and characters appeared three-dimensional through a graphical technique called axonometric projection—later popularized as "isometric perspective" by Blizzard North's *Diablo*—that displayed visuals from a slanted, top-down view, like looking down at a chess board from a corner instead of from one side. Copying *Zaxxon*'s perspective in *NFL Blitz* allowed Mike Mika to show a good chunk of the field so players could see where they were relative to their goal.

His next challenge was displaying all those characters. The conversion needed to display a certain number of athletes on the screen at once, but more than ten sprites on one of the screen's horizontal lines would cause flickering. "Sprites couldn't pull that off," Mike recalled, "so I went to an old trick I'd seen on NES all the time. I didn't like it, but you'd do flickering: Any time there were too many sprites on a single line, I'd alternate drawing half the sprites on one frame and the other half on the next."

While *Blitz*'s graphics on Game Boy Color didn't come anywhere near to conversions of the game on more powerful hardware such as Nintendo 64 or PlayStation, the artificial intelligence of Mika's port was up to par. He poked around at all the plays in *NFL Blitz*'s source code—Safe Cover, Stuff It, Kombat, Black Rain—and found a scripting language Midway's programmers had used to carry them out. By translating the data, he was able to make the plays work on Game Boy. The only thing he couldn't carry over was the arcade game's over-the-top tackles. Once again, he targeted spirit rather than replication by recording video of impacts in the arcade version of *Blitz*. The videos were more like quick takes, flashing two or three frames before the game reverted to its isometric view, but it was better than leaving tackles out completely.

Safeties brought everything crashing down. No matter how hard he tried, he couldn't wrap his head around how to make the complicated plays work in code. Midway took pity and offered to send two QA testers to work on-site with him. That gave Mika pause. His bosses at *Next Generation* knew he had two jobs, whereas Midway, one of the biggest coin-op and console studios in the world, did not. He picked up his new workmates from the airport and, once pleasantries were out of the way, dropped the bomb.

"Look," he said as he pulled back into traffic. "I have a one-bedroom apartment with very little room. During the day, I work at *Next Gen*."

The two testers shrugged. "We won't tell anybody."

Mika's stress melted away. "I loved *Blitz* because I didn't have to know football to enjoy that game. They walked me through what needed to be done to get the game to where it needed to be. They were fantastic and such a great help."

Critics took the Game Boy Color port of *NFL Blitz* to task for slow gameplay and for the video-like presentation of tackles. However, Mika chalked the project up as a win on two fronts. The first was financial. "While it wasn't the best quality in the world, it sold extremely well. That was the moment we realized, 'You know what? The Game Boy is such a big platform that people are forgiving.' Even though reviews weren't very good, people were buying my game because they were just happy to have a form of *Blitz* they could play on a bus or at school."

The second win came three months later, as Mika was browsing the video game section at a Toys R Us. A mom stood nearly with her son as he selected *Disney's Tarzan*, another Game Boy game. Mika happened to notice and spoke up. "Oh, cool. I made that game."

The mom shot him a dubious look. "What?"

"No, really." Mika turned around and grinned at the gasps of surprise from the mom and son. On the back of his t-shirt was the logo for Digital Eclipse, the same logo on the box held in the boy's hands.

"Oh my God!" the mom said.

A clerk overheard their conversation, and Mika smiled as the other two customers filled him in. "That's so cool!" the clerk said.

"He bought one, and they bought one, and they had me sign them. I was on cloud nine," Mika remembered. "I was thinking, *I can't believe these people want my autograph.* I was as excited to see them buying it as they were excited about meeting me."

***

YEARS EARLIER, A Digital Eclipse t-shirt would have looked nothing like the one Mike Mika happened to wear during his Toys R Us outing. It would have displayed a logo, and likely a hard drive with an Apple symbol near it.

Based in Emeryville, California, Digital Eclipse was founded in the early nineties as a company devoted to building hardware and software for Macintosh computers. A sound app let users replace default sound effects. Another application compressed hard drives according to a proprietary algorithm. Looking to branch out, the company explored opportunities in porting games. Then Jeff Vavasour, Digital Eclipse's lead tech engineer, had a thought: Instead of porting a game, what if they went a level deeper?

Simulation, or emulation, was more complex than porting. A port involved making changes to source material—graphics, sound effects, artificial intelligence, and other content—to get the title working on another platform. Emulation was the process of getting a game to look, play, and sound exactly like it did in its native environment "This was before MAME and everything else [in emulation]," explained Mika. "They said, 'If we simulate the registers on this old hardware, modern hardware might be fast enough to do it. We'd just run the original ROMs.'"

Vavasour wrote an emulator designed to replicate three of Midway's classic arcade games: *Joust*, *Defender*, and *Robotron*. Once all three were working, Vavasour, Ayre, and a few other managers packed a laptop and flew to Chicago to take a meeting with Midway. Waiting in the lobby, Vavasour unpacked the computer and showed off his emulator to people as they walked by. Larry DeMar, then Midway's lead engineer, noticed a crowd and strolled over to see what had captured everyone's attention.

"He knew immediately what it was and flipped out," Mika said. "Midway was super-excited, and they signed a deal to let Digital Eclipse publish those games under a license. That opened up the direction of Digital Eclipse from that point forward: The company focused entirely on arcade game ports."

Digital Eclipse existed on a steady diet of arcade re-releases for the next several years. Products such as *Williams Arcade Classics*—also known as *Williams Arcade's Greatest Hits*—bundled *Defender*, *Joust*, *Sinistar*, and other games together and, through emulators like the one Vavasour had programmed, effectively shrank arcade cabinets down into cartridges and discs published on platforms from Sega Genesis and Super Nintendo to PC, Dreamcast, PlayStation 2, and Xbox 360.

Digital Eclipse was able to release anthologies on so many platforms due to the control it exercised over publishing rights. "In effect, Midway sold DE all their digital-game rights," Mika explained. "Midway no longer owned those for a little while, until someone at Midway realized that and came back to the table. In good faith, DE sold them back, but said, 'Okay, just give us right of first refusal on doing classic game collections.'"

DE's work with Midway opened the door to other projects. Capcom permitted them to re-release games such as *Ghosts 'n' Goblins* and *1942* on Game Boy Color. Nintendo's colorful handheld, which ran on the Zilog Z80 8-bit processor that had powered several arcade titles, was the soil in which Digital Eclipse planted its flag. Every successful conversion brought in new opportunities such as Mika's conversions of *NFL Blitz* and *Mortal Kombat 4*. One of the trickiest ports was *Dragon's Lair*, a coin-op game that played as an animated movie drawn by veteran Disney artist Don Bluth. "We had to translate twenty minutes of video to this underpowered machine to get it to play the real arcade game," Mika said.

Digital Eclipse's staff went the extra mile on anthologies by packing in bonus materials like design documents, concept art, and video interviews with the designers who had created the original arcade games.

By the mid-2000s, however, coin-op companies viewed ports and emulation in a different light. Because those projects had quick turnarounds, publishers could afford to pay DE less than it would have had to spend on to make a brand-new title. As anything retro became a hot-ticket item for collectors, publishers paid DE less so they could pocket even more of the profit. DE's managers argued that extra work such as video interviews and concept illustrations added value to packages. To publishers, more extras meant more time, and more time meant more money out of their pockets.

"To be fair, we weren't that far removed from the era when those games came out," Mika admitted. "I think they were looking at it like, these are still really fun games, and still modern enough that people would pay again to play them. Now we're at a point where if you're going to put *Joust* or *Robotron* out there, there needs to be extra value. For DE, that means the educational side: We try to put in background information, videos, and everything else to build up the value of our package. But back then, there weren't that many years between when *Defender* came out and when we were releasing them on [newer] consoles."

Digital Eclipse added to its income stream by diversifying. A 2003 merger between DE and ImaginEngine resulted in Backbone Entertainment. Soon, the DE brand was lost in the shuffle of yet more mergers and acquisitions. Later that year, Mika and Ayre co-founded Other Ocean Group. Other Ocean took on a variety of ports until 2015, when one of the co-founders spoke a question that had been on everyone's mind. "We said, 'I wonder what it would take to bring DE back,'" Mike recalled. "We were entertaining the idea of, 'If we got DE back, what would we do with it that's different?'"

Mika stepped up as the studio head of the new Digital Eclipse. He, Ayre, and Frank Cifaldi, a gaming historian who'd been writing for *Gamasutra*, already had their first project. For the past year, they'd been pitching Capcom on bundling more classic titles into tidy packages. "It'd be amazing to do something with any of your old IP," Mika remembered saying to one manager. "*Street Fighter* in particular, but whatever we can get."

"Well," the manager said, "we were thinking of doing something with *Mega Man*."

Mega Man had been Capcom's flagship series until *Street Fighter II* became a global sensation in 1991. The first *Mega Man* was released in 1987 for the NES, and introduced nonlinear gameplay to side-scrolling action games by letting players blast their way through stages in any order. Every stage ended in a boss fight against a Robot Master with a unique power, such as bombs or beams of lightning. Defeating a boss yielded its weapon, leading to a paper-scissors-rock system where certain bosses were weak to specific weapons.

Capcom signed *Mega Man Legacy Collection,* an anthology of the six titles from the NES era, to Other Ocean Group. Cifaldi recalled landing the project as the moment when he and the others gave serious thought to creating a new—or new-old—label. "Other Ocean is a work-for-hire game developer," he explained. "We'd done a bunch of mobile apps, port work we're barely credited with. We do everything, so there's not really a brand associated with Other Ocean. I felt that the sort of Criterion Collection thing we were starting with *Mega Man Legacy Collection* needed a brand."

IMAGE COURTESY OF FRANK CIFALDI.

Cifaldi aspired to put together collections that functioned more like interactive documentaries than video games. Ayre and Mika agreed. "We said, 'Let's use DE as a way to push our game preservation agenda as fast and hard as we can,'" Mika recalled.

He communicated that intent when he, Mika, and Ayre announced the return of Digital Eclipse in 2015. "I wrote our snooty marketing text on the old website in the very serious tone I wanted to make people stand up and pay attention. It wasn't, 'Hey, kids! Remember this?' No. It was, 'We are presenting this as art, and we're studying it and taking it very seriously.' That's what I wanted that Digital Eclipse brand to be."

Curating the definitive anthology of *Mega Man*'s 8-bit glory days galvanized Cifaldi. Digging through archives, hitting up his sources for old design documents, concept artwork, old code, anything they might have—that was his specialty. The company opened its vault to Cifaldi, who came away with an extensive database of characters and lore that had only been published as part of *Rockman Complete Works*, a repackaging of *Mega Man 1* through *VI* for PlayStation exclusively in Japan. "It had this database feature that had every enemy in the game with all their stats and a little bio," Cifaldi said. "Those bios had never been translated, so that's something I worked really hard—outside of scope; nights-and-weekends sort of thing—to get in there because I thought it'd be cool. I didn't want to include all of the features from old re-releases, just the ones that made sense, and that, to me, made sense, because it gave more context to the worlds you were running through."

The centerpiece of *Mega Man Legacy Collection* was a challenge mode that strung together screens from levels across all six games. "I think of them as time traveling through levels," Cifaldi said.

Originally, Capcom wanted Digital Eclipse to build brand-new levels for *Legacy Collection* using assets from the six *Mega Man* titles. "We told them how much that would cost, and they said, 'Hmm. No. But can you do it anyway?'" Cifaldi recalled, laughing.

"So we came up with challenge levels as an alternative to creating new levels."

Mega Man Legacy Collection released to strong reviews. To Digital Eclipse's co-founders and growing team of engineers, positive feedback served as a sign that they were on the right track. "From that point forward, we said, 'Every product we do, we have to try to add something new to this experience that defines what DE is even more,'" said Mika. "We went from *Mega Man Legacy Collection* to *The Disney Afternoon Collection*. We added more presentation features, more museum features. By the time we got to *Street Fighter 30th Anniversary Collection*, we said, 'Okay, anything we can find. Let's try to beef this up as much as we can.'"

DE's team had been eyeing a *Street Fighter* anthology since getting the band back together. Frank Cifaldi, who'd left Gamasutra and Digital Eclipse to found the Video Game History Foundation (VGHF), would be involved as a historian and curator. When Cifaldi, Mika, and the others got in touch with Capcom about rounding *Street Fighter* titles, they were met with some hesitation. "Having worked on three Capcom projects like this, I think it's just luck of the draw: who's assigned to your project, and how much they care," Cifaldi said.

***

CAPCOM'S TWO CROWN jewels, *Mega Man* and *Street Fighter*, debuted in 1987. *Mega Man*'s nonlinear approach to action-platforming was novel, but the absence of a save system made the game less accessible. (Capcom corrected this in *Mega Man II* by introducing password-based progression.)

Critics were more enthusiastic about *Street Fighter*. A one-on-one fighting game, *SF*'s maiden outing cast players as Ryu, a Japanese martial artist, in the game's single-player mode. Ryu faced off against eight opponents in different stages such as back alleys and trainyards, culminating in a battle against Sagat, a Muay Thai master. None of the challengers Ryu faced in the single-player mode were available in multiplayer. Instead, a second player assumed the role of Ken, an American student who learned alongside Ryu, for a one-on-one match. Ken and Ryu played identically, and had access to three special attacks: a fireball, a leaping uppercut, and a spinning kick. Stiff controls and an inherent demand for frame-perfect timing made special attacks tough to pull off, but who who managed to land special attacks were rewarded by dealing massive damage.

Capcom released *Street Fighter* in two cabinet styles. The standard edition featured an eight-way joystick and six buttons, three for light, medium, and hard kicks, and three for punches in the same flavors. The game's deluxe cabinet paired the joystick with two pressure-sensitive rubber pads. That led to the obvious outcome of control panels being damaged by players guilty only of trying to convince their avatars to hit just a bit harder.

Street Fighter enjoyed modest commercial success in arcades, leading Capcom producer Yoshiki Okamoto to begin work on a sequel. An early version of the game was shown at trade shows under the title *Street Fighter '89*. The title confused buyers. *Street Fighter* had been a one-on-one fighter, but the *'89* sequel was a brawler like *Double Dragon*, where one or two players selected a character and walked left to right beating up enemies. Okamoto knew what he was doing. He'd been enthralled by *Double Dragon II: The Revenge* and had cut his game from the same cloth, but with several technical modifications. Attacks had better feedback. Backgrounds were more detailed, such as a subway station where lights flickered on and off. Character sprites were larger and more animated. When arcade operators expressed concern over buying a sequel that looked nothing like the original game, Okamoto conceded and renamed his brawler *Final Fight*.

Final Fight was a success, but many developers within Capcom felt they'd left the depths of one-on-one fighting games unplumbed. Among them was Okamoto, who wanted to design a sequel that fleshed out the original. Approximately forty developers formed a team to make *Street Fighter II: The World Warriors*. Noritaka Funamizu took the reins as producer, while designer Akira Nishitani and character artist Akira Yasuda, both of whom had worked on *Final Fight*, headed up their disciplines.

Street Fighter II entered production in 1989. Capcom's team didn't give much thought to game balance. Their communal goal was to make the game deeper and more fun than its predecessor by creating characters that moved and fought with fluid animations like an animated film. Their choice of hardware, the CPS I (Capcom Play System), facilitated that objective. Using the board, programmers and animators could design characters that consumed varying amounts of memory: a certain amount for Ryu, a warrior clad in a karate *gi* and wandering the world in search of his next fight, and a little more Zangief, a taller and more muscular character covered in bloody marks attained over his career wrestling bears.

SFII went through several design phases before developers settled on eight "World Warriors." Unlike *Street Fighter*'s versus mode, all eight were selectable in single- and multiplayer contests. Every character had three types of punches and kicks, plus unique special moves such as fireballs, a blur of slapping hands or kicking feet, wrestling piledrivers, and aerial maneuvers such as a flipping kick and rising uppercut. Dealing enough damage caused opponents to grow dizzy, a mechanic where characters staggered in place, giving their opponent a free hit. Novice players might land a jump kick or fireball on a dizzied opponent. Experts went for combos.

Combos, a rapid-fire chain of attacks, were created by accident. Producer Noritaka Funamizu was performing a bug check when he noticed it was possible to perform one attack and immediately connect with a second if he entered the follow-up's button presses and joystick movements fast enough. If he was successful, the first move would be interrupted mid-animation, and the second attack would execute right away.

Funamizu and the others designers made a game out of seeing who could pull off the biggest combos. What made combos shine was the fact that they were unbreakable if players unleashed chained hits fast enough.

After two years of development, the game became an immediate hit when it arrived in arcades in 1991. Players crowded around cabinets to marvel at the cartoon-like visuals and smooth animations. Almost overnight, players gravitated to one or another World Warrior based on factors like appearance and move sets. "*SFII* was the first game I remember having the total package—individuality and one-on-one competition," said Dan Amrich, former editor at *GamePro* magazine. "Your choice represented you, your style, your strategy. Other games before that didn't really offer that. Many female players I knew at the time played Chun-Li because they wanted to be represented as female. But at the same time, Chun-Li plays nothing like Ken or Zangief." That was a huge difference from other brawlers that did little more than change a few minor details in each character's design and attempt to sell them as being radically different from one another.

Street Fighter II was more than the king of fighters. It was the lord and savior of arcades. Once thriving during the 1970s and early eighties, coin-op games had come under fire from American parents and various associations who were concerned about kids spending so much time playing games. Those groups had been building steam for years. In 1981, 100 people protested outside an arcade in Franklin, New York, telling the New York Times that drug use and vandalism had increased since the gaming center had opened.

The North American videogame market crash of 1983 hit companies such as Atari the hardest, but arcades suffered too. Desperate to bring players back in, operators bought new games on credit only to be unable to pay them off when they failed to attract a crowd. Historians credit Capcom and *Street Fighter II* with giving arcades a second wind. From its release in 1991 through '93, Capcom sold over 200,000 *SFII* cabinets to arcades, pizza parlors, sandwich shops, and anywhere else owned by proprietors who realized the game was good for several hundred dollars a week. Within two years, Capcom had earned over $1.5 billion in revenue.

"I saw it as a resurgence," Amrich agreed of *SFII*'s effect on arcades. "Here was an experience that you had to go try for yourself to believe. And then when it came out on SNES, a lot of friends wound up practicing at home so they could show off in the arcade. The arcade remained the place to gain fame—make a name for yourself. You could practice at home all day long, but who's going to know you're good until you show up and prove it in public?"

Nintendo scored a major victory in the 16-bit "console war" against Sega when it locked down the exclusive console version of *Street Fighter II: The World Warrior* for Super NES in the summer of 1992. While there were myriad changes from the arcade—voice samples removed, soundtrack remixed, attacks altered or stripped out—the port quickly attained best-seller status, and remains Capcom's highest-selling game released for a single platform at 6.3 million units sold. (2009's *Resident Evil 5*, which has been ported to numerous platforms, is the company's best-selling game overall.)

The game's influence continues more than twenty-eight years later. Countless game developers who grew up playing *Street Fighter II* cited it as an influence on their careers. It established the structure of gaming tournaments set up between two or more human players, and many have pointed to the game as the origin of esports.

Ultimately earning over $10.6 billion in revenue, making it one of the top three highest-earning video games of all time, *SFII* opened the floodgates to copycats. Most were shallow and unsuccessful. Some, like *Mortal Kombat*, gave Capcom a run for its money. To stay ahead of competition, the company rolled out updates in quick succession. *Street Fighter II': Champion Edition*—referred to in Japan as *Street Fighter II Dash*—let players choose the same fighter, likely an acknowledgement of the feature's success in the first *Mortal Kombat*, as well as play as the four boss characters, bringing the roster up to twelve.

After an explosion of ROM hacks gave rise to illegal distributions of *SFII*, Capcom responded by releasing *Street Fighter II: Hyper Fighting*, an upgrade released less than a year after *Champion Edition* and featuring a faster pace, balancing for all twelve characters, and several new moves inspired by hacks, such as Chun Li's fireball and Ryu's and Ken's midair hurricane kick. Capcom ratcheted back the speed several months later in *Super Street Fighter II*, adding four more characters and reworking the game's color palette. Finally, *Super Street Fighter II Turbo* offered *Hyper Fighting*'s faster pace, super moves that players unleashed after filling up a meter, and a secret character, Akuma, who played like a souped-up version of Ken and Ryu. Collectively, *Street Fighter II* and its four updates have been ported to over eighteen platforms as of 2012, making it one of, if not the most-ported game in the industry's history.

Capcom eventually moved on from the *Street Fighter II* sub series. In 1996, *Street Fighter Alpha*, the first of a trilogy, took place between the first and second entries in the series and improved upon *SSFII Turbo*'s super moves. *Street Fighter III* launched a year later, and kicked off a sub-series of its own with *Street Fighter III: Double Impact* and *Street Fighter III: Third Strike*.

With the exception of a devoted following for *Street Fighter II*, casual players had left the franchise's 2D games by the wayside for newer, flashier versions such as 2008's *Street Fighter IV* and 2015's *Street Fighter V*. Digital Eclipse intended to bring back the classics in a big way—if, that was, its developers could persuade Capcom to use a little elbow grease.

Part II: Preserved or Lost

IT WASN'T THAT no one at Capcom cared about old *Street Fighter* games. Frank Cifaldi knew that. That said, they sure were dragging their feet.

Cifaldi and his collaborators at Digital Eclipse intended to make *Street Fighter 30th Anniversary Collection* a definitive compilation. It would include the original *Street Fighter*, *Street Fighter II: The World Warriors* and its four updates, the *Street Fighter Alpha* trilogy, and all three versions of *Street Fighter III*.

All that plus online play and rare finds like screenshots from a version of *Street Fighter II* for NES, a conversion that had never been released. "Capcom didn't even know they had an image of that in their archive, so we were able to throw that in there," said Mike Mika, studio head of Digital Eclipse.

Cifaldi also wanted to pack in a treasure trove of documents and artwork. He knew, for example, that the design document for *Street Fighter II* existed. Capcom had shown it off in the past. But when he touched base with his contacts at the studio, they expressed confusion. He even sent them scanned images from articles where they had shown it as proof that it was out there somewhere.

"No," Capcom's representatives said time and again. "We don't have that."

"I don't know if we had anyone in the Japan office who was nerding out about this stuff like we were," Cifaldi admitted.

"Whereas with *Disney Afternoon*, they surprisingly went all out on that one. They didn't have very much [extra content], but they scraped every last bit they could out of their archives for us. We're also working with American producers who are working with Japanese producers, so there's a game of telephone. It's almost like you have to know the right person who knows where to look or who to ask."

In the spring of 2018, a month before *Street Fighter 30th* was due to ship for Nintendo Switch, PC, Xbox One, and PlayStation 4, Cifaldi found an issue of *Pen*, a Japanese magazine, that had published scans of *SFII*'s design document. "The design document that they don't have? That's in a magazine in Japan instead of in our game. I don't know what the deal is. I suspect it's just finding the right person," Cifaldi said of working with publishers.

If *Street Fighter* artwork had been published anywhere, Cifaldi wanted it. In one instance, he asked Capcom to send a copy of an official art book, only to be told that no such art book existed.

"Of course it exists," Cifaldi replied patiently. "You guys published it."

Digital Eclipse extended its reach beyond Capcom by tracking down publishers, artists, and other creators who had contributed official materials to *Street Fighter II*, the crown jewel of the franchise, and of Digital Eclipse's collection. "There are often cases where Capcom or other publishers don't have some of this material anymore, but we know people who do. We either borrow that material and scan it, or buy it to make sure we have it all together," said Mika.

Cifaldi found the editor of the art book he was looking for, who responded with a doubtful and drawn-out "Maaaaaybe?" when Cifaldi asked if he still had a copy. After all, the editor pointed out, it was a book from almost thirty years ago. "That was the bulk of the job: figuring out every piece of artwork that existed, and then figuring out how to get at it, and getting approvals, or [denials] in some cases. Then from there, building the timeline out from that."

True to their mission statement, Digital Extreme's developers improved on themselves with *Street Fighter 30th*'s trove of historical artifacts. A sprite viewer let players scrub through character animations frame by frame to chart how their looks, moves, and signature styles changed from game to game. A timeline chronicled important dates such as the release of each *SF* arcade cabinet and home version. But the portion of *SF 30th* Cifaldi is proudest of is the interactive documentary of the making of *Street Fighter II*. "Step one was getting that delivery from Capcom that they said that was all the art, even though it wasn't. Step two was buying all the books, magazine back issues, and stuff to figure out what the other official assets were. Step three was kind of the stereotypical, conspiracy theory map on the wall with yarn and tacks: Finding all these connections and figuring out what stories to tell."

His idea for the documentary arose from the knowledge that the story he wanted to tell, and the story fans and developers cared about most, was how *SFII*'s two-year development cycle culminated in one of the most influential video games ever made. "What really made it exciting to me was the initial pitch document for *Street Fighter II* that they scrapped before starting over," Cifaldi said.

As the doc's producer, Cifaldi spent months gathering assets and piecing together the story of *SFII*'s creation. Capcom's scrapped pitch document detailed characters, levels, and game mechanics that had been left on the cutting room floor. Much of the material came from a hardcover book that had shipped with an official soundtrack for *Street Fighter II* in 1994. Cifaldi collected scans of the pitch document, fired up Photoshop to enlarge and clean them up, and had them translated to English for the first time. The final piece of the puzzle was a stack of books three feet high; resting on top was a Japanese-published book about the game's development he'd found on a Yahoo! auction. "We paid the guy who runs [fan site] Shmuplations to translate most of the developer commentary that was in the official sources," Cifaldi recalled. "Actually, I paid him out of pocket because I didn't want to deal with the paperwork. I just wanted to get it done because I didn't want anything to hold back my feature."

Cifaldi and Mika knew Capcom's staff and directors cared about *Street Fighter*. Like most publishers, however, they worked notoriously long hours. In the heat of production, they're not thinking about how someone may appreciate a sketch they dashed off on a cocktail napkin, or how a glitch had led to combos, a cornerstone of fighting games going forward. They're thinking about hitting milestones and shipping a product. After that, they immediately move on to the next project, and the next, and the next. Past work isn't viewed with fondness until much later, if at all.

That's where Digital Eclipse came in. "I think it helps with products, but that's our thing," Cifaldi remarked of including historical information with anthologies, remakes, and remasters. "That's a Digital Eclipse thing. I think publishers recognize the value of it, but I don't think they're in the same mindset as we are, where we think that's the lifeblood of a product. It's hard for a lot of publishers to understand that, I think."

"It's the whole thing where your day-to-day life seems mundane, but to someone else, it's magical," Mika added. "A lot of people work in game development, and it's a really hard job with long hours. You're thinking about getting the job done, and afterwards, you don't want to think about it for a long time. During that critical moment when you don't want to think about it, that's when a project is either preserved or lost."

Cifaldi and Mika had done their part to preserve the story of how *Street Fighter II* was made. To preserve the game and the multibillion-dollar franchise it had spawned, they turned to an engineer who already had years of experience keeping the game from fading.

***

DANIEL FILNER COULDN'T believe this was happening. He was seventeen years old, and he and his friend were hanging out at Skywalker Ranch, the center of George Lucas's Star Wars universe. "I was seven when Star Wars came out. This was amazing."

Filner's journey to that galaxy far, far away began at age eleven, the first time he touched Radio Shack's TRS-80 personal computer. His school had one, and his math teacher gave Filner permission to tinker with it because he was ahead of the rest of the class. Through middle school, he signed up for programming courses during summer vacations and learned BASIC on the Apple II.

Filner came by his proclivity for numbers honestly. His father, a scientist, didn't want his son wasting time playing video games on one of those Ataris or Nintendos he'd been hearing about. As a compromise, he bought him a TI-99/4A, Texas Instruments' personal computer released in 1981. For the modest sum of $525, the PC came with a three megahertz processor, 256 bytes of memory, and compatibility with storage media such as cartridges, floppy disks, and cassette tapes.

There, his father said as he finished setting up the PC. Now his son could learn practical skills instead of frittering away time on games. Naturally, the first thing Filner did with his new computer was write games. "By the time I was in seventh and eighth grade, I was trying to write *Donkey Kong* for the PET, and *Pac-Man* for TI994A, just trying to reproduce arcade games on home computers I had access to. I didn't do a great job, but that's how I started programming, just recreating arcade games on home computers, mainly because I didn't have twenty-five cents to put into an arcade game."

Pac-Man stumped Filner. He was programming in BASIC, and no matter how hard he tried, the four ghosts refused to roam freely, in real-time, while he guided the hockey puck-shaped character around the maze. First he moved, then the ghosts moved. "My mom actually liked it," he remembered. "I remember my mom playing it, and I was disappointed because the ghosts didn't move by themselves. But my mom found it more strategic because you had to cover the maze without wasting any ground."

Filner packed up his TI when his family moved to California. His new school had a Commodore PET, and he endeavored to recreate *Donkey Kong* on it to marginally better results. "Somewhere in my garage is a cassette labeled *Filner Kong*, which was *Donkey Kong*," he said.

Entering high school, Filner sought out more complex programming challenges. His father bought an Atari ST, and Filner progressed from BASIC to assembly language. His goal was to write his own BBS, or bulletin board system, an online message board where users could share messages and files. Then his friend Tim showed him a game called *Ball Blazer*, an action game made by Lucasfilm Games—later renamed LucasArts—for the Atari 800 PC. They liked it, and decided to port it to the ST. Filner uploaded the game to a BBS and was contacted by a guy who claimed to be working the dream job Filner had fantasized about since childhood.

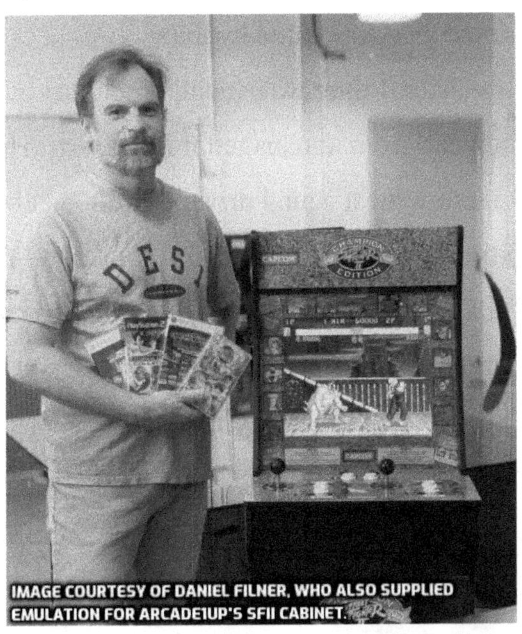
IMAGE COURTESY OF DANIEL FILNER, WHO ALSO SUPPLIED EMULATION FOR ARCADE1UP'S SFII CABINET.

"I'm seventeen, and he's a full-grown adult, and he knew I was a bulletin board operator in the neighborhood. He needed some work done on a BBS he was trying to get together, but it turned out he had been in the games industry, and he had connections. He saw what we were doing with our Atari ST version of *Ball Blazer*, and he got us in touch with Lucasfilm Games."

Lucasfilm invited Filner and Tim to Skywalker Ranch. After the grand tour, the executives presented them with a contract to finish *Ball Blazer* for the ST. It was fun while it lasted. "The total amount of money for the two of us might have been less than $2,000," Filner said. "We were high school kids. We finished it up and got it working, and it came out reasonably well. But it turned out they weren't going to publish it. It wasn't going to turn into a thing, and we were very disappointed by that."

A year later, Filner was attending classes at UC Berkeley when he got a call from a manager at LucasArts. He was looking for a programmer to write a sound driver—a file that brokered communication between hardware and software—for the Atari ST version of *Zak McKracken and the Alien Mindbenders*, a point-and-click adventure game that ran on the company's proprietary SCUMM (Script Creation Utility for Maniac Mansion) engine. The producer had reached out to Filner because he was one name on a very short list of programmers familiar with the ST. Just like that, he was a Jedi again.

"I mean, they sent me paper checks that had Yoda on them. I'm in college, and I'm making… not a living salary," Filner said after a pause, "but more money than a college kid needs, and I'm getting my computer science degree and already working professionally."

LucasArts continued developing point-and-click adventures on the SCUMM engine. Each new game introduced new features such as the ability to scale characters up and down as they walked closer to or further from the screen. Filner stayed on as a contractor, porting games such as *Loom* and *Maniac Mansion* to the Atari ST. Later versions of the engine forced him to keep his skills up to snuff by doing things like writing in a hybrid of assembly and C.

In university, one of his classes centered on learning to give presentations. Filner talked about his favorite subject: How to make video games. Around the same time, he enrolled in a course on assembly language. His professor greeted them the first day by saying, "You'll never really need to use this stuff" since high-level languages like C were far more prevalent in nine-to-five jobs like writing software for banks, but, he admitted, a few students might find it useful.

Filner smirked. "It was like, 'Well, actually, I'm getting paid to use this stuff right now.' It wasn't some hypothetical. It was actually what I was doing."

Following graduation, Filner got a job programming licensed games for a company called Equilibrium. He worked on a baseball game starring Bo Jackson, an action game that licensed the Attack of the Killer Tomatoes characters, and a title where players performed the slick moves of rapper Vanilla Ice. One afternoon, he got a call from a guy who asked if he'd be interested in working on a collection of old arcade games.

Filner was taken aback. He had no idea who this guy was or how he'd got his number—but, yes, he was interested.

The company was Digital Eclipse, and the assignment was to get *Defender*, *Stargate*, and other classic Williams games running on Sega Genesis. "The guy said, 'Okay. Here's the Genesis dev kit. Here's the source code for *Defender*. See if you can make *Defender* work.' It was like being handed the Crown Jewels: Looking at *Defender*'s source code and seeing how it worked. I was cross-translating from 6809 assembly to 68000 assembly," Filner explained, the latter being the dialect of assembly processed by the Genesis. "I had to understand the entire program top to bottom."

Every Williams game used a bitmap system that stored every pixel on the screen in a memory register. The end product displayed at a resolution that was more than good enough. Two weeks later, Filner called his contact at Digital Eclipse and said he'd gotten *Defender* working. "Great," the guy said. "Now do *Stargate*." Filner completed the job even faster. He moved on to *Robotron*, then *Sinistar*.

For his next job, Digital Eclipse wanted Filner to convert the same collection to the Saturn, Sega's CD-based console. This job, he knew, was a taller hurdle to jump. His Genesis conversions had been translations of a game from one language to another. The Saturn required an emulator. That would make each retro game in the collection arcade perfect, if Filner could figure out how emulators ran and how to write one. Fortunately, one of the engineers at DE gave him a primer. “You don't have to massage every single byte of every single line by hand,” Filner said. “You just the emulator to work, and then, boom—it comes out the right way. I don't think I've ever thought about it like this before, but I was right at the junction of having a game where the target system was not powerful enough to do an emulator, so I had to build an emulator for this game I already knew from top to bottom.”

Over the next several years, emulating classic console and arcade games became Filner’s specialty. He handled the *Capcom Classics Collection*, which included versions of *Street Fighter II*, an anthology of Sega Genesis games like *Sonic the Hedgehog* and *Golden Axe*, and more arcade titles by Midway. Many of those and other projects were given to him under contract by Digital Eclipse, who by that time had him on speed dial.

“When they got *Street Fighter 30th Anniversary Collection*, they knew right away that that was the kind of thing I could do,” Filner said.

***

DANIEL FILNER HOPED things would go a certain way when he worked with publishers. Hoped, but did not expect.

For instance, he rarely spoke directly to property-holders like Capcom, so he asked contractors such as Digital Eclipse to do his talking for him. His request for *Street Fighter 30th Anniversary Collection* was simple, and the same as every project involving porting or emulation: Get the source code. Having a game's source was like having a GPS on a long road trip. Without it, he just had to get in his car and drive. "Usually, it doesn't happen," Filner admitted. "It's super-difficult, because the source code is maybe missing completely or hard to access, and they don't understand or care that it's helpful, or they're paranoid about letting it out of their grasp. Sometimes it happens after the project is over."

Street Fighter 30th was a special case. Heading into the project, he already had a personal library of *SF* code he'd been amassing since the early 2000s, when he'd worked on various Capcom anthologies that included assorted flavors of *SFII.* He'd been work-for-hire at the time, so the emulator he'd written had belonged to his employer. Since then, he'd built his own from scratch, updating it whenever a *Street Fighter*-related project came along.

Every programmer went about writing an emulator in his or her own way. No matter the method, the goal remained the same. "Basically, an emulator pretends to be another piece of hardware," said Mike Mika, studio head of Digital Eclipse, and an engineer who'd written his fair share of emulators.

At the dawn of every emulation project, programmers consider the technical layout of the platform they want to emulate: its processors, its memory, its audio and video chips, and the language of the game's code, which executes the instructions that operate all that hardware. Most arcade games are written in assembly. The job of a game's main processor, the CPU, is to read instructions in code, one by one, and do what that instruction tells it to do: add values, subtract values, store a value, load a value, compare two or more values, branch into other sections of code. "An emulator does what the CPU does," Filner explained. "It has a number that points to the program counter, and it pulls the next instruction by reading from the game ROM."

Emulators are agnostic. They don't care what game the CPU is trying to run. They just wait for instructions and tell the CPU to act on them. "Each chip, whether it's a sound chip or anything else, follows the same basic pattern of doing a little bit of processing, producing output, checking the inputs—whether they're joystick inputs, a button being pressed, or input from some other chip," Filner continued.

Every frame of animation, emulators produce two types of output: an image rendered at the game's native resolution, and a stream of audio. Another part of the emulator decides what to do with that output. Usually, this means blowing up an image to fill the screen and directing audio to an output channel, most often a set of speakers. "The core of the emulator doesn't care what system it's on. It just produces a bitmap and a stream of audio samples," Filner said. "If you think about an arcade game that's eighteen inches square, maybe, and has thirty chips on it, one of those is the CPU, one might be a sound chip, and one might be another CPU to talk to the sound chip. An emulator just has to do what the hardware did."

Primordial games such as *Pong* were made up of circuits with gates that opened electronically and dispatched binary signals of yes or no, one or zero. That made them difficult to reproduce exactly, one-to-one, in code. When technology allowed engineers to make games from CPUs and RAM chips, most coin-op manufacturers bought those and other products off the shelf rather than reinventing the wheel. Every one of those chips and boards came with documentation that helped them to understand how to build what they wanted to build.

Writing emulators is still an arcane art rather than a science, but enthusiasts and career programmers like Filner have bridged the gap by following in the footsteps of coin-op manufacturers. When given an emulation project, they try not to reinvent the wheel. "If you think about automobile parts, these are like if you had a bunch of companies making automobiles, but the companies all got their parts from three parts manufacturers," Filner explained. "You might have an automobile with a Z80 and another with a 68000 processor. The outside could look like whatever they wanted, but the insides would look like the parts everybody knew how to use. If you know how to emulate those parts, it's all modular. The amount of unique hardware for each hardware system is still rather small."

In a way, emulating a game is simple. Once programmers understand a particular piece of hardware, they can write code so emulators such as MAME, the most popular arcade-machine emulator around, will support it. The tricky part comes when publishers request changes to be made. "Any time you need to modify original behavior in any way, it pierces the veil of the emulation. You can break things," Filner said.

Back in the heyday of *Street Fighter II* and *Teenage Mutant Ninja Turtles*, manufacturers like Capcom and Konami included a screen featuring the FBI logo along with a quote now synonymous with video arcades, *Winners Don't Do Drugs*. "Recently," Filner recalled, "some genius lawyer said, 'The FBI lawyer on that screen is a trademark of the US government. We're not necessarily still allowed to use that, so we'd better remove it.' What? No, that's part of the original game. Well, I'm not in the legal department so I don't get to ask those questions. They just say, 'Please take out the FBI screen.'"

Making a change as direct as ripping out a screen is easy when developing an original game. For emulation programmers without access to source code, classic games are black boxes. They could crack open the game's ROM, disassembling it, and sifting through code to find instructions pertaining to that screen, but that came with risks. Filner could accidentally damage other parts of the code. Instead, he tries to figure out how to hop from the instruction pertaining to the screen needing to be removed to the next instruction in line. Another option is to leave the screen intact, but implement a way to skip over it.

Publishers also tend to request that a game's copyright screen be updated to show the year of its re-release. That's less like performing surgery and more like defusing a bomb. "The copyright message is the first thing that would have boobytraps on it," Filner said. "When a programmer was trying to prevent bootlegging, they'd have checksums"—a sequence of characters the game verifies—"and checksums to check the checksums. If you're asked to change something that you think might have been boobytrapped, you have to be super-careful to make it so the emulator can't tell you've changed anything."

The approach Filner chose for *Street Fighter 30th* was to insert breakpoints, road signs that divert a program's execution without needing to even see legacy code, much less alter it. "Breakpoints mean, at this instruction, the emulator stops and calls this C++ function. The C++ function is essentially a magic watch that stops the world: It happens in between instructions, and you can change things without the original program noticing, if you're careful."

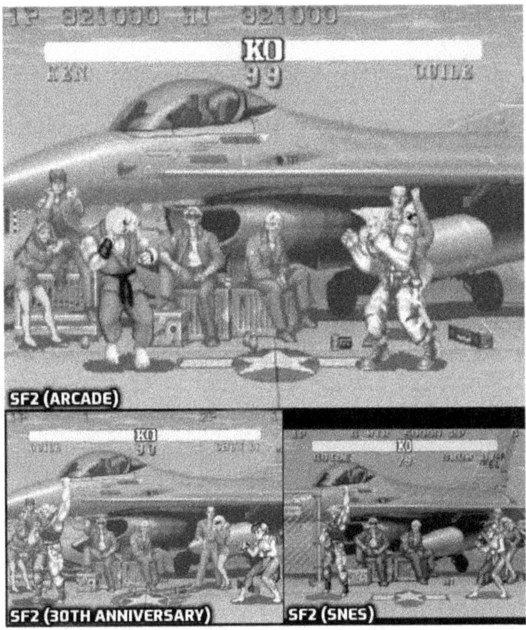

As Filner moved deeper into the code for the twelve games included in *Street Fighter 30th*, he had to make other changes requested by Capcom. Before each match, *Street Fighter* let players choose from a handful of stages themed after cities and countries. *SFII* expanded on that practice by designing a stage around each character's personality and the culture of their country: a dojo in Japan for Ryu, a U.S. Air Force hangar for Guile complete with a jet idling in the background and soldiers hanging around to cheer him on, a Chinese market for Chun Li, a temple for Dhalsim. Chun Li's marketplace is a hive of activity. Citizens pedal bicycles back and forth, a vendor throttles a chicken, and a family cheers from within the shade and safety of their shop. Behind the family sits a stack of crates decorated with Coca-Cola's white-swish-on-red-background iconography. Another offending item, a can of Coke, sits on the ground in Guile's hangar. "Capcom decided, 'Maybe we shouldn't have those because we didn't talk to Coca-Cola about it,'" Filner said. "I had to paint over or erase those crates so they didn't look like Coca-Coca [iconography].

The CPU of Capcom's CPS I board couldn't see the contents of image files. It just knew where it was supposed to unload them, like a truck driver who unloads boxes without knowing what's in them. *Street Fighter II*'s stages were made up of tiles stitched together in real-time as the CPU checked the tile number it was supposed to grab from memory and blasted it to the screen. All Filner had to do was isolate those pixels and paint over them. The CPU, blissfully oblivious to the fact that certain pixels had changed, went about its work. Boxes in single shades of gray or red were inserted in the marketplace stall, and the can of Coke was colored blue.

"There's something like 64,000 tiles for every one of these games, so there's this giant tapestry of tiles Maps and player-character sprites are generated from these lists of tiles," he said. "When it came time to make these modifications, I just inserted crate tiles that had been overlaid. The tiles are not actually stored as a big bitmap in the ROMs. In order to make these changes, I had to write a converter program to take the ROM image and convert it into a bitmap. Then I could edit the bitmap, and the tool had to convert the bitmap back into the ROM format."

Changing subtle details of decades-old game content gives Filner a different perspective of a career built on preserving games. "This particular topic isn't really preservation. This is corrupting parts of the original game to make it legally possible to [sell again]."

Getting *Street Fighter 30th Anniversary* running demanded more than painting over a few tiles. From the beginning, Capcom asked Digital Eclipse to include a training mode in core *SF* games, those being *SFII Hyper Fighting*, *Super SFII Turbo*, *SF Alpha 3*, and *SFIII Third Strike*. In training modes, one player can battle a CPU-controlled opponent to practice special moves, combos, timing, and other techniques. Training modes tend to come with lots of frills such as on-screen button symbols to show players exactly what they're pressing as they attempt moves, and options that force the CPU-controlled opponent to behave a certain way, such as blocking or jumping in place so players can practice specific scenarios such as trapping a blocking opponent in a corner.

"Capcom said, 'For training mode, we want to make it so that when you throw a punch, the other guy always blocks.' I said, 'Oh. How am I going to figure that out?'" Filner recalled.

Filner agreed readily, believing that adding a training mode would be simple. As time went on, he realized Capcom wanted a robust set of options, many of which they'd popularized in contemporary games such as *Street Fighter V*. Getting opponents to act or react in specific ways meant delving deep into layers of code he could not access easily. "The thing when you're working with an emulator is, you have to know how the game's chip works, but you don't have to know how the game itself works. And because you don't have to know, you usually don't bother learning the underlying logic."

Filner's early experiments proved fruitful… sort of. He was able to rig opponents to automatically block when he performed some attacks, but not all. Eventually he let Digital Eclipse know he was stuck, and Mike Mika got hold of contacts at Capcom to help out. "They'd worked on the PlayStation version, and found their old excerpts of code where they'd set up that blocking stuff," said Filner. "They gave me specific lines like, 'At this exact instruction, stick in these other things to make this happen, or if this happens, make this happen, and it will always block.' Those guys knew how the software worked down to the bottom, and they'd already worked all that out."

***

MORE THAN GLOSSING over logos, more than attaching puppet strings to characters, the most difficult part of emulation is optimization. Capcom's CPS I, which powered thirty-two coin-op games—closer to 134 if you counted revisions to those games such as *SFII Champion Edition* and *SFII Hyper Fighting*—had one primary processor, one secondary processor, two sound chips, a PPU (pixel processing unit), system RAM, and myriad other moving parts.

At a glance, emulating decades-old hardware on modern PCs and game consoles seems trivial. The CPS I's primary processor, a Motorola 68000, ran at ten megahertz, with later models ratcheted up to twelve. A Zilog Z80, the secondary processor, was clocked at 3.579 megahertz. Contemporary processors leave them in their dust by running several orders of magnitude faster, but those processors power machines juggling other work such as operating systems performing tasks in the background, sending and receiving data over the Internet, and multiple programs open at the same time. Arcade games were designed for a singular purpose. Consequently, even older games can run slow on machines that should be able to leave them in their dust. "The original system is doing things in parallel because it's got dozens of chips," Filner explained. "Every cycle of the original machine, those dozens of chips are doing things. Every piece of the original hardware is doing something every moment, and the emulator has to manage all of those pieces all the time."

"There's a reason those chips were independent originally," said Mike Mika. "They were able to do individual processing, and the sum of its parts delivered a really fast and crazy experience. So you have to optimize to get that same kind of performance."

Filner had encountered optimization issues before. "The PlayStation 3 wasn't fast enough to do proper emulation of the Sega Genesis," he remembered. He'd prioritized gameplay over audio by using WAV files for every game's soundtrack instead of emulating the Genesis's sound hardware. That solution did the trick in most games. *Sonic the Hedgehog* was one exception. "I think the worst case was, when Sonic gets the speedy shoes, the music is supposed to speed up. But we didn't have a way to do that, so I just didn't do it. We were using canned, pre-recorded music, so we couldn't just make it speed up in the middle. The more powerful a target system is, the less likely you are to have to cut corners in the emulation."

Audio is a sticking point in emulation optimization. On a sound chip, a channel is one outlet through which the chip can play a sample such as voices, sound effects, and music. Sound chips on arcade boards could output a few samples at once, or a dozen. Emulators that haven't been optimized to carry the load of a game's source hardware tend to fall behind in audio, resulting in errors such as sound effects lagging behind visuals. *Street Fighter II*'s CPS I and other arcade boards from the nineties produced sounds through circuitry that created wave patterns using complicated mathematical operations: comparing sines, performing fade shifts, modulating amplitude.

"There were six, or eight, or ten copies of the circuitry doing this sample by sample," Filner continued. "So every sample you want to emulate, you have six, or eight, or ten things going through mathematical operations just to generate a voice for the next sample. That tuns out to be CPU-intensive to emulate that circuitry sample by sample on a modern processor that doesn't have instructions able to do six things at the same time. There's a lot of parallelism: Every wire in the arcade machine was doing something, and the emulator has to do all of those at the same time. That's why emulators can bog down even really fast machines."

Then there's input lag, the delay between pressing a button and the game's response, such as moving a character or attacking. Input lag doesn't always come down to poor optimization. Manufacturers of arcade games had to accommodate one set of controls, usually a joystick and buttons, but sometimes special peripherals as well, such as a steering wheel, gearshifts and pedals, or a light gun. Emulators run on systems that let users plug in wired or wireless controllers, keyboards and mice, and joysticks or gamepads that require driver files to be recognized by an operating system. All those variables add up.

"You have all this lag you have to fight against to optimize your emulation," Mika admitted. "That's the thing we fight all the time: How much lag and latency can we reduce to make this feel like the original game? Sometimes we've turned down doing a game, or at least held off on it, saying, 'This can't be done now, but next generation will probably be the time we can do it.'"

"We also have a lot of people who are upset because they don't like the modern stuff," added Frank Cifaldi. "They think we're doing something to introduce more input lag than other emulated projects. It's like, 'No, that's how systems are, now. Sorry. We don't have extra input lag; we just have the regular input lag that everything has.'"

For *Street Fighter 30th Anniversary Collection*, Daniel Filner added in-game options to help players reduce input lag and accommodate as many input peripherals as possible. Setting input lag to a lower value in any game forced the emulator to register and react to input faster. One of the most important types of input lag reduction schemes, if not the most important, was cutting back on latency in online play. He knew the PlayStation 4, Xbox One, and PC versions of the anthology could handle the measures he'd have to take to cut back on lag online. Nintendo's Switch console, which Capcom had begun to support shortly after it sold millions of units upon its release in March 2017, was a bottleneck.

"What we ran into was, on the Switch, we had less room to work with in terms of CPU power, so I had to go further on the Switch to get things to work. Not in terms of cutting corners, but in terms of being more efficient: Skipping work that didn't need to be done, and doing the work that I was doing more efficiently."

Networking for online games tends to suffer on lower-end hardware. Cutting back on any and all forms of lag is crucial in fighting games, where a single frame of animation can mean the difference between a game-winning move or a character standing around like a dummy. *Street Fighter II* produced a new game frame every sixteen milliseconds to hit sixty frames per second, but that only pertained to players competing on the same console, or, online, the same network or perhaps country. A Guile player in Taiwan facing off against a Zangief player in America had an uphill battle on Switch, especially since the portable nature of the console encouraged play over WiFi, a less stable connection than plugging directly into a modem or router.

Filner did his best to mitigate input lag online by writing algorithms that predicted input ahead of time. If a Ryu player rolled from down to forward, the algorithm automatically assumed they would follow by pressing any of the three punch buttons to complete the maneuver for Ryu's fireball—waiting in the wings so it could be processed quickly. In other words, what players see happening in real-time already happened for the emulator several microseconds earlier.

"Predictively emulating into the future based on what you think the other player's joystick will be," Filner summarized. "It's not the best explanation, but you end up emulating more frames per frame than you would like. If your performance isn't good enough, you can't emulate as many frames as you'd want to."

Digital Eclipse studio head and fellow engineer Mike Mika referred to the process as network rewind. "You do multiple simulations, rewinding and simulating forward as fast as possible. That requires you to have six, ten, maybe twelve simulations of a game frame in a single game frame. That means you have to optimize the game code even more to be able to do that quickly so you're having the same experience, but online."

More than hardware struggles set the Nintendo Switch version of *Street Fighter 30th* apart from its Xbox One, PS4, and PC counterparts. Namely, it received an exclusive game, *Super Street Fighter II: The New Challengers – The Tournament Battle*, a special arcade-only version Capcom had produced in the mid-nineties. Based on *Super Street Fighter II*, *Tournament Battle* spans four cabinets that arcade operators must link together for the game to be used. Eight players, two per machine, compete in a tournament bracket, with winners and losers moving from one machine to another until only two competitors remain.

Tournament Battle was a novel idea, but arcade operators were less than impressed. They'd have to purchase and make room for four cabinets that wouldn't even work properly unless they had eight players to compete. And the machines had to be linked, so they had to be placed side by side by side by side, taking up tremendous amount of floor space for what was, in effect, a single game. Running a tournament also took a lot of work: drawing up and disseminating flyers to spread the word; raising a prize pool deep enough to attract lots of players, blocking out time for the event. *Tournament Battle* had a few pros but too many cons, and largely passed unnoticed.

Switch owners of *Street Fighter 30th* were treated to a version of *Tournament Battle* playable with four consoles. Filner understood the significance of dredging up an ancient game few people had played and restoring it to working order, but he didn't have much to go on. "MAME didn't have this working because nobody had information about it," Filner explained.

Luckily, he'd had the code base for *Super Street Fighter II* for years. From that, he figured out how to emulate linking machines together. "Within the microcosm of *Street Fighter*, it was an exciting development," he said. "Nobody who didn't have four of these special machines had seen this game. It was one of these really fun moments where you uncover something that hasn't been seen for a really long time, or maybe nobody's seen outside of the publisher."

Emulating *Street Fighter III* and its *Double Impact* and *Third Strike* updates was considerably tougher. The game ran on CPS III, the final arcade board designed by Capcom, and its most advanced. CPS III played games from CD-ROM, and game CDs contained encryption as well as a security cartridge that held the game's BIOS (the files that hardware needs to boot up), a game key stored in a special type of memory, and the decryption logic to unlock the game. *SFIII* featured beautifully drawn and fluidly animated characters, as well as features such as a camera that panned in and out when combatants drew closer to or further from one another. Shinji Mikami, director of *Resident Evil* and Capcom's senior planner in the mid-nineties when *SFIII* was in development, claimed the game's hardware and software were so complex it could never be brought to home systems.

That changed, of course, when Capcom brought iterations of *SFIII* to Dreamcast and other platforms. But emulation programmers had little experience with CPS III. "When you play *Street Fighter III*, the [characters] can get bigger and smaller smoothly," explained Filner. "Most of the older games couldn't do that. So the graphics system and CPU were from a new generation that worked quite differently, and the CPS III had CDs. If you owned one of these machines, you'd put a CD with the game on it into a drive, and the game would sort of install off the CD and into permanent memory. The new system had all these components, and it took a while for emulator writers to figure out how they worked. Obviously Capcom doesn't pass out documentation about how their stuff works. In fact, quite the opposite."

Capcom had good reason to be secretive. For coin-op developers, reusing hardware like the CPS I and CPS II was beneficial because they could sharpen their skills every time they reused it. However, Asian countries were notorious for ripping off arcade boards by learning their architecture and mass-producing them in factories. The demand for games skyrocketed after China and other eastern countries reported violent crimes being perpetrated by teens addicted to arcade games. When the government began banning coin-op games, arcade operators responded by going underground and hosting dozens of hacked consoles and cabinets. Dozens of illegal modifications spawned from *Street Fighter II* alone. *Rainbow Edition*, one of the most prolific bootlegs, was an unbalanced hack that let players do things like throw fireballs at a rapid-fire clip and switch between characters mid-match, all at a much faster, more exhilarating pace than the turgid *SFII' Champion Edition*.

"What that led to was, Capcom didn't want to use the same hardware for two games in a row," Filner said. "It's easy to copy EPROMs. An EPROM is essentially the arcade-game version of a floppy disk. You could copy a game off an EPROM and install it on other EPROMs. Arcade companies were going out of their way, from game to game, to make sure you couldn't just copy an EPROM and install it on old hardware."

Capcom escalated the war against pirates by equipping CPS II boards with "suicide batteries" that caused a game to cease functioning once the battery died. (Hackers came up with a way to "de-suicide" CPS II batteries, but the process is extremely technical.)

"So," Filner continued, "Capcom made little, itty-bitty changes in each generation of the system to prevent software transfer. That makes emulation a little more complicated, because you have to figure out what's different about this one from the last one."

Emulators exist in a gray area. Technically, they're legal. ROMs of commercial games are not. MAME's creators billed their foray into emulating arcade hardware deliberately. "The only legitimate excuse for MAME to exist is as a repository for information about how arcade games worked," Filner said. "Being able to play old arcade games is sort of a convenient side effect of having all this information, but the legitimate reason for it to exist is that people are figuring out how the games worked and preserving that information."

More programmers took an interest in CPS III. Finally, in June 2007, a coder by the name of Andreas Naïve cracked the encryption. MAME was updated to play arcade games that ran on the hardware. "By the time *Street Fighter 30th Anniversary*

Collection came around, the information was publicly available. I could just look up most of the technical aspects about how the hardware worked," said Filner.

***

STREET FIGHTER 30TH Anniversary Collection was a labor of love for all involved, but most definitely a labor. After months of re-painting pixels, fighting with various types of lag, and implementing new features such as training mode, the anthology released in May 2018. "Training mode ended up being the biggest iceberg. It didn't look too bad until the ship hit it," Filner admitted. "This was a prestige operation where it seemed like we'd have plenty of time, but the scope of a project will always expand to fill all available time. I think what we finished up with was pretty substantial, and much larger than what we'd planned."

Filner views the anthology with pride. He's proud of all his work, and his long association with keeping classic *Street Fighter* games from fading away. His pride and passion may be confusing for anyone who knows his tastes. He was born early enough to be enamored with games like *Defender* and *Pac-Man*, but he'd moved on to coding BBSes by the time *Street Fighter II* revolutionized game design. Even so, he recognizes the importance of his work.

"I like that people like these products. I tell people it's archaeology. Somebody asked me what credit I wanted on something I'd done, and I said, 'Digital Archaeologist.' We're digging through the remnants of old civilizations, picking up the bits and pieces and going, 'Ah, so this is how they lived back then."

To Mike Mika, all the speed bumps *Street Fighter 30th Anniversary* and other classic projects only served to validate Digital Eclipse's work. "That was part of the critical mission statement we had for DE: To make people aware of the problems we had with video game preservation. When they see something they haven't seen before related to *Street Fighter*, or *Mega Man*, or whatever, we wanted them to become interested in finding out, is there more than that? For us, we want, with every project, to point to the significance of preserving things."

For Frank Cifaldi, finding new ways to not only preserve history, but give users the chance to actively take part in it, continues to drive his efforts at the Video Game History Foundation as well as his involvement with Digital Eclipse. "I don't think people play old games like it's the eighties. I think of these as your toys: You should be able to play with them however you want. I want people to be able to access this content, to see it and appreciate the games without spending a month learning them. The idea of being able to see all the content easily, which started with *Mega Man Legacy Collection*'s challenge mode, evolved into the watch mode we have in *SNK 40th Anniversary Collection*."

Released in November 2018, *SNK 40th Anniversary Collection* features several of the Japanese developer/publisher's greatest hits. The "watch" mode Cifaldi and the team instituted allows players to alternate between playing the game themselves, and turning over control to a computer-controlled player. Rather than get stuck on a tough boss or stretch of enemies and give up, they can trigger watch mode, let the AI do the heavy lifting, then keep playing.

Cifaldi sees the feature as the next logical step in the journey that began with patching together screens from various *Mega Man* games in *Legacy Collection*'s challenge levels. "The path of least resistance, people being able to see everything, I think we nailed it for that game. I want people think of us as the special behind-the-scenes-stuff company. The audience I want is the audience that wants to go deeper and try to understand why we like these things as opposed to just rehashing them. I want them to go, 'Wow, that was an interesting moment in time. What was that? Let's think about this and learn what we got out of it, or should have gotten out of it.'"

With each Criterion Collection-like effort, Digital Eclipse's reputation grows. Mike Mika shared that many developers who had failed to recognize the impact they'd had on a certain game, genre, or company ended up contacting DE after playing an anthology, and asking if DE would be interested in taking a look at some of the old things—artwork, code, documents—they had boxed up in an attic or basement.

"We're always up against other products that are coming out which some people lovingly refer to as shovelware," Mika said. "It's really easy to put a bunch of emulated games in a collection and just ship them with an interface, and call it done. If we can educate people enough to value all the extras we try to put into these things, to the point that consumers almost demand it every time one of these collections come out, then we'll have completed our mission."

Chapter 11: Terminator 2: Judgment Day

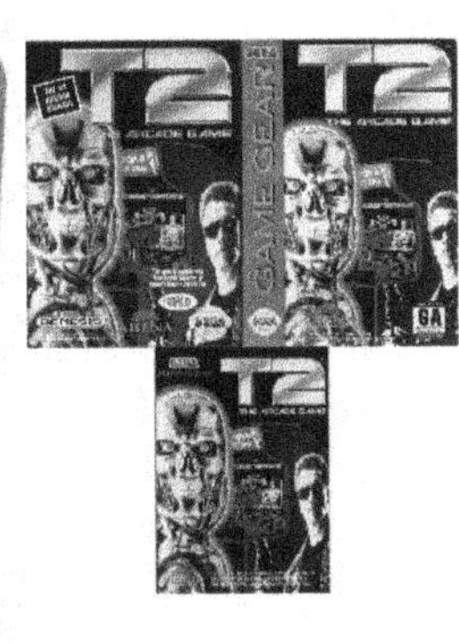

Part I: A Small, Very Precious Piece of Time

PAUL CARRUTHERS SAT in a dark room watching humanity die, one bullet at a time. When he reached the end of the videotape, he rewound it and watched again.

The future was bleak. A war-torn earth, survivors cowering behind charred bones and husks of buildings as cyborgs resembling humanoid skeletons laid waste with rockets and machine guns.

As another skeletal robot marched stiffly into view from one side and pivoted to aim a gigantic gun at the screen, Carruthers paused the tape. The image quivered as if in fear. He studied it for a moment, then turned around in his office chair and continued typing.

Before Carruthers had doomed the human race, he'd been a university student, coding games in assembly with a few mates in their spare time. It was a harmless hobby, not the sort of thing that could lead to the end of the world. Their machine of choice was the BBC Micro, a personal computer popular in the United Kingdom, especially among educators: By the time the sun set on the Micro in its thirteenth year of production, over eighty-five percent of British schools had at least one.

Released in 1981, Acorn Computer manufactured the BBC Micro—or the "Beeb" as it became known among hobbyists—to function as the beating heart of an initiative called the BBC Computer Literacy Project, a response to a television series that predicted microcomputers would reshape the UK's economy and industry in the coming years. The BBC considered several companies before selecting Acorn to develop its PC. They wanted a machine that could perform a wide array of tasks, from word processing and programming to graphics and artificial intelligence. Acorn's engineers responded by equipping the Beeb with an 8-bit, 6502 processor clocked at two megahertz, graphics hardware able to display eight simultaneous colors at up to an impressive 640x256 resolution, and high-performance memory that enabled programmers to do things like have video hardware access memory while the processor was still chewing through the last block of data it had received.

PAUL CARRUTHERS, ENGINEER ON MK1, T2: THE ARCADE GAME FOR SEGA GENESIS. (IMAGE (C) PAUL CARRUTHERS.)

Carruthers and his mates lucked out by bumping into an educational publisher looking for software designed to teach math to undergrads. "It was very fortuitous that we met these people. We made a slow move into making games full-time. They were small games, and we were barely making any money at all," he said.

As the job wore on, Carruthers learned new platforms such as the Commodore 64 and its successor, the Amiga. One afternoon, a friend telephoned with an offer. A contractor he knew was looking for someone to write *Alien 3*, a game based on the action-horror movie of the same name, to the Sega Mega Drive (known as the Genesis in the States). "He brought me in, and I spoke to Probe about the possibility of programming *Alien 3*. But for whatever reason, I wasn't offered that in the end. They offered me *T2* instead."

T2: The Arcade Game was, true to its name, a conversion of *Terminator 2: Judgment Day*, a coin-op shooter developed by Midway and released in 1991. The cabinet was massive and plastered with promotional artwork from James Cameron's blockbuster film: Arnold Schwarzenegger, looking buff in his spiky haircut, leather jacket, and sunglasses, armed with the shotgun he wields to negligible effect against the T-1000, a more sophisticated terminator model than Arnold's, and his nemesis in the film. Instead of a shotgun, the arcade cabinet was equipped with two jumbo-sized plastic machine guns that vibrated as players squeezed the triggers. The object of the game was to fire an endless supply of bullets at everything that moved while the screen scrolled along torn-up cities and warehouses under siege by the murderous machines of the future. Midway wanted its game to be as big a hit as its silver-screen source material. Schwarzenegger, Eddie Furlong, and Robert Patrick reprised their lead roles to appear in digital footage between levels.

Paul Carruthers was intrigued by the idea of converting a coin-op game, as well as intimidated. Midway provided no source code, but they did send a video tape of someone blasting their way through all seven levels. “With *T2*, I was operating from a videotape, and from the occasional trip to the arcades. I would play for about half an hour, and then all my coins were gone, so it was a hard process. The result with *T2* was a lot further away from the original.”

Arcade (left), Genesis.

The problem was that Carruthers, much like John Conner from the movie, was working under the gun. Probe had assigned another programmer to the project first, only for the coder to flake out. When Carruthers came on board, the project was a hot potato with only five months left in its deadline. “With these kinds of contracts, you have to do it on time. That's very, very important,” he said. The publisher would need time to print the code on ROM chips, manufacture Genesis cartridges, produce packaging, and ship software out to retailers.

Another, much larger problem was that Carruthers had no experience writing for the Genesis. Fortunately, he knew the Motorola 68000 processor, which had been used by computer manufacturers such as Apple and Commodore. Learning the console's inner workings became his priority. "You have to learn things like how joypad input is read, and you have to learn about the little tricks for putting sprites on the screen, and moving video memory around at a fast enough speed to be able to do what you need it to. That takes a bit of time."

He soon discovered several advantages to developing console games. "For example, if you write on a PC, and your program crashes, the machine would crash too, and you'd have to reboot. Whereas if your target machine is a console, and it crashes, it's a very quick process to just hit reset and restart it."

What he liked most was that the Genesis had no operating system. Every cartridge included boot instructions designed to help the console get up and running, a routine that had been provided to him by Probe. The rest of the cartridge was a blank slate. "On a computer, you have to make your game work around the underlying operating system. On the Genesis, it's blank. There isn't anything else in there, so you can use every bit of space," said Carruthers.

Carruthers' next objective was to duplicate what he saw on the videotape. To do that, he studied how the Genesis handled graphics. There were two pieces to that puzzle: the playfield, or backdrops; and sprites such as characters, items, and frames of animation. Both elements were made up of eight-by-eight pixel tiles, known as characters. The console's VDP (Video Display Processor) had memory to hold up to four palettes at once, for a total of sixty-four simultaneous colors out of 512.

As he studied, Carruthers knew he could pull off certain tricks. He could recycle sprites because duplicates took up less memory, something Genesis programmers labeled a type of image compression: Multiple images, but all more or less the same, and therefore only stored once. That was useful, because *T2* in arcades was an explosion of colors, albeit mostly blues, blacks, and reds, the color palette of sentient machines nuking humanity out of existence.

The Genesis displayed graphics by storing image data in memory and then pushing that data to the screen, like a patient being called from a waiting area into an exam room. *T2: The Arcade Game* scrolled the screen slowly to the right as the game progressed; that meant Carruthers needed a way to dispose of everything that disappeared off the left side, as well as to bring in new graphics from the right. He gave repeat objects first priority. "You have sprites that are used over and over again," he explained, "things like explosions and particular enemies. You load those all in before a piece of the level that includes those objects. After you scroll past the piece of the level where those objects appear, you move other bits in."

Displaying the playfield, a grid made up of eight-by-eight tiles, was a matter of taking those tiles and snapping them together so they formed the scene on the fly. "You might have five of those squares that look like a piece of grass, but your map has those five squares used over and over again," he said. "You're looking all the time for which background characters are in a part of the map that's coming up, and making sure all of those are in video RAM. You can only draw on the screen stuff that's in video RAM, so you're constantly moving information off the ROM and into video RAM just before the images appear on the screen. There's a bit of an art to it."

***

CARRUTHERS HIT SNAGS along the way. The Genesis was incapable of scaling images, so the artist Probe assigned to *T2: The Arcade Game* had to draw the same image at different sizes and pass them off to Carruthers to implement. Still, rendering graphics was a relatively simple process. The rub was handling *T2*'s controls.

In arcades, players fired plastic machine guns at enemies that ran in from either side or popped up from behind cover in the background. It was a nonstop blitzkrieg of gunfire and explosions. The Genesis port would be simpler. Every console shipped with a three-button controller, so Carruthers made it the default input device for his game. By the time development wrapped, he had become an expert in flying the cursor around the screen and shooting down rogue robots. But Sega had another idea. Nintendo had developed a rifle-shaped light gun for its Super Nintendo called the Super Scope 6. To compete, Sega's engineers answered with the Menacer, a handgun-style peripheral, in 1992.

Anticipating that Nintendo would insist on support for the Super Scope in the SNES conversion of *T2*, Sega told Probe it wanted the Genesis port to support the Menacer. "The light gun was a massive pain in the ass," Carruthers said.

Probe shipped Carruthers a Menacer along with instructions on how to implement it. Reading the instructions, he knew they wouldn't work. "We have a problem," he told his contact at Probe.

Their problem had to do with the vertical refresh. The fraction of time in which the electron beam moved from the bottom-right corner of the screen to the top-left was like an artist lifting her pencil. Carruthers needed that brief window to move the next batch of image data from the game ROM into video RAM so it would be ready when the artist returned her hand to the paper. "As long as you move stuff in and out of video RAM during that small opportunity in every frame, you won't get any glitching on the screen," he said. "That's a small, very precious piece of time for the programmer to be moving picture data into video RAM."

Carruthers relied on that period, but so did the programmers for the Menacer. In arcades, every time players squeezed the trigger, the screen was blanked, the target object was painted white, and a photodiode—a semiconductor that converted light into electrical current—stored in the gun's plastic read the white space. If players pointed at it when they fired, they scored a hit. Cathode ray timing, a technique used on CRT displays and favored by products such as Nintendo's Super Scope and Sega's Menacer, used a more complex method of reading and reacting to input from light guns. At the beginning of every vertical and horizontal refresh cycle, the screen sent a pulse to the console's CPU so it could track the electron beam—the artist's hand. When players fired a shot, the game's code, the CRT's circuitry, and the light gun's sensors launched an elaborate dance: the flash of light stirred up phosphor at a specific location; a timer in the game's code determined the position that changed based on where the electron beam was and how long it took to reach the affected position, which brightened ever so slightly; and a time was generated and sent through the peripheral's cord or through the audio/video (A/V) cable connecting the game console to the television. Based on all that data, the game code knew where the light gun touched and decided whether it collided with something there. If it did, players scored a hit.

"We had to tweak the speed of the code to match the physical speed of the video-update hardware. But it turned out that that was also how the light gun worked," Carruthers recalled. The operation was enormous, and there simply wasn't enough room to move the image data he needed into VRAM and run the Menacer's routines at the same time.

"It's technically impossible," he informed his contact.

"I'm sure it's possible," his colleague said. "If you tried a bit harder, I'm sure it would work."

Grinding his teeth, Carruthers rooted out places where he could make concessions. "I maybe don't have to use the whole of this period," he informed his contact, "but I need a big chunk of it." The Menacer's engineers wouldn't budge.

Carruthers invited the guy to fly out to his place and talk things over. The engineer obliged and, after reading through the game's code, huffed out a breath. "Yeah, that's a problem," he said.

Sega insisted they figure something out. *T2: The Arcade Game* was bound to drive sales of the Menacer. Over several sleepless nights, the two programmers reached a compromise. "The light gun was using all of that time, but it didn't have to," Carruthers said. "They were able to have a look every now and again, rather than just constantly looking. That allowed me a smaller amount of time where I could move pictures around. It kind of worked in the end, but it doesn't function perfectly as a light gun, and *T2* doesn't function perfectly as a game. It's a bit of a mess, really."

Critics responded more or less the same way. *T2: The Arcade Game* on Genesis shipped alongside versions for Super Nintendo, Game Boy, Sega Master System, and Game Gear in 1993. The Genesis port was grittier and more drab than the Super Nintendo's, a byproduct of Sega's shallower color palette. Art assets were missing, but that was to be expected. Carruthers had never received code or artwork, and five months was no time at all when one had new hardware to learn. "It's mostly there, but there are a few segments where there are very few enemies, or you'll run through a room and it's just an empty room. That's largely because we didn't have the time, and we didn't have the space. And we were working slightly blind as well," Carruthers said.

Though not his finest work, *T2: The Arcade Game* served as a launching point for Carruthers' early career in console games. He went on to do *Mortal Kombat*, *The Pagemaster*, and *Batman Forever*, all on the Genesis. His aptitude with the hardware evolved with each one. "By the end of all that, I looked back at the code I wrote for *T2* and thought, *Wow, how did that ever work?* It was awful code I'd written, very basic. But I was just hurrying along, trying to get something working in time. It got there in the end."

Part II: Coordinate Systems

DAVID LEITCH HAD come a long way since slogging through his port of *Double Dragon* for the ZX Spectrum. His next projects, conversions of *Shinobi* and *NARC*, turned out much better, so much so that after Binary Design went bust, Leitch posted up in London as a freelance programmer. A friend of his from the industry helped him land his first client.

"You know, you should talk to Tony," his friend said over drinks. Tony was Tony Beckwith, one of the chiefs at Mirrorsoft and someone Leitch had known from Binary Design. "They're looking for ZX-80 programmers to do games for the Master System." Sega's 8-bit console hadn't caught on in the US, but was popular in the UK, even outselling the NES.

Leitch got in touch with Beckwith and did a few projects for Mirrorsoft before it, as well as media baron and current Mirrorsoft owner Robert Maxwell, ran into trouble. "He died," Leitch recalled. "Fell off his yacht."

In the aftermath of the millionaire's accidental death, investigators uncovered questionable business practices. Mirrorsoft fell apart, and Leitch moved on. He landed at Virgin and converted a few Genesis games to the Master System and Game Gear, Sega's portable console. Eventually, Tony Beckwith got a job at Probe and called up Leitch. "The project he had was *T2*. That was my fourth Master System/Game Gear game."

Game Gear sat on the technical fence between old and new. Eager to cash in on the handheld craze popularized by Nintendo's Game Boy, Sega's engineers threw together a handheld based on Master System's hardware. While the Game Boy displayed graphics in black-and-white, Game Gear boasted a diverse palette of 4,096 colors, an exponential leap compared to the 64-color palette of the Master System. The handheld ran on a Zilog Z80 processor clocked at 3.5 megahertz and could display up to thirty-two colors at once at a resolution of 160x144.

Leitch wrote *T2: The Arcade Game* for Game Gear in a few months. He'd had to severely truncate the arcade game to make it all fit, but it was flashy and pretty, and the shooting—controlled using the Game Gear's two main buttons and its directional pad—was more than adequate. Ultimately, it would satisfy any consumers who wanted a shooter to play on the go.

Probe came back to Leitch and asked if he could convert his conversion to the Master System. Although Sega's 8-bit machine had ceased production in the U.S. in 1992, selling between 1.5 and two million units there, the majority of console owners in Europe still played Master System games in 1993.

Leitch knew he could get the game up and running quickly, if he could solve a coordinate problem. The Master System had a higher resolution than the Game Gear at 256x192. That only made sense, Leitch knew. The Master System was meant to be connected to a television. However, the difference in resolution conflicted with the way he'd written his code for the portable. "I'd made the coordinate system 8-bit, but to put it on a bigger screen, I had to change it to 16-bit, which was a real pain in the ass."

Because Master System's playfield was wider, Leitch had to optimize his graphics routines to load and display more sprite and background pixels as *T2*'s levels scrolled. The width of objects needed to be stretched as well. "Generally speaking, you'd want the X range to be something like the width of the playfield plus double the width of your largest object, so such an object could move smoothly on from either side of the screen," he explained. "It was basically a low-level optimization—and I use that word very loosely—that worked fine in the context of the original job, but wasn't fit for purpose on the Master System."

Arcade (left), Game Gear.

Early in the project, there was talk of adding support for the Light Phaser, Sega's light gun that released on the same day as the Master System in the U.S. in 1986. Probe and Sega nixed the idea, to Leitch's relief. Light-gun tech was fun, but inaccurate. Leaving it out did come at a cost. "The exciting part of the coin-op was you had these force-feedback Uzis," Leitch said of the arcade version. "That's what made it cool: You're blowing away these evil Terminators. On the Game Gear and Master System, you've got a joypad. It was less intense."

Every other aspect of the job was conventional. Characters and objects were sprites. Scenery such as silos and shattered walls were part of the character map, the grid of pixels that made up the background. He was even able to use parallax scrolling, a technique where one background layer scrolls at a different speed than another layer to give the illusion of depth. Bullets, rockets, characters, animation frames, explosions—all sprites. The screen wasn't as busy as the arcade version, but it was busy enough that flickering occurred. Leitch did his best to minimize it, with one exception: A sequence near the end which saw the T-1000 villain commandeer a truck carrying a cannister of liquid nitrogen. The player had to shoot the truck to keep it from gaining too much ground, while blasting other enemies.

"All the bullets are sprites, and you have to be able to point from your virtual position in the middle of the screen," Leitch explained. "You're drawing lots of sprites on a line whether you like it or not, because you have to have a line of bullets, otherwise it'll look really lame. For whatever reason, the truck that comes out at the end is also made of sprites. Large chunks of the truck will disappear because there are just too many objects to display."

Leitch recalled *T2: The Arcade Game* for the Master System as one of those projects where he was relieved more than professionally satisfied when he crossed the finish line. "You can go on YouTube and watch someone play it from beginning to end, and it's actually okay. It really shouldn't work, but it does."

Chapter 12: Mortal Kombat

Part I: Out of Thin Air

JEFF PETERS KNEW he liked video games. He also knew, on a theoretical level, that someone, somewhere, made the programs contained in the diskettes sold in his local electronics shop. He just had no idea who could do such a thing, much less how they would go about doing it. One of his friends demystified the process.

"One of my best friends at the time made a computer game and would sell it in Ziploc baggies, with the disk and instruction card, from the back of his truck to computer stores and individuals," Peters said.

Fascinated, Peters investigated the Radio Shack TRS-80 personal computer—somewhat affectionately referred to as the "Trash-80"—at his high school. He enrolled in the few programming courses on the curriculum and kept at it after graduation, moving on to PDP-11 minicomputers hooked up to mainframes in college. But programming was just a way to scratch an itch. He had no designs on making games professionally. How could he? That wasn't a real job. "I was going to be a lawyer. I was a speech-and-debate guy, and I was looking at law schools. I was going to go into corporate law because it intrigued me, for some weird reason I still don't understand. Then this video game phenomenon hit, and like everybody else, I went to arcades."

Arcade games enthralled him. Characters like Donkey Kong and Pac-Man were far more captivating than the spreadsheets and word processors he was using in school. With a few quarters, nimble fingers, and an eye for patterns, he was able to conquer their challenges. Peters got better with every quarter he dropped into machines, reaching later stages and demolishing high scores. He was the king of his arcade.

IMAGE COURTESY OF JEFF PETERS.

Twin Galaxies, an online repository of world records in video games, opened Peters' eyes to the fact that there were dozens, even hundreds of others like him. He kept playing, kept improving and, along with a few others including Twin Galaxies chief Walter Day, got his shot at worldwide fame when he became part of the U.S. National Video Game Team.

The National Video Game Team dated back to March 1983, when promoter Jim Riley pitched Walter Day on his interest in assembling a team of competitive gamers to travel the world and pit their reflexes and thumbs against all challengers. Day, who had grown in acclaim as Twin Galaxies' reputation exploded in parallel with that of arcades, agreed. He nominated Steve Sanders, then the world's most renowned *Donkey Kong* player, as team captain. Under Sanders, Day and Riley assembled a who's-who of the world's high-scorers, among them Eric Ginner, a multiple world-record holder who went on to co-develop *Ms. Pac-Man* for the Atari Lynx; and Billy Mitchell, a pinball nut who set his sights on *Donkey Kong* and *Pac-Man*, and who achieved global fame when he co-starred in the *King of Kong* documentary against babyface science teacher and aspiring *Donkey Kong* pro Steve Wiebe. (Mitchell was later stripped of his world records after it was discovered that he'd set many of his high scores using the MAME arcade emulator program instead of authentic coin-op hardware.)

Formed as the Electronic Circus, Day and Riley promoted their players as superstars but got off to a shaky start, crumbling just five days after launch. The Electronic Circus was no more, but the players continued as the U.S. National Video Game Team. New recruits such as Jeff Peters filled out the ranks. "We used to set up worldwide competitions, and we'd travel the world to take on other countries' videogame teams," Peters said. "We took over Twin Galaxies' international scoreboard, and got scores in the Guinness Book of World Records. That was my start of making money in the videogame business."

The team did more than compete. Observing a gap in the magazine market left by the folding of rags such as *Joystick*, Peters and Steve Harris founded *Electronic Gaming Monthly* as the official magazine of the U.S. National Video Game Team in 1988. At the start, they knew nothing about putting out a magazine. "We brought in all of our game-playing friends, mostly arcade and console players, and it was created from a labor of love," Peters explained. "*EGM* came not from a corporate point of view of, 'Hey, here's an industry, here's a theme, let's go create a rag,' but from fans of, 'This is the thing we want to read, so let's write what we want to read."

EGM took off, and Peters sought out his next challenge in the gaming industry: Development. "That was really my passion: I wanted to go make the stuff." He was hired at Sculptured Software, a small studio founded in Salt Lake City, Utah, by Bryan Brandenburg, George Metos, and Peter Adams in 1984. Sculptured's specialty was porting games from one platform to another. The scrappy team gained a reputation for their conversions of coin-op titles.

"The games we were doing were reaching the top of the charts," said Peters, who was project director at Sculptured Software from May 1992 until September 1997. "We were known as the Mode 7 studio, and were quickly gaining a reputation for being able to get the most out of the hardware."

Mode 7 was one of several graphics modes for Super NES. With it, developers could stretch and rotate backgrounds to create pseudo-3D effects. Sculptured Software put the mode to good use in games such as the *Super Star Wars* trilogy, a run-and-gun series where players flew through the Death Star's trench and blasted through ranks of Storm Troopers. One of the studio's most well-known titles was 1992's *NCAA Basketball.* Unlike competing hoops titles of the day such as Electronic Arts' *NBA Live*, which displayed on-court action from an overhead, isometric view, *NCAA Basketball* harnessed Mode 7 to render 3D-like graphics and gameplay: A behind-the-shoulder camera followed players, and the view rotated as they moved, setting the mold for how basketball games would look and play on future hardware such as Sony's PlayStation.

Other developers took notice of Sculptured's sales and critical acclaim, leading the studio to build and sell development kits to companies. Developers took advantage, largely because they had little choice. Nintendo wasn't in the habit of loaning or selling kits for its 8- and 16-bit consoles. Most studios were given a manual that explained the Super Nintendo's approval process for licensed software and how the console's architecture worked, and were left to assemble kits on their own. "Our tools were sold, assemblers and compilers in a physical box that allowed access," Peters said. "They became the industry standard for a while. If you were going to do NES or Super Nintendo development, you bought a hardware kit and the tools to do it from us. That implied we knew more about the hardware than anyone else. We were selling development kits for it."

Creating and selling middleware—an interface for software or hardware authored by someone other than the platform's manufacturer—was just a side gig for Sculptured. Its primary source of income was taking on contract work. In early 1993, Acclaim came to Sculptured with an offer: Port *Mortal Kombat*, a new one-on-one fighting game from Williams and Midway, to the Super Nintendo.

"They had a licensing deal with Midway, and brought the project to us," Peters remembered. They said, 'Are you guys interested?' At first, we weren't."

***

TWO ENGINEERS FROM Midway pulled their truck up to an arcade, threw open the shutter door, and rolled out a plain black cabinet. They wheeled it into the cool, dimly lit den of flashing screens and plugged it in near two of Capcom's *Street Fighter II* machines. Then they waited.

"It was like stepping into a ring against Mike Tyson at his prime. But, we flipped the switch and sat back and watched," said John Tobias, co-creator of *Mortal Kombat*.

At first, the cabinet just sat there. Then the attract mode ran. Grainy clips of digitized actors running through sequences of martial arts moves played out. The screen faded, and two characters squared off atop a narrow stone bridge set against a cloudy night sky. They moved toward one another, throwing kicks and punches—and then one crouched down and swung a right hook that connected under his opponent's chin, launching him into the air and splattering blood all over the walkway.

One of the players at the back of the line to play *Street Fighter II* stepped out of place, walked over to the black cabinet, and dropped in a quarter. A few seconds later, someone else wandered over. Two more joined them. Three more. By the end of that weekend, the *Street Fighter II* cabinets had been abandoned. "That's when we knew *MK* had the potential to become a phenomenon of its own," Tobias said.

On the surface, *Mortal Kombat* was one in a growing line of *Street Fighter II* clones. All were gunning for Capcom, the king of the one-on-one fighter. Thus far, no one had even come close. "I was a *Street Fighter II* fanatic. I was competitive," said Sculptured Software's Jeff Peters. "I would go to tournaments at local arcades, and it was, all right, how long can you hold the machine and take on all comers? It started the whole fighting-game frenzy: Everybody was knocking off *Street Fighter II*."

None of the knockoffs seemed able to capture *SFII*'s perfect storm of vibrant graphics, unique characters, and fast gameplay. Until *Mortal Kombat*. "From the game's inception we knew that it would not be a clone," Tobias said. "If we looked at *Street Fighter*, it was to study how not to do something in *Mortal Kombat*. I remember we just sort of conceded to the raw look of digitized footage. I think that was the right choice because it went a long way in making sure that our game would stand-out visually from *Street Fighter II*."

MK's most notable difference was its aesthetic. Where *SFII* looked like a cartoon, *MK* looked like an R-rated film. Its environments were grungy and dark. Its characters were lifelike thanks to a motion capture process that involved recording real actors performing all the moves. "I also think that the time we spent developing the characters and story, which was an odd thing to do in an arcade product, helped build a larger world in the minds of our players," said Tobias. "That impact lives with *MK* even in its most recent iterations. Of course, our brand of violence is in large part what gave us a seat at pop culture's table."

And *Mortal Kombat* had blood. The red stuff sprayed and splattered when players punched, kicked, and knocked each other into the air. But it was most abundant at the end of the match, when victorious fighters were given a short window of opportunity to perform a Fatality on their dizzied opponent. If the move was entered correctly, the screen darkened, and the blood flowed: the blue-clad ninja Sub-Zero tore off his opponent's head with the spinal cord attached; movie star Johnny Cage, a nod to Jean-Claude Van Damme from when *MK*'s original design starred the popular martial-artist-turned-actor, punched his victim's head clean off; and Kano, a master criminal with a metal plate covering half his face, ripped his opponent's still-beating heart from their chest.

Most impressively, *Mortal Kombat* had been made by a team of four, led by programmer Ed Boon and artist John Tobias. Five months in, they declared their dry run at a local arcade where *Street Fighter II* held sway a resounding success. The game was incomplete; Sonya Blade, *MK*'s sole female character, had yet to be added. Still, the fact that *Mortal Kombat*'s test version had pulled players away from *SFII* told Boon and Tobias that their David could hold his own against Capcom's Goliath. "We never knew for certain how successful the game would be. We only knew that we poured our hearts into it and that it was fun to play," said Tobias.

Street Fighter II had gained notoriety within competitive circles, but *Mortal Kombat* took a different tack. Its mechanics were solid, yet accessible. Former *GamePro* editor Dan "Elektro" Amrich recalled a friend complaining that *MK* was too easy because he could beat the computer-controlled opponents by performing jump kicks over and over. "And sure enough, I tried it—with Scorpion—and it was pretty effective," Amrich recalled. "So I always saw *MK* as more accessible and you could get lucky here and there, whereas if you studied *SF*, you could easily take any casual player. But *MK*'s real secret weapon was its willingness to push boundaries, to offer those fatalities and have players doubt that they even existed because who would do that? Are they even allowed?"

Mortal Kombat's fatalities were so graphic that they had to literally be seen to be believed. One kid would hold court on a playground and strive to convince a jury of peers that he'd seen one character rip off his face and breathe fire, reducing the other guy to ashes and bones. Another kid swore up and down that a fighter in a white jumpsuit and straw hat could zap characters' heads off with a bolt of lightning. "That breeds interest and foot traffic," Amrich said of the rumors surrounding *MK*'s gory finishing moves, "and before you know it, you have people looking closer because that controversial thrill was so unexpected. And that's going to be very powerful with kids whose media is largely—and rightfully!—gatekept by their parents. Here's a game you're know you're 'not supposed to play,' even if you haven't been strictly forbidden to play it. It tapped into the lure of the forbidden."

At first, Jeff Peters didn't know what to make of Acclaim's offer to contract Sculptured for a Super NES version of *Mortal Kombat*. Midway's bloody brawler seemed like just another *SFII* imitator. Below the surface, he saw something special. "Finishing Moves were different and funny, so that was another attraction point. And as a fighting game, it worked."

Putting his pro skills to work, Peters played the game and wrote up a detailed analysis of what *MK* had going for it, and what he saw as the biggest hurdles standing in the way of a successful port.

Arcade (left), Genesis (top), SNES.

Pros: It wasn't a shameless *Street Fighter II* copycat; it had a unique art style that would resonate with older players put off by Capcom's cartoonish visuals; and the violence was so over-the-top, so absurd, it was humorous and charming. There was no harm in fatalities and uppercuts, Peters concluded, because no one could possibly take them seriously.

Cons: The game's art style, hundreds of frames of animation, detailed backgrounds, and flashy special attacks, would be a bear to port. Nintendo's 16-bit hardware was robust, but paled in comparison to Midway's coin-op innards.

Managers at Acclaim took Peters' evaluation seriously. Acclaim was a marketing company, more versed in how to sell a product than how to build it. If Sculptured Software believed *Mortal Kombat* had a chance of dethroning *Street Fighter II*, they could throw a multimillion-dollar advertising campaign behind it. "My first analysis was that it would not reach the same level of *Street Fighter II* because of how different it was, the audience *Street Fighter II* had already built, the number of units it sold, all that stuff," Peters said.

However, he continued, *Mortal Kombat* didn't have to be the next *SFII*. It had more than enough pizazz to be as big a hit on home systems as it had proven to be in arcades. "I believed it could be a contender. It could stand on its own and have enough of a following that it could probably rise above all the knockoffs. That was the original analysis of, it's had the chance to rise above all the knockoffs, but it probably won't be the next *Street Fighter II*."

It was settled. Acclaim hired Sculptured to do the SNES port, while Probe, a studio based across the pond, would handle a Sega Genesis conversion. Farming out the same port to more than one studio was an unorthodox move, but one that Peters understood.

"By separating the two SKUs, Acclaim was hedging their bets. They were compartmentalizing the work that each developer would do. So, although it cost Acclaim slightly more money to have two different developers making two versions of the same game independently, it at least allowed for more focus. I think that helped get the project done within their time frame, because there definitely wasn't much time."

***

JEFF PETERS MANAGED the team charged with bringing *Mortal Kombat* to Nintendo's lead platform. He and a handful of developers had approximately six months to turn around their version. That would give Acclaim time to coordinate advertising centered on a specific release date: September 13, 1993, dubbed "Mortal Monday" by the marketing gurus. Almost right away, they hit a snag.

Sculptured Software's usual process for assigning teams to a project was for managers like Peters to hold planning sessions ahead of time to determine what resources—programmers and artists—were about to wrap up on a game and would be free to kick off the next. Before Peters could assess who was available and who wasn't, studio owner George Metos stepped in. "We get to that phase with *Mortal Kombat*, and George goes, 'Wait, I have this programmer who will do the work,' and he brings us Gary," Peters remembered.

Gary Lindquist materialized as if from thin air. No one knew anything about him: Where he was from, what his qualifications were. But Lindquist assured Peters he was more than capable of spinning off *Mortal Kombat*'s SNES conversion with time to spare, so Peters assembled a small team of artists around Lindquist and worked with his crew to establish goals. (Gary Lindquist could not be reached for comment.)

Every conversion was a numbers game: An arcade board's specs pitted against a home platform's meager resources. *Mortal Kombat* ran on Midway's Y Unit arcade board, which boasted a Texas Instruments' TMS34010 system board that incorporated a 32-bit CPU that could be clocked up to 50 megahertz, and separate graphics and sound processors with their own clock speeds. (Version 5.0 of the game ran on the upgraded T Unit board.) In comparison, Nintendo's Super NES crawled along at 3.58 megahertz and a paltry 128 kilobytes of RAM. On the plus side, its palette consisted of 32,768 unique colors, 256 which could be displayed on the screen at one time.

"We were literally trying to shove this into a really small box that this game was not designed to run on," said Peters. "But our goal remained the same: How close to the original can we make this? Every decision we undertook was about trying to achieve that goal and make a perfect arcade port."

Mortal Kombat was promising to be Sculptured Software's most ambitious—and potentially most lucrative—product to date. That called for unorthodox techniques to create as close to an arcade-perfect port as possible. "Our initial strategy was, let's convert the TI processor's assembly code into Super Nintendo assembly code. Literally line for line, instruction by instruction," Peters said. "We had an engineer who we talked to a lot, and he thought he could pull this off," he continued, referring to Lindquist.

Peters hesitated. Like every contract developer, Sculptured received payments according to milestones. When they submitted work on time, they got paid. Working toward milestones was not only traditional, it was a safe bet. Programmers coded prototypes every step of the way, allowing Sculptured and licensing partners such as Acclaim to see progress at any given moment. Doing a line-by-line conversion was exponentially riskier. Translating every line of code meant nobody would see the game running until every system—artificial intelligence, animation routines, processing button input—had been implemented. "Let's just say that scared the shit out of everybody," Peters admitted. "A game with a six-month development window, and nothing to show for almost half that time? That was scary."

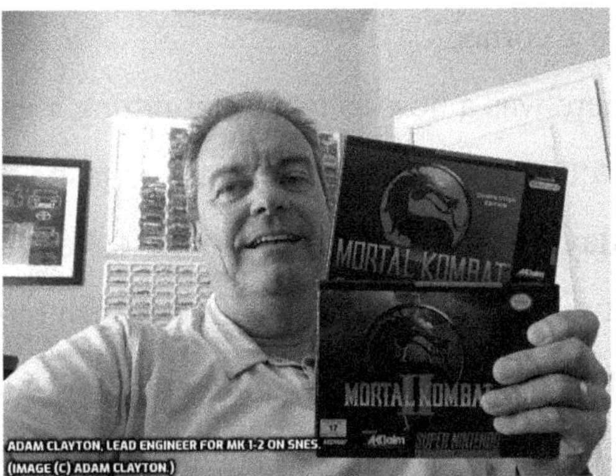

ADAM CLAYTON, LEAD ENGINEER FOR MK 1-2 ON SNES. (IMAGE (C) ADAM CLAYTON.)

Lindquist assured Peters he was up to the task. Curious, another programmer watched from afar. Adam Clayton had been at

Sculptured almost since its beginning. He'd have headed up *Mortal Kombat* if he hadn't been caught up in another game. Still, he kept tabs on every project, and right away he could tell Lindquist was in trouble. Clayton knew that working toward milestones meant writing code that laid groundwork for routines that would need to be written for the next milestone, and the next, and the next, and so on until a game was finished. Working on milestones was like building a house: draw up a blueprint, lay a foundation, put up a framework, and so on, always thinking about the bigger picture.

According to Clayton, Lindquist was working harder instead of smarter, hacking together one milestone only to have to tear most of it down later. "The next milestone was twice as hard because he hadn't thought about it until he'd finished the last one. He'd have to rewrite his code because he didn't write it to support what future milestones needed to do. Unless you really plan ahead, you can paint yourself into a corner."

If there was a how-to guide for getting a game done on time, Clayton watched Lindquist do the exact opposite. Instead of working during the daytime alongside everyone else, he'd pull shifts of seventeen, twenty, or thirty hours straight, then hibernate for days. On top of that, he was writing in a foreign dialect of assembly code that no other programmer could decipher, which meant no one could take over during his absences.

Lindquist also had an inefficient method of pushing art onto the screen. He'd written a custom tool in assembly that extracted art files from *Mortal Kombat*'s arcade board and dumped every pixel into the top-left corner of the screen. The problem was that jumbling all the sprites into one location threw off their alignment. "Normally, when you draw a character, you're saying, 'draw him relative to this point,'" Clayton explained. "All the boxes are relative to that point. Then you'd use the same point for the next one, and the next one, so the guy starts moving right, and each frame looks good against each other."

After several weeks of two-steps-forward-five-steps-back progress, Peters removed Lindquist from the project. "Gary had convinced George he could do everything," Peters said, "that there was no need for other engineers because he was a one-stop shop. The reality was not that. That's what you do as a producer, director, and manager: You go solve problems."

Now way behind schedule, *Mortal Kombat*'s already-tight deadline constricted further. Peters replaced Lindquist with three programmers. John Blackburn programmed Test Your Might, a mini-game in the arcade version where players mashed buttons to fill up a power meter and then chopped through material such as wood, stone, and diamond to earn bonus points. Dave Ross worked on the sound system. Adam Clayton was the Swiss army knife of the project: Anything else that needed doing, particularly finishing the conversion and figuring out how to pare down the arcade version's artwork, he'd do.

"All of this happened in very short succession," Peters said. "In a six-month project, there's not a lot of time to see how things play out. This was happening in real-time. Once the project started, the expectations for our time frame went up exponentially, like a tangent curve." The conversion had begun as a game that may or may not hit, only to grow into one of the season's most in-demand games as *Mortal Kombat*'s popularity swelled in arcades. "Literally every day involved major decisions, major strategy, major technical development," Peters continued.

Clayton was up to the task. As a teen, he'd been the first to write to Atari programmer Warren Robinett and reveal that he had discovered Robinett's Easter egg in *Adventure*, a secret room that spelled out his name in blocky letters, and thought to be the industry's first Easter egg. In 1987, he joined Sculptured Software as a fresh-faced twenty-two-year-old, designing games for the Atari 2600 before moving on to Atari's 7800 hardware, then Nintendo's Game Boy handheld, and finally the Super Nintendo. His experience with conversions dated back to the Game Boy, when he took the source code for the NES version of beloved 8-bit football game *Tecmo Bowl* and figured out how to translate it to the brick-sized portable. "All the functions they had, all the data tables—it all worked the same way as on the NES version," Clayton remembered.

"Once I got into that code and said, this is what a play is, this is how a play works—I didn't have to think about that; all I had to do was make my conversion do the same thing the original version was doing. We had the game playing exactly the same as on the NES. The timing and everything was perfect."

Peters gave Clayton a crash course in the challenges facing the *Mortal Kombat* team. Not only had the game fallen behind schedule, there was a ton of digitized speech that didn't fit into the Super Nintendo's dedicated, 64-kilobyte block of memory for storing music and sound effects in the S-SMP sound system—hardware designed by Sony employee Ken Kutaragi, who would go on to create the PlayStation console a few years later. The third and final problem was arguably the biggest: A gigantic amount of artwork. "There wasn't a cartridge made that was big enough to hold one-tenth of the art of the original arcade game," Peters said.

There wasn't enough time to finish Lindquist's hacked-together conversion, so Clayton opted for a hybrid approach, translating some code from the arcade machine and filling in blanks with custom routines. The result was a more traditional milestone-oriented progression that provided tangible progress to Acclaim.

Things got easier with the three-man programming team on the assignment, but they still faced an uphill battle. "I wanted to get it to where we could run as much code every frame as what the arcade did. And if we couldn't have done that, it would have been bad. There were times when we had to shortchange ourselves," Clayton said.

Lindquist had lost the "hot space" in the characters, the points at which the game registered connections such as overlapping sprites and collision detection for attacks. By dumping all the artwork to the same spot on the screen. Clayton painstakingly aligned sprites by hand to make sure the spider web-like intricacy of connections was in place. Lindquist's attempt had failed to include anti-aliasing, a graphics technique that smoothed the jagged edges of surfaces and character models to give them a more realistic look. "Johnny Cage would be moving, and his hair would disappear. It was just terrible," Clayton recalled. Characters had jagged edges in the product that shipped, like paper dolls cut out of pages with their perforations still in place, but it was the best Clayton had been able to do in the little time available to him.

As for the mountainous amount of artwork from the arcade, Peters worked with his programmers to arrive at a solution. "We had to compress the artwork into the maximum cartridge size we could use, and also fit within the RAM and VRAM of the Super Nintendo. Those were huge, huge challenges," he said.

One tool extracted Midway's artwork and downsized the game's color palette so it would fit the Super Nintendo's limitations. The arcade's larger-than-life characters had to be shrunk down and refitted into eight-by-eight sprites, like building blocks. Their animations had to be trimmed so they were less fluid—thereby consuming less storage space—but still crisp. For that, Sculptured Software used a tool known as *Chop*. "Its purpose was to take a large image and break it down into eight-by-eight pixel characters and convert those to palettes that we set up," Peters said. "And then—because in *Mortal Kombat*, you had so many frames of animation per character—go through each frame of animation and compare each eight-by-eight pixel character to see how many duplicates and such that we had so we could build a character set that made up all the animations."

Many processes were automated with certain goals in mind. The easiest way to cut down animations was to look for duplicate frames: Johnny Cage, for instance, didn't need three identical frames for his jump kick when one would do just as well, so the tool stripped out redundancies. From there, artists and programmers touched up artwork by hand to ensure that individual avatars stuck to the sixteen-color palette assigned them (with the rest of the on-screen colors being reserved for background artwork and special effects such as fireballs). "Unlike most games that weren't fighting games, you would use one, sixteen-color palette for this large character made up of eight-by-eight pixel sprites," said Peters. "We developed a process where one fighter could use multiple instances of these sixteen-color palettes. That allowed us to get a better color effect. That was a lot of back and forth: artistically selecting colors, doing touch-ups, recombining all these things."

Sculptured's developers set *Chop* and other programs to run overnight. By lunchtime, they'd have artwork to sort through and touch up by hand. The net result was characters that looked nearly identical to their arcade counterparts despite being smaller and lacking as many frames. "That became part of the ongoing development of doing fighters: making tweaks, doing touch-ups, getting artists involved, running the process again overnight, rinse and repeat," Peters explained. "We either ran out of time, or got something where we could say, 'Hey, this actually looks pretty good.' That was the process of how we got the characters to look as good as they did."

For the game's audio library, the programmers came up with an ingenious solution. The usual method was to build a sound bank, a chunk of memory to hold all the sound effects and music needed on a given level. But Peters and the team knew that the sound RAM for both Super Nintendo and Genesis was a bottleneck. It was just big enough to hold a few effects, but too small to hold all the sound samples of any given match in *Mortal Kombat*, such as characters names, sound effects, and the arena.

Their workaround was to do a resource budget for *Mortal Kombat*'s SNES cartridge. They knew X amount would need to be allotted for character graphics, Y amount for backgrounds, and so on. Another sizable portion was given over to sound samples such as digitized speech. Instead of limiting themselves by storing a much smaller selection of sounds for a level, the programmers suggested reading sounds from the cartridge one at a time and blasting them to a buffer in sound memory. It was a homegrown solution that Sculptured had used before. They had christened it blast processing. "That was before Sega adopted the slogan," said Peters. "We could just blast sound from the cartridge onto the game scene. That allowed us to keep the resolution and sample rate of the VO higher, as well as be able to have more sound samples to use in a given fight, or on a given level. By *Mortal Kombat II*, I think we'd perfected all this stuff, but *Mortal Kombat* was testing everything we'd learned about Nintendo's little box and our capabilities, especially given practically no time in which to do that."

Some problems were solved. Others, such as controls, fell victim to triage. Everything in the game was framed-based: Characters could punch or kick in midair after reaching a certain frame of animation in their jump; uppercuts and fireballs connected at a specific moment and location on characters. The ideal method for replicating those processes would have been to translate Midway's own table, but the SNES conversion's sloppy start and rapidly diminishing time table left the programmers with no choice but to guesstimate and code it by hand rather than fully converting

Midway's data. The outcome was a control scheme that was sluggish to respond, and sometimes failed to respond at all.

"Some of the offsets, the data and tables for those, had to be recreated by hand," Peters admitted. "We were stepping through frame by frame on the original game, saying, 'Sonya's in this position at this frame; we're going to copy the same thing proportionally to the Super Nintendo'—because the pixel ratios of the screens were different, so offsets like that had to be done by hand, and that seemed to be the quickest way to get it done. For those reasons, the controls felt slightly different."

All through development, Peters and the others kept in contact with Probe, the studio charged with the Sega Genesis version. Their respective owners, George Metos at Sculptured and Fergus McGovern over in England, were friends, and thought of their companies as friendly rivals. "There was also friendly competition over who could make the better version," Peters said. "Nothing [acrimonious], just the usual, 'We think we could do this better and faster than you!' That pushed both versions to be as good as they could be within our time frame."

Part II: ABACA-daBBra

PAUL CARRUTHERS HAD won the battle, but not the war.

His first conversion for the Sega Genesis, *T2: The Arcade Game*, had been almost as tough a battle as John Connor's rebellion against the machines of the future. After a few months of rest, Probe contacted him about converting *Mortal Kombat* to the Genesis. He could work from home, and go to Probe's office near the end of the project to fix any bugs the QA department found.

Carruthers went into *Mortal Kombat* with more optimism than he'd felt at the outset of *T2*'s conversion. "I had all the code. I kind of felt like I had to use that code, and emulate it on a much [less powerful] hardware platform. That was the approach I took there, and it actually worked out very well in the end."

For a few months, Carruthers' version dropped off the radar. That was necessary, he explained to his project manager, to do a one-to-one translation. Even with the source code, it was a slow process. He had to interpret Midway's version and figure out how to write it in the assembly dialect supported by the Genesis console's 68000 processor. The upside was that it worked. Everything, from the responsiveness of the controls to the arcade's devilish difficulty—designed, like all arcade games, to keep players feeding it quarters—worked on Sega's platform exactly as it had on Midway's arcade board. "Once that framework was in, the game happened in about a week. It all just fell into place because it was copying code."

Carruthers and the artists at Probe—led by Terry Ford, an ace at extracting and downsizing sprites and animation frames—had to cut corners. The Genesis had sixty-four kilobytes of video RAM (VRAM), same as the Super NES, but Nintendo's 16-bit console had more system RAM to work with. Consequently, Carruthers was only able to coax Sega's console to hold an arena and a frame or two of fighter animation in VRAM at one time. "As your characters animate, in every frame you're pulling in a whole frame of animation for that character during that refresh period," he explained. "Then the animation frame changes for the next scan. That filled up the entire refresh period, because those were big frames of animation, which meant there was a lot of video information being moved around every frame."

One problem was that an entire arena had to be stored in memory as well, since there was no way to tell when players would move left or right, at which time more of the arena would have to be displayed. "If you just take them and reduce them in an automated process, they end up looking poor," he said. "So we handed them off to an experienced artist who crisped up the edges a bit, and played with the palettes. I was involved in the process of cutting those pictures up into smaller chunks to make the sprites out of them." Carruthers used the Genesis' refresh period—the point at which the television's electron beam finishes painting the screen and resets to the top to begin its next sweep—to swap animations in and out, and keep the background loaded.

While the Genesis's conversion played identically to its coin-op counterpart, its limited color palette—512 total, sixty-four able to be displayed at once—turned out a grainier port. Backgrounds such as the Palace Gates, an elaborate courtyard consisting of a cobblestone path and décor such as a temple, statues, and vegetation, were truncated: instead of clouds drifting lazily overhead, the sky of the Palace Gates on Genesis was a single blue backdrop. There were more missing frames, too. Others, such as Sub-Zero's stance, were changed; the blue-clad ninja ended up sharing the stance held by Scorpion, his yellow-and-black-robed counterpart. "We were using every ounce of power and every byte of space, and having to throw out at least half of the animation frames," Carruthers said.

Compared to the SNES, the Genesis also fell short in terms of audio quality. On the one hand, the Yamaha YM2612 FM chip was outfitted with several channels, and each channel could be tapped to generate samples such as harp, strings, and percussion, as well as a rich, deep bass that sounded fantastic on high-end (for the time) stereo systems. On the other hand, the chip was slower than Super Nintendo's sound hardware. Sega had designed its console with two processors, with the Z80 carrying sound duties along with Yamaha's chip. The Super NES could send data directly to the PPU (pixel processing unit) and its audio processors—Sculptured Software's "blast processing"—and there was more audio RAM on board than on Sega's machine.

Graphics and the gameplay loop, all the logic necessary to play the game, received top priority. Any storage left on the cart went to audio. "Every time I talk to audio guys, they're horrified by this, that audio is the first thing that goes," Carruthers admitted. "You go, 'It's nice, but it's not absolutely necessary.' If there isn't any more room, audio gets cuts."

Mortal Kombat's audio palette on Genesis is even more limited than its visuals. While the Super Nintendo version was missing voiceovers such as "Flawless victory" and "Fatality," the Genesis had been scrubbed of nearly everything else such as the name of the winner at the end of a round. Screams and battle cries were squished down to generic grunts. "We did as much as we were able to. The audio hardware in the Genesis isn't great," Carruthers admitted.

Late in the process, Probe asked Carruthers to convert his Genesis code for the Sega CD, a disc drive add-on for the 16-bit console. On paper, the Sega CD version of *Mortal Kombat* should have been much closer to the arcade source. CDs could hold an order of magnitude more data than a cartridge. Unfortunately, the frustrating process turned out a version subpar compared to the Genesis. Unlike cartridges, which contain ROM chips that can be modified, CDs are a closed media. "You have to bring all of that off the disc and put it into RAM so you can move it in and out of video RAM," Carruthers explained. That, coupled by limited memory on the Sega CD hardware, resulted in choppy experience. "We were just about able to do that by having fewer animation frames, and we made everything a bit smaller as well," he continued. "The backgrounds weren't quite right. There were bits missing out of them. What was particularly hard was Shang Tsung, the bloke at the end who can morph."

Shang Tsung was *Mortal Kombat*'s final boss. At a glance, he seemed like a pushover: Thousands of years old and in possession of only one special attack, hurling flaming skulls across the screen. His real power was the ability to transform into any of *MK*'s other characters, even its sub-boss, the four-armed Goro. Shang Tsung's morphing power required every other fighter's animation set to be at the Sega CD's disposable. At a moment's notice, players might decide to morph into Sub-Zero, or Johnny Cage, or Sonya. Those animations couldn't be swapped in and out of system memory quickly. Every time Shang Tsung morphed into another fighter, and then, around twenty seconds later, morphed back, sprites had to be loaded in and out, halting gameplay for several seconds at a time. The disc made a loud, painful *whirring* sound as it spun furiously, retrieving and sending data to memory.

"It was just incredibly slow," Carruthers said. "It ended up as an awful product, absolutely dreadful. It isn't a problem I found an answer to. There was no answer. We had to use fewer animation frames, which means it looks worse than the [Genesis version], and the whole idea of that more powerful machine was that it should have looked better. It was a shame."

Part III: "Something Either Really Cool, or Satan Incarnate"

JEFF PETERS ENJOYED his quiet life. The tranquility of the suburb where he lived provided a pleasant contrast to the long hours and crazy demands of his work at Sculptured Software. His neighbors were friendly, and tightly knit by the bonds of Mormonism, the dominant religion for large swathes of Utah. Every morning on his way to the office, he'd make small talk with friends out watering lawns, fetching the paper, or getting ready for their own commute.

One morning, Peters said hello to a neighbor and got a chilly stare in return. Peters went cold. *They know*, he thought.

"I was ostracized in the neighborhood I lived in because they found out I worked on *Mortal Kombat*," he said.

Peters didn't realize he'd been cut out of the inner circle right away. Every now and then, his doorbell would ring, and he'd find one of the neighborhood kids peering in. "Do you guys do drugs?" one blurted. Startled, Peters said no. The kid scampered home.

"Do you worship Satan?" another tyke asked.

"Are you really gay?"

"My mom says you're going to hell. How come she says that?"

His all-time favorite question never failed to brighten his mood. "My mom says we can't play *Mortal Kombat*, but can we come in and play it at your house?"

Mortal Kombat's violence bled into every aspect of the lives of developers assigned to its conversions. "One of the key things that Sculptured and Probe had to solve completely different was the whole violence thing," Peters recalled. "This gets into the backdrop of things going on with the gaming industry."

Things were touchy at the office. One of the programmers went to Peters and insisted he could only work on *Mortal Kombat* if his name was not attached to the project. "If his family came to visit the studio, we'd tell them he was working on something else," Peters said. "Half the studio had grown up here in Utah and refused to have anything to do with *Mortal Kombat*. This stigma, depending on your worldview, made *Mortal Kombat* something either really cool, or Satan incarnate."

Mortal Kombat's gore was a sensitive subject for American society at large. The moment word of fatalities spread beyond arcades and into schools, homes, and churches, parents and politicians went on the warpath. Editors at magazines like *Time* wrote special features that questioned whether video games, formerly the domain of happy-go-lucky cartoon characters like Nintendo's Mario, had finally gone too far by depicting graphic death with character models that resembled real people instead of mushrooms and turtles. Senator Joseph Liebermann of Connecticut joined forces with other politicians to crack down on *Mortal Kombat* and other adult games, opining that their gruesome content was no different than an R-rated movie and shouldn't be marketed toward children.

Nintendo was firmly on the side of politicians like Liebermann. The Japanese game maker had built a reputation as a purveyor of fun for the whole family. Court hearings that devolved into reps from Sega and Nintendo hurling insults at each other eventually led to the formation of the Electronic Ratings Software Board (ESRB) in the summer of 1994. Moving forward, games were assigned ratings intended to give parents a heads-up about their content.

But late in the summer of 1993, with Mortal Monday fast approaching, the ESRB was still nearly a year away. Sega and Nintendo gave their consent to hosting *Mortal Kombat* on their platforms as long as Probe, Sculptured Software, Midway, and Acclaim held to certain rules. Sega's compromise was sticking an "MA-13" rating on the Sega Genesis version, the rough equivalent of a PG-13 rating on a movie.

Nintendo went further than trusting parents to decide if their kids were mature enough to handle *MK*'s bloodshed. An internal division called The Mario Club exercised nearly total control over the publishing process. "You'd actually get game and feature criticism as well," said Peters. "You'd get it from their gaming analysts. First, you'd get approval to make the game. Then you'd submit the game for approval. Then they would give you bug reports, and then they'd give you qualitative reports of, 'Here's the stuff that's good, here's the stuff that's bad.'"

While content creators such as Midway owned their IP, the Mario Club, on behalf of Nintendo exercised control over what form that IP could take on Nintendo platforms. Content the analysts deemed unfit, for any reason, had to be changed. "Nintendo's goal of their new publishing agreements was to avoid what happened with the [the market crash of '83]," Peters explained, "by controlling and regulating the content so that shelves weren't filled with unsold crap again."

Extreme fatalities were changed. Johnny Cage kicked through his opponent's chest instead of punching off their head, Sub-Zero froze his defeated foe and shattered them into blocks of ice, Rayden electrocuted his victims into a pile of ash, and Kano punched through their chest and ripped out an amorphous gray blob that could have been anything, but was not explicitly a beating heart. Tamer fatalities—with the definition of "tamer" being at Nintendo's discretion—such as Scorpion's flame and Sonya's fireball kiss went untouched.

Sculptured's small team came up with the substitute fatalities, but had to run them by Nintendo. Hiding the fatalities behind a cheat was out of the question. “Acclaim and Sculptured would have been sued for everything that they had,” said Peters. The developers were so paranoid at accidentally leaving a trace of a taboo fatality in the code—their approach of a partial conversion meant one could have slipped in before they understood what its code was used for—that they checked and rechecked to make sure they were dropped. “The fear of somebody on our team accidentally or intentionally putting in a code that turned blood on or bringing in original fatalities—that was real,” Peters continued.

“We developed coin-op games for the arcade crowd, which in our experience skewed older than console players at the time,” added *Mortal Kombat* co-creator John Tobias. “But, in hindsight the industry itself was maturing and it took a while for us to see that happening. Unfortunately, I think Nintendo tried to take advantage of opportunistic politicians looking for headlines to gain an advantage over their competition with Sega and it backfired. Thankfully, when the dust settled the ESRB was the result and I think that it was a reasonable reaction to the whole dilemma. It was pretty much an acknowledgement of video games as a legitimate form of entertainment that caters to all ages.”

Sega operated under looser guidelines. Higher-ups knew that catering to older players would make Sega’s version more appealing to that demographic. The product’s engineer, Paul Carruthers, was in charge of making it happen. Carruthers was on-site to help with bug testing near the end of production when permission to sneak blood and gore into the game came down from on high. "I moved down there for a period of maybe a month, three months at the worst," he said. "They would put me up in a bed-and-breakfast in Croydon, and I became an honorary employee. It was close to the end that we found out things like Nintendo wouldn't allow blood in the SNES version, and they wouldn't allow blood in Germany. There was this backlash against what was, at the time, a very violent game."

By default, *Mortal Kombat* on Genesis was clean, without even a drop of the sweat found in the SNES version. Sega had voluntarily scrubbed out blood and replaced fatalities with replacements even tamer than those designed by Sculptured Software: Johnny Cage kicks his opponent across the screen, and Sub-Zero simply uppercuts them, sending them flying higher than usual before they crash to the ground. That would satisfy the politicians and parents up in arms over the game's violence, and it was the responsible thing to do. But at the main menu, players could press down, up, left, left, A, right, down, spelling out DULLARD, to reveal a cheat menu. In the secret screen, they could do things like enable blood, which also reinstated the original arcade fatalities, and choose which arena to fight in.

"I came up with DULLARD, because it just amused me to arrange everything that was at your fingertips: A, B, C, and D, U, L,

R for the movement. There's not much more you can do with that," said Carruthers.

Later, someone at Acclaim worried that DULLARD would be too hard for players to remember. "The ABACABB code was forced upon me: I was instructed to put in a code word that only used A, B, and C."

He wanted a mnemonic, but the limited number of buttons on the Genesis controller—three by default, though players could pay extra for a six-button controller—left him without much wiggle room. He settled on ABACABB, a nod to the album "Abacab" by rock band Genesis. At a screen just before the main menu, players could press A-B-A-C-A-B-B to enable all the blood and gory fatalities from the arcade hidden behind the thin veil of censorship. (All other cheats remained hidden in the DULLARD menu.) Carruthers' last-minute addition became known as "the blood code" among fans and journalists, and remains one of gaming's most infamous cheats.

Sega and Probe knew the existence of ABACABB and DULLARD would incur the wrath of Liebermann and parental groups. They kept both codes secret, trusting that some enterprising player would discover them. From there, word-of-mouth would imbue the Genesis version with a mystique that—fingers crossed—would give Sega an advantage over Nintendo in the 16-bit "console war."

Future GamePro editor Dan Amrich and a friend were among the first to crack the DULLARD code. Amrich had just graduated college and had pre-ordered Mortal Kombat for the Genesis, his console of choice. It was due to release on September 13, but his local store broke the street date and sold Amrich's friend Carl Elston a copy of the game early. Elston called up Amrich and mentioned that someone on Usenet, a bulletin board system where users could post messages about virtually any topic, claimed there was a code for the Genesis that made it nearly identical to the arcade. He was unable able to test the code, so he asked Amrich to do it.

"DULLARD opened a developer debug menu that let you not only toggle the blood on and off, but several other dev-test things, like making Reptile appear," said Amrich, referring to *Mortal Kombat*'s secret character.

Amrich entered the menu and found switches that could be toggled on or off. Some, like "Blood," were obvious. Others were head-scratchers; Flag 0, Flag 1, Flag 2, and several others were set to on or off, but contained no context as to what they enabled or disabled. "The only way to determine what they did was to go through, methodically, and test them. So I did that basically all weekend and came up with the definitive guide for what seven of the eight flags did."

Amrich wrote up an exhaustive document that detailed the functionality of each flag. He asked his dad to fax it to *GamePro*, his favorite magazine, which gave a free t-shirt to anyone who sent in a cheat that could be verified. “A few days later I got a phone call from one of their editors, asking me how I got the code and if I was using this on a retail copy of the game. They had the EPROM for review, but they hadn't received final retail versions yet. I assured them that it was legit and told them how I'd figured out all the flags.”

The editor who called was Lawrence “Scary Larry” Neves. (It was *GamePro* policy for each editor to write under multiple pseudonyms to make the magazine’s scrappy editorial team appear larger than it really was.) Neves thanked Amrich for his submission, and complemented him on his writing. Neves informed him that the cheat would run as a two-page spread due to all the hype surrounding *Mortal Kombat*. As a bonus, he paid Amrich the ultimate compliment. “We don’t usually get cheat submissions that are this clear and complete,” he said.

Amrich mentioned that he just happened to be looking for freelance work. Neves said the magazine didn’t have the budget for it at the moment, but he was welcome to try again in the future.

Several weeks later, Amrich’s t-shirt arrived in the mail. It was too small. A few years later, Amrich landed a job at the magazine. His first official act as a *GamePro* editor was to claim what was rightfully his. “I remember finding a *GamePro* shirt in a storage area and loudly proclaiming, 'This is mine! You owe me this!”

***

MORTAL MONDAY WAS coming.

On September 13, 1993, *Mortal Kombat* would storm the Sega Genesis, Sega Game Gear, Super Nintendo, and Nintendo Game Boy platforms. Every day leading up to Mortal Monday was as exciting for consumers as it was stressful for the teams at Probe and Sculptured Software.

There was more on the line than getting the code, artwork, and audio ready. Cartridges for Super NES had to be ordered directly from Nintendo and were shipped from Japan by boat. That meant Acclaim had to estimate how many cartridges it could sell on each system. It was a requirement that could lead to financial disaster. Orders had to be placed approximately six months out from a release for the shipment to arrive on time. If a publisher overestimated, they were stuck with cartridges they'd bought but couldn't sell. If they underestimated, they had to wait for another batch to arrive from Japan; by the time it came into port, consumers might have moved on to the next hot game.

Acclaim left nothing to chance. Executives put in orders for every cartridge ROM chip that could be manufactured in the world. "For Mortal Monday, there wasn't a discussion of, 'If we could have made more, we would have,' or 'It's too bad they only put in an order for this many million.' No," stated Jeff Peters. "They bought up the worldwide production. That's the pressure we were all under."

By August 1993, the pressure was so great that Acclaim sent producers to work on-site alongside both teams to make sure production finished with enough time to manufacture and ship out cartridges. “Them being a marketing company, there wasn't much they could do other than maybe decisions that would affect the marketing campaign,” said Peters. Moreover, the producers couldn’t measure up to the developers’ schedule. Sculptured’s team worked around the clock, and the producers burned out in days. Acclaim sent backup so the producers could work in shifts.

“From their point of view, they were protecting their investment,” Peters continued. “Or if there was a decision to be made, one of Acclaim's people could make it faster on the ground with us than out in New York. It was just funny to us that they couldn't keep up with our pace.”

At an Electronics Boutique store where he worked, Hughes Johnson lugged the red binder over to the counter and dropped it with a sigh. It landed with a thud. To Johnson and his colleagues at Electronics Boutique, this binder was their bible. It contained pre-orders for upcoming games. During every shift, customers would add their name and phone number to the binder, guaranteeing that the store would hold a copy for forty-eight hours. The notion of claiming a copy of a video game before its release was still new. Last year, *Sonic the Hedgehog 2* became the first video game to release at the same time around the globe when Sega had coordinated shipments of product around Tuesday, November 24, 1992, a day the company dubbed "*Sonic 2*sday."

Acclaim's effort looked to pay off: As Mortal Monday approached, Johnson estimated that pre-orders for Genesis outnumbered Super Nintendo players ten to one. Acclaim had a big investment to protect. Over the last several months, over 70,000 consumers had called the studio to inquire after a release date for *Mortal Kombat*. The demand was so great that the company set up pre-orders with retailers to get a better idea of how many copies they could expect to sell for each of the four main platforms: Super Nintendo, Sega Genesis, Nintendo Game Boy, and Sega Game Gear.

Promotion escalated in parallel to fevered anticipation. Comic books were plastered with advertisements showing gameplay and thumbnail graphics of the fighters with text commanding players to *Prepare Yourself* for Mortal Monday. Gaming magazines ran several ads per issue. A television commercial showed teenagers tearing through streets while pumping their fists and shouting "MORTAL KOMBAT!" at the top of their lungs. All summed up, Acclaim had invested $10 million in the game's advertising, and it seemed poised to pay off.

"I have to say that while *MK* was born in a way that was completely organic, literally a black box with a game in it that drew hordes of players without any advertising, the marketing folks at Acclaim recognized its viral nature and went all in with their ad campaign," says co-creator John Tobias. "That took some foresight because they poured big-time dollars behind the marketing effort which catapulted something that was already very popular into something that became a pop culture phenomenon."

Tobias, who was head-down on *MKII*, heard about Mortal Monday from friends and family who had noticed ads in the subway or on TV. He remembered getting involved in the campaign only once: When someone at Acclaim accidentally mirrored the franchise's dragon emblem so it faced the wrong direction.

"Ed and I lost our shit. I remember giving them the analogy that just like you should never mess with Superman's 'S,' so they shouldn't ever mess with our dragon icon. They bought that feedback and the next iteration was a perfect version of the dragon icon from our arcade game. Everything from that point forward became about authenticity with the arcade source material. I think Acclaim saw the value in that."

As the weeks leading up to Mortal Monday dwindled to days, store owners checked reserve lists. At most locations, a handful of customers had plunked down cash for the Sega Genesis version for every one looking forward to the Super Nintendo cart. "We knew we had our hands tied behind our backs with Nintendo," said Peters, who braced for the fallout. "We knew fans wanted the blood, wanted the fatalities, and there was no escaping that. Our expectation was that just because of the blood [code], the Genesis version would probably outsell us. All we could do was make the best game we could, and hope people could appreciate it for what it was, under the constraints and rules of engagement we were given."

Their predictions panned out. Word of the Genesis version's blood code spread, and Sega more than made up the lead Nintendo had gained by securing exclusive rights to the console port of *Street Fighter II* a year earlier.

"Pre-review career, I was a Genesis guy," said former GamePro editor Dan Amrich. "I was in college when I got my Genesis, having missed the entire NES cycle because, as my mom put it, 'You have all those Atari tapes.' Most of my SNES friends fell into the *SFII* camp because they got such a good version of that game and they had it so early. *MK* felt like a win for 'the other guys' and kind of silenced the smugness from my SNES friends. 'Who needs blood?' Well, to me, that forbidden, adult aspect was part of the appeal, and I wanted it. I wound up owning both systems before too long because I started my game review career around that time, but I never bothered to pick up the SNES *MK*—I figured I had the definitive home version already."

Paul Carruthers gave little thought to his Genesis port's impending arrival. He was already working on other conversions, and expected *Mortal Kombat* to come and go like any other game. One night, he met up with friends to see Jurassic Park at the local cinema. Taking their seats, they asked him how work was going.

"I've been working on this fighting game," he told them. "It's called *Mortal Kombat*, and it's supposed to be a big deal." They smiled and nodded.

When the lights dimmed, trailers for upcoming films played. Next up was an advertisement for *Mortal Kombat*. One by one, his friends slowly turned to Carruthers wearing shocked expressions. "Isn't that your game?" one asked weakly.

"A lot of the people I work with now were born after this came out," he said. "It's not very important to them. They don't understand what a big deal it was. So I don't think about it very often. It's only when people like you phone up and want to talk about it," he finished, laughing.

Jeff Peters remembers his time spearheading *Mortal Kombat* on Super NES fondly. The port sold well, because anything *Mortal Kombat* sold well. But what he remembers most is the stage of history on which the saga around Midway's premier fighter played out.

"It definitely hit a very specific time in the industry where a whole bunch of things happening in the background affected the development of this game in particular. So from an industry and historical point of view, it's a really interesting time. Not just the game, but everything that was going on behind the scenes, too."

Chapter 13: NBA Jam

Part I: Through Your Eyes

JOOLS WATSHAM HAD to be dreaming. He wanted to pinch himself, but was afraid he'd wake up.

An undergrad taking a lunch break between classes, Watsham had been strolling down a street of nondescript buildings when he'd seen the EMAP Images logo on one of them. It was the same logo on the gaming magazine rolled up and clutched in one hand. "I had a copy of the magazine on me at the time that was called *The One*. They did reviews and news on Amiga and Atari ST games, which I was really into," Watsham said.

It was a warm spring day in May 1991. London's streets were bustling, as they bustled every day. But that day was different, because even though he was just a college kid too young to legally drink, he was wise enough to realize he stood at a crossroads. He could stand here for a moment longer, continue thinking, *Wow, that's cool. That's where they make my magazine*, and then hustle back to campus to make his next class. Or he could march in and ask for a job.

"Obviously, I walked in and asked for a job. I got one as a trainee staff writer because I was cheap and enthusiastic."

Watsham was smart enough to seize an opportunity that had literally been right in front of him. He was also self-aware enough to know he was a terrible writer. His managers seemed to know this, because they steered the upstart away from editorial and assigned him to capturing and organizing the in-game screenshots that accompanied articles published in EMAP's magazines. "Back then, screenshots in the magazine were photos of the screen that we would take in a dark room. We'd print the photos, add it to acetate, then send them off to the printers to couple them with the magazine layout. There were hundreds of negatives and photos in complete disarray. I had to organize them, and I was more than happy to do so because I was working at a video game magazine. It was really amazing, and a great opportunity."

IMAGE COURTESY OF JOOLS WATSHAM.

Over the next year, Watsham became a sponge. He talked with other editors about writing and the games industry, learned how to put together eye-catching layouts, and assembled an art portfolio he stored on a single, 3.5-inch floppy disk. He also kept his ear to the ground. Editors were always talking about this or that studio making the game they were assigned to cover for next month's issue. In the spring of 1992, he submitted his art portfolio to one and landed a gig as a pixel artist, touching up backgrounds and sprites for games released on 8- and 16-bit game consoles.

A year later, he applied to Iguana Entertainment. It was a good fit. Like Jools Watsham, Iguana founder Jeff Spangenberg had skipped college and taught himself a skill, programming in his case. He'd got his start as the lead designer at Punk Development until he left to found his own studio in 1991. The company was based in Santa Clara, California. Spangenberg hired a staff of twenty, including many friends. At first, his startup had no name. Then Jay Moon, development support manager, took a closer look at Spangenberg's two pet iguanas, Spike and Killer, that stayed in an aquarium in the lobby, and pitched Iguana Entertainment.

Iguana paid the bills by converting games to the Super Nintendo and Sega Genesis. The team's big break was a homemade intellectual property called *Aero the Acrobat*, a humanoid bat that swooped and leaped through levels. When the exorbitant cost of living and running a company in the San Francisco Bay Area grew untenable, Spangenberg announced the company would be relocating. He and his team scouted cities including Seattle, the home of Nintendo of America, and Austin, Texas, which a few developers visited in May 1993. They reported that Austin had a burgeoning tech scene ripe for companies like Iguana. All but one employee made the trip. (That developer was David Brevik, who wanted to stay in the Bay Area, and who went on to co-found *Diablo* and *Diablo II* studio Condor, Inc.—which became Blizzard North—with Max and Erich Schaefer.)

As Iguana grew, Spangenberg expanded by opening international offices, including one in North England where Jools Watsham was hired. Shortly after starting, he was shipped out to the Austin, Texas-based office for three months of training. He's been in the United States ever since. "I was nineteen at the time, and that was a good way to trick a nineteen-year-old to going over to the States. If they'd have asked, 'Hey, do you want to go over there?' I'd have probably said, 'Hmm, I'm not sure.'"

Other employees who transferred from England joined Watsham at Iguana's headquarters in Austin. Far from being homesick, the staff was caught up in the thrill of making games by day and partying by night. "It was a young studio trying to do things professionally, but not in a stuffy way," Watsham recalled. "Everyone was really close outside of work. It was kind of like your college years, in a way."

Although he was still working as an artist, Watsham had been thinking a great deal about design. Iguana and most other studios lacked a formal designer role. Design was a collaborative effort, with programmers establishing game mechanics and artists conjuring characters and levels. By late 1993, that began to change. "We were trying to form the game designer role within our studio as a discipline," he said. "It needed to be a person rather than something that happens by accident. Even though I started in the industry as an accident, I tried to move over to the game design role as quickly as possible."

Genesis (left), SNES.

With every project, Watsham's desire for a career change grew stronger. He had done sprites for 16-bit games from *Aero the Acrobat* to *Pirates of Dark Water* and *Side Pocket*, a billiards title. "At that time, I felt very much like a hired gun to do artwork for someone else's game. That's probably how most video game artists feel: I'm doing stuff for someone else's vision. I felt detached. It was a foreign experience for me, even though the whole thing was foreign to me."

During breaks, he'd unwind by meeting up with friends and playing arcade games scattered around the office. *NBA Jam*, a two-on-two hoops title from Midway, was a recent favorite. The game's development had been spearheaded by Mark Turmell, a programmer who, like *Mortal Kombat* co-creator Ed Boon, experimented with game ideas in his own time. Turmell had been the lead on *Total Carnage*, a shooter that had fallen short of sales expectations, and wanted to make something with broader appeal. He liked basketball, and was dazzled by the digitized graphics Boon and John Tobias had incorporated in *Mortal Kombat*. When managers took notice of prototypes for a basketball game he'd been building, they pitched the NBA on securing a license to use the likenesses of real players such as Scottie Pippen, Mark Price, Shaquille O'Neal, and nearly every other player from the 1993-'94 NBA season. One notable exception was Michael Jordan, whose contract with Nike precluded him from participating.

The NBA was reticent to mix its multi-billion-dollar industry with video games, and turned them down. Turmell and the team revised their pitch and sent in another video game. This time, the NBA said yes, making *NBA Jam* the first NBA-licensed coin-op game.

Turmell wasn't interested in creating a realistic simulation. He dreamed of fast and fantastical play: a turbo button for players to move at superhuman speeds, gravity-defying moves like dunks that launched players fifteen feet or more in the air and shattered backboards and rained glass over the court, and two-on-two contests to make every step, pass, and shot count. During development, one designer came up with an ability to grant athletes who scored three baskets in a row unlimited turbo and preternatural accuracy when shooting, a state called "on fire" that set the ball aflame and burned the net to cinders after each basket.

Budding voice actor Tim Kitzrow, who got involved on a lark, added even more personality. Kitzrow was polishing his acting skills at Second City and running his own improv group in New York City when he happened to be working a side gig across the street from Midway in Chicago. Jon Hey, Midway's musician and a good friend of Kitzrow's, was working alongside him when Turmell wandered over and chanced upon an acting exercise featuring Kitzrow. Impressed, Turmell asked Hey to talk to Kitzrow about lending his voice to *NBA Jam*. Kitzrow accepted, and Hey wrote a script consisting of lines such as every NBA team name and the names of players. Hey also took cues from NBA announcers such as Marv Albert, who'd make quips like "He's heating up" and "He's on fire!" when an athlete was playing well. Kitzrow improvised others, such as "From downtown!" when players shot three-pointers, and "Boomshakalaka!" after spectacular dunks.

NBA Jam dunked arcades in 1993, shortly before Midway's *Mortal Kombat II*. The cabinet was impressive, featuring a huge screen set in front of control panels for four players to compete in heated two-on-two contests. The game appropriately caught fire, selling over 20,000 machines—with one machine holding the world record for most money made in a single week at $2,468—and netting Midway north of $900 million in revenue purely from quarters.

Following the smashing success of *Mortal Kombat*'s "Mortal Monday" campaign promoting the game for home systems, conversions of high-earning Midway titles became all the rage. In fact, *Diablo* co-creator David Brevik had tried to convince Iguana head Jeff Spangenberg to pitch Midway on porting the game for Super NES and Genesis, only for his boss to express doubt that the game would ever step out of *Street Fighter II*'s shadow. Determined not to miss another golden opportunity, Spangenberg secured rights for his UK-based studio to port *NBA Jam* to Genesis and Super NES.

Jools Watsham and other developers at Iguana's Austin location were jealous, but good-naturedly. *NBA Jam* was their favorite game to play on breaks. Match-ups often became competitive, with developers taunting and whooping as the score swung back and forth. Several months into UK's work on the project, management announced they would be sending several artists across the pond to help their colleagues wrap up the project. Watsham eagerly volunteered.

***

BY THE TIME Jools Watsham and the rest of Iguana Austin's cadre of artists arrived, Iguana UK had made significant progress on both conversions. The visiting artists' job was to assist with odds and ends such as creating a custom font for the Super NES and Genesis that matched the style of the arcade's text, and creating and touching up elements of the interface such as team names and point totals. "A lot of people hate it, but I still enjoy it," Watsham said of the tasks.

There was lots to do: menus for things like options that weren't part of the arcade game; touching up the portraits of athletes on each team; making sure eyes in each portrait were white instead of accidentally taking on a player's skin tone. "Whatever details exist on the player's face or hair, you have to get in there by hand and make sure they pop," Watsham explained. "It was a tremendous amount of work, a much of it was very technical more than creative."

Despite his growing desire to lead design, Watsham was thrilled to work on *NBA Jam*'s conversions and absorbed all he could from teammates who'd been working on the game for months. He knew, for instance, that the Genesis version had likely had a head start. Although the Genesis's graphics hardware couldn't hold a pixelated candle to the Super NES's rich color palette and multitude of display modes, Sega's machine pushed out graphics at the standard resolution of 320x224, perfect for the screen ratio of 4:3 used by televisions. "You could create a square on your development PC, and it would look like a square when you got it over to the Genesis. The Super Nintendo wasn't that way," explained Watsham.

Nintendo's engineers had designed the Super Nintendo to output at resolutions from 256x224 through 512x448. That gave it a much broader range than Sega's, but the default size of most SNES games started at the lowest resolution, which squashed pixels and the sprites intended for other outputs. Without artists touching up graphics by hand, a game running on SNES would look fatter than its Genesis counterpart. Consequently, developers at Iguana usually started multiplatform projects on Genesis to give them a firm idea of how a game's visuals were supposed to look.

Player-characters had undergone dozens of iterations by the time the artists from the US arrived, letting them focus the bulk of their efforts on touching up sprites and painting UI elements. Watsham and the others extracted sprites from *NBA Jam* and used Deluxe Paint—the games industry's art software of choice in the days before Photoshop and Maya—to modify them for the two consoles. Assets were arranged on a grid within the program. A single keypress in Deluxe Paint switched to a scaling mode, and artists adjusted assets click by click. By the time artists finished a sprite, their sizes on SNES would be indistinguishable from those running on Sega hardware. Only sprites could be scaled. *NBA Jam*'s background consisted of a grid of tiles, which could not be modified.

The next step was transferring graphics over Iguana UK's Internet connection to a Genesis or Super Nintendo hooked up to a TV. From within Deluxe Paint, an artist could press a combination of keys to art-send, as they called the transfer. "That was an amazing tool, not only for aspect ratios, which was handy, but for colors," Watsham said. "You could see how that console deals with the pixels you've created on your PC, because the Super Nintendo and Genesis were going to handle it however they handled it, and spit it out on your TV through a crappy RF cable. But that's how everyone would experience it, so we wanted to experience it that way as well to see it through the player's eyes."

Most arcade games were drawn from a palette of 256 colors that could be applied to everything: sprites, backgrounds, special effects, the works. *NBA Jam*'s sprites were high-color creations that the artists downsized to a sixteen-color palette, standard on Nintendo's and Sega's 16-bit platforms. Out of those sixteen colors, artists would "have to reserve special colors for the jerseys, shorts, skin colors, and all that fun stuff, so you could modify them to match the colors of all the jerseys and players," said Watsham.

While the Genesis made for a great starting point due to its standard resolution, its limited color palette—512 total, sixty-one displayable at once—caused headaches for console developers, who knew their ports would never be as crisp as those of arcade and Super NES games. "It was still a lot of colors, more than the average person would think you'd need," Watsham admitted. "But when you were trying to get fine shades for jerseys and skin colors, a very specific color, it may just not [be possible] on the Genesis, and you may have to find the next closest thing."

Although the color palette of the Genesis could be tripled using special display techniques, many colors available to Super NES simply did not exist on Genesis. That was all the more reason to start Genesis ports first. Artists used it to create a baseline so that, when they turned to the Super NES, they could broaden the palette from there. Skin color, for instance, consisted of three to four shades, not counting the color applied to the character's head. Artists would export a sprite from *NBA Jam*'s arcade hardware and isolate all bits of memory that held values for skin colors, like surgeons probing for a hard-to-spot bit of tissue. As they isolated those bits, they assigned them RGB (red, green, blue) values in memory and set them aside as part of the sixteen-color selection used for player-characters. Those shades could then be referenced to create bodies for any character in the game.

"Let's say there are three color values per skin," Watsham said. "You have those in code, and you can say, 'Great, this is Charles Barkley's skin, Mark Price's skin,' or whomever. And then you can use that when that player is used. Same with jerseys, shoes, the rest of it. It gets down to a science."

Blasting sprites from their computers to a console connected to the TV using art-send let Iguana's artists see how it looked on Super NES compared to Genesis. If Sega's less robust palette turned out ugly sprites, they could make adjustments. By the time *NBA Jam* shipped, Sega's colors looked nearly identical to those on the Super NES. Graphics were crisper on Nintendo's version, but Sega's port didn't look as washed out and muddy as, say, *Mortal Kombat*'s. "You'd have to mess with it until it looked right, but at least you'd know exactly what the player would be seeing. Art-send was a great tool," Watsham said.

Acclaim, once again the publisher for a Midway title, channeled the success of "Mortal Monday" to create Jam Day on Friday, March 4, 1994, when *NBA Jam* hit the Super NES, Genesis, Game Gear, and Game Boy. Great tools and passion for the project led to a slam dunk for Iguana. In fact, the studio's art director, Matt Stubbington, changed the logo to show one of Spangenberg's titular pets spinning a basketball on one finger.

The Super NES port edged out Sega in review scores, but both versions sold well in no small part due to which camp players preferred. "Because I loved the arcade version, I think *NBA Jam* for Genesis was my personal favorite," said Dan Amrich, former editor at *GamePro* magazine. "That was in no small part because I used an XBAND modem to play online with *NBA Jam*, and not a lot of games supported that peripheral. *NBA Jam* was pretty close on 16-bit—'close enough' for sure—and got right up to par with 32-bit hardware's ability to do sprite scaling."

The demand for *NBA Jam* was not lost on Jools Watsham, who reveled in being able to bring the game from arcades into living rooms. He went on to make good on his ambitions, rising from "hired gun" artist to producer and director at several companies before founding Atooi, LLC, in 2015, where he oversees art and design on the company's retro-themed titles.

"Back then, arcade games were very relevant," he said of his experience converting *NBA Jam*. "They were the pinnacle of video games at that time, because all you had at home were Super Nintendo and Genesis. Arcades gave you the best hardware, the best audio, the best gameplay experiences, the best everything. So at that time, we felt like we were trying to outdo arcade games, or at least equal them. For *NBA Jam* to be coming to home consoles, and to be involved with it in any way, was very special for everyone involved. I was just a hired gun; the main team did a ridiculously good job. It's a fantastic port of a fantastic game. Everyone was killing themselves to make it as great as possible."

Part II: On the Fly

WHEN CHRIS KIRBY thought video games, he thought *Space Invaders* and *Missile Command.* Mattel, the toy manufacturer that made Barbie dolls and Hot Wheels cars, did not come to mind. The Mattel Aquarius, a keyboard-sized personal computer contained in a plastic shell and sporting a rubber keyboard, changed his outlook.

"Mattel made these little computers back when everyone was making computers," he said.

IMAGE COURTESY OF CHRIS KIRBY.

Personal computers were all the rage. Software to run—and play—on them was not. If he wanted to play games on his snug little box, which housed a Zilog Z80 processor, 1K of RAM, and the BASIC language, Kirby would have to write his own. So he did, following along with the manual that came with the machine. His next computer was a Z81, and again, he was left to craft his own entertainment. When he upgraded to a ZX Spectrum, he advanced his coding skills by learning assembly. "I wrote little demos for the machine in assembly language, trying to push it to its limit."

After school, he got a job at a company looking for someone fluent in assembly. After six months, he interviewed for a game programmer role at Optimus Software, a little studio in the quaint village of Stockton, England. He took his portfolio of demos to the interview, wowed the managers, and was hired on the spot.

The job was far from illustrious. Optimus had a partnership with Codemasters, manufacturer of the Game Genie, a plastic device that attached to game cartridges and let players input cheat codes. Finite lives became infinite, gravity was an afterthought, enemies died in a single blow or bullet, and player-avatars became invincible. "What they needed was someone to hack all the games and create codes. That was a massive job," Kirby said of his position at Optimus.

Game Genie worked by associating the codes players typed in with blocks of memory where game values such as health, remaining lives, and jump height were stored. As the game software ran, the Genie sat idly by until it detected a change in those values, such as players taking a hit from a monster, at which point it intercepted the value and replaced it with one that carried out the cheats it had been given: lost hit points were instantly restored, jump heights were modified, and so on. Kirby's job involved sorting through a massive box of cartridges and, using a Commodore

Amiga, disassembling a game's code to figure out what values could be changed. "When I found something I wanted to test, I'd change those two bytes, run the game, and test it. I did the SNES version," he said.

Kirby was a contractor who held aspirations of full-time work. Between hunting through reverse-engineered code and creating cheats, he programmed his own game to impress his bosses. The software he wrote for the Atari ST computer ran at sixty frames per second, leaps and bounds ahead of other games on the platform. He got his full-time spot, and moved up from hacking games to writing custom software that would be published by Codemasters. One morning, he showed up at work to discover the studio had been purchased by Iguana Entertainment. "The reason why they wanted to buy a company in England was because if they had a company in England that was over five years old, they could do inter-company transfers, and transfer people from the UK to the States, making it easier to get a green card."

Optimus was older than five years, and the staff was small, only half a dozen developers including Kirby. "We expanded really quickly, and the first big license we got was doing *NBA Jam*," he said.

While artists such as Jools Watsham saw to 16-bit versions of Midway's two-on-two hoops game, Kirby was charged with putting the game on Sega's Game Gear portable. He was chosen for his expertise at coding for Z80 processors dating back to his ZX Spectrum. The Game Gear was a bit more powerful, able to hit approximately 3.6 megahertz, a resolution of 160x144, and drew from 4,096 colors with as many as thirty-two able to be shown on-screen at once.

Even if he'd been a Z80 rookie, Kirby wasn't under much pressure. "It wasn't a very high-profile version. There were other people doing the SNES and Genesis versions, but they gave me the Game Gear version, and I tried my best with it."

While he was familiar with the Zilog Z80, several differences separated the Game Gear from the home computers Kirby had programmed on growing up. The Spectrum used a single lump of memory to handle processor-specific tasks as well as pushing sprites and bitmaps to the screen. Game Gear had sixteen kilobytes of video RAM (VRAM) independent from the system's twenty-four K of memory, and artists drew characters and backgrounds by accessing special ports. "You would upload all your sprites into its special graphics memory, which were tiles," Kirby explained. Engineers at Sega had built Game Gear to display sprites as eight-by-eight or sixteen-by-sixteen blocks. To display a sprite, a programmer went to a tile's address in memory and gave it an X/Y screen coordinate. The problem was although Game Gear could display sixty-four sprites at once, it could only place eight on a single scan line. Nine or more caused the screen to flicker.

Rather than grow discouraged, Kirby viewed the Game Gear's strict graphics limitations as relative—far better than that of old PCs—and a challenge that would test his skills. He set about writing a tool to chop *NBA Jam*'s arcade graphics into eight-by-eight squares. The game supported four on-screen characters, two per team. Of course, all four characters were bound to occupy the same scan line as players dribbled, passed, and clashed over the ball. To mitigate flickering, he wrote a drawing routine that rendered all the animations for player one, then player two, then three, then four. Afterward, the routine would immediately begin again, this time drawing animations in reverse order, from player four to player one.

"So player one and player four would start flickering, but at least you could see them, which was better than them disappearing completely," admitted Kirby.

Game Gear.

Kirby had to take other shortcuts. For *NBA Jam*'s arcade version, Mark Turmell and his team had scoured magazines for headshots of players. To capture others, they videotaped NBA games and watched them over and over. On SNES and Genesis, in-game heads closely matched the real-life players they were based on. Game Gear was a different story. “For the Game Gear version, I just had a suite of heads, and I would say, ‘This one is close enough: It's a male with short hair.’ I didn't have the memory to store fifty players with different heads,” said Kirby.

The biggest shortcut he took involved recreating *NBA Jam*’s court as a facsimile of the arcade’s spacious play field. Midway had used a parallax effect to create a skewed, pseudo-3D environment. Players were able to run left and right, up and down, and diagonally over virtual hardwood. Artists pulled off the perspective using raster graphics, image data generally stored as a rectangular grid of pixels. As screens were refreshed, each line of pixels in the grid was drawn from top to bottom, with a delay between lines so short as to be unnoticeable to the human eye. Raster images enabled artists to divide the screen into layers.

An advanced raster process involved merging layers to create the illusion of depth of field, the same illusion seen in *NBA Jam*’s coin-op game. “I did loads of experiments, and I just couldn't get the Game Gear to do that. I was trying to interrupt at every line, but it was just impossible. It killed my processing time,” Kirby said.

An interrupt is a command to the processor to stop what it’s doing and do something else set to a higher priority. Some raster graphics used an interrupt to feed data into memory registers for a graphical operation. Kirby was stumped. Either the Game Gear wasn't up to the task, or his skills weren't, so he left the courts flat.

"I'd written one game for Game Gear before, but I still hadn't gotten a grip on the machine."

Kirby only written one title for Game Gear before being assigned to *NBA Jam*. He might have cracked his court-drawing conundrum if not for the project's tight deadline: The coin-op was a hit, and Midway and Iguana wanted home versions delivered as soon as possible. One more aspect of converting the game stuck in his craw. He was working on an Amiga outfitted with a seven megahertz processor and a green-screen monitor.

"I was using that to develop, and it was slow and cumbersome. We didn't realize how much graphical space the game needed. Also, the cartridge size was small." As a result, his conversion lost the blistering speed of the arcade game, rolling along at a sedate pace.

***

BY THE TIME *NBA Jam* for Game Gear dribbled onto store shelves on Jam Day in March 1994, Midway had already rolled out an upgraded arcade version called *NBA Jam Tournament Edition* boasting current rosters and new game modes. Iguana UK was scheduled to begin porting *Jam T.E.*, as players had taken to calling it, in roughly four months' time. Until then, developers either unwound from crunching on the first game, or began researching 3D graphics for the wave of 32- and 64-bit game consoles that would succeed 16-bit hardware.

Chris Kirby had no interest in planning for long-term projects. Not when his port of *Jam* continued to taunt him. He spent every minute during those four months rewriting his code and pushing Game Gear's hardware to its limits, tossing out hundreds of lines and writing new segments from scratch. When his managers assigned him to *Jam T.E.* for the portable, he was ready.

Kirby had a new PC to go along with his homemade tools, and a color monitor to boot. He fired up one of his tools, a picker that let him mark sprites one by one. "The first eight-by-eight sprite was the head, because I knew I'd need to change the color of the hair and skin tone. The next two sprites had to be feet, but couldn't have any shorts data in, because that would color the shorts wrong."

As the game ran, Kirby's upgraded code, lean and mean assembly, worked its magic. One routine changed sprites on the fly by uploading new data into memory and blasting it onto the screen. No more redrawing players in ascending and descending order. "It would generate players on the fly. I'd worked out that for every sprite, I could make seventy-two different variants of it in real-time. It would flicker, change colors, stretch the sprites to make them bigger, alter heads, change skin tones."

NBA Jam T.E.'s cartridge had 512K of space. Not a great amount, but enough for Kirby to deploy some of his experiments.

One was the option to bank data on the cartridge or in the portable's twenty-four kilobytes of system memory, then write assembly instructions to pull from banked data for faster processing. "We did tricks like, for each player, the same code was compiled four times in four different banks," he said. "To speed it up, I would switch the bank on the fly. The processor would be pulling instructions out, and one of the instructions would change the bank, which was where it would get the next instruction. It was really complex, but it was really quick, because it was faster to do that than to do a jump around memory."

Kirby's preparation bore fruit. By the time *Jam T.E.* for Game Gear was finished, the gameplay flowed as fast and almost as smoothly as its 16-bit conversions. "The artists would produce the sprites, and then I'd have to hunt and set things up as fast as possible. Some frames of animation would lose a bit, such as if a bit of shorts or an arm were sticking out. That would cost me another sprite to do more pixels, so I'd drop that bit off because I knew it'd only be displayed for a split second, and speed was more important. There were lots of compromises, but that's how I increased the speed."

One experiment was shelved early on. Before moving on to *Jam T.E.*, Kirby had been asked to dump his Game Gear port of the original game to the Sega Master System. The similarities in hardware specs meant the conversion shouldn't take long. Under their respective hoods, both systems were practically identical. Their input methods were a different matter. *NBA Jam* used three buttons: one for turbo, and two others that changed functionality depending on whether players were on offense or defense, such as shooting, passing, stealing, or blocking. The Game Gear only had three buttons, labeled 1, 2, and Start. Most developers reserved the Start button for pausing, but Iguana made a special case to Sega that the Start button would have to be mapped to a gameplay function because two buttons weren't enough to replicate the arcade's functionality. Sega consented.

Unfortunately, the Master System's controller, consisting of only two buttons, hadn't been designed for a game as complex as *NBA Jam*. "We spent most of our time working out special combos: double-tapping a button to pass, holding a direction and pressing a button," Kirby recalled. "Eventually we said, 'We can't do this. It's just not fun without three buttons.'"

Iguana cancelled the project midway through development. Years later, a consumer reached out to Kirby with surprising news. He'd bought a development cartridge for Master System believing it contained an early version of *Super Hang-on*, a racing game, only to discover the half-finished *NBA Jam* conversion.

"He dumped it, and now it's on the Internet for you to download. It was bizarre, because when they got in touch with me, I'd forgotten all about it," said Kirby.

Part III: "Such an Amazing Thing"

NO ONE KNEW where the box came from. One of the managers hauled it onto a desk and called a team meeting. Everyone gathered around, wide-eyed and excited. The box was massive, Chris Kirby noted. He got a look at the shipping label. Some words were written in English. Others were Japanese kanji.

Whispers broke out, a single word repeated over and over. Each intonation sent a chill up Kirby's spine.

PlayStation.

Inside the box was a development kit, a console engineered to read and run code. It would launch in Japan in December 1994 followed by a U.S. release in September.

Kirby gaped in astonishment as one of the managers turned to him and announced his next assignment: A port of *NBA Jam: Tournament Edition* for Sony's console, due to release as a launch title next September.

"I was eighteen at the time, still just a kid, really, with the most powerful console hardware on the planet. It was just amazing."

The PlayStation, and Kirby's big chance to play with it, would never had happened if not for a chain reaction of political backstabbing triggered by Nintendo. In the late 1980s, Ken Kutaragi was an engineer at Sony who had answered a call from Nintendo to design the Super NES's SPC700 sound chip. He did so by flying under the radar: Sony would never have sanctioned development of outside hardware by one of its engineers. When his bosses found out, they immediately moved to fire him.

They would have succeeded if Norio Ohga, Sony's president, had not admired Kutaragi's work on the incomplete chip. Far from canning him, Ohga gave authorization for him to continue.

Kutaragi became something of a golden child within Nintendo after executives marveled over the SPC700, a masterclass in audio engineering that would go on to pump out soul-stirring scores for the likes of Squaresoft's *Final Fantasy III* (known as *Final Fantasy VI* in Japan). His moonlighting opened channels of communication between Sony and Nintendo, the latter of which drew up a contract for Kutaragi to lead development of a CD-ROM add-on for the Super Nintendo called Super NES CD-ROM System, or SNES-CD. The SNES-CD would be sold separately from the SNES, while another console, this one bearing Sony's iconography, would ship with the CD-ROM drive installed and be branded the Play Station.

As development progressed, Nintendo president Hiroshi Yamauchi grew dissatisfied. The terms of the contract gave Sony control over the SNES-CD's disc format. Sony would claim all royalties, only giving Nintendo a portion of profits from hardware sales. Worse, leaders at Sony had assured Nintendo it would be creating non-gaming software for its CD-ROM hardware, such as encyclopedia and business applications. The contract told a different story: Sony never specified in writing what type of software it could make for the SNES-CD and Play Station. Nintendo had put itself in the position to let another company publish games on a system bearing its name, and it wouldn't see a cent of royalties. Sony's contract effectively broke Nintendo's control over determining which studios could publish games and how many they could publish in a year.

Shortly before the public announcement of the partnership, Yamauchi deployed Minoru Arakawa, president of Nintendo of America and his son-in-law, along with NOA lawyer Howard Lincoln on a secret mission to Europe.

The particulars of their secret mission were revealed at the June 1989 Consumer Electronics Show in Las Vegas. As Lincoln took the stage and announced that Nintendo would partner with a company who would help usher them into the age of optical media, Sony executives, along with Ken Kutaragi, grinned in anticipation. Just last night they had been showing off their Play Station prototype to developers and suits. Then Lincoln named Philips, one of Sony's biggest competitors, as its partner.

Kutaragi was livid. More than that, he was mortified. He had built the bridge between Sony and Nintendo, and Nintendo had demolished it in the most public way possible. Now, he believed, his bosses would make a quick and quiet exit from the video game industry, which they'd never wanted to dabble with in the first place. Not so, he was told by management. Ohga, even angrier and more embarrassed, had never wanted to make games, true. Now he refused to leave the business. Sony was coming for Nintendo, Ohga said, and gave Kutaragi permission to continue working on the Play Station.

Sony's opening salvo was battling Nintendo in court for ownership of the Play Station name. It won, and sandwiched the two words into one. Nintendo fretted: The first iteration of the platform had been constructed with SNES-compatible technology. Fortunately for Nintendo, whose developers were petrified of another company being in possession of their tech, only 200 were manufactured before Sony pulled the plug. Kutaragi desired to build a more powerful box, one capable of pushing out 3D graphics made from polygons instead of sprites. Ohga gave his consent, and Kutaragi earned the moniker "Father of the PlayStation."

The PlayStation that shipped to US retailers in late 1995 left the Super NES in its dust. It sported a 32-bit processor clocked at 33.9 megahertz, two megabytes of system RAM and one meg of video RAM, a 3D graphics engine still able to deftly manipulate up to 4,000 sprites at once, a color palette of 16.7 million, and up to

360,000 polygons a second. Kirby wracked his brain trying to tame the beast. It was far and away the most powerful platform he'd ever worked on. It was also the most esoteric. He would need to learn a high-level language, meaning one further removed from a machine's inner workings, but easier for humans to understand than assembly, a low-level language. "PlayStation One was the first [platform] I ever used C for. It was about ninety percent C, and ten percent R3000A assembly," he said of *NBA Jam T.E.*

Kirby pored over the Texas Instruments manual that pertained to the PlayStation's 32-bit processor. He and every other developer getting a jumpstart on PlayStation games felt like they were in kindergarten again, learning how to spell, count, all the basics. "At the time, the libraries were just a total mess," Kirby said. Libraries are files written in code that expedite certain functions, such as outputting date and time, and blasting graphics onto the screen.

"It was all in Japanese, and there was no real documentation. It took us a whole day to get it hooked up and compile code."

Every PlayStation development unit came with a disc packed with demos engineered to show off the console's power. One demo was called *Balls*, and it delivered what it promised. Selecting *Balls* from the menu cleared the screen before drawing a single ball made up of sixteen-by-sixteen pixels. The ball moved in one direction until it hit an edge of the screen, then rebounded according to physics computations. Pressing a button on the PlayStation's controller spawned another ball. A counter on the screen ticked up to *2*. Another button press, another ball, another increment to the counter. Kirby mashed buttons and the screen filled with colorful bouncing spheres. The frame rate never dropped below sixty. "Whoa," he muttered, and kept mashing buttons.

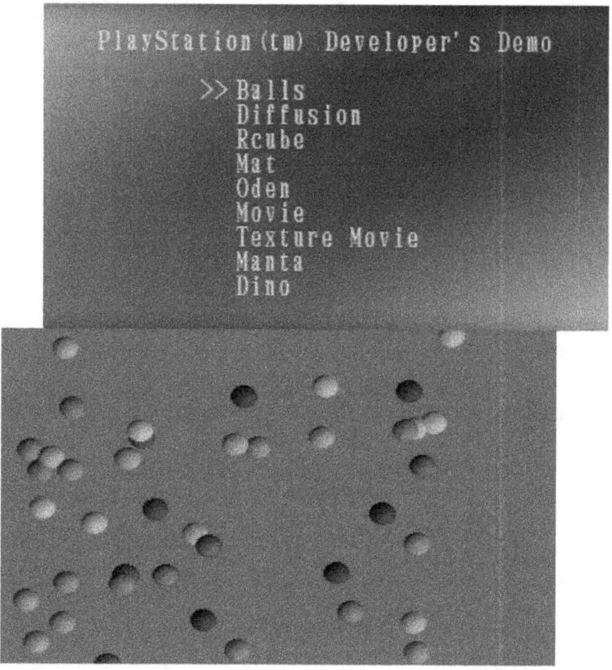

Twenty balls became 100, which grew to 200, then jumped to 300, finally 8,000. "We all stood there looking at each other, our jaws on the floor. We'd just drawn 8,000 sprites in a frame, and we'd done it at sixty frames per second," Kirby remembered.

PlayStation was more than capable of producing an arcade-perfect version of *NBA Jam T.E.*, or so Kirby thought at first. He and a team of artists dumped the coin-op's code and extracted art assets. The code for the game's main loop could be exported wholesale and rewritten. "That's why our conversions were so accurate: We copied the main player loop pretty much line by line," Kirby said.

The only obstacle to porting *NBA Jam T.E.* to PlayStation without a hitch, was the PlayStation. Kirby and the other engineers toiled for weeks to make heads or tails of the console's libraries. Then Kirby realized the answer was right in front of him. *Balls*. He could dump that code, study it, and change its routines to those of *Jam T.E.*

"The first thing I did was I went and got the arcade graphics for the court," he said. Kirby and the artists converted *Jam T.E.*'s basketball court so each line was a sprite measuring five-by-twelve pixels. He took one of those lines and dropped it into the demo's code. Instead of a bouncing ball, his bit of court bopped here and there. He rewrote more lines until the routine *Balls* used to draw the titular objects rendered *NBA Jam*'s court instead. "The final game was still compiling to an executable called *Balls*," he said, laughing. "We never changed it. I built the whole game off that demo. You find that a lot, actually. Many people did the same thing when learning new, unfamiliar hardware."

Kirby dabbled with polygons even though *NBA Jam* had been made using sprites. He was curious. As 3D images scrolled on PlayStation, polys distorted in a subtle-but-noticeable swimming effect. That was due to how the console calculated the angles and screen positions of polygons. "When you moved around, those numbers would jump, and you could see the swimming effect. But sprites are just flat on the screen. It was a great machine for that."

Kirby sped up *NBA Jam T.E.*'s sprite-rendering capabilities, already zippy thanks to the PlayStation's graphics hardware, by accessing the machine's scratch pad, a reserved space in memory that took in and pushed out data faster than normal. "You could write stuff to there and it'd copy it out really quickly instead of just throwing it in memory," he said.

NBA Jam T.E. stored the court in the PlayStation's one megabyte of VRAM, and the player sprites in system memory. "There were four players, so four sprites stored in video memory. I had to upload them every frame, and there were so many sprites in *NBA Jam*," said Kirby. To access them faster, he relied on the scratch pad and a handwritten compressor that packed and unpacked sprites using tight assembly code, which performed faster than C due to being low-level. "I spent weeks and weeks writing this decompressor so it was fast as possible. Every frame, I could upload one player sprite. That meant the maximum frame rate of animation was twelve-and-a-half frames of animation per second. That's why it's not completely arcade perfect: Because the arcade runs at twenty frames per second."

Other, more subtle differences cropped up as Kirby learned the ins and outs of the PlayStation. The console's resolution started at 256x224 and was able to increase to as high as 640x480. *NBA Jam*'s arcade hardware was set to 400x254, but the PlayStation port looked slightly less sharp than the source. The camera was closer as well, resulting in changes such as the camera quickly panning away from players after they throw the ball to follow its arc.

PlayStation's CD-based storage medium forced Kirby to carefully consider how to read and write data. As the game ran, data was unpacked from the disc and sent to VRAM. To minimize load times, a natural consequence of disc-based media, he arranged the data linearly so the PlayStation's laser eye that read contents from the disc wouldn't need to jump around to gather assets and code. "The worst thing on CDs is seeking. Drives can seek quickly on a single track, but if the head moves, you wait a few revolutions for the head to sync and work out where the disc is. The fastest way to load data off a CD is to continually read, so I tried to read everything as fast as possible without much jumping around. It was as fast as I could get it at the time."

One of Iguana's and Kirby's top priorities for the PlayStation conversion of *Jam T.E.* was making use of the Multitap, a peripheral into which players could plug in up to four controllers. By default, the console included two ports. Four-player gameplay on PlayStation would make for the most authentic arcade *Jam* experience yet, if

Kirby could decipher the Japanese instructions that explained how to add code that enabled support for Multitap.

Frustrated, he phoned Sony and was connected to Ken Kutaragi. “Why isn’t this working?” he asked. “Hasn’t your software come across this same problem?”

Kirby could practically hear Kutaragi smile over the line. “No. You’re the first.”

Politely, Kirby hung up and stared at his phone. “Shit.”

On the bright side, he was no longer frustrated. Heading back to his computer, his face hurt from smiling. This was what he lived for.

“We were solving those problems on the fly, hacking into their software development kits, doing low-level assembly programming to fix problems in the hardware. For that reason, I've always loved the PlayStation One.”

***

NBA JAM TOURNAMENT Edition launched alongside Sony PlayStation when it debuted in the United States in September 1995. But all that was of secondary to Chris Kirby. His defining takeaway from the experience of developing one of the console’s maiden titles was a series of moments, all of which had transpired at a conference much earlier.

Kirby and hundreds of other engineers had converged on London for DevCon. PlayStation was on the tip of every game developer's tongue. One night, Sony threw a beer-soaked bash to celebrate the PlayStation's imminent arrival. Kirby's jaw dropped, and stayed that way for the rest of the night. He was just a kid, but here he was attending his first conference and hobnobbing with Ken Kutaragi and other celebrity game designers. There went Peter Molyneux, one of the UK's most outspoken and ambitious developers. Across the room stood the Bitmap Brothers, co-founders Mike Montgomery, Eric Matthews, and Steve Kelly, collectively one of the UK's most prolific publishers. Journalists from some of the twenty-four-hour cable news channels were talking to developers at the bar.

All night, Kirby talked, laughed with his peers, and drank. In the wee hours of the morning he staggered up to his hotel room. Before he went to bed, he sat in the dark and replayed the night. Had he really just returned from sitting around drinking with Peter Molyneux? With Ken Kutaragi? And had the hotel staff had to keep ducking into their wine cellar to cart out more bottles to keep up with all the game developers? Yes, and yes, and yes.

"The next day, they had to postpone the conference by three hours. Everyone was wrecked. It was such an amazing thing."

Chapter 14: Mortal Kombat II

Part I: Two Fighters and a Background

JOHN TOBIAS NEVER assumed he and Ed Boon would launch right into a sequel after finishing *Mortal Kombat*. In fact, by the time the game shipped to arcades, he and Boon were lobbying Ken Fedesna, general manager of Midway, to do a game set in the Star Wars universe. Fedesna looked at them like they were a pair of Ewoks.

"What are you talking about with Star Wars?" Fedesna said. "You guys are doing a sequel to *MK*."

Tobias was momentarily taken aback. The small team responsible for *Mortal Kombat* had been so focused on developing the original game that they'd had no idea it had become a *Street Fighter II*-sized phenomenon until Mortal Monday, the day of the original game's launch on home systems, had drawn closer. Two months later, Midway had shipped out over three million units of *Mortal Kombat* on Super NES, Sega Genesis, Game Boy, and Game Gear.

Boon and Tobias embraced the opportunity to expand their vision. Tobias in particular had grand plans for the game's fiction. The game's backstory introduced players to Shao Kahn, emperor of a realm called Outworld, a role inspired by the sinister Emperor Palpatine from Star Wars. Returning heroes such as Liu Kang, Scorpion, Johnny Cage, and Rayden teamed up with or fought against new faces such as Baraka, a grotesque, knife-wielding member of the Tarkatan race native to Outworld; Kitana, step-daughter to Shao Kahn and 10,000-year-old princess; Jax, a buff military man looking for his missing partner, Sonya Blade; Mileena, a clone of Kitana sporting the fangs of a Tarkatan beneath her veil; and a new Sub-Zero, out for revenge on Scorpion for killing his big bro, the original icy ninja.

ARTWORK EXTRACTED FROM MK2 FOR GENESIS. IMAGES COURTESY OF DAVID LEITCH.

ARTWORK EXTRACTED FROM MK2 FOR GENESIS. IMAGES COURTESY OF DAVID LEITCH.

Intriguing character biographies and endings that teased what would happen if a particular character defeated Shao Kahn became a staple of the *Mortal Kombat* franchise starting with *Mortal Kombat II*. It was another way for Boon and Tobias to set their property apart from *Street Fighter II*: Capcom was more focused on pushing out updates to *SFII* than it was building on lore. "For me specifically, there were lots of details that we embedded in our fiction that alluded to a larger world story and I was excited to have a chance to explore it further and expand on the themes," said Tobias.

Boon and Tobias's team received more time as well as new computers and equipment to build the ultimate sequel. The controls were snappier. Gameplay was faster and more fluid. Parallax scrolling let artists design layered backgrounds. *MKII*'s roster was beefed up from seven playable characters to twelve. Each fighter had two fatalities, doubling its predecessor's controversial finishers: defeated combatants could be decapitated, sheared or torn in half, impaled on knives and left twitching as they bled out, and exploded in a shower of blood and organs. Two new finishing moves, babalities, which morphed defeated fighters into infant versions of themselves, and friendships, which tended to involve the winner dancing or bestowing a gift on his or her victim, were included to placate all the parents and politicians moaning about violence, as well as for victors to humiliate their opponents.

"On the art side of development, there were things like color palette management and moving from an analog to digital camera capture with the characters that gave them a much cleaner look on *MKII*," Tobias added.

By late 1993, *MKII* was doing well in arcades, and Acclaim contacted Probe and Sculptured Software to port *Mortal Kombat II* to home platforms. Probe would tackle the Genesis and Game Gear versions, while Sculptured Software was assigned to the Super NES. Paul Carruthers, the engineer who had brought the first game to Genesis, was offered a contract for *Mortal Kombat II*.

"In fact, there was a point where Acclaim told Probe that they could only have the contract if I was doing it," Carruthers said.

Carruthers turned the contract down. "I was a bit bored of it. I said, 'I've done that once. I'm going to move on. There will be plenty of other games. We're all making money.' In retrospect, it was a bad choice. I should have done it."

Probe's next choice was Keith Burkhill, the programmer who had written *Mortal Kombat* for the Game Gear, but he was wrapped up in another project. David Leitch, fresh off *T2: The Arcade Game* for Game Gear and Master System, was available.

"I got *Mortal Kombat II* by default. I was the next monkey at a typewriter."

Like most freelancers, Leitch enjoyed working from the privacy and comfort of his own home. In December 1993, home was one in a line of quaint stone cottages in Weymouth, England. "I think I started it just before Christmas 1993," Leitch said. "Well, maybe not, because you never start a project just before Christmas. You end up starting it twice: You pretend to start it before Christmas, then you take a holiday, then you come back and really get started."

In mid-January of 1994, Leitch settled in to watch the United States Men's National Soccer Team challenge Norway. His producer, Robert O'Farrell, called him during a critical play. Leitch answered and said, "I'm not working on it right now. I'll call you back in ninety minutes."

Leitch wasn't fussed over *MKII*'s development schedule. He had five months to do the conversion, plus a month near the end for bug-testing. Plenty of time, and he had a head start: Midway had supplied Probe with the code from the arcade game, as well as Paul Carruthers' code from the first *Mortal Kombat* on Genesis. Leitch would use that code, which earned Carruthers a credit as an assistant programmer, as a foundation. "The structure of both coin-op games was very similar, so I used Paul's stuff as a kind of framework, and started adding new content. It served as a scaffolding, this thing I could use to build a new version of the game inside of."

The nature of *Mortal Kombat II* struck Leitch as simple. "The nature of this game is basically two fighters and a background, and then you're just implementing functionality: Get them walking, get them punching each other, get them jumping, and then you've got all sorts of special moves."

His overview served Probe's milestone schedule. Leitch—and the publisher—would get paid every time he submitted code and playable builds of the game, so he mapped it out in terms of characters. "The very nature of the game is modular. You can work on one character, get that done, and then you go on to the next one, which will probably be a slightly faster process because you've hacked out the code. That facilitates what a character can do, special-move-wise."

By the end of month one, he wanted two characters able to move and fight using basic collision detection. By the end of month two, he hoped to have three or four characters in, along with advanced functionality such as special attacks and fatalities. "Then you'd have Shang Tsung at the end, because he needs to be able to [morph in order to] do what everyone else does. Then you'd have the bosses, and then you'd be done with it."

Converting the game involved translating each line of the arcade version's assembly into the dialect understood by Sega's 16-bit hardware. "As translations go, it was very simple. The main interesting thing, from a programming perspective, was how Midway structured their game."

For *MK* and *MKII*, Ed Boon had used a style of programming dependent on co-routines, also known as multi-threading. The idea was to structure a program as a series of sub-programs. "With most programming, you read through a function or routine, it would do all the stuff there, and then the program would return from whence it came," explained Leitch. "The way Midway's stuff worked was, a function would run up to a certain part, then it would say *sleep*, and that's where it would stop. The task dispatcher would go off and execute another little program that might need to be woken up from a sleep state."

Sub-programs ran one after another after another, like workers on an assembly line performing specific tasks toward a greater whole. "You'd have a program, for example, for each of the characters," added Carruthers, who had experience with Boon's code. "You'd have a program for each of the special moves, and a third program for the background, and another program that was reading the joypad."

Leitch used Liu Kang's fireball projectiles—able to be executed from standing or crouched stances—as an example. The moment a fireball was generated on-screen, a sub-program kicked off. The fireball sub-program held instructions to move the projectile, then to check for collision against anything, namely the opponent. If it connected, the sub-routine played animation of the fireball bursting apart, and dealt its damage. Then the program would go to sleep, its task performed.

What fascinated Leitch about Boon's sub-programs was they were able to exercise precise control over themselves rather than running through their instructions from beginning to end. A sub-program consisting of 200 lines of code could, say, perform a check for a condition at line fifty, and sleep there if it needed to hand off control to another sub-program.

"The entities were managing themselves. It was the first time I'd come across that, and it took a little while for me to get my head around it. Subsequently, I used it on pretty much everything else I did from that point onward, because it was a really nice way of doing games."

"It took me quite a bit of time to make the underlying structure work," Carruthers added, referring to his conversion of *MK1*. "But once it was working, I was able to pretty much translate from the original code line by line. That made everything much easier."

Leitch's port moved at a steady clip. After translating the code and getting characters up and running, he turned his attention to figuring out how to cram twelve characters, several arenas, hundreds of frames of animations, and dozens of sound effects and music tracks onto a Genesis cartridge.

***

DAVID LEITCH WAS one of a handful of freelance developers Probe enlisted for *Mortal Kombat II*. While Leitch translated assembly language, artist Terry Ford extracted art assets from the coin-op's EPROMs.

Leitch faced a problem unique to conversions. Artwork had to be pruned so the game would fit on a Genesis cart, but animations, poses, and other visuals couldn't be trimmed down too much, or the game would lose its personality. As with the first game, audio was the first to go on the chopping block. "It's just data management," said Leitch. "That was the crux of that project: Deciding what to leave out. 'Is leaving out this Scorpion sample going to piss off more people than if we left out this Sub-Zero sample?'"

Mortal Kombat II's audio palette on Genesis was even more barebones than its predecessor's. No character names, no fanfare such as "Flawless Victory" or "Fatality," and generic grunts and cries replaced the wide array of screams from the coin-op. Only a select few samples such as Scorpion bellowing "Get over here!" after hooking an opponent with his spear survived the programmer's axe.

Some reductions were obvious: decrease the size of each fighter's sprite, remove a pillar here and a tree there from the background. From there, decisions were based on how many animations could fit onto the cartridge. The only way to proceed, Leitch knew, was to implement some form of compression. In the end, he used two.

The word "compression" may call to mind visions of programmers squeezing code between their hands like a vice. The reality is more complicated. Computer science defines compression as encoding data so that it uses fewer bits, much like abbreviating a word. From there, the discipline branches off into techniques. The type used by programmers who need to cram a lot of data into a small box is known as lossless compression, keeping information intact while shaving off bits and bytes so it consumes less space. Lossless compression is commonly applied to discrete information, data meant to hold specific types of values, such as documents, spreadsheets, and certain types of images and videos.

Leitch had years of experience doing conversions, but he was green in the field of compression. To assist, Probe put him in contact with Greg Michael, a fellow engineer. When Michael was put on another assignment, Nick Pelling stepped in. "The problem the main *MKII* developers faced was that the game had so much animation, so many sprites, that it would only fit in the largest size of cartridge," Pelling explained. To most publishers, the idea of paying more money to increase a cartridge's ROM was out of the question: Why spend more on production when a hotly anticipated game was going to sell millions of units no matter what?

"They were in a bind," Pelling continued. "However, I had designed and implemented a number of bespoke compression systems for home computer games, that combined good compression ratios with short decompression times. And this was basically exactly what they needed for *MKII*."

Pelling wrote his compressor/decompressor pair according to a lossless compression scheme. The compressor packed files in, and the decompressor unpacked them on the fly as they spooled from the cartridge ROM into the Genesis's system memory. Pelling's methodology was to target duplicate frames of the same color—usually repeated frames in Liu Kang's jumping kick or Scorpion's victory pose, for instance—and strip them out. His algorithm also scanned for blank spaces around sprites, like images from a children's coloring book that hadn't been cut precisely around their outlines, and removed them. "The main win was from all the empty spaces around the sprites, but it had to decompress really fast too, so a well-optimized decompressor was also part of the delivery," he said.

Leitch and Terry Ford, Probe's artist, still had to do lots of editing by hand to make sure every sprite, background, and animation frame functioned correctly or didn't accidentally get sniped as Pelling's compressor/decompressor handled it. "Conspicuous stuff, like the fighting stances, had to be truncated," explained Leitch, "but they had to be tight, because that's one of the things players see much of the time. In more elaborate animation sequences, you can chop out two or three frames without anyone knowing the difference. You just sustain a frame where a new one would have gone. So, animations are the same, but less fluid."

Leitch kept an archive of all the sprites extracted from *Mortal Kombat II*'s arcade board—every fighter, every portrait, every background, every fireball and Scorpion-spear and ice blast and explosion—as well as sprites from his Genesis port. For example, Liu Kang's animations were spread across 248 sprites, each constituting a single frame, all resized and color-reduced to work on the Genesis. Kang's walking and stance animations were mostly preserved, because Leitch and Ford knew diehard fans would pay attention to them. "Nearly everything else got nobbled to some extent," he said.

For instance, when Liu Kang leaped toward or away from his opponent, he flipped through the air before landing on his feet. That flip-jump was slashed from eight frames to five on Genesis. In total, the animation lost fifty percent of its frames.

Objectively, Leitch found the approach convenient. "It was quite a nice system to use, because it was easy to swap stuff in and out depending on feedback. But the overall trend was most definitely towards 'out,' and it meant a significant amount of extra work, more so for Terry than me."

Subjectively, he found it galling, but necessary. If Acclaim had approved more storage capacity, Leitch wagered the Genesis version could have matched the arcade frame for frame. Sacrifices had to be made.

One of Leitch's favorite fatalities was Liu Kang transforming into a dragon—personifying *Mortal Kombat*'s signature image—and biting his opponent in half. "I remember when I first implemented Kang's dragon fatality and it used all the animation frames," he said. "And I was so impressed with it—and myself, ho-ho!—that I sent a build straight off to Probe. And everybody there loved it. But later, we had to start chopping the fucking thing to bits. Okay, that's an exaggeration, but nearly 50 percent of it got removed in the end."

A point of pride for Leitch was the speed of his Genesis version. The system's Motorola 68000 processor ran at 7.61 megahertz, just over double the processing speed of Super Nintendo's CPU. That, combined with its Zilog Z80 co-processor running at four megahertz, preserved the arcade's brisk gameplay, and rarely if ever suffered from slowdown. "There were no hitches, no frame drops, no hiccups whatsoever. The compression system was not so computationally expensive that it got in the way of the action. The movement speed of the animation processes was consistent with the coin-op, because the game program was very easy to translate."

Slightly less blood accompanied each blow and fatality, however. It was a concession made to avoid taxing the Genesis by drawing more than twenty sprites per scan line. Leitch could have allowed more sprites, but overflowing the maximum would have caused the visuals to flicker. "You don't want your character's legs disappearing because there are all these other sprites taking up priority. The blood was probably decided on that basis: Enough to make sequences look more effective, but not so much that it slows things down."

Elsewhere in the United States, Sculptured Software tackled challenges of its own.

Part II: "WOW!!!"

THE FIRST *MORTAL Kombat* had taught Sculptured Software a harsh but vital lesson: Always vet your team. Jeff Peters was determined to learn from history. Returning as project director for *Mortal Kombat II*'s Super NES port, Peters did not allow studio co-founder George Metos to throw everything out of whack by appointing a programmer at the last minute. There was really only one choice for lead engineer. "As a technologist, Adam Clayton was one of the backbones of the company. If there's a problem, Adam can step in and help."

Clayton had been more of a firefighter on *MK1*. After Gary Lindquist had bitten off more than he could chew, Clayton had been the principal engineer called in to salvage the gameplay loop as best he could, to mixed results: crisp, nearly arcade-perfect graphics, at the expense of poor controls and, thanks to Nintendo's family friendly policies, bloodless *Kombat.* Sega and Probe had dominated at retail thanks to the inclusion of secret codes that enabled all the gore and fatalities from the arcade.

Clayton and Peters were bound and determined that this project would be different. So, apparently, was Nintendo. Fans eager to rip out heads and beating hearts at home had pelted Nintendo with angry letters and phone calls, outraged that the family-friendly company had seen fit to decide what they could and couldn't see. Nintendo got the message, and revealed in *Nintendo Power* magazine that *Mortal Kombat II* on Super Nintendo would contain every drop of blood from the arcade game that the cartridge could fit.

All that remained for Peters and Clayton was to decide how to approach the conversion. In October 1993, just one month after Mortal Monday, Clayton went to Peters with his suggestion. "We're just going to convert this game. We'll build these systems, but we'll convert the code line by line."

Sculptured's port of the first game had started out the same way, but had gone off the rails. Not this time. Clayton would work at a calculated pace, and would ensure that the defects of the original port would be nonexistent. The downside to one-to-one conversions was the time it would take to see so much as a single fighter in an arena.

Every system, every line of code, would have to be translated before any gameplay could be seen.

Mortal Kombat's popularity had caught everybody by surprise, but *Mortal Kombat II* had ridden a wave of hype into arcades. Anticipation ballooned when word came that home versions would be available in late summer of 1994. Acclaim needed to know its golden goose was laying eggs on schedule. That meant sticking to milestones and showing playable builds of the game every step of the way.

Jeff Peters shielded Clayton from Acclaim's worrying so the engineer could do his thing. He appeased Acclaim's executives by sending assets such as backgrounds and fighter sprites extracted from the arcade and mapped to the Super Nintendo's robust color palette. "That was how we told them, 'Hey, stuff is happening. This isn't a game build, but stuff is happening,'" Peters said.

Even then, extracted assets amounted to a small step across a huge valley. "We converted the code, but we had to get all of the artwork for the characters so we'd have an engine to display them; we needed to have the artwork converted and scaled, so we needed all those bits," Clayton recalled. "The problem is the idea of saying, 'I need to show a character on the screen.' Well, it's hard to do that, because you're writing all this code just to show that; you should really concentrate on working on the final product. That's what we were trying to do: We've only got so much time, so we've got to hurry and get it done."

Every time Acclaim requested an update—preferably something that could be played—Peters smiled and had an answer at the ready. "The thing we kept saying was, 'Look, this is going to go from you seeing nothing, to the game working overnight.' We'd earned trust to give that a shot. We knew it was going to work. We had the right talent. We just needed time."

***

TO EXPEDITE HIS conversion, Adam Clayton wrote an editor that pulled code from chips on *MKII*'s arcade board and translated it into 65816 assembly, the dialect used by Super NES programmers to tap into hardware resources such as graphics modes and moving data in and out of memory.

Once the editor did its job, Clayton massaged it line by line, squeezing as much as he could out of the Super NES. He also wrote tools that extracted artwork and scaled it to match the console's 256x224 screen resolution, drawing sprites to be wider than they were tall so the picture wouldn't get cut off.

Clayton's translation also mimicked the arcade's memory registers while making sure they conformed to the Super NES's procedures for storing and saving objects. In general, that meant writing two or three lines of Super NES code for every one line of Boon's source. Gary Lindquist's approach on *Mortal Kombat* had been to move data from sub-programs in and out of memory. Clayton's approach was cleaner and smoother.

Sculptured Software's team had their own way of compressing data. "We had this tool that would look at all the sprites, because we had to make a character set of all the unique eight-by-eight pieces, and we had a way to balance how good the characters looked against how much space they would consume," Clayton said. "You had to scale at a certain ratio and still have it look good. And of course, you had limited colors, too. There was a lot of work there."

Every sprite was made up of eight-by-eight blocks of pixels, one of the most common sizes used on the Super Nintendo. The fewer eight-by-eight blocks, the less space a sprite took up on a cartridge. "We needed to go through and compare all these eight-by-eight squares," Peters explained, "saying, 'This one looks close enough to that one. Let's use one and throw away the other.' Then you create this massive look-up table that says, 'I need this [image] character,' so you go look for the character set, pull this eight-by-eight pixel, and shove it into this slot in real-time. That was our best form of compression for the fighters."

When designing *MKII*'s arcade version, co-creator John Tobias had taken aim at improving the raw, digitized aesthetic of levels in the first *Mortal Kombat*. Environments were more richly colored, as were the game's twelve combatants. "We did coordinate the colors of our characters in contrast to the backgrounds so that they wouldn't get lost," Tobias said. "Characters were typically composed of flesh tones and a primary color or two, which let us cut loose on the environment visuals. I think that in combination with improvements in how we captured footage of the actors added up to what gave *MKII* its unique visual approach."

The Super Nintendo's larger color palette and special graphics modes for rendering backgrounds afforded Sculptured's team the ability to capture the detail *Mortal Kombat II*'s artists had put into each arena, such as hooks and chains hanging from the ceiling of a dungeon set within a pool of acid, a wasteland where refugees of Outworld huddled around bonfires, and a sky palace where players clouds zoomed past a window in the background. Still, Sculptured's team was selective about what they culled. "Something used only once on the far side of the screen? No one will ever know that's missing," explained Peters, "plus it will take up forty [sprite] characters, so we'll just remove it. You end up having to make decisions like that, but you try to make them in a way that people won't notice it. If they don't have the arcade and the cartridge sitting next to each other to do a pixel-to-pixel comparison, you want to get it close enough to where they think, Oh, yeah, this is exactly what I remember."

Mortal Kombat II's use of parallax scrolling posed an intriguing challenge. The arcade machine stored environments as bitmaps, seamless images of an entire arena, like a tapestry on a wall. The Super Nintendo broke backgrounds into tiles, and Clayton wrote a table of indices that the game referenced as it loaded backgrounds and scrolled the screen. "You have to provide the illusion that the background is a huge bitmap, but it isn't. That's why there's a lot of repetitiveness when you look at backgrounds: You'll see the same patterns repeatedly, because it's tiled."

Clayton figured out how to switch graphics modes on the fly as the TV's electron beam repositioned itself from the bottom corner of the screen to the top. "The Super Nintendo had all sorts of different modes you can set it to," Peters said, describing Clayton's process, "and the modes had to do with—from a hardware point of view—how many backgrounds can I display at one time? How many colors can I use per background? How can I regiment my palettes to use those things? We could have all the health meters and [interface] at the top of the screen, using a mode that used four-color backgrounds, then switch to another mode that used sixteen-color backgrounds with a bunch of sprites."

As the big picture took shape, Clayton and the artists were able to give thought to small-picture details. "With the arcade machine, one thing they did was they could have a bunch of stuff overlapping, and we could not do that," Clayton said in regard to displaying names. "We had to put the names [below the meters] because the SNES could not do that."

The Super Nintendo port of *Mortal Kombat* had rendered each fighter's health bar as a sprite. Nintendo's 16-bit console was capable of rendering 128 sprites per line—thirty-two per scan line, or up to thirty-four eight-by-eight tiles per line. For *MKII*, the team's goal was to reserve sprites for fighters and their animations while still turning out detailed backgrounds. That meant drawing health bars and other interface elements as parts of the background layer.

Other oddities crept in. In the arcade, inputting a fatality darkened the screen before the grisly finisher unfolded. Afterwards, the word *FATALITY* oozed down in bloody letters that bled onto the floor. On the Super NES, *FATALITY* pops up in a blood-red color; droplets spill onto the floor, but the letters remain frozen instead of wriggling. “To animate it meant a lot of frames of animation, which meant taking up more space on the cartridge,” Peters said. “We probably decided having the memory for the fighters and the audio was more important than a word animating.”

On the bright side, the Super NES port contains virtually every sound sample found on the arcade board: all fighter names, all fanfare such as “Fatality” and “Flawless Victory.” To make room for high-priority samples, grunts and screams were downsized. Even so, Sculptured Software’s blast processing—the term their developers coined to describe playing audio directly from the cartridge—made the conversion’s soundscape nearly as rich as the coin-op’s.

“We could throw out more VO [voiceover samples] than any Super NES or Genesis cartridge that wasn't made by Sculptured at that time,” Peters said. “We knew that was so much a part of the game's character, but again, it was a priority, both in how we mapped out memory on the cartridge to how we prioritized technology. We wanted to create as much as we could, through all the limitations we had, asking how close to the arcade version we could get.”

***

ADAM CLAYTON’S ONE-to-one translation took approximately six months. In April 1994, three months before the deadline, Peters sent Acclaim a playable version of the game. “What we had was one of the levels where all the art was converted, and two characters in there with everything running 100 percent: collision detection, game feel—all the code had been converted and was working fine," he remembered.

The executives were so impressed, they sent it along to Midway. A few days later, Clayton received a fax from the coin-op development team praising his work on the translation. "I don't know if that comment would've happened the first time we played it," said John Tobias, "but certainly by the end of development I remember thinking they did a fantastic job with *MKII*."

Ahead of schedule, Sculptured's team gave their version an Easter egg in the form of a game mode exclusive to the Super NES. At the main menu, players could enter a combination of buttons to play an eight-fighter, elimination-style tournament. "Because converting the code was our starting point, that gave us extra time to add modes to the Super Nintendo that weren't in the arcade game," said Peters.

"At that point, they just left us alone. They never had to send anyone out," he added, referring to Acclaim assigning producers to hover over the team's shoulders during work on *Mortal Kombat*. "We just got it done, and it went really well. I kept some of the magazines that said, 'This port is amazing.' A large amount of that was, you just had to know how to convert the code."

APR-14-1994 15:59 FROM WILLIAMS BALLY MIDWAY ENG TO 918014672905 P.01

To: Adam Clayton at Sculptured Software April 14, 1994

From: Midway MKII Design Team

Re: SNES Mortal Kombat II

Hi Adam,

We just got our first pass of MKII for SNES.

WOW !!!

The entire video department here at Midway is absolutely blown away at how well you have matched the "feel" of our arcade version on MKII. We can already see that this will be the version to have as the graphics and gameplay are awesome!!

The Midway Guys

PS - Say hi to Gary Penacho !!

COURTESY OF ADAM CLAYTON.

Part III: Talking Points

IN 1982, AUSTRALIA-based Beam Software carved out a name for itself when designers Veronika Megler and Philip Mitchell dazzled players with a rendition of J. R. R. Tolkien's *The Hobbit*. The game was a text-adventure, a genre predicated on parsers that processed simple combinations of verbs and nouns, such as GO NORTH or TAKE BOOK. Megler's parser was far more robust, able to understand and carry out grammatically correct sentences. She circumvented another failing of text adventures such as Sierra On-Line's *King's Quest* by allowing players to treat everything as an object rather than forcing them to find the exact verb-noun combination required to pick up and use an object on the screen—objects often so crudely drawn that many players struggled to find the right noun for pixelated, unrecognizable blobs.

The Hobbit's full-bodied parser made it a more engrossing puzzler. It sold over one million copies for Beam Software, a fact of which Megler was unaware; she was busy graduating from college and hunting for a job. Beam continued putting out games until a shake-up in 1987, when parent company Melbourne House was sold to Mastertronic. Beam's catalog was scattered far and wide, farmed out to various publishers such as Firebird, which distributed 1988's *Samurai Warrior*, a fighting game in the vein of *Street Fighter II* and *Mortal Kombat*.

Cameron Sheppard was one of several developers who rode out the transition from Melbourne House, where he'd worked part-time on titles for Nintendo's upcoming Game Boy handheld, and Mastertronic. The bulk of his job was researching and poking at the Game Boy to learn as much about its workings as he could. During one project, Gary Liddon, a producer at Probe, flew from England to Australia to visit the office. Liddon and Sheppard got to talking and, over drinks after work, Liddon explained that his boss, Probe founder Fergus McGovern, was looking for a programmer to convert *Mortal Kombat II* to Game Boy.

Back at Probe, Liddon went straight to McGovern to talk to him about Cameron Sheppard. "He's the best programmer in Australia. You should put him on *Mortal Kombat II*."

Arriving at Probe's London office on January 28, 1994, Sheppard battled a case of nerves. Liddon naming him the best programmer in an entire country was high praise, and he'd need to live up to it to overcome the stigma of the first *Mortal Kombat* on Game Boy. No one had expected the handheld, black-and-white version to look or play as well as it had in arcades. Unfortunately, it fell far below the already-low bar with input that was even sloppier than the Super Nintendo port's. "I don't want to put it down, but you had to be very slow with the controls to do special moves," Sheppard said of the first game.

The reason, he discovered, was the game's main core. Drawing sprites was a major part of any game loop, but the Game Boy's slow processor got bogged down trying to process button inputs while continually refreshing the on-screen action.

Sheppard was given three months, from early February until the end of April, to port *Mortal Kombat II*. His first move was to rewrite the core to display fighters and backgrounds more efficiently. The first game had rendered characters using sprite masks, a graphics technique that hides or reveals groups of sprites at certain times. For *Mortal Kombat II*, Sheppard voted against sprite masks. Yet even pared down, *MKII*'s fighters were too detailed for the Game Boy to process. "It was very limited. You couldn't draw two characters using sprites. You could only have ten sprites per line," he said.

Instead, Sheppard rendered characters as background objects. "I rewrote the routine to be three times faster. Just really, really inline and pushing the Game Boy. That's how I improved the speed of *Mortal Kombat II*, which increased overall playability many fold."

Sheppard's technique called for him to prune characters so they wouldn't conflict with other parts of the background, namely the arena where fights unfolded. For instance, every fighter was bordered by white space that could prove problematic. "For instance, if I was to draw Mileena, around her head would be white, and the background would disappear. That's because she would overwrite the background, because she's part of the background." His solution was to read the arena from an array of pixels called the character map, then mask-out the area for a fighter's head as the player moved around the screen, and then render the head. "That way the background around her head was still there. Because the code was running faster and you could enter moves faster, it made the whole game faster."

To improve responsiveness when players pressed buttons, Sheppard wrote an interrupt, a separate block within the core that wouldn't clash with drawing routines, a problem that had hobbled the first Game Boy port. "That was a better way to do it because my key-reading had priority, and wasn't affected by any slowdown in the main loop."

There were consequences to Sheppard's solution. "The fighters were background animations, so there was a limited amount of [space] left over for backdrops." The Kombat Tomb, a balcony overlooking a fiery sky, was modified to display a flat gray color instead, so it looked more like a featureless stone wall. Players would not expect arcade-perfect translations of the arenas in a portable version anyway, Probe reasoned, and it was a small price to pay for a sequel that was exponentially more responsive than the first game. Plus, the approach freed up the Game Boy's sprites to be used to draw special moves. "Basically, because both characters were being masked in as software sprites, that freed up all the hardware sprites to be used for that," Sheppard explained. Hardware sprites referred to the maximum number of sprites the Game Boy was able to display: forty on-screen, ten per line. "All throwing objects—fireballs, Scorpion's spear, Sub-Zero's ice—were separate, and drawn as hardware sprites," said Sheppard.

The game's roster was small, containing eight fighters out of the full twelve. Palette swapping, a common graphics technique where an image already in memory is given a different color scheme without consuming extra memory, made it possible to pad out the roster with ninjas such as Scorpion, Sub-Zero, and Reptile—included as a hidden character, as he'd been in the first *Mortal Kombat*—and Mileena and Kitana. "You had the core frames for standard moves," Sheppard said of palette-swap characters such as Kitana and Mileena, "but each palette-changed character had a few frames of their own," he continued, referring to the way Mileena stands with one arm raised while Kitana balls her fists near her waist.

Fatalities were cut up and reimagined to accommodate the Game Boy's lower color palette—four monochrome shades—and its limited capacity for sprites. Sheppard was given directives for new fatalities from management. Liu Kang's fatality that transformed him into a torso-chomping dragon was changed so his dragon form breathed fire, causing the body to burn until it exploded, after which the bones scattered off-screen. Out of sight, out of mind and memory. "That was a background frame that was carefully drawn to not use up too many background squares as possible," he said of the dragon. Acclaim insisted on including the dragon, so Sheppard made it happen, with the transformation occurring in a single frame of animation. "It's one of those things where you want to push it in because it could become a talking point for the game."

***

SHEPPARD'S GAME BOY port turned out so well that, several months later, he was charged with bringing the game to Sega's 32X add-on. "Most of my time was spent R-and-D-ing the 32X because it was brand-new at the time. Our dev kits were the size of mini fridges, for some reason. I don't know why they were that big. It was very strange."

Like the Sega CD, the 32X attached to the Genesis. It dramatically increased the 16-bit console's processing speed and color palette: Not only could the 32X choose from 32,768 colors, like the Super Nintendo, it could display that many colors at once, a much greater amount than the SNES's maximum of 512. On the flip side, it pushed pixels out slower than the Genesis's sixty-four on-screen colors.

Developers compensated for the 32X's programming by recruiting the Genesis as a co-processor. Sheppard did just that for his conversion of *Mortal Kombat II*. "The 32X was, basically, a video layout over the Genesis. All that was going on was the game code, the AI and instructions and anything, ran on the Genesis, and that was Dave Leitch's code," Sheppard explained.

With more cartridge space and a much broader color palette, the 32X port of *MKII* rendered backgrounds, sprites, and animations that had been extracted from the coin-op game. There were exceptions where Genesis animations were used, such as Kitana only raising her arms halfway when throwing her fans, and Baraka pausing halfway through his victory animation so he appears to bow—an honorable gesture wholly out of character for the bloodthirsty killer—rather than raising his knives and displaying his jagged teeth in a chilling grin. Strangely, the 32X offers a larger selection of sound effects—more screams, more grunts—but draws from the soundtrack used by the Genesis game. The resultant aural experience is mixed, but close enough to the arcade version.

Graphically, however, the 32X version is demonstrably superior to the Genesis cart. "I was just grabbing where his sprites should go, and inserting my own high-res, higher-colored versions in, because the 32X had better video capability," he continued.

Part IV: Nothing Can Prepare You

IF *MORTAL KOMBAT*'s "Mortal Monday" campaign marked the arrival of a controversial hit, *Mortal Kombat II*'s debut on Genesis, Super Nintendo, Game Gear, and Game Boy on Friday, September 9, 1994, was a global phenomenon. Backed by a $10 million marketing campaign from Acclaim, Midway's stock jumped six percent to forty-two cents a share and earned $101 million in its second fiscal quarter thanks to sales of the adaptations for home systems.

This time, Nintendo came out on top. According to sales charts, the Super NES version of *MKII* outsold its rival two to one. It was graphically superior, and despite jags of slowdown due to the console's slower CPU and graphics processor, the gameplay and gore matched the arcade much more closely than the Genesis port. Critics appreciated the zippier speed on Genesis, but were disappointed by the flat color palette, sparse backgrounds that had been trimmed of décor—the Dead Pool stage, for instance, had fewer chains dangling from the ceiling—and shallow selection of audio samples.

"It felt like a level playing field since the content was what gamers really craved," said Dan "Elektro" Amrich, former *GamePro* editor. "You buy a home conversion because you want the arcade experience at home, so when you know one company is saying 'We won't allow that level of accuracy,' that stings if you've decided that

SNES is part of who you are, and your Genesis friends can say 'you made the wrong choice.' There is no better example of 'Genesis does what Nintendon't.' So with *MKII*, that became moot and I'm glad it did—suddenly the SNES fans didn't feel like second-class citizens anymore, and it was around then—as we worked our way closer to 32-bit hardware anyway—that it became less of a big deal which system you were using for *MKII*. It fell into the same old tribal preferences because 'they both have blood now.' And it helped that both conversions were pretty darned good."

Differences aside, both versions had strengths. The Super NES game offered a more complete package, but the faster pace on Genesis more closely matched the back-and-forth momentum of contests in the arcade. "To my shame, I don't think I've ever played the SNES version," admitted Genesis coder David Leitch. "If you go on YouTube—and I'm not saying this is the measure by which everything should be judged—the SNES version seems to come out the winner. I mean, I'd rather the result be the opposite, but it's water under the bridge."

Leitch had no complaints. The months he spent converting *MKII* in his stone cottage marked the fulfilment of his geek story: A kid who'd grown up wanting to make video games for a living. "I should say I wasn't the first candidate to do it, but I think I did very well with it. And it's a really good game, and I think a good piece of work. That's the nature of conversions: You spend the whole time fighting with hardware so that the best parts, the money shots of the game, are worth it. That's a tough job."

His impact on pop culture was driven home when, like Paul Carruthers before him, he went to the cinema with friends and was surprised and pleased to see a commercial for *Mortal Kombat II* before the feature rolled. "*MKII* seemed like an event game, a huge game. In hindsight, its release was the biggest event I've participated in during my career."

Nintendo may have won the *MKII* theater in the 16-bit console war, but Sega scored a point thanks to Cameron Sheppard's nearly arcade-perfect 32X port, which released in 1995. But Sheppard is most proud of his Game Boy adaptation. Like Adam Clayton at Sculptured Software, he'd received word from Midway that Ed Boon had praised his work as the best handheld conversion of a game he'd ever played. "I was working such long hours, sixteen-, eighteen-hour days, going into the office in the early morning and leaving in the early morning, doing nothing but working. To get that praise from Ed Boon was brilliant. Recently I went online and watched YouTube videos, and comments on them were quite favorable. I didn't realize this until a few years ago, when I decided to search for them. It was quite an achievement to get *Mortal Kombat II*."

Sheppard also got an attaboy from Probe chief Fergus McGovern. McGovern—who was the subject of an Easter egg in

Leitch's Genesis version, wherein players could perform a *Fergality* to summon a character that had his head—died suddenly in 2016 when he suffered a cerebral blood clot following a transatlantic flight. He was only fifty years old. Obituaries from developers and games journalists flooded the Internet, all reminiscing fondly about the co-founder's cheerful demeanor and work with charities.

***

MIDWAY THE CORPORATE entity profited from *Mortal Kombat II*'s success, but so did developers of the console ports. Royalties on cartridges was becoming a thing of the past, so Adam Clayton counted himself lucky when he was able to put some money away in savings as well as buy a 1995 Subaru, a car he still drives today. "Royalties were not that common. After this, game projects got bigger, and you had more people involved. They stopped doing it, because the pie was divided into too many pieces."

David Leitch came into an unexpected windfall. Initially contracted to port *MKII* to Game Gear and the aging Sega Master System. Probe boss Fergus McGovern modified the contract by scribbling out *Game Gear/Master System* and writing *Sega Genesis* instead. The problem for McGovern, and the boon for Leitch, was that Leitch had been promised a higher-than-average royalty from sales, since the Game Gear and Master System carts were projected to sell significantly fewer units than the 16-bit versions.

"I got this tip-top royalty deal out of it—four or five times the amount I originally expected to make. Fergus, God bless him, really begrudged paying it out to me, but it was his mistake, and it was amicably resolved in the end, but I'm sure he never did anything like that again."

Clayton made out well, but questioned if the payout was worth it. *MKII* was grueling, calling for him to work six to seven days a week for up to sixteen hours a day. He'd crunched since the early days of his career, but was finding that he had less endurance for it as he got older, and especially since he and his wife had had children. After *Mortal Kombat II* shipped, Clayton approached his managers and asked for extra time off. He was denied. There were more projects to ship.

Since leaving Sculptured Software and continuing in the games industry, he's worked on products such as the *Disney Infinity* line of toys-to-life games made by Avalanche Software. But no matter the scope of or anticipation for a game, work-life balance is his top priority. "I felt like I was strengthened by being order to do that game and still manage my family at the time," Clayton said of *MKII*. "It was a good game, but it taught me a lot about making sure my family needs to be taken care of, too."

Jeff Peters watched royalties slip away, and saw it as an unfortunate sign of the times. Sculptured Software didn't employ hundreds of people. Teams were smaller, so everyone did a little bit of everything. Some employees were more appreciated than others. “It was a very tech-driven company from its earliest culture, and very proud of that heritage. That also meant programmers were highly valued. It took a lot of years to value the artists. They weren't valued... well, at all, to be honest,” Peters admitted.

He recalled a conversation he had with Sculptured co-founder George Metos after *Mortal Kombat* had shipped. They were chatting in the hallway when Metos met his eyes and said, “You know, that $35,000 you spent on art? I bet you could have spent only $20,000 and nobody would have noticed.”

Peters was speechless. The artists had worked as hard as the programmers, and had been instrumental in helping extract art from the arcade board and scale down animation frames and color palettes. “That was the culture of the company at the time. It was a long, hard slog to get Sculptured to value artists. It was just a tech-driven company.”

John Tobias, Ed Boon, and the rest of *MKII*’s coin-op division raked in royalties after the game become a global sensation. Tobias left Midway shortly after the release of *Mortal Kombat 4* and *Mortal Kombat Mythologies: Sub-Zero*, a spin-off game starring the icy ninja. Today, he appreciates the money, but is more grateful that had a hand in creating a franchise enjoyed by so many, a legacy carried on by NetherRealm, the company formed by the *Mortal Kombat* team after Midway went bankrupt in 2009.

"I think *MK* is a forever franchise," Tobias said. "I felt that way when I left Midway and I feel that way today especially with Warner Brothers' acquisition of the property. Like any franchise it may have ups and downs, but it is engrained in popular culture because of its birth in the nineties and will remain a staple as longs as it's dusted off and kept polished. Its relevance today is entirely due to the great work being done at NetherRealm."

Chapter 15: Street Fighter Alpha

Part I: Laidback

IT WAS TOO much. The dark, gloomy cave. The blood and grime smeared along the walls. The skeleton, its bones yellowed with age, suspended from manacles against the stone.

Keith Burkhill had no objections to the violence in *Mortal Kombat*, nor to the bleak atmosphere of the cavern-turned-torture-chamber where Goro, the four-armed, half-human-half-dragon beast had taken on—and brutally murdered—all comers for 500 years. It was too much for the Game Gear, Sega's handheld console.

Burkhill had gone from releasing *Missile Defence*, his clone of *Missile Command*, to doing platform games on the Sega Master System as a contract programmer for Probe. Right away he'd been given hot properties such as *Back to the Future 3* and *Alien 3*. Next up was *Mortal Kombat*, and to Burkhill, it was just another job—at first. "I had the arcade machine at my house," he said. "That was a nice thing to have. I got paid more than I had on the previous games as well. That made me think it was probably going to be a bit bigger."

Probe's port of *MK* to the Master System was flying under the radar. All the advertising copy—magazine ads, posters plastered on the backs of comic books, TV commercials—touted the Super NES, Genesis, Game Boy, and Game Gear versions as releasing on

"Mortal Monday," September 13, 1993. Fergus McGovern, the boss over at Probe, was interested in Sega's handheld. Game Gear's hardware was similar to Master System's, making a port relatively simple. "Later on this new thing called the Game Gear came out, and he wanted a quote for how much it would cost to put on there," Burkhill remembered of McGovern. "I gave him quite a high sum and ported it in a week. I got one over on him, there."

Like the Game Boy adaptation, *Mortal Kombat* for Master System and Game Gear catered to the lowest common denominator of home platforms. Artwork for all seven fighters from the arcade game wouldn't fit on cartridges for the 8-bit machines, so the higher-ups at Probe made cuts. Kano, the mercenary who ripped out opponents' still-beating hearts, got the axe on Master System and Game Gear. Johnny Cage, the flamboyant movie star whose signature move was performing a split and punching his opponents in their most sensitive area, was removed from Game Boy.

Under contract, Burkhill worked from home. An engineer at Probe extracted *Mortal Kombat*'s artwork from an arcade cabinet and sent all the backgrounds to Lee Ames, the artist at Probe assigned to the project. Ames downsized the number of arenas from six down to two for Sega's 8-bit platforms, leaving Burkhill with The Pit and Goro's Lair. The Pit fatality, knocking defeated opponents into the spikes below, was removed, as was some of the macabre décor of the cave.

Burkhill pruned diligently, removing frames of animation to maximize efficiency and cartridge space. "That was the first game I'd written using machine code on a PC," he said. "I used machine code [assembly] to do everything back then. I hadn't heard of this new language called C. I wrote my own compression algorithm."

Without source code to work from, Burkhill wrote *Mortal Kombat*'s logic from scratch. Computer-controlled fighters were simple to fight as a result, but the full-color backgrounds, fighters, and blood—enabled via a cheat code—elevated the Master System and Game Gear versions above the Game Boy port. There was only one sticking point. "The only problem with that game was the low frame rate," Burkhill admitted.

The lower framerate was due to the large size of character sprites. They were gigantic, especially on Game Gear, but he believed the tradeoff was worth it. Larger sprites resulted in a high level of detail—despite the loss of animation frames—uncommon on Sega's 8-bit systems. Unfortunately, the lower frame rate made the game floaty in execution. "Ed Boon, one of the originators of that game, was always complaining to me about the slow frame rate," continued Burkhill. "I think in retrospect, making the characters big so they would look good was nice, but to get the game to play better, we should have made them a bit smaller."

Technical hiccups aside, *Mortal Kombat* sold well on Game Gear, leading Probe to contract Burkhill to adapt home versions of

Mortal Kombat II. "I was begging to work on the 16-bit version," he said. Probe had a pecking order. Paul Carruthers had adapted *Mortal Kombat* to Genesis and had done an excellent job, making him the primo choice, but he'd chosen to move on to other projects. David Leitch was next in line for the Genesis version. That left Burkhill to convert *MKII* to Game Gear. "David Leitch and Paul Carruthers got paid a lot more than me, probably ten times as much," he said.

Burkhill had his code from the first game, so developing the sequel was a matter of substituting artwork. As before, cuts had to be made. Probe winnowed *MKII*'s roster from twelve to eight, leaving behind fan favorites like Baraka and Kung Lao. The two arenas, The Pit II and The Tomb, were as detailed as the Master System and Game Gear could afford to make them, but Burkhill managed to carry over The Tomb's fatality, punching an opponent onto spikes jutting down from the ceiling like stalactites.

MKII played identically to the first game on Master System and Game Gear: large, detailed sprites in exchange for a lower frame rate that was good enough for low-end hardware.

"It was pretty exciting. There was quite a bit of advertising on TV when it came out. But for me, it was ultimately just a job. I did what I was paid to do. It was still cool to be working on it."

Back-to-back conversions of fighting games for handheld platforms prepared Burkhill for the two projects that would simultaneously represent the highest high and lowest low of his career. After wrapping up a few additional products, he received a call from Cameron Sheppard, a friend and the Probe contractor who had converted *MKII* to the Game Boy. Sheppard had gone on to found a development studio, Crawfish Interactive, and pitched Burkhill on an enticing project, porting *Street Fighter Alpha* to Nintendo's Game Boy Color. Burkhill agreed.

***

AFTER THREE YEARS and five updates to *Street Fighter II*, Capcom was ready to move forward—and, in a way, backward.

Instead of announcing *Street Fighter III*, Capcom put designers on *Street Fighter Alpha*, a prequel chronologically set between *Street Fighter* and *SFII*. Its placement on *SF*'s timeline opened the door for a roster stacked with competitors from the first game and its world-renowned sequel. Fan favorites such as Ryu, Sagat, Chun Li, and Ken were present, as was Charlie, an army buddy of Guile's. *SFI* alumni Adon and Gen, a Muay Thai pupil who trained under Sagat and an ancient master of Chinese martial arts, respectively, joined the fray, as did Sodom, a powerfully built "Japanophile" (a foreigner obsessed with all things Japan) who fought with sais the size of katana blades and wore a mask to hide his identity, and Birdie, another hulking world warrior sporting steel-toed boots and a canary-yellow mohawk. Lastly, the pink-*gi*-wearing Dan fought similarly to Ryu and Ken, but his special moves were weaker and goofier, such as fireballs that dissipated almost immediately after leaving his hand. Dan's haplessness was by design: Capcom's designers created him to mock rival developer SNK's *Art of Fighting* franchise, which they considered a flagrant and uninspired rip-off of *Street Fighter II*.

Arcade (left), Game Boy Color.

Mechanically, *SF Alpha* was a huge evolution over *SFII*. Players still controlled characters by manipulating an eight-way joystick and six buttons split between punches and kicks, but attacks could be blocked in midair, more moves could be chained together to create longer and more impressive combos, and an upgraded power bar imported from *Super Street Fighter II Turbo* could be used to unleash powerful attacks that dealt huge damage.

Street Fighter Alpha hit arcades in 1995. Home versions were released for the Sony PlayStation and Sega Saturn, and the sophisticated hardware in both consoles turned out arcade-perfect ports. Carrying over the game's trappings to Game Boy Color was a thornier process. "My previous game had been done on a Saturn, so I thought going back to this very slow, tiny handheld was a backwards step," said Burkhill.

Alpha's deep mechanics and beautiful visual direction, taken from recent Capcom one-on-one fighters *Darkstalkers* and *X-Men: Children of the Atom*, would not translate well to the Game Boy Color. Burkhill harbored doubts about the project until he sat down to read through the arcade game's code. "I noticed that the Capcom had made everything very simple," he explained. "They forced coders to follow certain policies, which I could replicate. All these processes were using the same sort of structures, and I could replicate that on the system's Z80-based CPU."

Better still, Burkhill had two powerful tools at his disposal. The first was Nintendo's official development kit for Game Boy Color. The second was No$gmb, an emulator that ran ROMs for virtually any game released on Nintendo's family of handhelds. Not only could it play software, it included tools for programmers such as a debugger with a slick user interface, breakpoints that halted code if certain conditions were met, and warning messages that alerted coders to routines that could be inefficient or unstable.

Burkhill couldn't always make heads or tails of what the arcade's code was doing, but he didn't have to. Performing a one-to-one conversion, he replicated Capcom's programming, done in C, into assembly that could be processed by the Game Boy Color's Z80 processor. The conversion took longer, but came with several benefits. "It was quite different from *Mortal Kombat*, which I had to write the AI and movement code for myself. It was quite a rush, actually, when you'd get it to work and see it playing exactly the same as the arcade machine."

Not every component of *SF Alpha* could be recreated by translating Capcom's code. For one, multiplayer was out. There was no room on the cart for a mode where players could link their Game Boy Colors and go head-to-head. The larger obstacle was *Street Fighter*'s control setup. An eight-way joystick and six buttons had become synonymous with the franchise. Expert players grasped nuances such as throwing a fireball with a hard punch, which propelled it across the screen faster than if they'd pressed medium or light punch. The Game Boy Color had two buttons, and Burkhill had to cram all six basic attacks plus special moves into them.

His solution presented the best possible outcome. Tapping A or B performed a fast strike, while holding a button longer executed slower, harder-hitting attacks. Diagonal inputs were stripped out so moves could be entered quicker and more accurately. For instance, the maneuver to cast a fireball with Ryu became down-forward-punch instead of down-down/forward-forward-punch. "It wasn't based on the Capcom code. I just muddled through as best I could.

We eventually got to something which the testers said was acceptable," Burkhill recalled.

Street Fighter Alpha's graphics were in the capable hands of Kevin McMahon, one of Crawfish's best artists. McMahon reproduced startlingly detailed arenas that evoked rather than replicated their arcade counterparts, an impressive accomplishment considering the gulf between the arcade's hardware and the handheld's. Characters were less detailed in some ways, such as nondescript faces, but their animations were instantly recognizable and, despite being truncated to reduce frames, astonishingly fluid.

Street Fighter Alpha released for Game Boy Color in 2000. It didn't score as highly as ports on better hardware, but Crawfish and Capcom expected that. Their goal had been to develop an above-average conversion for players who wanted to throw fireballs on the go. "It was a very laidback project. I don't remember being stressed out about it," Burkhill said.

Besides the handheld's hardware, one impediment to *Street Fighter Alpha* on Game Boy Color was the size of the cartridge. "Back then it cost a lot of money to make these cartridges," Burkhill said. "Sega and Nintendo would charge a lot to their customers, so we'd get these ridiculously small cartridges, which compromised everything, really. That was a big consideration on *Street Fighter Alpha 3*. That's what caused it to be such a nightmare."

Part II: "The Best Thing I Ever Did"

RATHER THAN PUMP out updates for *Street Fighter Alpha*, Capcom turned out numbered sequels in record time. Released in 1996, *Street Fighter Alpha 2* retained the art style and mechanics of the first game while adding more characters and a custom-combo system that consumed a portion of the power meter to pull off a flurry of punches, kicks, and special moves. *Street Fighter Alpha 3* was widely considered the deepest *SF* game upon its release in 1998. Based on the NAOMI arcade hardware Sega designed in conjunction with its forthcoming Dreamcast console, *SF Alpha 3* boasted crisp, flowing animations, backgrounds rich with color and detail, and a walloping twenty-eight characters.

Ports to consoles such as PlayStation and Saturn were a given, but Capcom had its eye on the handheld market as well. Nintendo's Game Boy Advance, the successor to the aging Color device, sported a higher resolution, the ability to display 32,000 colors at once, and a 16.78 megahertz processor, putting the handheld nearly on par with the Super Nintendo and representing an evolutionary leap forward in the portable market. Crawfish was ready to take advantage. Studio founder Cameron Sheppard met with Capcom executives to discuss bringing *Street Fighter Alpha 3* to the GBA. Impressed with Crawfish's work on *Street Fighter Alpha* for the Color, Capcom agreed.

Sheppard knew just the programmer for the conversion. "I was the logical choice, as I'd done the previous Capcom game," said Keith Burkhill.

Arcade (left), Game Boy Advance.

Normally, Crawfish's developers juggled multiple projects to meet overlapping deadlines. Burkhill, who worked on nothing but *Alpha 3*, was the exception. Game Boy Advance was set for a fall 2001 release, and Crawfish and Capcom wanted *Alpha 3* on shelves day and date with the portable to capitalize on sales. Sheppard paired him with the same artists who had worked alongside Burkhill on *SF Alpha*, figuring that the small team could turn out gold once again. Burkhill had grown into a seasoned coder, and something of an expert on converting fighting games to handhelds. *Alpha 3*'s lead artist, Kevin McMahon, was a passionate *SF* player, and had even put together the mock screenshots for *Alpha 3* that had sold Capcom on signing Crawfish to the job.

Almost right away, however, Burkhill hit a speed bump. "Why can't we have a sixteen-megabyte cartridge?" Burkhill asked Sheppard on several occasions. He knew the answer as well the first time he asked as he did the last time. “Capcom didn't want to pay Nintendo all the money for bigger cartridges, even though they would have recouped it because the game was going to be successful,” Burkhill remembered.

Game Boy Advance cartridges could hold up to 256 megabytes of data, significantly more data than Game Boy or Game Boy Color carts, and roughly one-third the capacity of a CD-ROM. With a bigger ROM, he could produce an arcade-perfect port. The only obstacle would be the GBA’s four buttons, although they would map the arcade game’s six buttons much better than the Color’s two.

Sheppard wouldn’t budge—not because he didn’t want to, but because he couldn’t. According to Burkhill, Crawfish had promised Capcom they’d make the port work in eight megabytes. “I thought that with sixteen megabytes I could have squeezed everything in there, but eight megabytes was just a nightmare,” Burkhill said.

Game Boy Advance.

Burkhill wielded his coding skills like a machete. Stages were removed. Voice samples were deleted or downgraded. World Tour, a mode added to the PlayStation port that let players spec out fighters as they defeated opponents, was slated to be included in the GBA version, but was cut to make space for high-priority features. “They were really pissed off that we hadn't squeezed that into the eight-megabyte cart,” he said of Capcom.

Besides several cuts and downgrades, Burkhill managed to submit a robust version of *SF Alpha 3* to Capcom. All characters from the arcade game were accounted for, as were four new characters plucked from *Capcom vs. SNK 2*, a mashup of the *Street Fighter* and *Art of Fighting* franchises. Sprites had been trimmed, but animations remained smooth, and the four-button controls were more than adequate.

Capcom responded with pages upon pages of bug reports, all in Japanese and in need of translation, and most of which weren't glitches or errors, but complaints that this or that feature was missing and must be included. Rather than push back and help Capcom understand the reality of their constraints, Crawfish's managers tasked *Alpha 3*'s leads to address the issues. Burkhill threw up his hands: The issues couldn't be addressed unless the ROM size was increased, which Capcom and Crawfish refused to do.

Burkhill kept working. In lieu of voice samples that had to be dropped, existing samples were tweaked. Sakura, a teenage martial arts student determined to follow in Ryu's footsteps, shouted when she threw her fireball, but the shout was a higher-pitched version of Ken's—Ryu's rival—battle cry. Other problems came to light as the project dragged on. Crawfish management believed that one of Capcom's internal teams was sandbagging their port out of envy that an outside studio had been given *Alpha 3*.

"They made things as difficult for us as possible," recalled Burkhill. "They wouldn't give us their tools. I had to develop all my own tools to create the AI for these new characters they wanted to put in. The main problem was memory, but I also had to develop this AI and write a bunch of tools."

He also wrote custom software to extract graphical data from a *Street Fighter 3* arcade board when Capcom refused to hand over source materials. Characters, backgrounds—everything required its own special tool. "Every process was slightly different," he continued. "A tool to extract backgrounds and store them in such and such a way; the sprites of the fighters were stored with all their offsets encoded in the art, so the full-size sprites had to be scaled with Photoshop, supplied them to me, and I needed a tool to extract the data from there."

Street Fighter Alpha 3 languished in its beta phase. Every time Crawfish solved bugs, Capcom came back with more, with most related to missing content. When the Game Boy Advance's fall 2001 launch came and went, executives from Capcom summoned Cameron Sheppard and Mike Merren, the director of development at Crawfish, to their offices, where they were chastised and informed their royalties would be cancelled for missing the promised deadline.

Crawfish was battling internal problems as well. While Burkhill and another programmer, brought on to write compression algorithms, waded through *Street Fighter Alpha 3*, the rest of the company's developers were spread thinly over multiple projects that were falling behind. Management had signed too many contracts without enough resources to go around.

Burkhill caught most of the flak. He was *SF Alpha 3*'s lead programmer. Making the game work was his responsibility, never mind that he wasn't the one who had made impossible promises to the publisher.

Sheppard, too, was stressed to the max. Barring a miracle, Crawfish was going to sink.

***

STREET FIGHTER ALPHA 3 for Game Boy Advance limped into retail in 2002. From there, it soared.

Critics were amazed at the portable title's graphical detail, smooth animations, and deep gameplay. Sure, some stages had been axed, but thirteen survived, and every character from the arcade—and then some—was on deck. The game sold well, but Crawfish received no royalties.

Problems continued to mount. Not only had *Alpha 3* been a zero-sum game for Crawfish, Cameron Sheppard had struggled to sign new contracts through late 2001 into early 2002. The Game Boy Advance was a new platform, and as with every new platform, publishers tended to hold off on contracting developers to make games until they'd had time to monitor how the system performed at retail.

Desperate, Sheppard negotiated an acquisition offer from a publisher in late 2002. When the deal fell through, Crawfish fell with it. Much of the blame was piled atop Keith Burkhill's shoulders. "Going over by a year finished Crawfish, and it pretty much finished me as well. That's the last decent project I did, really. Since then it's been low-status, low-paying jobs. A lot of people wouldn't talk to me after that."

Burkhill suffered personal losses as well. By his account, Cameron Sheppard refused to work with him again. That caused a cascade effect, with Probe head Fergus McGovern, a friend of Sheppard's, swearing off Burkhill as well. Within months, he had become persona non grata in the games industry. "A lot of people must've thought I'd lost a step and thought they couldn't trust me with projects."

Burkhill still works as a programmer, though he prefers not to discuss particulars of his job. Thirteen years later, looking back on *Street Fighter Alpha 3* twists the knife in his heart.

"It's still the best thing I ever did," he stated.

Chapter 16: San Francisco Rush 2049

Part I: Crossing the "T"

SAN FRANCISCO'S STREETS were not made for driving.

One block of Lombard Street is a steep, zig-zagging stretch of hairpin turns that attracts over two million tourists every year, all eager to pick their way down the "world's crookedest street." Stretching from New York to the San Francisco Bay Area and serving approximately 300,000 vehicles every day, I-80 is one of the busiest highways in the United States, but the most highly trafficked stretch is found in San Francisco's Eastshore Freeway. TRIP, a transportation group based in Washington, D.C., published a report in August 2018 that granted San Francisco the dubious honor of hosting the worst roads in the United States: eighty-seven percent of its major roads and highways are in "poor or mediocre condition," and motorists pay an average of $1,049 in repair costs every year.

Driving conditions weren't much better in the Bay Area back in the mid-nineties when developers from Atari Games chose San Francisco as the setting for their upcoming racer. The idea was quickly revised. Atari's team wanted players to be able to reach speeds of 150 miles per hour or more, something not even the fantasy of arcade racing games could make plausible in the Bay Area, so they exercised creative license and created a fantastical version of the city for *San Francisco Rush*.

Rush sped into arcades on Christmas Eve of 1996. The game let players race eight tricked-out cars across three tracks. Players could hit speeds up to 160 miles per hour and shoot off ramps to fly through the air. Atari capitalized on the popularity of *San Francisco Rush* by contracting a development team to convert it for the Nintendo 64 and PlayStation. Ed Logg, veteran creator of arcade hits such as *Gauntlet* and Tengen's ill-fated NES port of *Tetris*, was assigned to the project as a programmer. "I had just completed *Wayne Gretzky's 3D Hockey* for the N64, so I knew the N64 very well. I was a contract employee at the time for Tengen, and they asked about porting the coin-operated *SF Rush* for the N64."

Logg and the developers carried over the arcade version's three tracks and added five more: three tracks, bringing the game's normal racing circuit up to six, plus two secret courses. Players can even switch things up by racing through mirrored and reverse layouts of each course.

Arcade (left), Nintendo 64.

San Francisco Rush 2049, the third game, was set in a futuristic San Francisco. Players half-drove, half-flew space-age vehicles in races. Wings were used to adjust trajectory while in midair, and up to eight players could sit in cockpits kitted out with wheels, pedals, gear shifts, and a keypad that created and stored passwords for each player.

When Midway, which had purchased Atari Games in 1996, prepared to bring *Rush 2049* to the Nintendo 64 and Sega Dreamcast, Logg once again served as a programmer. Both versions were ported at the same time, and had unique goals from the arcade material. “For example, I did not have to worry about getting the player the right amount of time for his quarters, but instead had to add enough to make them buy the cartridge in the first place,” said Logg.

Little mystique surrounded Nintendo’s 64-bit hardware as it had with Sony’s 32-bit PlayStation, though experiences varied from studio to studio. Developers who wrote games for the N64 reported that the process just kind of worked as if by magic. The hardware was zippy and flexible, and even shoddy work tended to run and play better on Nintendo 64 than on PlayStation. Still, the road to learning and acting on a new system’s features could be bumpy. Late Nintendo president Satoru Iwata got his start as a programmer, and commiserated with developers who had to wrestle with learning how to render 3D graphics while juggling the hardware’s limitations.

The biggest limitation, besides a debugging program that could be as glitchy as the software it was supposed to be helping programmers patch up, was the fact that software was stored on a cartridge. Nintendo had skipped compact discs as a storage medium for the console, a decision that caused an outcry among developers and consumers. CDs were cheaper to mass produce and held exponentially more data than cartridges. Consequently, many developers swore off the N64 and stuck to PlayStation. Nintendo explained its decision to develop N64 games on cartridges instead of CDs, pointing to lengthy loading times on discs compared to near-instantaneous loading from ROM chips as one of the biggest factors.

Another restriction was the number of polygons that could be drawn on the screen at one time. *San Francisco Rush 2049*'s arcade hardware ran on a 3Dfx Voodoo3 graphics card capable of drawing objects such as trees, signs, and roadways far in the distance to avoid pop-in, the sudden appearance of objects on the horizon. While the N64's Reality Coprocessor (RCP)—made by Silicon Graphics specifically for the Nintendo 64—couldn't match the level of detail of *Rush 2049*'s Voodoo3 card, it pumped out polygons fast enough to replicate the arcade's sense of speed. It couldn't draw as far ahead as the Voodoo3, however, not without sacrificing critical frames per second and slowing down the game. "I had to create a system that would only allow certain sections of track to be processed until it came time to be needed," Logg explained. "The N64 had a problem with 'crossing-the-T,' as I would call it."

A vertex is a point on a geometric shape where two or more lines, curves, or edges meet. Crossing the T refers to the vertex of one polygon cutting into another. This occurred when the view changed in *Rush 2049* on the N64: A vertex would pull away from the edge, causing a tear that allowed background colors to seep through. "I could not work around this without redoing all the track art so we did not fix it," Logg said.

Another way Logg compensated was by devising a fog system that cloaked areas still in the process of being rendered. "This was San Francisco, which I thought added something to the realism," Logg said of the overcast city. "Of course adding the fog helps this too because if there was pop-in you would not notice it. There were some areas where it could not be helped so I would not say I eliminated it completely."

Issues such as crossing the T and fog that hid the wizard frantically assembling courses behind the curtain prevented the N64 port of *San Francisco Rush 2049* from reaching arcade perfection. The Dreamcast, Sega's latest—and ultimately final—game console, suffered no such limitations.

Part II: Beyond Perfection

IF THE CONSOLE war between Nintendo and Sega could be thought of as Mario and Sonic going fifteen rounds, the attitudinal hedgehog had grown winded in the middle of the third.

Sega threw its hat into the ring of game consoles with the Master System, an 8-bit machine that was popular in Europe but failed to gain traction in the United States. The Japanese company's second console was a different story: By the time the Sega Genesis—known as the Mega Drive outside the U.S.—ceased production, it had sold 30.75 million units worldwide. Nintendo ultimately won the 16-bit console war by putting 49.1 million Super Nintendos in homes. But what mattered to Sega, and to retailers and consumers, was that a viable challenger had emerged to loosen Nintendo's chokehold on the industry.

Sega's third console, the Saturn, stumbled out of the gate. On May 11, 1995, Sega of America president Tom Kalinske took the stage during the first-ever E3 trade show and dropped a bomb: The previous announcement that Sega would launch the Saturn that September was a smokescreen to obscure its true release date—right then, immediately, due to "high consumer demand." Sure enough, 30,000 Saturn consoles materialized on store shelves at Toys R Us and other retailers for $399. The first of many problems the Saturn encountered was distribution. Sega had failed to ramp up production to meet the demand that greeted its surprise announcement; as a result, retailers who tried to order it received only a few consoles, if any, and consumers went store to store only to leave emptyhanded. Even worse for Sega, retailers caught off-guard by the announcement and unable to order stock grew chilly toward the company.

Despite a few setbacks, the Saturn seemed primed to succeed. It was a 32-bit system that played games on CD-ROM, which kept the price of software reasonable. Developers from Sega's arcade division were assigned to develop games for the Saturn, and a nearly one-to-one "arcade perfect" port of *Virtua Fighter*, Sega's polygonal challenger to *Street Fighter II* and *Mortal Kombat*, shipped alongside the console. Before Sega could gain a foothold in the 32-bit space, Sony disrupted the industry with the PlayStation, a machine priced $100 cheaper than the Saturn. PlayStation received a warm welcome from retailers due to the oft-delayed debut of Nintendo's 64-bit console, and because of the damage Sega had done to its reputation by releasing the poorly supported Sega CD and 32X add-ons for the Genesis, and for springing the Saturn on retailers before its manufacturing was ready to meet their demand. Sony put out a fantastic arcade port of Namco's *Ridge Racer*, built from the ground up to take advantage of PlayStation's hardware. Critics were less favorable toward Sega's conversion of *Daytona USA* on the Saturn, preferring the graphics, controls, and audio of *Ridge Racer*.

Sony's sudden popularity troubled Sega executives. The Saturn was beloved among players for its arcade ports, but arcades were in trouble. Cutting-edge machines like PlayStation and Saturn were demonstrably on par or superior to arcade hardware, giving players less reason to leave the house to play video games or grow excited over home versions of arcade games they'd never bothered to play.

Focusing on that dwindling audience, Sega split into two teams to develop its next console. IBM engineer Tatsuo Yamamoto spearheaded the team working on the American hardware, codenamed Black Belt and equipped with 3Dfx's Voodoo graphics tech. Back in Japan, Genesis designer Hideki Sato engineered White Belt—later named Katana—using NEC's PowerVR graphics chip. The American project came undone when Katana was chosen as the console to develop moving forward, and 3Dfx sued for breach of contract.

Arcade perfection was a focal point for the console that became the Dreamcast. Sega engineered NAOMI, or New Arcade Operation Machine Idea, a board outfitted with the Dreamcast's technology but with significantly more RAM and processing power for arcade games. The Dreamcast's specs were designed to handle NAOMI-based coin-op games: a 128-bit, 200 megahertz processor, 16 megabytes of system RAM and eight megabytes of video RAM, and a color palette of 16.7 million bolstered by being able to crunch three million polygons every second.

Ports of arcade games had moved beyond their source material years ago in terms of gameplay. Konami's *Contra* run-and-gunner on NES featured tighter controls and better pacing than the coin-op original. *Teenage Mutant Ninja Turtles IV: Turtles in Time* on Super NES added a new boss fight that, while not a major update, forced players to master fighting techniques beyond mashing the attack button, namely stunning Foot Soldiers and throwing them at the screen. *Ninja Gaiden* was a bland, forgettable hand-to-hand brawler in arcades, but on the NES, it added tough platforming and more fluid movement that made the game much more difficult yet deeply increasing satisfaction in players able to master it.

Those and other games share one thing in common: While they improved upon the gameplay systems of their respective coin-op forebearers, arcades had always been graphically superior to home systems. When the Dreamcast launched on September 9, 1999, it marked the first time a home console could not only deliver arcade perfection, but go beyond it. Namco's *Soul Calibur*, a 3D fighter and a sequel to *Soul Edge*, was rebuilt from the ground up for the console. Not only was a new game mode added, but animations were smoother and crisper, characters were more defined with fewer sharp edges, the roster was doubled from ten to twenty, and arenas boasted more geometry, giving them a more three-dimensional look than the arcade's blend of polygons and 2D backgrounds.

"Simply put—*Soul Calibur* was perhaps the first port of an arcade game to greatly outshine the original release," wrote John Linneman, expert hardware editor at Eurogamer's Digital Foundry website. "The age of arcade perfect had come to an end—we were in an era beyond."

***

ED LOGG AND the *San Francisco Rush 2049* team at Midway were prepared to take the Dreamcast port into the next era of console games as well. "I liked it better than the N64 because the visuals were so much better," Logg said of Sega's hardware. "I found the colors on the Dreamcast were more vibrant, which is why I like the Dreamcast version of *Rush 2049* so much more."

Arcade (left), Dreamcast.

Like all consoles, Dreamcast had its quirks and special features. While other systems had supported modems and online networks in the past, such as the XBAND that let consumers play certain Super NES and Genesis titles online, Dreamcast was the first console to include a modem built into the machine, as well as an online network for multiplayer games. Sega also required developers to write routines in code designed to prevent pirates from bootlegging discs. "I remember this because I added a feature that would detect and try to prevent [pirating]," Logg said.

Despite what Sega may have considered its best efforts, piracy ran rampant on the Dreamcast. When Logg visited his son in Seattle sometime later, his son's roommate proudly showed him a bootleg of *San Francisco Rush 2049*. "He said it was the hardest game he had been able to hack," Logg remembered. "I did not have the heart to tell him if he saved any high scores, there was a bit I set that would tell if this came from a hacked disc. We never did look through the database to see how many hacked high scores there were."

Like its N64 counterpart, *San Francisco Rush 2049* for Dreamcast packed in every feature from the arcade, as well as extra tracks, vehicles, and ways to play. Both ports featured battle arenas that were as popular in some college dorm rooms as the game's default racing options. *Rush 2049*'s battle mode was pitched by an executive from Midway's Chicago office who had come to check in on the port's progress. He mentioned, just thinking out loud, an idea he'd had where, instead of racing, players sped around large areas gathering weapons and hunting each other down, like deathmatch in *Doom*, but with cars instead of flesh-and-blood marines.

Logg and the team loved the idea. They went even further by including a stunt mode where players could sharpen their skills before challenging other players. "By the end of the project, we felt the battle mode was the most innovative while the driving gameplay was good, but had been done before," said Logg.

Word got back to Logg's team that their colleagues at Midway's San Diego office enjoyed battle mode so much, they were holding daily tournaments during lunch. Some of those developers paid Logg and the others a visit at their studio in Milpitas, California. They exchanged courtesies before holding a contest: two developers from Midway San Diego, two from the Milpitas office, to decide which team was the best. "Todd Papy, an artist for *Rush 2049* and avid game player, and someone else played their two hotshots. Of course we slaughtered them every time," Logg remembered.

***

SAN FRANCISCO RUSH 2049 parked on Sega Dreamcast, Nintendo 64, and Game Boy Color in early September 2000, just shy of Dreamcast's one-year birthday. Critics from leading outlets such as IGN and GameSpot gave the Nintendo 64 port one thumb-up. Unsurprisingly, the Dreamcast got two. "The Dreamcast version is hands-down the best version available—even killing the arcade version in looks, playability, and sheer lasting play. Every mode in this game is also in four-player split-screen mode—and not a bit of fun is lost in the reduced screen [size]," wrote an editor from IGN, who awarded the game a 9 out of 10 score.

For Ed Logg, who got his start developing games for coin-op hardware before seeing less sophisticated facsimiles make their way to home platforms, the fact that consoles seemed on the verge of rendering arcades obsolete was bittersweet.

"This is one of those good news bad news situations. Arcades were a place to come and see your friends and play games that you could not play at home. With the introduction of the PC and PC game market, the arcades lost some of the social status. The Internet also reduced the need to go to a place to play with and against your friends. As the consoles got better the arcades lost their basic, sole purpose in my humble opinion. Of course the consoles are so realistic now and very impressive. It is hard to imagine competing with them."

Epilogue: One last Quarter

ARCADE PERFECT. ONE to one. Mirror match.

If game development is a science—and it is, as much if not more so than game design is an art—arcade perfection is a problem we can consider solved.

Arcades are on the brink of death, if not dead already. But that's okay, because several times a year, publishers like Capcom, Konami, and Digital Eclipse grace us with anthologies of arcade games from yesteryear, a phrase I'm sorry to tell you is, in this context, redundant.

But it's not the same, is it? All these re-releases are fantastic, and publishers such as Digital Eclipse have found ways of enhancing those experiences far beyond what fifty cents or a buck got us twenty-plus years ago.

What I mean is, playing with a controller or a keyboard isn't the same. It never has been. In fact, playing *Street Fighter II* in front of a television or at my desk is more convenient, yes, even comfortable. But it's not the same thing, as Tastemakers president Scott Bachrach knew.

Even manufacturers of arcade cabinets in all shapes and sizes—tabletops, uprights, wall-mounted fixtures, portables—admit that they aren't able to capture the exact look, feel, and experience of playing coin-op games. And how could they? The reason brands like Arcade1Up, New Wave Toys, and MyArcade exist is because they offer affordable alternatives than full-size machines which can't be moved without a dolly.

I'll go one step further: You could track down and buy every arcade cabinet that ever meant anything to you, and you'd still fall short of the white whale you're chasing. Maybe you don't even know you're chasing it. That white whale is a hot commodity at flea markets, trade shows, and on YouTube. The worst part is, it's intangible. It's an idea, a moment in time more than a cabinet or a set of joysticks and buttons.

I'm talking, of course, about nostalgia.

Think back to the first time you played an arcade game. That first time occurred when you were young—or at least younger—and life was simple. For me, that discovery took place when I was in elementary school.

Back then, I didn't have a care in the world. No money, but no bills. No freedom, but I had people to make decisions for me.

Back then, I hadn't gone through rough patches in my marriage.

Back then, I hadn't had to go to my mom, hat in hand, and ask to borrow money—much more than a few quarters—because I'd been laid off again, and writing jobs in 2008 and '09 were scarce, and rent was coming due.

Back then, I still had my dad. Every Friday or Saturday night, he'd take the family to the mall and give my little brother and me money for the "game room," as it was called in the House of Dad. Then, a just before I turned twenty, he died, and I never got to know him as one adult to another.

Maybe you were a little older than I was when you discovered arcades. Maybe you were a teenager with a job, like a paper route, or a little older and flipping burgers or stocking shelves. But even if you were an adult with a mortgage, a spouse with personal and financial obligations to your partner and/or children, a job you loved or hated or something in between, arcade games were still magical.

Why?

Because you could only find them in arcades.

During the 1970s and eighties, busybodies painted arcades as dens of iniquity. They had to blame something for everything wrong in the world. The more things change, and all that.

Arcades were magical. Stepping out of a tiled mall corridor and into the dimly lit, cavernous space aglow with flashing screens and the air alive with beeps and trills and digitized voices, was like taking that first step out of the wardrobe and into the soft, untouched beauty of Narnia, or allowing Calypso to waylay you on the island of Ogygia. Except instead of Turkish delight or soul-achingly beautiful meadows of violets and parsley, there were video games.

Video games, everywhere you looked. Wall to wall. So many there was no room for anything else. You could play games at home, but home wasn't as magical. Home was where homework waited, or your sister was hogging the TV, or your parents were fighting. Arcades existed outside of time, chambers holding nothing and no one but fun.

Places where you waited while your mom shopped for adult things that would consume your life when you were older.

Places where you can remember your dad and Friday nights out with the family.

That's why I miss arcades, and why I miss conversions that differed in ways great and small.

Because when conversions were a thing in my life, responsibility, pain, and loss were not.

Because conversions were the same, but different, opening my eyes to the idea that day to day, minute to minute, second to second, nothing in life would ever be exactly the same, but that was okay. Different can be synonymous with intriguing, alluring, and exciting, not scary, or disappointing, or bad, or wrong. Different can be better.

Or just different. And that's okay, too.

-David L. Craddock

5 July 2019

Attract Mode: Bonus Interviews

IT NEVER FAILS.

I map out one of these books. I send out emails, Facebook messages, tweets, LinkedIn requests, ravens, and smoke signals to coordinate interviews with dozens of people. Those dozens of people and I talk for dozens of hours. Our conversations are wonderful and insightful, spanning dozens of topics—not all of which, unfortunately, have a place in the story I'm looking to tell.

Rather than leave that material on the cutting-room floor, I thought an "attract mode" for a book about arcade games and their conversions was fitting. In this section, you'll get to read a smattering of my favorite conversations, lightly edited for clarity. Each conversation delves deeper into subjects such as life in the games industry, development woes and triumphs, and, in some instances, topics hardly related to games at all.

Outstanding Ideas: Ed Logg on Asteroids and Gauntlet

IF YOU FED quarters into arcade cabinets during the 1980s, you've probably played at least one of Ed Logg's games. In his time at Atari, he designed classics from *Asteroids* and *Centipede* to *Gauntlet* and, under Atari's controversial Tengen label, coin-op and NES versions of *Tetris*.

Arcades wound down in the mid-nineties, but Ed was just getting started. He stayed ahead of the curve by developing console ports of games such as new installments of *San Francisco Rush 2049* for Midway and left his mark on other hits through compilations such as *Midway Arcade Treasures 2*.

Seven years before I spoke with Ed about his work on *Tetris* for this book, I picked his brain about *Gauntlet* and *Asteroids* for another project. My intent was to include that interview as a bonus chapter. After I decided it didn't fit with the material as well as I'd initially thought, I set it aside. Years later, I deemed it perfect for *Arcade Perfect*.

***

David L. Craddock: What led to your interest in video/computer games?

Ed Logg: I was always doing games. When I first started programming in high school I used games as a means of learning of how to program and to answer questions about the games themselves (the best strategies or what are the odds of….). This carried on to college and my jobs thereafter.

Craddock: What did you do before creating video games?

Logg: I worked at Control Data Corp. (CDC) which was across the street from Atari. Of course I was the one at CDC that did all the games, had the most complete list of printable art, Snoopy calendar programs, complete list of etc. For example I did conversions of the original Adventure and Star Trek between CDC Fortran and the IBM Fortran. So although I was paid to support CDC software and I often did games on the side.

Craddock: How did you receive the opportunity to work at Atari?

Logg: A co-worker had gotten a job at Atari and encouraged me to come over. I do not remember who this was. But I did and as they say the rest was history.

Craddock: What was Atari's culture like when you started?

Logg: I had only one "real" job before Atari and it was dominated by a corporate structure that was out of state. So I only had this job to compare it to. In any case I liked the smaller company atmosphere, although in 1978 Atari was not really a small company anymore. I did not have to go through security every day and Atari was connected to Warner Bros. At the time so I could get LPs at a discount at the company store.

Craddock: You're famous for designing some of the industry's most successful coin-op games. Did you enter Atari as a designer?

Logg: I was hired to program video games. Atari has just recently switched over to using a microprocessor to implement games instead of using just hardware. I worked in a group led by Dave Stubben. This group had two programmers, myself and Mike Albaugh, one engineer, and two techs. My job was to replace Dennis Koble who had moved over to the consumer division. So I got to help release Dennis' game of Avalanche and continue work on his game Dirt Bike.

Now, programming in those days was very interesting. The development system did not have a compiler or any means to save our source code. This was all done on a PDP system and there were two ladies who did all the data entry. We provided a listing or marked up sheets of paper and they made the desired changes to the game code and provided us a listing and a paper tape (as best as I can remember it was paper tape) for us to load into the "black box" development system. This system would allow us to stop and start the program as well as examine memory.

Craddock: How did you receive the opportunity to design *Asteroids* alongside Lyle Rains?

Logg: Lyle called me into his office and said he had an idea for a game. The idea came from a previous game which failed miserably. The previous game had a large asteroid (for lack of a better description). People would shoot this asteroid but nothing would happen because it was just there to provide cover for the other player. In any case Lyle suggested we do a game that allowed the players to shoot these rocks and blow them up.

I am not sure why Lyle suggested this idea to me instead of others in engineering. Lyle was head of engineering at the time I believe so he could have chosen anyone. I had some success by that time with *Super Breakout*, *Video Pinball*, and *4-Player Football,* so maybe he felt I could do the job better than anyone else. There were other projects I worked on that did not make it into production, but that is another story.

Craddock: The idea of floating around in space and shooting rocks to dust seems simple, but it was revolutionary at the time. How did you and Lyle hit on that idea, and *Asteroids*' specific implementation?

Logg: I would certainly give Lyle the credit for idea for the game. However, the meeting I remember was more of a brainstorming session. For example I believe I suggested several ideas like breaking the rocks into smaller and smaller pieces so there would be a strategy other than just shooting wildly. In other words shooting all the big rocks just leaves more objects that could hit you. I also believe I suggested the saucer that would come out and shoot you if you did not shoot some of the rocks in a timely fashion.

Craddock: What were the advantages and disadvantages to designing *Asteroids* as a vector-graphics game?

Logg: This was another idea which I suggested in the meeting with Lyle. I had played *Space War* and I had done some work on the vector hardware we had so I knew the advantages. The most important was the higher resolution, 1024x768 instead of 320x240. I felt we needed the extra resolution to show where the ship was aiming.

Also the color masks on the displays at the time were not good, so a color pixel would be larger and less clear than on a vector screen. The black and white monitor also had a slow phosphor so that the shots and ships left a trail which actually added to the appeal of the game but this was not part of any design.

The only disadvantage was the game was going to be black and white, but being in space, that was not going to be a problem.

Craddock: Was creating *Asteroids* as straightforward as its design appears?

Logg: It was actually very straightforward. There were no difficult or technical issues. Of course there were limitations such as the amount of stuff I could draw and still update the game at 60Hz. The limited RAM also limited the number of asteroids I could draw so you may see some large asteroids go away with a single shot if the screen if full.

There was issue of the spot killer that was interesting. The spot killer was a feature added so that if the game crashed when the beam was on that it did not burn a hole in the phosphor on the screen. Thus I needed to have enough deflection on the screen so the spot killer did not turn off the beam. Therefore I put the copyright on the bottom of the screen and the scores at the top.

However, no one told me how much deflection was actually needed and I found out later this was not quite enough, so on some games the screen would dim if the player ship and the3 remaining asteroids were at the right spots on the screen.

I enjoyed myself during the development. I enjoyed watching the game come to completion. I enjoyed watching others having full play the game and I certainly enjoyed creating Atari's most successful game.

Craddock: As you mentioned, *Asteroids* went on to become Atari's most successful coin-op game. How did you become aware of *Asteroids*' success in those days? Going to an arcade and seeing people crowding the machine?

Logg: I knew early that the game would be popular because those at Atari would ask when I was going home (so they could play the game). Also you come in each morning and see a bunch of new high scores.

But I certainly knew when we field tested the game in the arcades especially after many weeks when the earnings stayed at a high level. I never heard any stories about operators adding larger boxes.

Craddock: Fast forwarding a bit, the home video game market crashed in 1983. How did that affect your work in coin-op games, if at all?

Logg: We had layoffs and it was the first time we had layoffs in the coin-operated division. It was hard to see many coworkers leave. Our market had a serious problem too around that time due to over saturation of games. We were definitely seeing reduced sales.

Craddock: What led to your interest in creating a hack-and-slash arcade game?

Logg: My son had been bugging me for some time about doing a *D&D* game since he enjoyed it so much. I could not figure a way to do it until I saw the game *Dandy*. A coworker had brought the game in and we played it at lunch. This game gave me the idea on how to make a *D&D* game fit into the coin-operated market.

I was working on another game at the time so I had to finish that before I started but more important I had to figure out how to do the game with our existing hardware. We did not have hardware that allowed us to do this game so I asked for a set of features to be added to make this game possible. Unfortunately we were short of engineers at the time and the engineer assigned to the game could not work on it for more than nine months.

By that time I had lost my co-programmer. Fortunately a new engineer, Pat McCarthy, was assigned and he created the hardware necessary to put all those monsters on screen.

Craddock: Strip away the frenetic real-time gameplay and *Gauntlet* had much in common with roguelikes such as *Rogue* and *Moria*: clear dungeons of monsters to level up, survive to reach the next level. Had you played any roguelike-type games before making *Gauntlet*?

I have not heard this term before, nor the games *Rogue* or *Moria*. I certainly played many dungeon games before like *Adventure*.

Craddock: What was *Gauntlet*'s process of generating mazes? Did you consider adding an element of random, or procedural generation to keep arcade players guessing?

Logg: We had a maze editor that allowed anyone in engineering to create mazes. In fact Lyle Rains created many mazes for *Gauntlet* while I was away on sabbatical. So we had a fixed number of mazes and I had an algorithm that would sequence through all the mazes except the first 6 levels I believe. So the only random part of this was the starting point in the set of mazes.

Craddock: Each of the game's four characters had distinctive characteristics, such as the Elf having the fastest movement rate. Did you want one class to have an edge over all the others, or were they meant to be balanced?

Logg: I felt the wizard was most powerful although I could not prove it. Later when the game was released in Japan it was determined that the wizard and warrior could play forever on one quarter as long as no other players joined the game.

Craddock: *Gauntlet* didn't include final bosses or a goal besides survival. Did you worry that players would balk against playing within a video game structure, such as the growing template of ending levels with a boss fight? Or, was there even a "video game structure" at the time?

Logg: There was a considerable amount of discussion about this issue. I had this question come up often. I could not come up with a solution for those players who may have just joined or what to do with the money they have left in the machine. So I took the course of least resistance and did not provide an end to the game or a final boss to defeat.

Craddock: *Gauntlet* was lauded in large part for its fun co-op for up to four players. This was during an era when most multiplayer coin-ops supported two players at most. What led to incorporating play for up to four?

Logg: The fact that it was co-operative play came from the basic fact you had to co-operate to get to the next level and to fight the monsters and generators successfully. I would also create *Dandy* with the credit for 4 players and co-op play.

There another reason that four players were added and that has to do with the coin-operated industry. We could not increase the cost of play at the time because 50 cents was resisted by most players. Of course reducing the time per play was out of the question so the only logical solution was to have more players playing at the same time. Therefore I could earn four times more money with four players playing at the same time over any other game with one player playing at a time.

This was one of the most outstanding ideas for *Gauntlet*. This also proved hard for me to convince marketing that this was going to work. Fortunately the field test results spoke for themselves.

Craddock: The game was undoubtedly popular among friends. Did supporting four players require any extra game balance?

Logg: Unfortunately I did little to tune the game between one- and four-player play. I felt that having more players would increase firepower thus requiring less food so it would somewhat balance out. This proved to be wrong as the players in Japan showed me. So I later created a version of the game that would reduce the food if there was one player playing.

Craddock: *Gauntlet* was also known for its narrator, which both praised and goaded players. What led to the incorporation of the narrator's voice?

I added the voices to mimic the Dungeon Master that would normally be part of any *D&D* game. Many phrases were added to provide comic relief and to provide a little competition to see could eat all the food.

Craddock: Outside of balancing, did you have any strategies in mind for players who were going to enter *Gauntlet*'s dungeons with three friends? Or was the general approach—kill monsters, eat food—more or less the same regardless of how many players were up?

Logg: Each level needs to be learned so that you can expose the generators at the right time. For example shooting in their direction and then scrolling so that the shot hits the generator before it has time to generator a monster is a great strategy. Of course it helps if everyone cooperates.

Craddock: Was there any concern within management or marketing that a cabinet built to support for players would have trouble attracting so many to justify any extra engineering or manufacturing costs?

Logg: This was another major issue that marketing would ask me at any review. They were not convinced although I was. The doubt was dispelled the very first week of our very first field test. The game earned so much and increased the earning of the arcade that it created word of mouth excitement in the industry.

In fact I had to pull the game after the first week because all our competitors were coming to check it out. This is the only time I have ever heard of this happening.

Craddock: *Gauntlet* featured a barebones story, at least in the arcade release. Was this intentional? How important do you view player-controlled storytelling in games versus a more traditional, linear narrative?

Logg: I never felt games needed a story in the coin-operated industry. Coin-operated games needed to be played by those who could take one look at the screen and know what they needed to do. I felt *Gauntlet* met this criterion and added many features such as cooperative play that I did not need to add an explanation as to why you were there or where you were going.

Craddock: What was the most difficult feature to implement in *Gauntlet*?

Logg: The hardest part of this game was getting the hardware done. This alone lead to many of the 5 patents *Gauntlet* was awarded. However, what most people do not know and cannot see if the changes required making the printed circuit board (PCB) for *Gauntlet*.

At the time we only made 2 player PCBs. This made the board too big. So we looked into making a four-layer PCB. This had never been done and it was feared it would not be cost effective but in the end it was. It also required Atari to redo their layout software to allow smaller traces and required changes in manufacturing to auto insert the components in the board.

The four-layer PCB also reduced our emissions to the point I believe where we did not need to put the PCB in a cage. After all this effort Atari would use 4 layer PCBs for all new games.

Craddock: What is your favorite aspect of, or feature in, *Gauntlet*?

Logg: It is always hard to pick one aspect of this game because it had so many new features. However, I always thought the thief was an interesting idea to steal away the power-ups the players gathered during play.

Craddock: Were there any features you wanted to add to *Gauntlet*, but couldn't? What were they, and why couldn't you add them?

Logg: There were many ideas we had and most of them made its way into *Gauntlet II*.

Craddock: Countless players have enjoyed your games over the years. They have their favorites. Where does *Gauntlet* rank in the gameography of properties you've worked on and, in this case, created?

Logg: It was by far the highest earning game I ever made. I had operators thank me. There was one operator in Toronto who said his *Gauntlet* made over $2400 in one week! It also the game that is most responsible with creating so many look-alike games.

Craddock: You were credited for *Gauntlet*'s game design, which later caused problems with *Dandy* creator John Palevich. What is your take on the dispute?

Logg: I did not know anything about problems with *Dandy* or John Palevich. I know Atari was very sensitive and lawsuits so it was not right to speak out about *Dandy*. I do know John Palevich did approach Atari about *Gauntlet* and I heard it was resolved to everyone's satisfaction. Perhaps I am wrong on this account.

I have not heard how John Palevich feels about this nor have I read anything on the subject. And you can see from my answers above I give much of the credit for the idea of *Gauntlet* to *Dandy*.

Craddock: Besides the first game's financial success, what factors led to you designing a second *Gauntlet*?

Logg: There were some ideas I had after *Gauntlet* was released and I thought the additions to *Gauntlet II* were compelling enough to make the game worthwhile, especially the secret levels and the Contest!

I believe we had a sufficient collection of new ideas that the game would add additional appeal. Besides this game was so successful we just had to create a sequel even if nothing more than to add new levels.

Craddock: Was creating a sequel something you wanted to do? Or was it a financial move?

Generally I do not like doing sequels especially in the coin-operated market. I believe *Millipede* was the only one I did and only because I had many ideas which I thought would add to the game play. The only idea I had for *Centipede* which I did not include was the colored area at the bottom of the screen to indicate where you were allowed to move. All the other ideas came later.

In the consumer market sequels are a different matter. I did several sequels for *San Francisco Rush*. The last one, *Rush 2049*, I was very happy with.

Craddock: Many players favor *Gauntlet II* over the first game for the sequel's mechanical improvements. For example, more than one player can control each hero type, a mix of starting positions, and random food and potion placement. Did you want to stick these features in G1 but were unable to do so?

Logg: With *Gauntlet* I wanted to create a *D&D* style of game with different characters. Only when I realized after its release that people have favorite characters they want to play and the best way to handle this was to allow them to select their character.

Craddock: Do you prefer *Gauntlet* or *Gauntlet II*? Why?

Logg: I guess I prefer *Gauntlet II* because I can play the wizard from any position.

Come in and Play: Hanging Out in Paul's Gamerzone

AS I PULLED up to Paul's Gamerzone in Canton, Ohio, a colorful sign caught my eye. It was stippled with pictures of dozens of gaming consoles from Atari to Nintendo 3DS and the Switch, to VR headsets. At the top, in large, bold letters, was a warm invitation: *Come in and Play.*

Nicholas Paul wants you to feel welcome. He is the owner and sole proprietor of Paul's Gamerzone, which he proclaims is the oldest video game lounge in Ohio. I did my homework, and Internet sleuthing seems to back up his claim. Locations such as Old North Arcade, the DK Effect, and Quarter Up have only been around for a few years. The closest is 16-Bit Bar, which opened the doors of its flagship location in Columbus the same year Paul's Gamerzone put controllers in patrons' hands. But there's a difference. 16-Bit, DK Effect, and the rest are arcade-bar combos. You eat, you drink, you drop quarters in coin-op games from *Street Fighter II: Champion Edition* to *Hydro Thunder*.

Paul doesn't charge by the quarter. He doesn't even charge by the hour. For a $10 charge at the door, customers can get their hands on any game in Paul's massive library from the time the Gamerzone opens—around five p.m. Eastern every night—until midnight or later. Along the left wall as I entered, a group of four played *Dark Souls III* on Xbox One. Further back, a large area had been cleared to give players space to flail around playing VR games. A dimly lit corner hosts an Atari VCS/2600. Tables in the center are occupied several times a week for Pokémon and Yu-Gi-Oh collectible card game (CCG) tournaments. Birthday parties, on-the-spur-of-the-moment get-togethers—Paul does it all.

I talked with Paul about his history with games, how his father inspired him to own his own business, his staggeringly extensive work history, and the type of atmosphere he and his associates work to foster within the Gamerzone.

***

David L. Craddock: How long have you played video games?

Nicholas Paul: I've played games since I was two. My very first console was the Sega [Genesis], but the first console I played was the Nintendo. My older brother was a Ninja Turtles fan, so we would play the first *Turtles* [from Konami].

Craddock: I'm still feeling residual stress from playing that damn dam level.

Paul: [laughs] Yeah, it was rough. My brother and I spent a whole vacation trying to get past that level. It was nice because that's how I bonded with my brother. If it wasn't for my brother, I never would've been into video games. His name's Chris. He's seven years older than I am.

Craddock: What made you want to become an entrepreneur, and to open a gaming lounge specifically?

Paul: I was eight years old, and my dad was a business owner. He owned a factory. He put over half a million dollars into it, just a lot of money. My parents were divorced, and I never got to see my dad; he was always working since he was a business owner. I just wanted to hang out with my dad. One night, when I was at his place for the weekend, my dad was really upset and stressed out. I asked him why he was so stressed out, and he said, "We don't have enough employees." His factory was huge. I said, "Well, I'll work for you."

My dad laughed and said, "You're too young." I said, "Dad, let me at least help you. Gimme a try." I did that just so I could hang out with him. So he did, and he kept me on. Between the ages of eight and 14 years old, he was teaching me how to start up a business, how to do taxes, how everything worked. By the time I was 14, he let me become a manager. I'd be there four, five, sometimes six days a week. Right after school, I'd make sure I did all my homework, did chores around my mom's house, and then go to my dad's. In my eyes, this was a reason to go see my dad. I felt good because I was helping him.

But what I didn't know was my dad was paying me for the work. He saw me as an employee, because I was doing what all the other employees were doing. He paid me and everything. I was a manager of 25 people in my section. But my true love was gaming. Whenever I had time, I'd be playing on my Game Boy Color. When Pokémon came out, I was huge into that.

I was an only child on my mom's side, so after my parents divorced, I didn't have anyone to play with. I said, "It'd be cool if I made something like this." I had this idea when I was nine or 10, right around there, because my dad was teaching me how to start a business. When I was 14, I quit working at the factory because my dad started a landscaping business. The factory was up and going, but my dad was always looking to start businesses. I did that from 14 to 16.

Then I told my dad, "It's nothing against you." My dad is an awesome guy, but when I was 16, I wanted to experience childhood. As a high school student, I wanted to have a regular job apart from my dad, because a part of me always wondered, *How would I do anywhere else*? In everybody else's eyes, my dad was holding my hand. I was tired of hearing that, so I said, "I'll go get my own job."

I worked at Chuck E. Cheese, Glenmore Country club, and Lakeside Center Banquet Hall. I became a manager at Glenmore and Lakeside, did that for a couple of years, and still working at Chuck E. Cheese. The crazy thing was that before working there, I hated kids. I'd been around adults throughout my childhood. But when I worked at Chuck E. Cheese, I saw how kids were so honest. They were so innocent, and just nice. They were good kids, and were always telling me how they wish there was a place to go where they could play lots of video games.

I was 18, and I quit everything. I quit every job, and it was my senior year: All I did was work, and I wanted to just enjoy my senior year. I graduated, and I was going to go to school for business. I thought, *I know everything about this. I can't fail*. But that's the thing: I went to school, and I wasn't learning anything knew. So after my first year of college, I said, "What's the point of school?" And I'm not saying college is bad. Education is always good, but...

Craddock: But everyone walks their own path.

Paul: Exactly. I said, "I'm going to do this. I'm going to make this happen, because what they're teaching me is exactly what my dad taught me, so why am I going to school?" I started my own asphalt business. I was working on highways, driveways, roads, parking lots, all that kind of stuff. I had some good contracts and was making a lot. I was doing very well, but I always got done at 5:00. The sun goes down, and the air cools, so you can't really lay asphalt. So I'd go home and say, "I want to play a game." After a while, I was bored. I was by myself. I had my online friends, but that wasn't the same as being with people in a social environment.

I said, "I'm going to make Paul's Gamerzone." I'd get to work and kids were coming into my shop, having a blast. It was rough at first because nothing like this was around. There were moments when I wanted to quit, because those kids told me, "This is where we go. We didn't have friends, but here we do." That touched my heart. These kids were outcasts, and this was a place where they belonged and felt safe. So I decided to stick around.

And today, those customers are still coming in regularly, six years later. We've just been working and doing pretty well.

I'm hoping that if something ever happens to me, my son would want to take over. Right now, he's only a year and nine months old. But he knows how to use Netflix, phones...

Craddock: They grow up on screens these days

Paul: Yeah. I think that's cool that he learned so quickly.

Craddock: How have you seen your business, and this type of business, change over the last six years?

Paul: It was actually the very first video game lounge in Ohio. We have had a lot of people try to copy what we do, and that's sad because that brings up competition where we have to hurt each other's [profits]. I don't want that. I made this business because it's one of a kind. Now they're popping up everywhere. Our store is still strong, but the difference between when I founded this place, the difference between then and now, is everything is so competitive. These places are called "esports lounges."

To me, the point of video games is to have fun enjoying them with your friend. Now, they're so competitive. They're coming out with all these battle royales, and if you're not good at the game, no one wants to play with you. It's kind of like school: If you weren't good at basketball, or volleyball, or whatever, you'd be the last one picked.

The nice thing we have here is that we [foster] that vibe. We do esports stuff, but we also have a lounge scene where people can just come in and enjoy themselves. Nobody judges anybody. If you're good, if you're bad--people just want to have fun with you. That's what makes this place a lot different than other places.

Craddock: You've got so many games and generations of hardware here. What was it like starting out?

Paul: It was all my stuff. I was a collector. I'd been a collector, even of Pokémon cards, Yu-Gi-Oh cards, Magic cards. If I beat a game, I'd save it, because that [save file or high score] was like my trophy for finishing it. I had one shelf for the games I'd finished, and one for the games I hadn't.

When I'd beat a game, I'd go get another one. I just kept collecting.

Craddock: When you started out, you said you had a rough go. I know owning a business is difficult, but what specific problems were you running into?

Paul: When I started, it was one of a kind. Even the zoning of a video game lounge had never been considered. The city didn't know whether to label me as an arcade, or an Internet cafe. The difference is, an arcade is where you've got the machines, and you get tickets for prizes. We're not that. And Internet cafes are just computers where you pay for time. We're not that, either. We didn't know what to call ourselves.

It was rough because zoning wouldn't let us get certain locations, and we had trouble finding one. When we finally did find one, people thought we were a gambling place. We don't serve alcohol. I want a place that's safe for kids, where it's safe for everybody. But this was such a new idea, it was hard to make people aware that it existed. People didn't even know to look for us.

As we became more known, we've had people from California come to check us out. Now they're doing this out in California. This is the only Paul's Gamerzone, but people, in general, have realized that this is the modern-day arcade. From arcade machines to today and into the future, I see this continuing to grow. Younger kids, even my son--he's so young, but he knows how to operate Netflix and iPads. When I was his age, I could barely work a TV remote.

Craddock: I was outside playing with sticks.

Paul: [laughs] Exactly! Outside playing in the yard, rolling down hills in boxes. It's changing. It's evolving in a good way, but maybe also in a negative way. The good way is because games bring people together, and more people than ever are playing. Back then, when we were kids, you were a nerd. A geek. In school, you were considered a loser.

Nobody wants that, so people were quiet about the fact that they played games. Nowadays, younger kids are playing Fortnite, and they're the cool kids. That's a huge difference compared to 10 years ago.

Craddock: What's the negative?

Paul: It's competitive. If you're no good, nobody wants to play with you. It's very rare for someone to say, "Hey, I'll play with you so you can get better." That right there is the point of video games: playing together, having fun, enjoying your time.

Craddock: That's what was great about arcades: They were communal. The first time I saw *Mortal Kombat*, one player was Kano, and he ripped the other guy's heart out. I was just a kid, but I approached him and said, "Could you tell me how you did that?" And he explained it to me. Sharing information was fun.

Paul: Yeah. And now it's like, "Ha! I beat you! I win!" I feel like that's rude.

Craddock: How do you try to foster that communal atmosphere in here?

Paul: The nice thing is we allow kids to come in, and they can pretty much play whatever they want. They can play together; they can go against each other. Either way, they get to know each other. This is a place for people to meet each other, make friends, and play together.

We do competitions for competitive players, and they play against casual players. But when that happens, they learn from each other: different communication skills and so on.

Craddock: What sorts of events do you run?

Paul: All sorts of stuff. We do Apex Legends. We do card games like Final Fantasy and Pokémon. Transformers just became a card game, so we're going to get into that. Board games--anything that's a game, we like to offer our customers.

Craddock: How many video games do you have?

Paul: We have over 2,000 hard-copy games and hundreds of digital games. We have handheld games for DS, 3DS, Vita, Nintendo Switch, all those platforms. I would say, with everything put together, I would say it's between 3,000 and 5,000 games. A lot of newer games can only be downloaded on the newer-gen consoles.

Craddock: What's the oldest console you have hooked up right now?

Paul: We've got an Atari 2600 in back. We've got an Atari, and everything up until now. We're one of the only video game lounges in the US that offers every console. A lot of places in the US, they'll only offer retro, or only Nintendo, or only Xbox. We've got VR and a little bit of everything.

Craddock: Do you try to offer new games right away?

Paul: Yep. We're getting the new *Mortal Kombat* [*11*] tomorrow and start doing *Mortal Kombat* nights. Those will be on Thursdays, and we're thinking of calling it "Paul's Gamerzone: Fight Night." On Thursdays, we also play the newest *Smash Bros*.

That's what's cool about having all the different generations in here. We cater to everybody.

Craddock: What's hot right now? What's bringing people in?

Paul: Battle royale games, definitely. Last year was all about Fortnite. The year before that, it was PUBG. This year, so far, it's all about Apex legends. It's hot right now, but there will always be something new in the future. That's what's nice about this place: We stay on top of things and know how to get involved.

***

A few of Paul's associates happened to be around on the evening I visited the Gamerzone. They were kind enough to share with me their appreciation for Paul and the environment he offers them, as well as how they contribute to the business, and to the goals they share with their friend. To respect their privacy, I've only used their first names.

Craddock: How'd you discover Paul's Gamerzone?

Mae: I was making some copies at Office Max [next door]. I pulled out, looking both ways, and I happened to see the sign. I pulled back in here and talk to him, and he showed me around the whole place. Everything was smaller. We've upgraded with shelves and stuff like that. I came in around 9:00 the first time, and he said, "Since it's your first time, I won't charge you. Just look around and see what you like."

I've been here just about every day since. [laughs]

Craddock: What are you working on right now?

Mae: Right now I'm helping Nick schedule some posts for our Facebook page. I post things to let people know what days are *Smash* [*Bros.*] days, what days we'll be holding Pokémon card competitions, and big events like Fortnite battles. We got a lot of people during spring vacations; around 60 people showed up one day because they saw our Facebook post.

I went to school for graphic design and have passion for that stuff, and I'm happy to do it. I love this place, and there's nothing else I'd rather be helping out with.

Craddock: What keeps you coming back?

Mae: What Nick does with this place--other than rent, you know, and paying for the building--really comes back to the community and to the customers. That's what I absolutely love. If somebody comes in and wants a certain game he doesn't have, he'll go out of his way to get that game. A lot of old games can be really expensive.

Right now, a lot of new games are $60. But when the new Smash Bros. came out, he went and bought five Nintendo Switches and five copies of Smash Bros. just so people could all play at the same time. We have all-nighters, which gives us a boost at the end of the month. It's so nice to see everybody come together to keep us going.

What I like to tell people is this is a community, a family, more than a business.

Craddock: I notice you like to use "we" and "us."

Mae: Yeah, I do. Because when I come here, I know I'm among friends. I consider these people family more than I do some members of my [blood] family. We joke around and have fun. On the rare chance when somebody says something out of line, you just explain it to them, and it's all good. It's a really fun, communal place. People of all ages can come in here and play what they want.

I also love it because it gives me interaction with people I'd otherwise never meet. I have gaming consoles, but I'd rather come in here and play with somebody than I would go online.

Craddock: Talking to a screen name is different.

Mae: Yeah. You get experiences like if somebody beats you, you can give them a playful punch on the shoulder. You can say, "That was a good game. Let me buy you a drink." It helps you grow more as a person when you're around people.

Craddock: Anthony and Jen, how long have you been coming here?

Anthony: I'm trying to think, actually, but I can't remember. Maybe 2015.

Jen: I had a friend who helped out at the very beginning, and I came in on opening day. That's how long I've been here. I slowly got to know the owner. How I really got to know this place was, the next day was really slow, so I came in and said, "Hey, can I play Dragonball?" He said, "You like this game? Cool, I'll join in."

Anthony: Some friends invited me to come here, and I've been coming ever since.

Craddock: What's brought you back for so many years?

Anthony: I help run a Pokémon [card] league here. We play every Wednesday.

Jen: I get interaction with more people. That helped me out a lot in the beginning, because I was home schooled. First I went to public school, but when I started home schooling, I lost all that [social] interaction. Discovering this place helped me meet more people and feel more comfortable. I still love coming in and interacting.

Craddock: Jen, what special events do you like to participate in?

Jen: There's Super Smash Bros. on Thursdays. On Fridays, I'm in a group that plays Dungeons & Dragons. There's other random things we like to do. New players, just remember that you'll mess up, but something cool will always happen. We've got a bad D&D player in our group--

Anthony: I know who you're talking about.

Jen: He puts player knowledge into his character. That's a big no-no. I looked at my DM and said, "Hey, whenever he does this thing, could I do this to mess with him?" He said, "That's character knowledge. Go for it."

Making Magic: Susan G. McBride on Life at Atari

WHEN I BEGAN researching this book and contacting developers for interviews, most of the teams looked the same: white males, intelligent, geeky, driven to create. Susan G. McBride stood out. She paved a path for women in the games industry as well as adjacent creative fields, and she's still going strong.

But McBride didn't stand out to me because she's a woman. After finding her name on *Ms. Pac-Man* for the Atari Lynx, I googled her LinkedIn and read her resume to get a little background before reaching out. I read. And read, and read, and read.

As an artist, designer, inventor, producer, director, and about a dozen other roles, McBride has worked with brands that make up the bedrock of the games, television, and movie industries. She has over 90 games to her credit, including licensed games that defy the stereotype of licenses: *Batman*, the coin-op based on the 1989 Tim Burton flick; *Road Runner*, starring Looney Tunes' creator Chuck Jones' famous speedy bird and hapless coyote; *Star Wars: Return of the Jedi*, and more.

When I couldn't connect with McBride through LinkedIn, Jerome Strach, co-programmer on *Ms. Pac-Man*, put me in touch. My objective at the outset was to pick her brain about *Ms. Pac-Man* on the Lynx, information found in that game's chapter. But I couldn't pass up the opportunity to talk with her about the laundry list of other arcade and home classics she's worked on, many of which had a profound impact on me as a kid, as well as in my adulthood.

I'm pleased to present my conversation with Susan McBride below. We discuss arcade and consumer-grade technology, go on a whirlwind tour of her gameography, reflect on her friendship with Jerome Strach, and talk candidly about how she left—and is still leaving—her mark in the "boys' club" of video game development.

***

David L. Craddock: How did you get started in the games industry?

Susan G. McBride: I actually started out with Atari, in the arcades [division]. I was majoring in art at San Jose State University, but I really wanted to see my art move. I got into animation, and that gave me a full load of credits for my major. Then I went off and did another six units at a junior college because they were the only ones [teaching] animation in the Bay Area at the time.

My professor there recommended me to Atari based on an award-winning international film I had called *Muncha Muncha*. It was kind of a precursor to *Pac-Man*. Atari interviewed me, and they hired me on the spot when they saw my film. I worked at Atari's arcade division for numerous years. I started as an animator, doing computer graphics on some of their first systems. That was all arcade games. I worked on titles such as *Crystal Castles*, *Gauntlet* 1 and II, *Hard Drivin'*, *Indiana Jones*, *Paperboy*, *Pit Fighter*, *Pole Position*, *RBI Baseball*, *Skull and Crossbones*, *Star Wars: Return of the Jedi*, *Tetris*, *Toobin'*, *Batman*, and others, all in the coin-op division.

Craddock: That's quite a resume in itself! How did you get involved in Atari's home division?

McBride: What happened was, the home division offered me a job, and I went over there to help establish the internal development department for Jaguar, the first 64-bit system, and development for Lynx as well. While I was there, I became the director of computer game graphics and game design, so I was a game designer, too. That's where I helped convert *Gauntlet*, *Police Academy*, *Batman Returns*, *Ms. Pac-Man*, *Paperboy*, Rampage—all for Lynx.

The games I worked on for the Jaguar include *Tiny Toons*, *Tempest*, and several others. I have over 90 games in my portfolio.

Craddock: Before we dig into *Ms. Pac-Man* for the Lynx, I wonder if you could take us on a whirlwind tour of some of the other companies and brands you've been involved with.

McBride: I went to work on a startup after Atari. That was with Steven Spielberg and Andy Grove, working with some of the first Pentium [processors], and we were doing voice over the Internet in 3D environments. I became their director of content, and produced stuff there. I left to become a vice president [at Velocity Inc.], which gave me the opportunity to work with id Software and other gaming companies.

Then I went to Mattel, and I was brought in more as a senior producer to work on their Nickelodeon and Fisher Price products. Back then, we were doing PlayStation, Nintendo, and CD-ROM media. I got to work on all the Nickelodeon titles, and a few Barbie titles. Then from Mattel, I went to their competitor, MGA.

Craddock: [laughs] You defected!

McBride: [laughs] Well, for the record, Mattel had The Learning Company, and with that, they had to close their interactive department. I loved Atari—it was one of my favorite places to work—and I loved Mattel, too. I would have stayed there longer. But at MGA, I became an inventor of patents, and was senior director of product development for games, and got to oversee all their game development. I actually worked on a Pac-Man conversion for toys there, and got to work with Namco and other big gaming companies. Mostly, we were doing interactive toys and some PlayStation products for Bratz.

Craddock: Even by that time, you'd accumulated experience working for big and small companies. Did you have a preference?

McBride: I have a habit of liking to go do startups, because the arcade business made me love new hardware. Back in the day, when you worked on arcade games, you were developing new hardware for your products. I have a love for technology. Any time there's some new tech, I have to see it. I actually left MGA to go work at TimePlay Entertainment, where we were trying to develop some kind of hardware that would go into movie theaters. It ended up going into casinos, and I said, "Okay, I'm a gamer. I'm gonna leave."

From there, I worked at Say Design, and then to enVie Interactive. At MGA, I'd created a massively multiplayer online game for kids, and at enVie we were creating another MMOG, which was Vie The Game. Then I went to Inhance Digital and started working with more Fortune 500 companies, and from there to Age of Learning. I was a senior producer for Interact Games For Kids, which involved math, English, and other languages. I oversaw a [catalog] of over 75 games there.

So, that's kinda me in a nutshell.

Craddock: You said earlier that you didn't just want to draw. You wanted to see your drawings move. Were you already leaning toward video games? Or were you interested in movies at first?

McBride: Back in the eighties, games weren't as huge as they are now. I remember my dad bringing *Pong* home, and playing it on the TV. That was super-exciting, even though it was just a couple of paddles and a ball going back and forth. But I was very fortunate because my father was into electronics, and I got my technology drive from him.

I just found it very fascinating to make my characters come alive. I love to draw and design, and the idea of characters actually moving was like, "Wow, that's fascinating!" I knew about animation from my love of Walt Disney as a kid. I've been a cartoon fanatic since my childhood, so I wanted my characters to move, too.

So, I played some games like *Pac-Man*, but it wasn't anything like we have nowadays. It was actually my professor who got me into Atari. Otherwise I probably would have gone into [film] animation. It was Atari that opened my eyes to all that was out there in video games.

Craddock: I know the games industry, new as it was, was very much a boys' club back then. How would you describe Atari's culture as one of few women working there?

McBride: When I first started, it was 100 engineers, all guys, and me. It was an experience. There were a couple other women, but they were working for an animator. It was an awesome experience because they were looking for people who knew how to make stuff move. We were working on this pixel processing system, and everything was developed in-house. There were no art tools back in the day. Engineers had to create our art tools, which was awesome. We had a great group of engineers back in the day. Even today, every engineer I work with, I'm in awe of, being from an artist's background.

It was definitely a boys' club. All of management was male. I would say the video game industry stayed that way for a long, long time.

But what I found most fascinating was that I admired programmers and engineers for what they're capable of doing—and I won't say it was a stereotype because I don't believe in stereotyping anyone—but at first, their social skills were very much... When they get into code, they're in that world. Interacting with people was not everyone's forte. I believe [my managers] had to get approval to hire me because I was a female coming into this environment. There was already another female there, so I was going, "What's the problem?"

It was interesting because at first, the guys didn't know what to do or how to act. Once we broke that barrier, it was like, "No, you don't have to open doors for me. You can go first." I became part of their social interaction because I'm a geek at heart, too.

It was great. I loved everybody I worked with. To be a gamer, you have to have love for it. We all were creative, and just wanted to make the best products we could. When you get people who are like-minded, it shouldn't matter what your gender is.

Craddock: Based on your experience, how have things changed for women in the games industry? Or have they?

McBride: If you worked on *Gauntlet*, you've been around a while. [laughs] I don't have a big problem with my age, but for my benefit, I don't like to reveal it. It's probably somewhat about being a female in the industry, too. I use whatever I can to do the best that I can. I do know what the industry is like, but I also know what I'm capable of. So I don't fret about it too much.

My mom also never told anyone her age, so it's also probably something that was passed down. Growing up, I'd hear her say, "You don't ask a woman that question." I'd go, "Why? Why?" My sister worked in engineering, too. She was probably one of the first foremen in the utility industry, and she definitely had a lot of experience and knew how hard it was. She's 12 years older than me, and made my life so much better when I started my career.

I feel very fortunate and lucky. I'm proud of what I've done. The fact that I even get to say that I'm an inventor and that I have a patent is great. Honestly, though, anything I've done is a team effort. Anyone who thinks it's just one person is crazy. In my career, I've been so fortunate. When I worked on *Road Runner*, I met Chuck Jones and worked with him. I spent the day with him, and what I found as a kid, being all googly-eyed, was that he was the most humble human being I'd ever met. All the people I've met are super-humble, because they know it's not just them. Everybody worked together to make magic happen.

Craddock: What was your first project at Atari?

McBride: I remember having to make E.T. look like E.T. That was a challenge in pixels, but it worked. We were lucky. We had 16 bits versus the home games, which had around four colors to work with. We could even work with 32 colors sometimes! [laughs] I remember when we went to 16-bit [consoles], people were saying, "What are you complaining about? You have all the colors in the world!"

Craddock: You mentioned that back then, artists were involved in helping to build and define arcade hardware. What did that entail?

McBride: For one thing, when it came to hardware in arcades, I was not the engineer. I didn't design the hardware, but I did get hardware specs, and try to figure out what we could make from that. It was more understanding what the hardware was, and what types of graphics and game design we could do with it. Also, suggesting ideas of, for *Gauntlet*, a four-player game, what kind of interactions can we do? What will the hardware allow?

As another example, when I was doing *Return of the Jedi*, I remember they had never worked with eight 256K ROMs. I asked them, "Why can't we do this?" and they said, "Well, we've never done this before." I was more the one who would help challenge the engineers, saying, "Can we make this happen?" When they asked why, I would say, "So we can do this," with an example. When we were doing the battle on the planet Endor, I wanted to go from space back to the ground. They said, "Why do we have to do this?" I said, "It's in the movie! It'll be fun game design." Our game was great. Dennis Harper and our team were awesome. Dennis said, "Yeah, why not?" We all worked to get the hardware to do those kinds of things.

I was always driven by what the moment-to-moment player experience would be. I wanted to help make the graphics be the best they could be for the player. We didn't have early on what would be called a *game designer* in the [arcade division]. Usually the leads would get together and design a game: lead animator, lead programmer. It was much more of a team effort. Trust me: Our game design documents [from back then] were nothing like what they are now. Now they're bibles, which is awesome, but it took a lot of years to get things like that to happen.

For Jaguar development, Leonard Tramiel [son of Commodore International and Atari Corporation founder Jack] would call me in and say, "We can produce all the colors in the world, but the system has limitations." So I'd say, "Let's work with what the human eye sees." We see more greens and reds, so I'd go for more of a green palette. I always concentrated on what the visual experience would be for the player.

Craddock: That's what I like most about game development. There were the halcyon days of one programmer working in his or her basement and doing everything: art, audio, code, game design. But it very quickly became a team effort, and that's important to remember. Speaking of, what was it like working with the *Gauntlet* team to create that title? It set the mold for so many dungeon crawls.

McBride: I loved it. Ed was fabulous. He's brilliant. He let me do some of the level design. I always loved working with Ed, because what he taught me was, "It's about the gameplay. Not necessarily the graphics or tech, just the moment-to-moment experience." If Ed Logg knows anything, he knows what the player wants. I'm always happy when I can see him, because most of the time now I only get to see him and others when we're all at a conference or something.

When I worked with Dennis Harper on *Star Wars: Return of the Jedi*, I did all the graphics on that project, and he wrote all the code. That was rare. Early on in my career, even when I worked on *Crystal Castles*, Franz Lanzinger did most of the programming, and Barbara Singh and I did the graphics. There were a few other people, but the *Star Wars* product was the one where I had the smallest group. *Gauntlet* was a much larger product: six or seven artists, several programmers. Back then, it was so huge. But that's so teeny compared to nowadays.

Craddock: Since you had experience working in Atari's coin-op and home games divisions, I wonder if you could elaborate on some things I've heard about those institutions. For instance, I know many developers received royalties on sales of cartridges based on arcade games, which understandably upset many arcade developers who'd come up with the technology and concepts on which the home games were based.

McBride: I do a lot of journaling. In the industry, we're very quick to say, "This person came up with this idea." I guess that's just how we are. But I found that in the games industry, people would take credit for stuff they didn't do. I used to jot down a lot of information because at the end of projects, we got our bonuses based on [our role], and royalties based on how well a product sold.

When it was time to determine who would get what percentages, people would say all these things, then I'd pull out a journal and say,

"No, actually, so-and-so did this." I was all about the right people getting credit.

Craddock: Since you've worked with so many iconic brands such as Star Wars, is it still exciting to get those opportunities?

McBride: That's very exciting. Anytime in my career when I get to do something like work on *Return of the Jedi* and visit Lucasfilm—it's so exciting. Working with Batman was great, and when I worked with Nickelodeon's brands, I got to fly over and meet people who made the Nick products. Meeting Namco people, meeting these creators—you're just in awe, because you realize that [opportunity] means your company believes in you enough to create these products.

For me, it's also exciting because one thing I take pride in, and am known for, is staying true to brands. When I worked on *The Incredible Hulk*, I had Marvel come to me and say, "Susan, you got The Hulk correct. How'd you do it?" Well, I found out where they did their 3D modeling, and I got hold of those models and put them into our product.

But also, many times early in the industry, people would work with characters they didn't have on spec. One thing I love to do is to make sure I stay true to an original image [and design]. If you're even a few pixels off, you're still off. That's something I was very excited to do because I found it a great challenge.

Craddock: How do you stay true to a vision when you're confined to such limited hardware?

McBride: Ah. [laughs] Well, the truth of it is, you have to have your world bible and use your resources. Some people have their books that they give you and say, "This is what you need to stay true to the character," but back in the day, they didn't have much of that kind of stuff at all. Unless it's [a major company like] Warner Bros., because they're film people and know what a model sheet is, for example.

What we had to do was get products and look at them, really concentrate on [the vision]. One of my fortes is, we were doing a lot with third-party developers who'd bring in art that I'd have to modify and show them, "This won't work." It was an educational experience for people, because you have to have a trained eye. The greatest joy I had was educating the rest of the team by saying, "This is how you can tell it's on-model. Look for these things that may not be happening."

Craddock: You've had a remarkable career so far. It was a pleasure talking with you about it. How has all that experience shaped your current work, and what you hope to accomplish in the future?

McBride: I've been so fortunate to work on the products I've been able to work with. I've worked with so many great managers and teams. The Tramiels, for example: They gave us opportunities to do what we could dream. Management was saying, "Go for it. Create what you can create." You could always smell success on a good product. There was a magic to it. Those of us making products were there all hours of the day and night, and we couldn't get enough of playing them. That's how we knew we were on to something. I remember us meta-gaming each other in *Gauntlet*. Sometimes, when we wanted to win, we'd tap each other's food supplies. There was the game, and then there was the [meta] game between the players.

I've just been lucky enough to work with such wonderful people and expertise in the industry. To have access to all the different technologies was very rare. Working at Atari gave me so many magical times in my career, and I'll never forget those great people. We all had mutual respect, excitement, and love for what we did. The passion was definitely there.

That's what drives me now. If people have a passion and a dream, they can turn anything into reality. That was the opportunity when working on these products: Making these dreams come to a great reality, and knowing that I got to help people out there—kids, adults, anyone—experience fun. To be able to have the opportunity was definitely a gift.

Pro Tips: Ex-GamePro Editor Dan "Elektro" Amrich on Arcade Perfection

DAN AMRICH AND I are grizzled veterans of gaming's first virtual war. It was fought on playgrounds and in retail stores. Countless articles and more than a few books have been written about it, including this one in an indirect fashion. Years later, starting out as a cub freelance writer, I got a contact at Official Xbox Magazine that pointed me in Dan's direction. He was a senior editor at the magazine, and accepted or dismissed pitches from freelancers like me.

He earned my respect immediately. This, I discovered, was "Dan Elektro," his pseudonym at GamePro magazine, one of my favorite rags as a kid. And I'm pleased to say we got along well. I turned in my stories on time, and Dan was firm but kind in his critique of my writing. Like I said, I was still cutting my teeth, and needed all the help I could get. Dan provided it in spades. We've stayed in touch over the years. Back in 2016 I interviewed him about his coverage of cheat codes in their heyday, and I talked to him just recently about arcades and conversions.

Yes, Dan and I have enjoyed a long professional relationship. Which is why I'm so sad to announce that I must cut ties with him, effective immediately. Because although Dan and I found our way back into civilian life after the 16-bit console war, I've only recently discovered that he and I fought on opposite sides.

Don't blame me, Dan. It's a matter of principle.

Okay, Dan siding with a blue hedgehog over my man Mario is a forgivable sin. After all, *my side won, Amrich! What now? Huh?!*

Sorry.

The thing is, Dan had a few years on me. As you'll discover in the following interview, he was launching his writing career while I was grinding through middle school. I was too old to fight the good fight for Nintendo on playgrounds, so I took my arguments to gym class, where my then-best buddy and I found ourselves divided by the war. I had *Super Mario World* and *Street Fighter II*. He was a Sega fan, and spent his nights ripping out spines in *Mortal Kombat* thanks to the original game's blood code.

Our arguments were fierce. We even stopped sitting next to each other on the bus. Hey, we were thirteen. This was serious business. (Also, it bears repeating that *my side*… Never mind.)

Those arguments are a thing of the past. The fact is, console wars are no longer really a thing. Xbox One and PS4 have the same library of multiplatform games, and aside from middling differences that only the most rabid soldiers on either side will ever care about, they're more or less the same. Is that a good thing?

Dan and I put aside our old differences to talk about the heyday of the arcade scene, what he looked for when he put on his critic's hat to evaluate conversions, and whether the differences that separated ports of the same game made each version worth owning, or if consumers and critics alike would have been better served playing the same game on all platforms.

Dan got his start in the games industry as a writer for several of the industry's most popular consumer magazines, notably GamePro and Official Xbox Magazine, where I met him when I was starting out as a freelance writer. If you read GamePro, you probably read Dan's work under his pseudonym byline, Dan Elektro, game critic and purveyor of cheat codes, the subject of our first interview several years ago.

When I decided to write a book about converting arcade games to home platforms, Dan was the first person I wanted to talk to. I reached out to him before I began contacting developers. While I was a kid during the 16-bit "console war" between Nintendo and Sega, Dan was cutting his teeth as a writer, giving him a front-row seat to the console war's theaters: Nintendo landing an exclusive home version of *Street Fighter II* for Super Nintendo; a secret blood code hidden in the Sega Genesis port of *Mortal Kombat*, leading to Nintendo taking a beating in sales; and the many, many versions of classics such as *Space Invaders* and *Pac-Man* on early platforms from Atari 2600 to Apple II to ColecoVision, platforms exponentially less powerful than arcade boards.

Dan was gracious enough to go into detail on his time covering home conversions as a critic, to convey again how the Genesis version of *Mortal Kombat* and a wee bit of serendipity paved his path into the games industry, and whether the differences that separated ports of the same game—the gray "sweat" of *Mortal Kombat* on SNES versus all the blood and fatalities from the arcade version on Sega Genesis, for instance—were good or bad for the industry, and for consumers.

***

David L. Craddock: Before home consoles and PCs were ubiquitous, arcade games ruled the gaming roost. What was the core attraction of going through the chore of leaving the house to play an arcade game?

Amrich: You went because you knew you were getting an unparalleled experience. I have never fallen out of love with the primary attraction of arcade gaming: a 400-pound plywood box built to play one game. There is a dedication to a three-minute entertainment experience from both parties, the creator and the consumer. Nothing could ever beat that.

Arcade games were always new, often unique, and always considered the real thing; home ports were close approximations. And you knew they were compromises, but you still wanted them, because it was the only way to get a piece of that magic experience at home. I still loved them because it was as close as I could get.

The standard impossible dream for most kids at that point was owning an arcade machine. I mean, could you imagine? It was the impossible dream. One of my friends in grade school bragged that his dad, a doctor, had an Asteroids machine in his office, so he was able to go in and play for free any time he wanted. He was lying, and we realized, wow, if you can't even get an arcade game when you're a doctor…!

This is why owning an arcade machine remained a dream of mine right up until the day I got an *NBA Jam* cabinet in my living room. I never expected to enjoy such luxury.

There were very few ways to learn about new games outside of Electronic Games magazine, word of mouth, and personal experience. Just going to the arcade or pizza place meant a fair chance of discovering something that hadn't been there before. You would often stumble upon something amazing and thrilling that you never knew existed—all you needed the ability to make the pilgrimage to the holy temple and enough quarters to experience what it had to offer.

Craddock: What was the earliest home conversion you played—as a consumer, a critic, or both—where you felt that, while parity between arcade and home hardware had not yet been achieved, consoles had finally come close, or close enough, to replicating an arcade experience?

Amrich: I distinctly remember telling my mother that Super Mario Bros. was "exactly like the arcade" and that we should get it because I would save all those quarters she was talking about. She didn't go for it, but I remember being absolutely astounded that Nintendo would release the same experience at home as they had in the arcade. *Galaga* on NES is still one of my favorites; the only real difference is the aspect ratio is horizontal instead of vertical, but here I am with one of the recent MyArcade toys on my desk, right now, featuring that NES-on-a-chip tech.

NBA Jam was pretty close on 16-bit ("close enough" for sure) and got right up to par with 32-bit hardware's ability to do sprite scaling. I don't think people realize that the next NBA coin-op, NBA Hangtime, was running at 60fps—which was something home devs were not even dreaming of doing yet. I think that was the kind of difference-maker that the devs were trying to put into coin-ops in the late 90s. They knew they had to do something to keep that arcade experience special and give people a reason to go to a location.

Craddock: As a critic, what were you looking for in a conversion of an arcade title on consoles (a question specific to handhelds can be found below)?

Amrich: I expected accurate gameplay, sounds, and graphics. If it looked and sounded and felt like I remembered—and critically if I was able to apply the skills I'd acquired in the arcade to the home version—then it was worthy. So I guess I was looking for not just as simulation but a re-creation of what I remembered. It became a lot easier once the publishers began simply writing emulators for the original ROMs, like Namco Museum and whatnot.

There was no doubting the accuracy, as long as the hardware could reproduce it correctly. And of course, if booting up started with the same RAM checks as the arcade versions, it was clearly legit on a software level—it was just a question of whether there was slowdown, or if it was still fun and felt right with a home controller.

This might be irrelevant but it came to mind: I did a lot of the retro arcade reissue reviews at GamePro in the late 90s and early 2000s as an ill-tempered rabbit in a leather jacket called Bad Hare. While there was no real difference between BH and Dan Elektro, because I was the only person who wrote under either one. If you cared enough to look at the prose you'd see it was still my voice; I decided to keep Bad Hare as the retro reviewer. He was sort of a projection of the grumpy old-school gamer. I had the old-school arcade expertise, but I generally only expressed it through Bad Hare, so he would have a consistency as an expert in that field with the readers.

Craddock: Obviously, parity between arcade and console hardware was not possible until much later. When did a conversion's differences from its source material become dissimilar enough to warrant taking points off its score, literally or figuratively?

Amrich: I knew there was always going to be a compromise—sprites were redrawn, sound effects might not be exact—but if it still felt right, that was the biggest factor. If a key sound effect was really out of spec and annoying, then I might ding it, because it was part of the experience. But even by the 16-bit era, I was seeing fairly accurate conversions, or close-enough products that did the original game justice.

I'm sure this is something you're dealing with overall, but the home version can never be "the same" unless it's running the same ROM. If the emulator is up to the task, then you can get something that is as close to replicating the original experience as you can ever hope for. So for 16-bit conversions, they weren't always using the ROM, and I tempered my expectations accordingly. It's usually a best guess and whatever reverse engineering the devs can manage on their own.

Craddock: What are some conversions you played that introduced new features or alterations from the source material that, in your view, made the conversion equal to or better than the original?

Amrich: Tempest 2000 comes to mind immediately, though I think I liked *Tempest 3000* on PlayStation even more. Jeff Minter did a great job reinvigorating that with new elements and a truly evolved presentation while keeping the original spirit and gameplay there. I have vague memories of *Defender* and *Robotron* updates, but they didn't charm me the same way, and that's why they remain vague. *Donkey Kong* on Game Boy gets a nod here too, for extending without ruining the arcade original.

Craddock: As a critic, did you do your best to remain impartial when reviewing multiple versions of the same game? Or did you tend to lean toward one platform or another for reasons of your own?

Amrich: If I felt one version was more accurate or more satisfying, I would give that a nudge—I mean, that was my job as a reviewer, to assess and rate. If I felt there was something I could point to that made one version more satisfying or special than the other, I would be duty-bound to mention it. If it didn't matter enough to mention, it'd probably get the same score from me. And that's assuming we're talking something like SNES vs Genesis, systems that were "equitable" in the market if not necessarily in power or specifics. Whichever one felt more accurate might get a higher score, but it could be either platform and it would always be dependent on that title.

Beyond that, if there were things where you knew the hardware was capable of doing more—like the 32X version of *NBA Jam Tournament Edition* or *MKII*—then you have to review it as a different animal from the 16-bit versions, because the hardware and probably the engine or code base is different. I would expect more arcade accuracy from a console with more power.

Craddock: Some conversions of arcade games were so different as to be considered a completely different game, such as *Mortal Kombat* on Game Boy and Game Gear. As a critic, was it fair to weigh a portable conversion against its arcade original, or did you look for other factors?

Amrich: Portables were a different playing field and I tended to judge them based on what the hardware could not, not a hardline of what the arcade version delivered. I never expected accuracy but I was thrilled by any details that made it over. *Street Fighter II* on Game Boy is still one of those games that stunned me as to how good it was, and how much of the game they managed to translate in an accurate-feeling experience.

Same for *Donkey Kong* on Game Boy—wow, that was "just like the arcade" even if the gameplay was expanded and the levels were in different orders and the screen dimensions were totally different.

Craddock: To this day, what is your favorite home conversion? And along the same line, what do you consider to be the best conversion?

Amrich: Because I loved the arcade version, I think *NBA Jam* for Genesis was my personal favorite. That was in no small part because I used an XBAND modem to play online with *NBA Jam*, and not a lot of games supported that peripheral. I am also partial to the N64 version of *NBA Hangtime*, but that is purely because I am in it!

Pigskin was one of my favorite arcade games—sort of medieval football, a clear precursor to *NFL Blitz*—and the home version of that came with Jerry Glanville's trendy endorsement, which was weird (black-and-white photos of him are laid over the menus, which are otherwise cartoony and colorful). But the game plays well and it was one of my favorite home conversions simply because the original game was so tough for me to find. I still get worked up over playing that either as a MAME ROM or the Genesis cart.

Galaga NES, as mentioned, always struck me as the gold standard for NES arcade conversions, up there with *Super Mario Bros.* in terms of quality. I think the NES port I valued the most—and still do—is the Tengen version of *Tetris*, which was far more accurate to the arcade than the Nintendo version, even though all my friends felt the Nintendo version was the default version. Coming from an arcade background, I resisted that outlook—the arcade is where things are born! Even if *Tetris* was really born on a mainframe in Russia, *my* version of *Tetris* would be the one Ed Logg worked on, dammit.

And to this day, I don't enjoy the Nintendo version of *Tetris* for NES—single-player, pastel colors. Why go for that when you can have bold primary colors and two-player competitive mode, with arcade details like the Cossack dancers and the arcade music? To me, Tengen's *Tetris* is the definitive version and I'm taking my cartridge to the grave. That made me aware of all the other Tengen cartridges, many of which were arcade conversions via Atari, and I sought them out because the brand came to represent arcade accuracy to me.

Soul Calibur for Dreamcast was fantastic, as was *Crazy Taxi*. I might need to paw through the games in my garage to determine some more answers. I might surprise myself with what I saved!

Craddock: Since the PS2 era, arcade conversions on multiple platforms have achieved near-perfect parity. That could be considered a good thing: I can buy, say, Street Fighter 4 on Xbox 360 without feeling like my buddy playing on PS3 got the better version. But what have we lost by no longer getting to choose between editions that vary, oftentimes wildly, from one another, and from their source material?

Amrich: We have lost the desire to fight over stuff that does not matter. I never enjoyed the console wars despite being a veteran on the front lines. If everybody can have the same satisfying experience on different hardware, that's utopia to me.

Craddock: Is it too far-fetched or hyperbolic to say that the "console war" of the 16-bit era was fueled in large part by the differences in conversions of arcade games such as *Street Fighter II* and *MK*?

Amrich: I think that's a bit too far, personally, and I wouldn't agree. I think *MK* and *SF* are the biggest examples of home conversions being difference-makers, but I think first-party exclusives—Mario vs Sonic—and original content built for each platform (*Super Metroid*, *Ecco the Dolphin*, *Pilotwings*, *Toejam & Earl*) were bigger drivers of the divide. *MK* and *SF* are the undercard to the main events.

Craddock: How did parity in terms of speed, graphics, features, artwork, and more change the job of critics?

Amrich: Well, it got easier if you knew they were using one engine to power both versions. If the middleware used could work with multiple systems, then you knew they only had to build it once, then try to optimize for each platform according to its architecture. And sometimes, of course, it makes more financial sense not to make it different—some folks just wanted it to run smoothly no matter what it was running on.

So if you understand their goal is "same everywhere," you don't have to look as closely as a critic—it comes down to hardware executing that same core software. And sometimes it wasn't equal, so you'd find slowdown here or a glitch there. When ROMs came in, it was even easier.

Craddock: Objectively, did the differences between ports of the same game amount to a good thing for the industry? For publishers? For critics? For players? Why or why not?

Amrich: You're always going to have some completist fans who need it on every platform. (I am guilty of being the guy who wants Monopoly on every platform, but even there, I'm often dealing with wildly different interpretations and presentations based on the same ruleset.) That said, each first-party publisher is always going to say "our version is the best because it's the same as the arcade, purists will want our version because it's authentic down to the pixel" or "our version is the best because it's different and therefore more interesting, here's a reason to try our version because we give you more than you expect."

Like, no matter what, someone's going to spin it as a win. So I'm not sure if it was a good thing or a bad thing—it was merely business as usual to me. I always felt like it was bad for consumers, because they had to choose one (in most cases) and that always feels bad. If you loved *MK* but had a SNES, you had to feel like you were getting the shaft. If you loved SF but had a Genesis, you didn't even have a version of the game for another year or so after *SFII* hit SNES. So, considering that the audience has a limited budget and likely limited buying power—because they're kids who get games for annual holiday gifts or by saving up their money from allowances and jobs—I don't think it was a good thing for most players, because they always felt the grass was greener on the other side of the fence.

It's only when "core" versions of the consoles came down to $100 that most gamers could consider buying both and finding out for themselves which one was "better"—and even that's subjective.

For critics…hey, that was my job, to make judgment calls. It was certainly more interesting to consider the differences and relative merits of two different conversions, so it was fun from an analytical perspective. But my goal was always to try to guide someone who cared about that arcade game as much as I did, and help them make the decision that was right for them.

Craddock: Hypothetically, suppose arcades were still profitable enough to be as commonplace today as they were in the early '80s. Would "arcade perfect" conversions still be cause for excitement, given that most consumers would expect a one-to-one transference?

Amrich: No way—it'd be expected as a default, and any game that wasn't arcade-perfect would be lambasted. There did come a time in the Dreamcast and Xbox/PS2 era where "arcade perfect" started to be expected, too. You hear all these specs and all these capabilities coming out of this generation of systems: "The PS2 is powerful enough to launch missiles! Saddam Hussein bought 70 of them, he's probably using them to launch missiles!" Or, more likely, he has an extended family and every kid got the best present from their powerful uncle. You start to think, "Well, if you can't give me a spot-on version of *Samurai Shodown*, how powerful are you, really?"

That expectation is natural—and yet we never got a home version of Midway's *The Grid*, which was so darned good as an arcade deathmatch game. The Dreamcast version was planned but never materialized. So maybe there were still frontiers left to explore.

Tyson in His Prime: John Tobias on How Mortal Kombat Challenged Street Fighter II

MORTAL KOMBAT WAS as big an influence on me as ThunderCats, Teenage Mutant Ninja Turtles, Sesame Street, and Mr. Rogers' Neighborhood. I was 10 years old when the first game roundhouse-kicked arcades, and was drawn to the weighty hits, huge character sprites, gritty art style, and, yes, the fatalities.

Senators Joseph Lieberman and Herb Kohl, the government officials who led the charge on hearings concerning violence in video games, wouldn't look favorably on kids putting *Mortal Kombat* on the same pedestal as Fred Rogers. That's okay. I believe their efforts to push the then-nascent gaming industry into codifying videogame content was important. Irresponsible parents shouldn't let their kids play games like *Doom* or *Mortal Kombat.* But my parents were not irresponsible. They monitored the books I read, the TV shows and movies I watched, and the games they played. While they certainly did not care for *Mortal Kombat*, they had no issue with me playing it, as long as I understood that it was a fantasy.

Besides, *MK*'s buckets of blood and absurdist fatalities were surface-level attractions. I was more interested in what they game didn't want to show me than the sight of Sub-Zero ripping out Scorpion's severed head with dangling spinal cord for the umpteenth time: its secrets (Who was this Reptile, and where could I find him?), its graphics (How did they make Liu Kang, Sonya, and the rest of the characters look so real?), and its moves.

Mortal Kombat gave me my first paid writing job. As soon as my mom bought me a strategy guide for the first game, I memorized every move and fatality, and wrote my own guide at school. While other kids spent time in the Mac Lab learning the fundamentals of typing, I was surreptitiously printing off dozens of guides and selling them for a quarter apiece.

Mortal Kombat and its sequel influenced the writing of this book. Even though I'd been playing games for years by the time *MK* arrived on home consoles in September 1993, the differences between the four main versions—Game Boy, Game Gear, Super NES, and Sega Genesis—intrigued me. Why couldn't each version look, play, and sound identical to the arcade? What was each machine capable of, and where did each fall short? It was time to find out.

Arcade Perfect took shape from there, with *Mortal Kombat* serving as its beating heart. (Let me know if you see Kano lurking, yeah?) I was fortunate enough to get John "Saibot" Tobias, co-creator—or is that ko-kreator?—of the franchise, to weigh in on the game's creation, the input he and Ed "Noob" Boon contributed on the home versions, and the impact of the game's $10-million-dollar marketing campaign, "Mortal Monday," on his career.

David L. Craddock: How did you get started in the games industry?

John Tobias: I was hired at 19 right out of art school. My first game was *Smash TV* where I got to work with Mark Turmell (NBA JAM) and Eugene Jarvis (Robotron, Defender, Stargate, etc.).

Craddock: How did you meet Ed Boon?

Tobias: I met Ed when he moved down from the pinball department to join us in the video game department. I shared an office with John Vogel and Ed moved into the office next door. He played his music way too loud.

Craddock: What was the most difficult part of creating, moving, and animating Goro?

Tobias: The only experience I had with stop-motion animation prior to Goro was on a film short that I did with my brother as kids using our Star Wars action figures and a super-8. Any difficulties I had with Goro were due to inexperience. The mini-stage setup for Goro was incredibly crude, but I suppose it got the job done. I think the concept of incorporating a stop-motion puppet with digitized actors in a video game was novel enough to give us a pass on quality. No one had done it before as far as I know.

The Goro puppet itself was amazing. The sculptor, Curt Chiarrelli, did a great job of interpreting my drawings. The one thing that made it somewhat difficult to animate was that Goro's armature was built with wires. It worked okay, but would've worked better had we done it with ball and socket joints as I believe Curt had suggested.

I think we were looking to save time and money so we cheaped out. We should've listened to Curt because on our later puppets for *MK3*, Motaro and Sheeva, we went with full skeletal armatures which made it so much easier to pose the figures.

Craddock: What was your involvement in the new, bloodless fatalities given to characters such as Sub-Zero, Johnny Cage, Rayden, and Kano on SNES?

Tobias: I believe we shared ideas on what to do in lieu of the original versions, but I remember sort of conceding that, "Okay, these are going to suck, so let's do the best we can with the existing art we have available."

Craddock: One of my objectives with this book is to point out how ports of arcade games differed from their source material, and explain how the technical limitations of consoles, PCs, and handhelds were responsible for those differences. What were your thoughts on the differences between the Genesis and SNES versions of *MK*?

Tobias: Back in those days the technology in coin-op games was so far advanced compared to the home consoles that I remember just settling with, "Well, I guess that's the best they could do." Not so much with *MK*, but just with games in general. It was that way for me since I was kid and I think that was still the case in the early to mid-'90s.

Given that attitude I think Sculptured and Probe did a commendable job of capturing the spirit of *MK*. If you could excuse the differences in graphic quality, which were at the mercy of console limitations, then I think the games were pretty good ports.

Craddock: Were you aware the Genesis and Game Gear versions would include a blood code?

Tobias: I only vaguely remember being aware of a blood code and I don't remember whether that was during the course of conversion development or after the release. Ed was much closer to the code side portion of the ports and if I learned of the codes it would've been through him.

Craddock: For *MKII,* was Kintaro easier to create, move, and animate after that initial experience making Goro?

Tobias: John Vogel animated Kintaro in *MKII*. In fact, I remember John buying action figures and cutting up and gluing parts of armor onto the new puppet that Curt had created. The puppet was created the same way as the original Goro. I think John did a better job of animating Kintaro than I had done with Goro.

Craddock: Who came up with the Noob Saibot character?

Tobias: That was Ed! He was created specifically for *MKII*. I gave Ed a bunch of random color palettes for the ninjas and he snuck Noob Saibot into the game entirely on his own. I added fiction and history to the character later, but Ed was responsible for the inception.

Craddock: How often did you get to see updates to the console versions of *MKII* while they were in development?

Tobias: I remember our level of involvement with the *MKII* home ports being similar to the first game. Again, we provided feedback less often at the beginning and then more often toward the end. I remember that maybe we were more critical throughout the process only because we felt the need to protect the property.

Craddock: *MKII*'s home release came eighteen months after its debut in arcades. That seems like an exceptionally long time between arcade and console releases. Do you know if there as any particular reason for that on Midway's side?

Tobias: I don't remember why that would've been other than maybe having to do with the release of the arcade game. I think the coin-op was officially released in the spring time and so it's possible that the port would not have been ready in time for that holiday season.

Also, that would've only been several months from the arcade release, which would've upset arcade operators who were dependent on coin-drop. There was a feeling that the home release could affect their earnings and our relationship with the distributors and operators was very important.

Craddock: How soon after *MKII* released in arcades did you and the team break ground on *MK3*?

Tobias: I don't recall exactly. I know after we locked down software and began manufacturing the coin-ops I turned to creating the *MKII* comic book that we advertised in the arcade game. That was great fun for me and a good break from pushing pixels. Also, the team probably spent some time decompressing before we rolled on to *MK3*. But, we didn't float too long. It was business as usual for us. We had that blue collar Chicago work ethic engrained in our souls.

Craddock: Ed Boon says Scorpion is his favorite character. Who's your favorite?

Tobias: I love all my children!

Craddock: I love the speed and gameplay of *MK3*, but I've always been curious why its violence was even more over-the-top. For instance, a single character would explode and shower the screen with multiple skulls, rib cages, and more than four limbs. Fatalities were more over-the-top, too, such as Jax growing into a giant and stepping on his opponent. Why was this more cartoonish style chosen?

Tobias: Because bigger is better! Honestly, I don't know that we were [cartoonish] on purpose as much as just wanted to be more over the top with the violent aspect.

Craddock: Arcade and console hardware seemed to exist in a symbiotic relationship: Conversions of coin-op games gave consumers reason to spend money on a game once and play it at home, but arcade games were graphically superior to consoles, and boasted unique apparatuses such as cockpits and huge screens, giving console owners reason to venture back into arcades. Was this relationship as symbiotic as it seemed?

Tobias: Actually, in my experience it was quite the opposite. For me it was the unique peripherals that made arcade games special. It was the seat and steering wheel of a driving game or the actual molded gun of a shooting game. For fighting games the pads of home consoles were inferior to the feel of an actual joystick and mounted buttons. I think that's true to this day.

But, in the late '90s and early 2000s when the graphic quality of the consoles caught up with what we could do in the arcade, that's when players began to stay home. Today the arcade experience has kind of had a resurgence. Not so much with the bar/arcade retro scene as much as the new location-based event games you find in places like Dave & Busters.

Craddock: I've learned a lot about the obstacles console and PC programmers faced in bringing arcade experiences into the living room. Pac-Man for the Atari 2600, for example, was incapable of rendering circular dots—at least at the time Tod Frye worked on the conversion—and TV screens were wider than they were long, forcing Frye to rejigger Pac-Man's maze. Frye's conversion was judged harshly, and was considered partially responsible for the North American video game market's crash in the '80s. Do you feel conversions like Pac-Man and programmers like Frye were judged too harshly then or now, given that consumers—and most critics—couldn't understand the restraints that developers charged with home conversions had to work within? Or should that not matter?

Tobias: It's funny you mention the 2600 *Pac-Man* game because I remember being bent as a kid that it differed so wildly from the arcade version. I remember flipping through the manual and reading the dots described as wafers to kind of explain away the square shape. My view on that changed when I began actually working on games and understanding how hardware limitations can put a pretty low ceiling over your head.

For what it's worth, I loved every game I played on our 2600, even the bad ones! That was a magic time for me. Even the crash was magical for me because the games were discounted to $2 or $3 bucks!

Craddock: Of all the *MK* games you worked on, which is your favorite?

Tobias: For nostalgic purposes I'd say *MK1* was my favorite only because we were so innocent and had no idea of the success that was ahead of us. That's a very rare experience for anyone who embarks on a creative endeavor. It was just us. No one told us what to do or how to do it. We had absolute creative freedom.

Bibliography

THE FOLLOWING WORKS were helpful in writing this book:

The Ultimate History of Video Games: From Pong to Pokémon and Beyond : the Story Behind the Craze that Touched Our Lives and Changed the World by Steven Kent

Replay: The History of Video Games by Tristan Donovan

Gamers at Work: Stories Behind the Games People Play by Morgan Ramsay

Game Over: Press Start to Continue: The Maturing of Mario by David Sheff

Vintage Games 2.0 by Matt Barton

Notes and Citations

I CONDUCTED DOZENS of interviews over countless hours to write this book, and combined those interviews with research to write it. Interviews were conducted in-person, over email, or—most commonly—via Skype or the phone. After transcribing interviews, I organized all the transcripts into an outline to write each chapter.

This book contains new information gleaned from interviews with the following individuals, listed in alphabetical order, are: Allan "Al" Alcorn, Dan "Elektro" Amrich, Pete Andrew, Richard Aplin, Scott Bachrach, Steve "Snake" Palmer, Keith Burkhill, Paul Carruthers, Frank Cifaldi, Adam Clayton, Michael Cranford, Daniel Filner, Tod Frye, Rob Fulop, Eric Ginner, John Jones-Steele, Chris Kirby, Garry Kitchen, Franz Lanzinger, David Leitch, Ed Logg, Susan McBride, Mike Mika, Eric Mooney, Nick Paul, Jeff Peters, Cameron Sheppard, Jerome Strach, Simon Street, John Tobias, and Jools Watsham.

The following notes reflect all supplementary sources cited throughout the book. When magazines, newspapers, and other dated materials could not be furnished, I relied on digital archives.

Introduction

I also noticed a big difference in the number of colors: "NES Classic Edition: Developer interview – Volume 1: Donkey Kong," Nintendo, https://www.nintendo.com/nes-classic/donkey-kong-developer-interview/.

Chapter 1 – Pong

Bushnell told Alcorn he'd landed a contract with General Electric: Kent, Steven, The Ultimate History of Video Games: The Story Behind the Craze that Touched Our Lives and Changed the World, Prima Publishing: Roseville, California.

Alcorn's prototype consisted of: Ibid.

because Atari supplied him with pinball games: Ibid.

Gaddis kept Atari informed of Pong's growing: Ibid.

patrons were starting to visit the bar just to play the game: Ellis, David, Official Price Guide to Classic Video Games: Console, Arcade, and Handheld Games, 2004, New York: Random House.

which was pulling in thirty-five to forty bucks a day: Helgeson, Matt, "The Father of the Game Industry Returns to Atari," Game Informer.

A few days after Bushnell left, Alcorn received a call: Kent, Steven, The Ultimate History of Video Games: The Story Behind the Craze that Touched Our Lives and Changed the World, Prima Publishing: Roseville, California.

and inspected the milk carton he'd set up inside: "10 Things You Might Not Know About Atari," Mental Floss,

http://mentalfloss.com/article/31624/10-things-you-might-not-know-about-atari.

they were able to charge operators three times as much: Kent, Steven, The Ultimate History of Video Games: The Story Behind the Craze that Touched Our Lives and Changed the World, Prima Publishing: Roseville, California.

ranted about the copycats, referring to them as jackals: Ibid.

had been working on the Odyssey since 1966: "Genesis: How the Home Video Games Industry Began," Ralph Baer, http://www.ralphbaer.com/how_video_games.htm.

and had even signed his name in the guestbook: Kent, Steven, The Ultimate History of Video Games: The Story Behind the Craze that Touched Our Lives and Changed the World, Prima Publishing: Roseville, California.

In April 1974, Magnavox filed a lawsuit against Atari: "Magnavox Sues Firms Making Video Games, Charges Infringement," The Wall Street Journal, 17 April 1974.

only to later recant and say that he had attended: "The Story of Computer Games," Discovery Channel Documentaries, 1 January 2003, https://www.thetvdb.com/series/discovery-channel-documentaries/episodes/4113032.

he circulated an internal memo that outlined: "Pong For Your Home TV - Part 1," Atari Museum, http://www.atarimuseum.com/videogames/dedicated/homepong.html.

that Magnavox had the home market locked down: "First-Hand:The Development of Pong: Early Days of Atari and the Video Game Industry," Engineering and Technology History Wiki,

https://ethw.org/First-Hand:The_Development_of_Pong:_Early_Days_of_Atari_and_the_Video_Game_Industry.

little box was a way to sell more televisions: Ibid.

he showed up at Atari's factory in Los Gatos dressed to impressed: Ibid.

Nolan Bushnell hopped in a box and rode it down a conveyor belt: Kent, Steven, The Ultimate History of Video Games: The Story Behind the Craze that Touched Our Lives and Changed the World, Prima Publishing: Roseville, California.

included hot tub parties and passing around marijuana: Ibid.

they arranged to store it at a friend's apartment for the night: "Pong For Your Home TV - Part 1," Atari Museum, http://www.atarimuseum.com/videogames/dedicated/homepong.html.

In January 1975, Alcorn and a few others: "First-Hand:The Development of Pong: Early Days of Atari and the Video Game Industry," Engineering and Technology History Wiki, https://ethw.org/First-Hand:The_Development_of_Pong:_Early_Days_of_Atari_and_the_Video_Game_Industry.

when Tom Quinn stopped by and asked how things: Ibid.

including a prototype that featured breast-shaped: "Sex, Pong, And Pioneers: What Atari Was Really Like, According To Women Who Were There," Kotaku, https://kotaku.com/sex-pong-and-pioneers-what-atari-was-really-like-ac-1822930057.

a line of credit to finance production at a bank Sears owned: "Pong For Your Home TV - Part 2," Atari Museum, http://www.atarimuseum.com/videogames/dedicated/homepong/homepong-pt2.htm.

became Sears' most successful product to date: "Atari Pong," Centre for Computing History, http://www.computinghistory.org.uk/det/4007/Atari-PONG/.

video games after Space Invaders took Japan by storm: "Master of Play," The New Yorker, https://www.newyorker.com/magazine/2010/12/20/master-of-play.

Chapter 2 – Space Invaders

It was a dream. It was a video game: "The Gamespy Hall of Fame – Space Invaders," GameSpy, https://web.archive.org/web/20080408152913/http://archive.gamespy.com/legacy/halloffame/spaceinvaders.shtm.

were behind the technological curve of other countries: Ibid.

allowing for better graphics and smoother animations: Staff, "Nishikado-San Speaks," Retro Gamer.

Over the next year, he designed and rounded up tools: "Classic GI: Space Invaders," Game Informer, 2008.

more concerned about factors such as the cost of hardware: "The Gamespy Hall of Fame – Space Invaders," GameSpy, https://web.archive.org/web/20080408152913/http://archive.gamespy.com/legacy/halloffame/spaceinvaders.shtm.

he kept the invaders' faster movement and touted it: IN THE MAKING: SPACE INVADERS, "Arcade Sushi," https://arcadesushi.com/in-the-making-space-invaders/.

strips of orange and green cellophane over the screen so the: Ibid.

first three months on the market did not bode well: "Ten Things Everyone Should Know About Space Invaders," 1up.com, https://web.archive.org/web/20090226064943/http://www.1up.com/do/feature?cId=3168373.

cleared out their arcades and stocked the game exclusively: Ibid.

the first game to save a high score, tacitly challenging: "IGN's Top 10 Most Influential Games," IGN, https://www.ign.com/articles/2007/12/11/igns-top-10-most-influential-games.

the first game where players could take cover: "How Cover Shaped Gaming's Last Decade," Kotaku, https://kotaku.com/how-cover-shaped-gamings-last-decade-5452654.

had sold over 100,000 machines and earned the equivalent: "Thirty-five years ago today: Space Invaders conquer the Earth," The Register, https://www.theregister.co.uk/Print/2013/06/05/feature_space_invaders_at_35/.

that Japan suffered from a shortage: "The Gamespy Hall of Fame – Space Invaders," GameSpy, https://web.archive.org/web/20080408152913/http://archive.gamespy.com/legacy/halloffame/spaceinvaders.shtm.

fewer 100-yen coins than usual over 1978 and ’79: "Space Invaders Targets Coins," Academia.edu, https://www.academia.edu/2568838/Space_Invaders_targets_coins.

Atari programmers looked around for games to make: "Reminiscing from Richard Maurer," Giant Dad, https://dadgum.com/giantlist/archive/maurer.html.

first few months at Atari studying documentation for the 2600: Ibid.

and was surprised when no one seemed interested: Ibid.

more valuable than clones of arcade hardware: Ibid.

making that port the first arcade game licensed to a console: Kent, Steven, The Ultimate History of Video Games: The Story Behind the Craze that Touched Our Lives and Changed the World, Prima Publishing: Roseville, California.

For reasons he could not comprehend: "Reminiscing from Richard Maurer," Giant Dad, https://dadgum.com/giantlist/archive/maurer.html.

who had sketched them out on graph paper: Ibid.

wincing as he cut features and routines he was proud of: Ibid.

the first game to hit the vaunted one-million-units-sold milestone: "The video games boom has yet to come," Google Newspapers, https://news.google.com/newspapers?id=fC5VAAAAIBAJ&sjid=npQDAAAAIBAJ&pg=4131,3188851.

the first "system seller" or killer app for a game machine: Kent, Steven, The Ultimate History of Video Games: The Story Behind the Craze that Touched Our Lives and Changed the World, Prima Publishing: Roseville, California.

a maximum of ten sprites on a line: "Game Boy Programming Manual Version 1.1," Archive.org, https://archive.org/details/GameBoyProgManVer1.1.

Chapter 3 – Missile Command

making Night Driver the first first-person driving game: "Night Driver [Upright model] Arcade Video game published 43 years ago by Atari, Inc.," Arcade History, https://www.arcade-history.com/?n=night-driver-upright-model&page=detail&id=26054.

The nightmare. Always the same: "THE CREATION OF MISSILE COMMAND AND THE HAUNTING OF ITS CREATOR, DAVE THEURER," Polygon, https://www.polygon.com/features/2013/8/15/4528228/missile-command-dave-theurer.

satellites built with state-of-the-art radar screens: Ibid.

make a game that used a radar to track missiles: Ibid.

Create Armageddon, the title of the game: Ibid.

focus on bases that could be saved: Ibid.

Theurer pointed out that no one could spell it: Ibid.

ended up being too complicated and were cut: Ibid.

born of the Cold War nightmare: Ibid.

the idea that Missile Command was telling a story: Ibid.

a player who shared his find in a letter to the editor: "From the Editor," Atari Age, July/August 1982.

was removed in later versions of the cartridge: "Rob Fulop interview," Atari Compendium,

http://www.ataricompendium.com/archives/interviews/rob_fulop/interview_rob_fulop.html.

one of the top ten bestselling games on the system: "TOP 10 BEST-SELLING ATARI 2600 GAMES," IGN, https://www.ign.com/articles/2008/08/26/top-10-best-selling-atari-2600-games.

comprising a memory map of 704 positions: "CHAPTER 17 Graphics," World of Spectrum, http://www.worldofspectrum.org/ZXBasicManual/zxmanchap17.html.

an innovation from previous models of ZX computers: "The ZX-Spectrum screen layout: Part I," Overtaken by Events, http://www.overtakenbyevents.com/lets-talk-about-the-zx-specrum-screen-layout/.

start to crack down on blatant clones such as Apple Invaders: Craddock, David L., Break Out: How the Apple II Launched the PC Gaming Revolution, Schiffer Publishing: China, 2017.

Chapter 4 – Pac-Man

players lasted ten seconds or less their first time out: Bang, Derrick, "Beating the Classics," Computer Gaming World, May–Jun 1983.

became an honor worthy of bragging rights: Kent, Steven, The Ultimate History of Video Games: The Story Behind the Craze that Touched Our Lives and Changed the World, Prima Publishing: Roseville, California.

Athletics, acting—nothing appealed to him: "The Story of... Pac-Man on Atari 2600," Retro Gamer (read via PressReader.com), https://www.pressreader.com/@nickname12310913/csb_2qTPIedQ

UIQumQK1bYp4NgU8fbBD1ZpBMRjgM_lfSIogcroUthNAfn_DF5 ZdCVXs.

when he cut class, he could often be found: Ibid.

dropped out of high school during his junior year: Ibid.

to create coin-operated children's rides: "Namco founder and 'Father of Pac-Man' has died," Ars Technica, https://arstechnica.com/gaming/2017/01/namco-founder-and-father-of-pac-man-has-died/.

swooped in and bought the company for $500,000: Ibid.

first arcade game to use multicolor sprites: "Namco's founder and 'father of Pac-Man' dies at 91," Polygon, https://www.polygon.com/2017/1/30/14438064/father-of-pac-man-obituary-masaya-nakamura-namco.

rounding out the Kanji character for mouth: "Toru Iwatani, 1986 PacMan Designer," Programmers at Work, https://programmersatwork.wordpress.com/toru-iwatani-1986-pacman-designer/.

Japanese players paid little attention to Pac-Man: "Pacman: The Phenomenon - Part 1," GameSpy, https://web.archive.org/web/20071016203822/http://classicgaming.gamespy.com/View.php?view=Articles.Detail&id=249.

players spent over $1 billion in quarters on Pac-Man: Wolf, Mark J. P., The Video Game Explosion: A History from PONG to Playstation and Beyond, Greenwood: Westport, Connecticut.

arcade cabinets in North America in 1980: "Pac-Man Sublicenses Extend Bally's Profits," The New York Times,

https://www.nytimes.com/1982/02/16/business/pac-man-sublicenses-extend-bally-s-profits.html.

secured exclusive licensing rights to distribute cartridge: Ibid.

Namco's arcade board sported a Zilog Z80 processor: Bogost, Ian and Nick Montfort (editors), Racing the Beam: The Atari Video Computer System, The MIT Press: Cambridge, Massachusetts.

vertically mounted, nineteen-inch monitor: "Midway's Pac-Man: Parts and Operating Manual," Fix Your Pacman, http://www.fixyourpacman.com/wp-content/uploads/2016/01/Pac-Man.pdf.

company-wide policy that only space games could use: "Inside Atari's rise and fall," TechCrunch, https://techcrunch.com/2018/06/21/inside-ataris-rise-and-fall/.

that phosphor would cause a burn-in effect: "The Great Market Crash," Atari Compendium, http://www.ataricompendium.com/archives/articles/crash/crash.html.

myths about me being pressured to have it done for Christmas: "Pac-Man," Atari Protos, http://www.atariprotos.com/2600/software/pacman/pacman.htm.

the first magazine devoted to consumer video games: "The Great Market Crash," Atari Compendium, http://www.ataricompendium.com/archives/articles/crash/crash.html.

Journalists had been writing about games in newspapers and magazines: Wolf, Mark J. P., Encyclopedia of Video Games: The Culture, Technology, and Art of Gaming, Greenwood: Westport, Connecticut, 2012.

and told him that he and Warshaw had been offered jobs: "The Great Market Crash," Atari Compendium, http://www.ataricompendium.com/archives/articles/crash/crash.html.

feared a repeat of the disgruntlement that had led employees: Ibid.

Frye and Warshaw were the only two senior programmers: Ibid.

billed April 3, 1982, as National Pac-Man Day: "Today is 'Atari National PAC-MAN Day'. No, Seriously, it is," Kotaku, https://kotaku.com/today-is-atari-national-pac-man-day-no-seriously-i-5898908.

the game's on-sale date was elastic depending on when retailers: "The Story Of Atari's Pac-Man Day & Game Launch - Gaijillionaire's Club: America - GTV," YouTube video, 21:59, GTV Gaijillionaire, June 15, 2017, https://www.youtube.com/watch?v=VzhI4IGRP8I.

received ninety-six copies each in mid-March: Ibid.

cranking out millions of cartridges in anticipation of: "Mar 1982 - Pac-Man is Released as an Arcade Port for the Atari 2600," World History Project, https://worldhistoryproject.org/1982/3/pac-man-is-released-as-an-arcade-port-for-the-atari-2600.

Seven million of those cartridges found their way: Ibid.

of the twenty million 2600 consoles they had sold to date: "Pac-Man," Next Generation, April 1998, https://archive.org/details/NextGeneration40Apr1998/page/n41.

but in time, pundits cited it as one of the key failures: Bogost, Ian and Nick Montfort (editors), Racing the Beam: The Atari Video Computer System, 2009, Cambridge: The MIT Press.

Chapter 5 – Donkey Kong

introduction of the number zero in India between 300 and 400: "The Origin of Zero," Scientific American, https://www.scientificamerican.com/article/history-of-zero/.

Viatron Computer Systems' coining of the term microprocessor: "System 21 is NOW!," Bit Savers, http://bitsavers.org/pdf/viatron/ViatronSystem21Brochure.pdf.

Intel engineer Ted Hoff invented the microprocessor: "The man who invented the microprocessor," BBC, https://www.bbc.com/news/technology-13260039.

answered a job ad for a circuit designer at Rockwell: "DP Interviews Mark lesser," Digit Press, http://www.digitpress.com/library/interviews/interview_mark_lesser.html.

George Klose and Richard Cheng, two of the division's engineers: Ibid.

determined that a single chip from an LED calculator: Ibid.

redesigned the chip and wrote a multiplexing: Ibid.

executives believed the games were too rudimentary: "Mattel's Football (I) (1977, LED, 9 Volt, Model# 2024)," Handheld Museum, http://www.handheldmuseum.com/Mattel/FB.htm.

over 500,000 units were being sold per week: Ibid.

a billiards-style toy, and patented his work: "Electronic pool game," USPTO Patent Full-Text and Image Database, http://patft.uspto.gov/netacgi/nph-Parser?Sect2=PTO1&Sect2=HITOFF&p=1&u=%2Fnetahtml%2Fse

arch-
bool.html&r=1&f=G&l=50&d=PALL&RefSrch=yes&Query=PN%2F4346892.

the most expensive of 1977's 'holy trinity' of personal computers: "Improbable PC Pioneer: Commodore's Jack Tramiel, 1928-2012," TIME, http://techland.time.com/2012/04/09/improbable-pc-pioneer-commodores-jack-tramiel-1928-2011/.

was shipping out 4,000 cabinets a week: Kent, Steven, The Ultimate History of Video Games: The Story Behind the Craze that Touched Our Lives and Changed the World, Prima Publishing: Roseville, California.

playfield had to be completely redrawn to reflect movement: "STELLA PROGRAMMER'S GUIDE," Classic-Games, http://www.classic-games.com/atari2600/stella.html.

they assumed the color of their respective player objects: Ibid.

were the first to get it working on the 2600: "Keys to the VCS's Longevity," Atari Compendium, http://www.ataricompendium.com/archives/articles/longevity/longevity.html.

game to be released that utilized the technique: Ibid.

rumors that Coleco sabotaged its ports of licensed games: "The History of 'Donkey Kong' Ports is the History of the Gaming Industry," *Variety*, https://variety.com/2018/gaming/opinion/donkey-kong-country-tropical-freeze-2-1202794862/.

sold over six million copies of Donkey Kong: Sheff, David, Game Over: Press Start to Continue: The Maturing of Mario, 1999, Wilton, Connecticut: GamePress.

turning over five million in royalties to Nintendo: Ibid.

many consider it one of the worst arcade-to-home ports: [Author's note: https://www.ranker.com/list/worst-arcade-video-game-ports/collin-flatt , https://www.ign.com/articles/2006/06/28/top-10-tuesday-worst-coin-op-conversions , and https://www.watchmojo.com/video/id/11402 just for starters.]

Chapter 6 – Ms. Pac-Man

verified by a referee from Twin Galaxies: "Centipede Scores," Twin Galaxies, https://www.twingalaxies.com/game/centipede/arcade/points-tournament-settings/.

verified his score of 1,081,900 points in Burger Time: "Burger Time Scores," Twin Galaxies, https://www.twingalaxies.com/game/burger-time/arcade/points/.

The law came by its name ironically: "Atari Tempest: Dave Theurer's Masterpiece," Arcade Blogger, https://arcadeblogger.com/2018/01/19/atari-tempest-dave-theurers-masterpiece/.

the first arcade games to feature an ending: "Crystal Castles," The International Arcade Museum, https://www.arcade-museum.com/game_detail.php?game_id=7456.

It was faster, and much more affordable: "Chip Hall of Fame: MOS Technology 6502 Microprocessor," IEEE Spectrum, https://spectrum.ieee.org/tech-history/silicon-revolution/chip-hall-of-fame-mos-technology-6502-microprocessor.

when Macrae, who ran a pinball room out of his dorm: "THE MAKING OF MS PAC-MAN," Retro Gamer,

https://www.retrogamer.net/retro_games80/the-making-of-ms-pac-man/.

dropped out of MIT and were renting a house in Brookline: Ibid.

They had a different take: It sucked: Ibid.

estimated that temperatures spiked by Pac-Man fever: Ibid.

continue selling conversion kits, but with Atari's consent: "Classic Game Postmortem: Ms. Pac-Man," YouTube video, 1:02:02, GDC, January 13, 2017, https://www.youtube.com/watch?v=rhM8NAMW_VQ.

spun it off into a separate game, Pac-Woman: "The MIT Dropouts Who Created Ms. Pac-Man: A 35th-Anniversary Oral History," Fast Company, https://www.fastcompany.com/3067296/the-mit-dropouts-who-created-ms-pac-man-a-35th-anniversary-oral-history.

the game's name was finalized to Ms. Pac-Man: Ibid.

its distribution deal with Midway fell apart: "Ms. Pac-Man," The International Arcade Museum, https://www.arcade-museum.com/game_detail.php?game_id=8782.

sales of over one million units, a prestigious accomplishment: "RETRONAUTS EPISODE 91: RETRONAUTS EAST - SEGA'S GOLDEN ARCADE ERA, PT. 1 Expand Menu," Retronauts, https://www.podcastone.com/episode/retronauts-91.

first personal computers to use sprites for graphics: "Atari 400," Old Computers, http://www.old-computers.com/museum/computer.asp?c=76.

the engineers who had created the Commodore Amiga: "THE MAKING OF BLUE LIGHTNING," Retro Gamer,

https://www.retrogamer.net/retro_games80/the-making-of-blue-lightning/.

action games that sold well on the Commodore 64: "A Time of Endings, Part 2: Epyx," The Digital Antiquarian, https://www.filfre.net/2016/12/a-time-of-endings-part-2-epyx/.

prototype for a handheld system called the Potato: Ibid.

but passed on making deals: Ibid.

Tramiel gave Warner no money for the company: "WARNER SELLS ATARI TO TRAMIEL," The New York Times, https://www.nytimes.com/1984/07/03/business/warner-sells-atari-to-tramiel.html.

thanks to rocky finances at Epyx, he had designs on scooping: "A Time of Endings, Part 2: Epyx," The Digital Antiquarian, https://www.filfre.net/2016/12/a-time-of-endings-part-2-epyx/.

reduced to the status of a “software partner,” no different: Ibid.

lengthy battery life and pack-in copy of Tetris: "A Time of Endings, Part 2: Epyx," The Digital Antiquarian, https://www.filfre.net/2016/12/a-time-of-endings-part-2-epyx/.

threadbare release schedule, virtually nonexistent marketing budget: "The Next Generation 1996 Lexicon A to Z: Lynx," Next Generation, March 1996.

and tendency to chew through batteries doomed it: "A Time of Endings, Part 2: Epyx," The Digital Antiquarian, https://www.filfre.net/2016/12/a-time-of-endings-part-2-epyx/.

Chapter 7 – Double Dragon

it boasted an updated version of Sinclair's: "Sinclair ZX 81," Old Computers, http://www.old-computers.com/museum/computer.asp?c=263.

custom Ferranti logic chip designed to handle input and: "SINCLAIR ZX81 home computer for a minimum prize [sic]," Computer Museum, http://computermuseum.50megs.com/brands/zx81.htm.

and, in the mid-eighties, several budding studios: "About," Gameopolis, http://gameopolis.org.uk/about/.

that made budget-priced titles published by bigger names: "Binary Design, Ltd.," Giant Bomb, https://www.giantbomb.com/binary-design-ltd/3010-496/.

first game to center on fisticuffs: "The Tao of Beat-'em-ups Part 2: A fight is not won by one punch or kick. Fighting from '85 to '93," Eurogamer, https://www.eurogamer.net/articles/a_taoofbeatemups_pt2_retro.

and popularized martial arts-themed games in arcades: Ibid.

allowed players to move up and down the screen: "6 November 2007 Evolution of a Genre: Beat 'Em Ups," ABC, http://www.abc.net.au/tv/goodgame/stories/s2067970.htm.

Double Dragon ushered in a golden age of beat-em-ups: "The Tao of Beat-'em-ups Part 2: A fight is not won by one punch or kick. Fighting from '85 to '93," Eurogamer, https://www.eurogamer.net/articles/a_taoofbeatemups_pt2_retro.

cemented the game as more than just another game: " Hall of Fame - Double Dragon," GameSpy, https://web.archive.org/web/20090818045122/http://www.gamespy.com/articles/488/488826p1.html.

a feat made possible by graphics engineer Richard Altwasser: "Colour Clash: The Engineering Miracle of the Sinclair ZX Spectrum," Paleotronic, https://paleotronic.com/2018/09/29/loading-ready-run-sinclair-edition-the-zx-spectrum/.

after being touted on BBC's The Computer Programme special: Ibid.

In order to meet an affordable price point: Ibid.

each block held two bytes' worth of values: Ibid.

all a manifestation of color clash: Ibid.

promised it would revolutionize home computer storage: "Infinite loop: the Sinclair ZX Microdrive story," The Register, https://www.theregister.co.uk/2013/03/13/feature_the_sinclair_zx_microdrive_story/.

budget line of titles starting at £1.99: "A History of Mastertronic," Guter, https://web.archive.org/web/20060830193907/http:/www.guter.org/mastertronic_history.htm.

Norman Tebbit laid out plans to train the unemployed: "Youth Policies in the UK: A Chronological Map," Keele, https://web.archive.org/web/20081006195150/http:/www.keele.ac.uk/depts/so/youthchron/Education/8090educ.htm.

away from potential careers and into unpaid positions: "Setting the record straight on YTS," The Guardian, https://www.theguardian.com/society/2012/feb/19/setting-record-straight-on-yts.

after one man's wife bought him a ZX-81 computer: "THE KEYBOARD WARLORDS - A profile on M.C. Lothlorien," Crash Online, http://www.crashonline.org.uk/08/lothlorn.htm.

quite a feat on the Atari ST: "Scrolling on the Amiga," Blog, https://uridiumauthor.blogspot.com/2017/12/scrolling-on-amiga.html?view=classic.

a technique for which the Genesis was becoming well-known: "SEGA GENESIS/MEGA DRIVE VDP GRAPHICS GUIDE V1.2A (03/14/17)," Mega Cat Studios, https://megacatstudios.com/blogs/press/sega-genesis-mega-drive-vdp-graphics-guide-v1-2a-03-14-17.

Chapter 8 – Tetris

Stubben would test hardware like controllers by beating: "Chatting with the original Atari Paperboy team," Arcade Museum Forums, https://forums.arcade-museum.com/showthread.php?t=279827.

but it failed Atari's field test: "ASTEROIDS DESIGNER ED LOGG HONORED WITH PIONEER AWARD," Wired, https://www.wired.com/2011/11/ed-logg-pioneer-award/.

became the first coin-op title to use a microprocessor: "From Transistors to Microprocessors: This Classic Arcade Game Was the First and Last of a Generation," The Franklin Institute, https://www.fi.edu/blog/from-transistors-to-microprocessors-classic-arcade-game.

arcade games need anywhere from 150 to 170 transistors: "The Apple Story - Part 1: Early History - An Interview with Steve Wozniak," Byte Magazine, https://archive.org/stream/byte-magazine-1984-12/1984_12_BYTE_09-13_Communications#page/n461/mode/2up.

promised Jobs a $700 bonus if he could build the game: "How Steve Wozniak's Breakout Defined Apple's Future," Game Informer, https://www.gameinformer.com/b/features/archive/2015/10/09/how-steve-wozniak-s-breakout-defined-apple-s-future.aspx.

Over four sleepless days, Woz worked with Jobs: Ibid.

Jobs mentioned nothing about the royalties he would earn: Ibid.

and became Logg's first commercial hit: "Chapter 6: Interview: Ed Logg," Flylib - Game Design: Theory and Practice (2nd Edition) (Wordware Game Developers Library), https://flylib.com/books/en/4.479.1/.

a move he admitted was "stupid" in retrospect: "Atari Founder Was 'Stupid' To Sell The Company," Kotaku, https://kotaku.com/atari-founder-was-stupid-to-sell-the-company-5610033.

wearing a suit on his first day only to be greeted by Bushnell wearing: "The Replay Interviews: Ray Kassar," Gamasutra, https://www.gamasutra.com/view/feature/134733/the_replay_interviews_ray_kassar.php.

This was California, where everybody lit up: Ibid.

claimed the decision was mutual in his account of the incident: Ramsay, Morgan, Gamers at Work: Stories Behind the Games People Play, 2012, New York: Apress.

Atari couldn't operate at tip-top efficiency: "The Replay Interviews: Ray Kassar," Gamasutra, https://www.gamasutra.com/view/feature/134733/the_replay_interviews_ray_kassar.php.

which Bushnell had wanted to put out to pasture: Ibid.

called the programmers “high-strung prima donnas” in a comment: Ibid.

spent five hours listening to a programmer read poetry he’d written: Ibid.

he had programmed on his own had generated over twenty: "The History Of Activision," Gamasutra, https://www.gamasutra.com/view/feature/129961/the_history_of_activision.php.

pitched Kassar and other executives on a compensation plan: Ibid.

Their cohort had made Atari over $60 million: Ibid.

no more important than the workers on assembly lines: Ibid.

The “Gang of Four,” as they became known: Ibid.

the first third-party publisher to release games: "Stream of video games is endless," The New York Times, https://news.google.com/newspapers?id=nwsdAAAAIBAJ&sjid=QX8EAAAAIBAJ&pg=3635%2C1989311.

Atari’s second-bestselling game on the 2600, after Tod Frye's Pac-Man: "IAM David Crane, creator of Pitfall! and co-founder of Activision," Reddit AMA, https://www.reddit.com/r/IAmA/comments/yli88/iam_david_crane_creator_of_pitfall_and_cofounder/?limit=500.

the communications giant to weather a loss of $425 million: "WARNER SELLS ATARI TO TRAMIEL," The New York Times, https://www.nytimes.com/1984/07/03/business/warner-sells-atari-to-tramiel.html.

Over 7,800 Gauntlet cabinets were sold in '85: "Atari Production Numbers Memo," Atari Games, https://web.archive.org/web/20130120084806/http://www.atarigames.com/index.php?option=com_content&view=article&id=47%3Aatari-production-numbers-memo&catid=5%3Aatari-inter-office-memos&Itemid=5.

making it Atari's most lucrative coin-op title: "Synopsis," Allgame, https://web.archive.org/web/20090308030532/http://www.allgame.com/game.php?id=15438.

and the seventh highest-grossing coin-op video game of all time: "Top 10 Highest-Grossing Arcade Games of All Time," USgamer, https://www.usgamer.net/articles/top-10-biggest-grossing-arcade-games-of-all-time.

to release no more than five titles per year: "Happy 30th anniversary, Tengen! Your anti-DRM NES chip fought the law, and the law won," The Register, https://www.theregister.co.uk/2015/07/25/happy_30th_anniversary_tengen_you_fought_the_video_game_law_and_the_law_won/.

Pavlovsky noticed sixteen-year-old Gerasimov: "Tetris Story," Oversigma, https://vadim.oversigma.com/Tetris.htm.

a collection of their work, which they called a computer funfair: Ibid.

expanded the idea so two players could challenge each other: Ibid.

there were shortages of the ROM chips that held code: "NOW, PLAY'S THE THING," The Washington Post, https://www.washingtonpost.com/archive/lifestyle/1988/11/25/now-plays-the-thing/616dbc27-d77d-407e-a5a4-d610b6b581f4/?utm_term=.6660163cc074.

walked into Tengen's lab and asked the three engineers huddled: "Tetris... forever," Atari HQ, http://www.atarihq.com/tsr/special/el/el.html.

added a competitive multiplayer mode as well as: "A Tale of the Mirror World, Part 6: Total War," The Digital Antiquarian, https://www.filfre.net/2017/07/a-tale-of-the-mirror-world-part-6-total-war/.

Logg helped them get the code up and running: "Chapter 6: Interview: Ed Logg," Flylib - Game Design: Theory and Practice (2nd Edition) (Wordware Game Developers Library), https://flylib.com/books/en/4.479.1/.

offered five million in exchanged for the rights: "A Tale of the Mirror World, Part 6: Total War," The Digital Antiquarian, https://www.filfre.net/2017/07/a-tale-of-the-mirror-world-part-6-total-war/.

the Japanese gaming giant would make up any differences: Ibid.

That same day, Atari announced that Tengen: Ibid.

company responded by countersuing Atari for patent infringement: Ibid.

software manufacturers in North America sympathized with Atari: Ibid.

were prohibited from selling any home version of Tetris: "COMPANY NEWS; Atari Is Blocked From Selling Game," The New York Times, https://www.nytimes.com/1989/06/22/business/company-news-atari-is-blocked-from-selling-game.html.

estimated that 50,000 copies of the game: Ibid.

Hundreds of thousands were returned: Ibid.

Chapter 9 – Teenage Mutant Ninja Turtles

filed for bankruptcy in 2009 after being unable to climb: "Midway Files Chapter 11," IGN, https://www.ign.com/articles/2009/02/12/midway-files-chapter-11.

Mortal Kombat, the Midway logo, and another title for $49 million: "Midway's Chicago HQ closing, final buyout price $49 million," GameSpot, https://www.gamespot.com/articles/midways-chicago-hq-closing-final-buyout-price-49-million/1100-6213488/.

Arcade1Up received the coveted Tech Toy of the Year Award: "Arcade1Up Wins Coveted Toy of the Year Award," PR Newswire, https://www.prnewswire.com/news-releases/arcade1up-wins-coveted-toy-of-the-year-award-300797036.html.

by manufacturers and distributors as the Oscars of their industry: "About The Awards," Toy Awards, https://www.toyawards.org/toyaward/about/toyaward/the-awards.aspx?hkey=c897f648-a33a-466b-b0e6-1278139ea024.

licensing issues caused both games to be pulled from Xbox Live: "TMNT Re-Shelled no longer available in US after June 30," Engadget, https://www.engadget.com/2011/06/23/tmnt-re-shelled-no-longer-available-in-us-after-june-30/.

acquired the rights to the property from co-creator Peter Laird: "Musings About the Sale," Peter Laird's blog, https://web.archive.org/web/20091026145019/http://plairdblog.blogspot.com/2009/10/musings-about-sale.html.

Chapter 10 – Street Fighter II

ran on the Zilog Z80 8-bit processor that had powered: "Other Ocean: Building the past, the future, and the present," Venture Beat, https://venturebeat.com/2017/09/22/other-ocean-building-the-past-the-future-and-the-present/.

introduced nonlinear gameplay to side-scrolling: "Gaming's most important evolutions," Games Radar, https://www.gamesradar.com/gamings-most-important-evolutions/5/.

announced the return of Digital Eclipse in 2015: "Digital Eclipse is back with a new mission: preserve classic games," Gamasutra, https://www.gamasutra.com/view/news/245465/Digital_Eclipse_is_back_with_a_new_mission_preserve_classic_games.php.

a repackaging of Mega Man 1 through VI for PlayStation: "Forgotten Gem - Jumping Flash," 1UP, https://web.archive.org/web/20070927211136/http://www.1up.com/do/feature?cId=3148848&did=3.

been enthralled by Double Dragon II: The Revenge: "Final Fight," Videogames.com, https://web.archive.org/web/19990223191246/http://www.videogames.com/features/universal/okamoto/okfinal.html.

expressed concern over buying a sequel that looked nothing like: Ibid.

who wanted to design a sequel fleshed out the original: "Interview: The Men Who Make Street Fighter II!," GamePro, June 1994.

Noritaka Funamizu took the reins as producer: "Street Fighter II - An Oral History," Polygon, https://www.polygon.com/a/street-fighter-2-oral-history/.

characters that consumed varying amounts of memory: "The Making Of... Street Fighter II," Edge magazine, March 2002.

perform one attack and immediately connect with a second: Ibid.

ceiling seemed to be four hits, but eventually rose: Ibid.

coin-op games had come under fire from American parents and various: "For Amusement Only: the life and death of the American arcade," The Verge, https://www.theverge.com/2013/1/16/3740422/the-life-and-death-of-the-american-arcade-for-amusement-only.

100 people protested outside an arcade in Franklin, New York: Ibid.

bought new games on credit only to be unable to pay them off: Ibid.

Within two years, Capcom had earned over $1.5 billion: "15 Things You Might Not Know About Street Fighter," Mental Floss, http://mentalfloss.com/article/64071/15-things-you-might-not-know-about-street-fighter.

there were myriad changes from the arcade: [Author's note: A comprehensive account of those changes can be found at http://wiki.shoryuken.com/Street_Fighter_2:_The_World_Warrior#Game_Versions and https://en.wikipedia.org/wiki/Street_Fighter_II:_The_World_Warrior#Super_NES.]

Capcom's highest-selling game released for a single platform: "Platinum Titles," Capcom - Investor Relations, https://web.archive.org/web/20150208030840/http://www.capcom.co.jp/ir/english/business/million.html.

ported to numerous platforms, is the company's best-selling game overall: Ibid.

cited the game as an influence on their careers: "The 25-year legacy of Street Fighter II, in the words of the experts," Gamasutra, https://www.gamasutra.com/view/news/264509/The_25year_legacy_of_Street_Fighter_II_in_the_words_of_the_experts.php.

established the structure of gaming tournaments: "EGM Feature: The 5 Most Influential Japanese Games Day Four: Street Fighter II," Electronic Gaming Monthly, http://www.egmnow.com/articles/news/egm-featurethe-5-most-influential-japanese-gamesday-four-street-fighter-ii/.

many have pointed to the game as the origin of esports: "The 25-year legacy of Street Fighter II, in the words of the experts," Gamasutra, https://www.gamasutra.com/view/news/264509/The_25year_legacy_of_Street_Fighter_II_in_the_words_of_the_experts.php.

earning over $10.6 billion in revenue, making it one of the top three: "World of Warcraft Leads Industry With Nearly $10 Billion In Revenue," Game Revolution, https://www.gamerevolution.com/features/13510-world-of-warcraft-leads-industry-with-nearly-10-billion-in-revenue#/slide/1.

ported to over eighteen platforms as of 2012: "The Port Authority: A Few Of Gaming's Most Ported Titles," *Game Informer*, https://www.gameinformer.com/b/features/archive/2012/07/24/the-port-authority.aspx.

a staff member at Capcom USA played a hacked ROM: "How hackers reinvented Street Fighter 2," Eurogamer, https://www.eurogamer.net/articles/2014-02-21-how-hackers-reinvented-street-fighter-2.

which powered thirty-two coin-op games: "32 official titles were released on this system between 1988 and 1995," Gaming History, https://www.arcade-history.com/index.php?page=articles&num=2.

closer to 134 if you counted revisions to those games: "Capcom CPS1 - Part 1," Arcade Hacker, http://arcadehacker.blogspot.com/2015/04/capcom-cps1-part-1.html.

arcade operators were less than impressed: "Tournament Battle is Capcom's gift to Nintendo Switch Street Fighter fans," Venture Beat, https://venturebeat.com/2018/03/18/tournament-battle-is-capcoms-gift-to-nintendo-switch-street-fighter-fans/.

the final arcade board designed by Capcom: "The Capcom Interview," Sega Saturn Magazine, October 1996.

claimed the game's hardware and software were so complex: Ibid.

demand for games skyrocketed after China and other eastern countries: "Gaming with Chinese Characters: Two Views From the Middle Kingdom," e:\> magazine, http://krishcat.com/edrive/wp-content/uploads/2014/08/EdriveZine_Issue1_August2014.pdf.

responded by going underground and hosting dozens of hacked: Ibid.

Rainbow Edition, one of the most prolific bootlegs: "This Bootleg Game Changed Street Fighter History," Kotaku, https://kotaku.com/this-bootleg-game-changed-street-fighter-history-1829103751.

came up with a way to "de-suicide" CPS II batteries: "Capcom CPS2 Security Programming Guide," Arcade Hacker, http://arcadehacker.blogspot.com/2016/09/capcom-cps2-security-programming-guide.html.

a coder by the name of Andreas Naïve cracked the encryption: "CPS3 Driver (preliminary)," Git Hub, https://github.com/mamedev/mame/blob/master/src/mame/drivers/cps3.cpp.

Chapter 11 – T2: The Arcade Game

over eighty-five percent of British schools: "How a BBC Micro shaped the course of GeekDad's life," Wired, https://web.archive.org/web/20111230170636/http://www.wired.co.uk/news/archive/2011-03/18/bbc-micro.

or the "Beeb" as it became known among hobbyists: "'Beeb' creators reunite at museum," BBC, http://news.bbc.co.uk/2/hi/technology/7303288.stm.

a response to a television series that predicted: "Acorn and the BBC Micro: From Education to Obscurity," Low End Mac, http://lowendmac.com/2007/acorn-and-the-bbc-micro-from-education-to-obscurity/.

have video hardware access memory while the processor: "The BBC Micro turns 30," The Register, https://www.theregister.co.uk/2011/11/30/bbc_micro_model_b_30th_anniversary/?page=4.

to hold up to four palettes at once: "Sega Genesis/Mega Drive - Console Information," Console Database, https://www.consoledatabase.com/consoleinfo/segamegadrive/.

labeled a type of image compression: "SEGA Genesis: Characters and Playfields," Schmid, https://www.schmid.dk/blog/2017-08-06-genesis-tiles/.

but was popular in the UK, even outselling the NES: "Total 8-bit and 16-bit Cartridge Consoles: Active installed base estimates," Screen Digest, March 1995, page 61.

selling between 1.5 and two million units there: "16-Bit Hits – New video games offer better graphics, action," Minneapolis Star

Tribune, October 15, 1991, archived from the original on November 10, 2013.

the majority of console owners in Europe still played Master System: Ibid.

Chapter 12 – Mortal Kombat

somewhat affectionately referred to as the “Trash-80”: "Please Don’t Call It Trash-80: A 35th Anniversary Salute to Radio Shack’s TRS-80," TIME, http://techland.time.com/2012/08/03/trs-80/.

The National Video Game Team dated back to March 1983: "U.S. National Video Game Team," US National Video Game Team, https://www.usnationalvideogameteam.com/history.

then the world’s most renowned Donkey Kong player: "The 'King of Kong' Gamer Just Had His Reigning King Kong Records Taken Away," TIME, https://time.com/5238168/billy-mitchell-king-of-kong/.

a pinball nut who set his sights on Donkey Kong: "The Perfect Man," Oxford American, https://www.oxfordamerican.org/magazine/item/622-the-perfect-man.

he’d set many of his high scores using the MAME arcade emulator: "Donkey Kong scoreboard strips Billy Mitchell’s high score claims [Updated]," Ars Technica, https://arstechnica.com/gaming/2018/02/donkey-kong-scoreboard-strips-billy-mitchells-high-score-claims/.

crumbling just five days after its launch: The National Video Game Team dated back to March 1983: "U.S. National Video Game Team," US National Video Game Team, https://www.usnationalvideogameteam.com/history.

got scores in the Guinness Book of World Records: "US National Video Game Team," Spy Hunter 007, http://spyhunter007.com/us_national_video_game_team.htm.

Electronic Gaming Monthly as the official magazine: "LOMBARD PUBLISHERS ACQUIRED," Chicago Tribune, https://www.chicagotribune.com/news/ct-xpm-1996-05-09-9605090299-story.html.

setting the mold for how basketball games would look and play: "SNES A DAY 93: NCAA BASKETBALL," SNES A Day, https://snesaday.com/2014/08/26/93-ncaa-basketball/.

loaning or selling kits: "You Can Own Sid Meier's SNES Development System, If You Have A Spare $9.5K," Nintendo Life, http://www.nintendolife.com/news/2015/05/you_can_own_sid_meiers_snes_development_system_if_you_have_a_spare_usd95k.

for its 8- and 16-bit consoles: "Nintendo Entertainment System 'Mission Control'," Handheld Museum, http://devkits.handheldmuseum.com/NES_MissionControl.htm.

they declared their dry run at a local arcade: "Mortal Kombat dev Ed Boon recalls the uppercut that started it all," Gamasutra, https://www.gamasutra.com/view/news/286864/Mortal_Kombat_dev_Ed_Boon_recalls_the_uppercut_that_started_it_all.php.

Sonya Blade, MK's sole female character: Ibid.

he'd been the first to write to Atari programmer Warren Robinett: "The True Story Behind The Original Video Game 'Easter Egg' That Inspired 'Ready Player One'," Forbes, https://www.forbes.com/sites/sethporges/2017/12/20/the-true-story-behind-the-original-video-game-easter-egg-that-inspired-ready-player-one/#36a3b59c2976.

hardware designed by Sony employee Ken Kutaragi: "The Nintendo PlayStation is the coolest console never released," Tech Radar, https://www.techradar.com/news/gaming/the-nintendo-playstation-is-the-coolest-console-never-released-1327988.

with the Z80 processor carrying sound duties along: "Sega's Original Hardware Developer Talks About The Company's Past Consoles," Silicon Era, https://www.siliconera.com/2013/09/18/segas-original-hardware-developer-talks-about-the-companys-past-consoles/.

Super NES could send data directly to the PPU: "WINNING THE CONSOLE WARS – AN IN-DEPTH ARCHITECTURAL STUDY," Hackaday, https://hackaday.com/2015/11/06/winning-the-console-wars-an-in-depth-architectural-study/.

questioned whether video games, formerly the domain: "Too Violent for Kids?", Time, http://content.time.com/time/subscriber/article/0,33009,979298,00.html.

their gruesome content was no different than an R-rated movie: "15 Most Influential Games of All Time - Resident Evil--PlayStation (1996)," GameSpot, https://web.archive.org/web/20100415183542/http://www.gamespot.com/gamespot/features/video/15influential/p14_01.html.

Sega and Nintendo hurling insults at each other: "July 29, 1994: Videogame Makers Propose Ratings Board to Congress," Wired, https://www.wired.com/2009/07/dayintech-0729/.

Sega's compromise was sticking an "MA-13" rating: Ibid.

The Mario Club exercised nearly total control: "Nintendo spins off 'Mario Club' quality control team," Engadget,

https://www.engadget.com/2009/09/16/nintendo-spins-off-mario-club-quality-control-team/.

knew that catering to older players: "Sega v Nintendo: Sonic, Mario and the 1990's console war," BBC, https://www.bbc.com/news/technology-27373587.

a nod to the album “Abacab” by rock band Genesis: "ABACABB," Metal Archives, https://www.metal-archives.com/bands/ABACABB/65892.

write under pseudonyms to make the magazine’s scrappy: "GamePro," GamingMagz, http://www.gamingmagz.com/magazines/usa/gamepro#.XRENHuhKiUl.

the first video game to release at the same time around the globe: "The Weird Reason Why Video Games Are Released On Tuesdays," Business Insider, https://www.businessinsider.com/why-video-games-are-released-on-tuesdays-2014-11.

Hughes Johnson logged the red binder: "My Loser Phase: Reflections on Video Game Retail from 1992-1997," Hugues Johnson, https://www.huguesjohnson.com/features/loser_phase/1993.html.

estimated that pre-orders for Genesis outnumbered: Ibid.

over 70,000 consumers had called the studio: "Video Violence: It's Hot! It's Mortal! It's Kombat!; Teen-Agers Eagerly Await Electronic Carnage While Adults Debate Message Being Sent," The New York Times, https://www.nytimes.com/1993/09/16/nyregion/video-violence-it-s-hot-it-s-mortal-it-s-kombat-teen-agers-eagerly-await.html.

invested $10 million in the game’s advertising: Ibid.

customers had plunked down cash for the Sega Genesis version: "In Mortal Kombat for Video Game Crown : Entertainment: Nintendo officials are likely to find out next week that holiday sales have given the title to rival Sega," Los Angeles Times, https://www.latimes.com/archives/la-xpm-1994-01-04-fi-8432-story.html.

more than made up the lead Nintendo had gained: Ibid.

Chapter 13 – NBA Jam

Iguana founder Jeff Spangenberg had skipped college: "A RETROSPECTIVE: THE STORY OF RETRO STUDIOS PAGE 2 OF 11," IGN, https://www.ign.com/articles/2004/12/18/a-retrospective-the-story-of-retro-studios?page=2.

hired a staff of twenty, including many friends: Ibid.

which a few developers visited in May 1993: Ibid.

David Brevik, who wanted to stay in the Bay Area: Craddock, David L., Stay Awhile and Listen: Book I Legendary Edition: How Two Blizzards Unleashed Diablo and Forged a Video-Game Empire, Digital Monument Press, LLC: Ohio, 2013.

experimented with game ideas in his own time: "The Rise, Fall, and Return of NBA Jam," 1up, https://web.archive.org/web/20130412043344/http://www.1up.com/features/rise-fall-return-nba-jam?pager.offset=1.

dazzled by the digitized graphics that Boon and John Tobias: Ibid.

license to use the likenesses of real players: Ibid.

whose contract with Nike precluded him from participating: "I am grizzled Game Designer Mark Turmell, and I'm here to tell you why I still use the coin-op NBA JAM techniques in the mobile Wizard of Oz: Magic Match game I make today. From my days making Apple 2, Atari VCS, Coin-op, and console, through todays mobile games – I'm Mr. 60FPS - AMA!," Reddit, https://www.reddit.com/r/IAmA/comments/61a0vl/i_am_grizzled_game_designer_mark_turmell_and_im/dfd14kh/. (Author's note: I probably could have shortened the article title, but it's hilarious, and I'm writing this book, so it stays.)

reticent to mix its multi-billion-dollar industry: "Hear the True Story of How 'NBA Jam' Almost Didn't Get Made," Mental Floss, http://mentalfloss.com/article/73416/hear-true-story-how-nba-jam-almost-didnt-get-made.

making NBA Jam the first NBA-licensed coin-op game: "THE GAMER BLOG: YOU DON'T KNOW JAM," ESPN, https://web.archive.org/web/20090212194701/http://sports.espn.go.com/espnmag/story?id=3668922.

he happened to be working a side gig across the street: "NBA Jam Announcer Tim Kitzrow on Voice Acting, Sports Games, and 25 Years of Boomshakalaka," Shacknews, https://www.shacknews.com/article/102805/nba-jam-announcer-tim-kitzrow-on-voice-acting-sports-games-and-25-years-of-boomshakalaka.

took cues from NBA announcers such as Marv Albert: Ibid.

selling over 20,000 machines: "11 Essential Talking Points on NBA Jam," Mental Floss, http://mentalfloss.com/article/62821/11-essential-talking-points-nba-jam.

most money made in a single week at $2,468: Ibid.

netting Midway north of $900 million in revenue: "BREAKING INTO THE INDUSTRY: TIM KITZROW," IGN, https://www.ign.com/articles/2000/02/16/breaking-into-the-industry-tim-kitzrow.

David Brevik had tried to convince head Jeff Spangenberg: Craddock, David L., Stay Awhile and Listen: Book I Legendary Edition: How Two Blizzards Unleashed Diablo and Forged a Video-Game Empire, Digital Monument Press, LLC: Ohio, 2013.

perfect for the screen ratio of 4:3 used by televisions: "Super Nintendo VS. Sega Genesis – Specs," Nerd Bacon, http://nerdbacon.com/super-nintendo-vs-sega-genesis-specs/.

a palette of 256 colors that could be applied to everything: "The Early 80's Arcade Aesthetic," CSANYK, https://csanyk.com/2012/05/the-early-80s-arcade-aesthetic/.

a sixteen-color palette, standard on Nintendo's: "SNES SPRITE ENGINE DESIGN GUIDELINES," Mega Cat Studios, https://megacatstudios.com/blogs/press/snes-sprite-engine-design-guidelines.

and Sega's 16-bit platforms: "Palette," Sega Retro, https://segaretro.org/Palette.

512 total, sixty-one displayable at once: Kent, Steven, The Ultimate History of Video Games: The Story Behind the Craze that Touched Our Lives and Changed the World, Prima Publishing: Roseville, California.

color palette of the Genesis could be tripled: "SEGA GENESIS/MEGA DRIVE VDP GRAPHICS GUIDE V1.2A (03/14/17)," Mega Cat Studios, https://megacatstudios.com/blogs/press/sega-genesis-mega-drive-vdp-graphics-guide-v1-2a-03-14-17.

the studio's art director, Matt Stubbington, changed the logo: "Obituary: Iguana Art Director And Freelance Illustrator Matt Stubbington," Gamasutra, https://www.gamasutra.com/view/news/123291/Obituary_Iguana_Art_Director_And_Freelance_Illustrator_Matt_Stubbington.php.

drew characters and backgrounds by accessing special ports: "Hardware Reference Manual for the SEGA Game Gear Console," Sega Retro, https://segaretro.org/images/1/16/Sega_Game_Gear_Hardware_Reference_Manual.pdf.

had scoured magazines for headshots of players: "BOOM SHAKA LAKA," Sports Illustrated, https://www.si.com/longform/2017/nba-jam-oral-history/index.html.

they recorded NBA games: Ibid.

did so by flying under the radar: "Farewell, Father," Eurogamer, https://www.eurogamer.net/articles/farewell-father-article.

Ohga gave authorization for him to continue: Ibid.

drew up a contract for Kutaragi to lead development: Ibid.

would ship with the console and be branded the Play Station: Ibid.

Sony would claim all royalties, only giving Nintendo: "The Weird History Of The Super NES CD-ROM, Nintendo's Most Notorious Vaporware," *Kotaku*, https://kotaku.com/the-weird-history-of-the-super-nes-cd-rom-nintendos-mo-1828860861.

Sony had assured Nintendo it would be creating non-gaming software: Ibid.

Sony never specified in writing what type of software: Ibid.

Sony was coming for Nintendo, Ohga said: "The Making Of: PlayStation," Edge magazine, https://web.archive.org/web/20120516003333/http://www.edge-online.com/features/making-playstation.

for ownership of the Play Station name: "Farewell, Father," Eurogamer, https://www.eurogamer.net/articles/farewell-father-article.

only 200 were manufactured before Sony pulled the plug: Ibid.

and up to 360,000 polygons a second: "Playstation Architecture, hardware and coding," Intel Assembler, http://www.intel-assembler.it/portale/5/playstation/hardware_tables_and_programming_ps1.asp.

and every other developer getting a jumpstart: "Developer explains what it's like developing for each console: PS3 being the hardest," Gaming Bolt, https://gamingbolt.com/developer-explains-what-its-like-developing-for-each-console-ps3-being-the-hardest.

Chapter 14 – Mortal Kombat II

You guys are doing a sequel to MK: Ed Boon's recollection of the story can be found at https://www.complex.com/pop-culture/2012/09/ed-boons-12-best-mortal-kombat-memories/.

Midway had shipped out over three million units: "Mortal Marketing," GamePro, 1994.

a role inspired by the sinister Emperor Palpatine: "In Konversation: Mortal Kombat Online vs John Tobias - Part 1," Mortal Kombat Online, https://www.mortalkombatonline.com//t/classic/in-konversation-mortal-kombat-online-vs-john-tobias-part-1/NDYXrilRqJV5.

critics and fans had complained about: "The First Fighting Game That Let You Just Be Friends - Mortal Kombat II," GameSpot, https://web.archive.org/web/20040219112446/http://www.gamespot.com/gamespot/features/all/greatestgames/p-17.html.

defines compression as encoding data: "Data compression theory and algorithms," Maximum Compression, https://www.maximumcompression.com/algoritms.php.

commonly applied to discrete information, or data meant to hold specific types: "Lossless Compression: An Overview," Stanford, https://cs.stanford.edu/people/eroberts/courses/soco/projects/data-compression/lossless/index.htm.

drawing more than twenty sprites per scan line: "Sega Genesis vs Super Nintendo," Game Pilgrimage, http://www.gamepilgrimage.com/book/export/html/10922.

pelted Nintendo with angry letters and phone calls: "Nintendo's Looser Stance on Violence Means a Bloody Mortal Kombat II," Los Angeles Times, https://www.latimes.com/archives/la-xpm-1994-09-09-fi-36631-story.html.

and revealed in Nintendo Power magazine: Nintendo Power, September 1994.

drawing sprites to be wider than they were tall: "Hardware Review: The SNES Classic Mini Is The Perfect Link To The Past," Nintendo Life, http://www.nintendolife.com/news/2017/09/hardware_review_the_snes_classic_mini_is_the_perfect_link_to_the_past.

one of the most common sizes: "SNES SPRITE ENGINE DESIGN GUIDELINES," Megacat Studios, https://megacatstudios.com/blogs/press/snes-sprite-engine-design-guidelines.

thirty-two per scan line, or up to thirty-four: "Super NES Programming/SNES Specs," Wiki Books, https://en.wikibooks.org/wiki/Super_NES_Programming/SNES_Specs.

able to understand and carry out commands: "Author of eighties classic The Hobbit didn't know game was a hit," The Register, https://www.theregister.co.uk/2012/11/18/hobbit_author_veronika_megler_reminisces/.

allowing players to treat everything as an object: Ibid.

so crudely drawn that many players struggled: "King's Quest Retrospective: I-IV," Gwen C Katz, http://gwenckatz.com/2015/11/22/kings-quest-retrospective-i-iv/.

sold over one million copies for Beam Software: DeMaria, Rusel and Wilson, Johnny L. High Score!: The Illustrated History of Electronic Games, McGraw-Hill: Berkeley.

a fact of which Megler was unaware: "Author of eighties classic The Hobbit didn't know game was a hit," The Register, https://www.theregister.co.uk/2012/11/18/hobbit_author_veronika_megler_reminisces/.

parent company Melbourne House was sold to Mastertronic: "A History of Mastertronic," Aguter Plus, http://web.archive.org/web/20180224213520/http://www.aguter.plus.com/mastertronic/mastertronic_history.htm.

the maximum number of sprites the Game Boy: "Making a Game Boy game in 2017: A "Sheep It Up!" Post-Mortem (part 1/2)," Gamasutra, https://www.gamasutra.com/blogs/DoctorLudos/20171207/311143/Making_a_Game_Boy_game_in_2017_A_quotSheep_It_Upquot_PostMortem_part_12.php.

to accommodate the Game Boy's lower color palette: "GAME BOY GAMES THAT PUSHED THE LIMITS OF GRAPHICS & SOUND," Racketboy, http://www.racketboy.com/retro/game-boy-games-that-pushed-the-limits-of-graphics-sound.

it could display that many colors at once: "Dr. DevSter's Guide to The Sega 32x '>>ALMOST<< Everything you wanted to know, that you never knew, and that you're going to know about the 32x'," Monkeeh, http://devster.monkeeh.com/sega/32xguide1.txt.

it pushed pixels out slower than the Genesis's: Ibid.

forty-two cents a share and earned $101 million: "WMS Industries Inc.'s fiscal second-quarter profit rose," Chicago Tribune, https://www.chicagotribune.com/news/ct-xpm-1994-01-26-9401260045-story.html.

the Super NES version of MKII outsold its rival: "US Platinum Videogame Chart (Games sold over Million Copies since 1995)," The Magic Box, http://www.the-magicbox.com/Chart-USPlatinum.shtml.

appreciated the zippier speed on Genesis, but were disappointed: "OC HIGH: STUDENT NEWS AND VIEWS : Mortal Kombat II; For Sega Genesis and Game Gear, Nintendo SNES and Game Boy," Los Angeles Times, https://www.latimes.com/archives/la-xpm-1994-10-14-ls-50167-story.html.

he suffered a cerebral blood clot following a transatlantic flight: "Obituary: Fergus McGovern," GamesIndustry.biz, https://www.gamesindustry.biz/articles/2016-02-29-obituary-fergus-mcgovern.

the co-founder's work with charities and cheerful demeanor: "Obituary: Probe Software and HotGen co-founder Fergus McGovern," Gamasutra, https://www.gamasutra.com/view/news/266847/Obituary_Probe_Software_and_HotGen_cofounder_Fergus_McGovern.php.

Chapter 15 – Street Fighter Alpha

Capcom's designers created him to mock rival SNK's: "The pathetic history of Dan Hibiki," Games Radar, https://www.gamesradar.com/the-pathetic-history-of-dan-hibiki/.

assigning the same artists who had worked alongside Burkhill: "Feature: The Making Of Street Fighter Alpha 3: Upper," Nintendo Life, http://www.nintendolife.com/news/2013/06/feature_the_making_of_street_fighter_alpha_3_upper.

all in Japanese, all of which had to be translated: Ibid.

but the shout was a higher-pitched version of Ken's: Ibid.

one of Capcom's internal teams was sandbagging their port out of envy: Ibid.

informed their royalties would be cut in half for missing the promised deadline: Ibid.

developers were spread thinly over multiple projects that were falling behind: Ibid.

Cameron Sheppard negotiated an acquisition offer from a publisher: Ibid.

Chapter 16 – San Francisco Rush 2049

over two million tourists every year: "Lombard Crooked Street," San Francisco County Transportation Authority, https://www.sfcta.org/projects/lombard-crooked-street.

serving approximately 300,000 vehicles every day: "THE 10 BUSIEST INTERSTATES IN THE UNITED STATES," Hotshot Warriors, https://hotshotwarriors.com/the-10-busiest-interstates-in-the-united-states/.

most highly trafficked stretch is found in San Francisco's Eastshore: Ibid.

eighty-seven percent of its major roads and highways: "San Francisco-Oakland Transportation by the Numbers - Meeting the Region's Need for Safe, Smooth and Efficient Mobility," TRIP, http://www.tripnet.org/docs/CA_San_Francisco-Oakland_Transportation_by_the_Numbers_TRIP_Report_Aug_2018.pdf.

an average of $1,049 in repair costs every year: Ibid.

the process just kind of worked: "Describe what developing for each console you've developed for is like," Reddit.com/r/gamedev, https://www.reddit.com/r/gamedev/comments/xddlp/describe_what_developing_for_each_console_youve/c5lg7px/.

even shoddy work tended to run and play better on Nintendo 64: Ibid.

render 3D graphics while juggling the hardware's limitations: "Sin & Punishment 2: Creator's Voice – Parts 1 & 2," Silicon Era (translated from Nintendo's Japanese site), https://www.siliconera.com/2009/11/01/sin-punishment-2-creators-voice-parts-1-2/.

caused an outcry among developers and consumers: "Retro: This Is Why We Should Probably Be Glad Nintendo Stuck With Carts For The N64," Nintendo Life, http://www.nintendolife.com/news/2017/02/retro_this_is_why_we_should_probably_be_glad_nintendo_stuck_with_carts_for_the_n64.

swore off the N64 and stuck to PlayStation: Ibid.

lengthy loading times on discs compared to near-instantaneous loading: "Sin & Punishment 2: Creator's Voice – Parts 1 & 2," Silicon Era (translated from Nintendo's Japanese site), https://www.siliconera.com/2009/11/01/sin-punishment-2-creators-voice-parts-1-2/.

ceased production, it had sold 30.75 million units: Ernkvist, Mirko (August 21, 2012). Zackariasson, Peter; Wilson, Timothy (eds.). The Video Game Industry: Formation, Present State, and Future. Routledge: New York, first published in 2012.

by putting 49.1 million Super Nintendos in homes: "Historical Data: Consolidated Sales Transition by Region," Nintendo, https://web.archive.org/web/20171026163943/https://www.nintendo.co.jp/ir/finance/historical_data/xls/consolidated_sales_e1703.xlsx.

due to “high consumer demand”: "This Day in History: Sega Announces Surprise Saturn Launch," 1up, https://archive.is/20130629122913/http://www.1up.com/news/day-history-sega-announces-surprise#selection-529.0-529.58.

30,000 Saturn consoles materialized on store shelves: Kent, Steven, The Ultimate History of Video Games: The Story Behind the Craze that Touched Our Lives and Changed the World, Prima Publishing: Roseville, California.

Sega had failed to ramp up production to meet the demand: Schilling, Mellissa A., "Technological Leapfrogging: Lessons From the U.S. Video Game Console Industry," California Management Review, 2003.

retailers caught off-guard by the announcement: Ibid.

Critics were less favorable toward Sega's conversion of Daytona USA: "ProReview: Ridge Racer," GamePro, September 1995.

Focusing on that dwindling audience, Sega split into two teams: "IGN PRESENTS THE HISTORY OF DREAMCAST," IGN, https://www.ign.com/articles/2010/09/10/ign-presents-the-history-of-dreamcast.

codenamed Black Belt and equipped with: "Hardware Classics: Sega Dreamcast," Nintendo Life, http://www.nintendolife.com/news/2015/04/hardware_classics_sega_dreamcast.

American project came undone when Katana was chosen: Ibid.

could not only deliver arcade perfection, but go beyond it: Ibid.

and then some when it launched day and date: "DF Retro: Soul Calibur on Dreamcast - beyond 'arcade perfect'," Eurogamer, https://www.eurogamer.net/articles/digitalfoundry-2017-df-retro-soul-calibur-dreamcast-beyond-arcade-perfect.

Namco rebuilt Soul Calibur's Dreamcast port: Ibid.

perhaps the first port of an arcade game to greatly outshine the original release: Ibid.

the first console to include a modem: "CONSOLE PORTRAITS: A 40-YEAR PICTORIAL HISTORY OF GAMING," Wired, https://www.wired.com/2007/06/gallery-game-history/.

piracy ran rampant on the Dreamcast: "4 hacker-friendly gaming consoles you should get right now," Gear Burn, https://memeburn.com/gearburn/2017/07/best-consoles-homebrew-hacking/.

The Dreamcast version is hands-down: "SAN FRANCISCO RUSH 2049," IGN, https://www.ign.com/articles/2000/09/08/san-francisco-rush-2049-2.

Acknowledgments

YOU'VE PAID YOUR quarters—or exhausted your continues—and, just when you thought you'd fall short of the finish line, you made it here, to the end. To the credits screen.

This book would not have been possible without the support of several important and special people.

Thank you to Milan Jaram, who has topped himself once again with this book's phenomenal cover, and to Chris Sanyk, who provided invaluable feedback during the revision process.

Thank you to Dan Amrich, John Tobias, Ed Logg, Nick Paul, and Susan McBride for going above and beyond to answer questions about their industries.

Thank you to everyone I interviewed about the games in this book, and every other arcade game and home conversion ever made. Your hard work made our lives better, one quarter or continue at a time.

Last but never least, thank you to my mom and my wife, Amie, who deserve more praise for their love, support, and encouragement than I will ever be able to give them.

About the Author

David L. Craddock lives with his wife, Amie Kline–Craddock, in Canton, Ohio. He is the author of several books including the bestselling *Stay Awhile and Listen* trilogy, and the critically acclaimed Gairden Chronicles series of epic fantasy novels for young adults. Follow David online at davidlcraddock.com, facebook.com/davidlcraddock, and @davidlcraddock on Twitter.

Stay up-to-date on David's latest releases by signing up for his newsletter: https://bit.ly/2PTDzLM.

If you enjoy *Arcade Perfect*, please consider leaving a review on Amazon and/or Goodreads: https://www.goodreads.com/book/show/46841504-arcade-perfect.

More Books by David L. Craddock

Fiction

Heritage: Book One of the Gairden Chronicles
Point of Fate: Book Two of the Gairden Chronicles
Firebug: War of the Elementalists

Nonfiction

Stay Awhile and Listen: Book I – How Two Blizzards Unleashed Diablo and Forged a Video-Game Empire
Stay Awhile and Listen: Book II – Heaven, Hell, and Secret Cow Levels (10/31/19)
Arcade Perfect: How Pac-Man, Mortal Kombat, and Other Coin-Op Classics Invaded the Living Room
Beneath a Starless Sky: Pillars of Eternity and the Infinity Engine Era of RPGs
Rocket Jump: Quake and the Golden Age of First-Person Shooters
Stairway to Badass: The Making and Remaking of Doom (TBD 2019)
Ascendant: The Fall of Tomb Raider and the Rise of Lara Croft (TBD 2020)
Shovel Knight (Boss Fight Books)
Break Out: How the Apple II Launched the PC Gaming Revolution
GameDev Stories: Interviews About Game Development and Culture
GameDev Stories: Volume 2 – More Interviews About Game Development and Culture
Once Upon a Point and Click: The Tale of King's Quest, Gabriel Knight, and the Queens of Adventure Games
Dungeon Hacks: How NetHack, Angband, and Other Roguelikes Changed the Course of Video Games
Dungeon Hacks: Expanded Edition
One-Week Dungeons: Diaries of a Seven-Day Roguelike Challenge
Making Fun: Stories of Game Development - Volume 1
Angels, Devils, and Boomsticks: The Making of Demons with Shotguns
Anything But Sports: The Making of FTL

Red to Black: The Making of Rogue Legacy
Everybody Shake! The Making of Spaceteam

Keep up with David's latest releases and announcements by subscribing to his newsletter: https://bit.ly/2PTDzLM.

www.ingramcontent.com/pod-product-compliance
Lightning Source LLC
Chambersburg PA
CBHW071353050326
40689CB00010B/1631

* 9 7 8 1 0 7 9 2 7 5 5 4 4 *